THE ECONOMIES OF CHINA AND INDIA
Cooperation and Conflict

Volume 1: China and India: The International Context and Economic Growth, Manufacturing Performance and Rural Development

THE ECONOMIES OF CHINA AND INDIA
Cooperation and Conflict

Volume 1: China and India: The International Context and Economic Growth, Manufacturing Performance and Rural Development

Editors

Manmohan Agarwal
Centre for Development Studies, India & Research and Information Systems for Developing Countries, India

Jing Wang
University of Western Ontario, Canada

John Whalley
University of Western Ontario, Canada & Centre for International Governance Innovation (CIGI), Canada & National Bureau of Economic Research (NBER), USA

World Scientific

NEW JERSEY • LONDON • SINGAPORE • BEIJING • SHANGHAI • HONG KONG • TAIPEI • CHENNAI • TOKYO

Published by

World Scientific Publishing Co. Pte. Ltd.

5 Toh Tuck Link, Singapore 596224

USA office: 27 Warren Street, Suite 401-402, Hackensack, NJ 07601

UK office: 57 Shelton Street, Covent Garden, London WC2H 9HE

Library of Congress Cataloging-in-Publication Data

Names: Whalley, John, editor. | Agarwal, Manmohan, editor. | Wang, Jing, 1974 April 21– editor.
Title: The economies of China and India : cooperation and conflict / editor-in-chief, John Walley; [edited by] Manmohan Agarwal (Centre for Development Studies, India & Research and Information Systems for Developing Countries, India), Jing Wang (University of Western Ontario, Canada)
Description: New Jersey : World Scientific, [2016] Contents: Volume 1. China and India: The International Context and Economic Growth, Manufacturing Performance and Rural Development -- Volume 2. Competitiveness, External Cooperation Strategy, and Income Distribution: Changes in China -- Volume 3. Economic Growth, Employment and Inclusivity: The International Environment.
Identifiers: LCCN 2016006686| ISBN 9789813100398 (hbk : set : alk. paper) | ISBN 9789813100534 (hbk : vol 3 : alk. paper) | ISBN 9789813100527 (hbk : vol 2 : alk. paper) | ISBN 9789813100510 (hbk : vol 1 : alk. paper)
Subjects: LCSH: Economic development--China. | Economic development--India. | China--Economic conditions--1949– | India--Economic conditions--1947– | China--Economic policy--1949– | India--Economic policy--1947– | China--Foreign economic relations. | India--Foreign economic relations.
Classification: LCC HC427.95 .E34135 2016 | DDC 330.951--dc23
LC record available at https://lccn.loc.gov/2016006686

British Library Cataloguing-in-Publication Data

A catalogue record for this book is available from the British Library.

Desk Editors: Herbert Moses/Yu Shan Tay

Typeset by Stallion Press
Email: enquiries@stallionpress.com

Printed in Singapore

Contents

Acknowledgement

The editors would like to acknowledge the support of the China Policy and Research Group (CPRG) at the University of Western Ontario (Canada) for the participation of Chinese researchers in the project. CPRG acknowledges supports from the Ontario Research Fund and Centre for International Governance Innovation (CIGI, Canada). The editors thank the staff at World Scientific Publishing, Herbert Moses, Xiao Qi, R. Raghavarshini, as well as Zvi Ruder for logistical and moral support. Editor Manmohan Agarwal also would like to thank the participants of seminars at the Centre for Development Studies Kerala where some of the papers were presented for helpful comments.

About the Editors

John Whalley is the Professor of Economics and Co-Director of the Centre for the Study of International Economic Relations at Western University; Research Associate at the National Bureau of Economic Research (NBER); Coordinator of Global Economy Group at the CESifo; and Distinguished Fellow at the Centre for Global Governance Innovation (CIGI). Professor Whalley is ranked No.1 in Canada among publishing economists in the RePEc rankings. He won the Hellmuth Prize for Achievement in Research, and also is 2012 Killam Prize Winner.

Manmohan Agarwal is the Reserve Bank Chair at the Centre for Development Studies at Thiruvananthapuram, Kerala, India. Earlier he had retired as a professor from Jawaharlal Nehru University, New Delhi, India where he taught for almost thirty years. Subsequently, he was a senior fellow at the Centre for International Governance Innovation (CIGI) at Waterloo Canada where he worked on issues of the world economy including the G20 and South-South cooperation. He is also a Senior Fellow at Research and Information Systems for Developing Countries, New Delhi and an adjunct senior fellow with the Institute of Chinese Studies. He also worked for a number of years at the World Bank and the International Monetary Fund. His research has been mainly in the area of International Economics and Development Economics.

Jing Wang is currently both the coordinator and research associate of the Centre for the Study of International Economic Relations at Western University. She was a Postdoctoral Associate in Department of Economics at Western University for years, and also held positions of associate research fellow in the Institute of Quantitative & Technical Economics at Chinese Academy of Social Sciences and editor of the Journal of Quantitative & Technical Economics.

List of Contributors

Manmohan Agarwal
Centre for Development Studies, India
Research and Information System for Developing Countries (RIS), India

Aritri Chakravarty
Centre for Development Studies, India

Hejing Chen
Western University, Canada

Upasak Das
Centre for Development Studies, India

Yue Gao
Shandong University of Technology, China

Sunandan Ghosh
Centre for Development Studies, India

Pei Guo
China Agricultural University, Beijing, China

Indrajeet Kumar
Centre for Development Studies, India

Chunding Li
Chinese Academy of Social Sciences (CASS), China
Western University, Canada

Jun Li
China Agricultural University, Beijing, China

Meeta Keswani Mehra
Jawaharlal Nehru University, India

Rita Pandey
National Institute of Public Finance and Policy, India

Keting Shen
Western University, Canada
Zhejiang Gongshang University, China

Haiyuan Wan
National Development & Reform Committee, China
Beijing Normal University, China

Jing Wang
Western University, Canada

John Whalley
Western University, Canada
Centre for International Governance Innovation (CIGI), Canada
National Bureau of Economic Research (NBER), USA
University of International Business and Economics (UIBE), China

Daqing Yao
Shanghai Academy of Social Sciences, China

Xiaopeng Yin
University of International Business and Economics (UIBE), China

Introduction

Manmohan Agarwal

The establishment, almost simultaneously, of the New Development Bank (NDB) by the BRICS (Brazil, Russia, India, China and South Africa) and the Asia Infrastructure Investment Bank (AIIB), fundamentally a Chinese initiative, though with a much larger membership, points to the elements of cooperation and conflict in the economic relations between China and India. China and India are both members of the two banks. But China has played a more active role in the establishment of the AIIB, canvassing members for it and has a larger say in its operations. The AIIB could completely overshadow the NDB, a more multilateral operation. On the other hand, economic relations between China and India in the areas of trade have been booming, despite a recent slowdown, and there are attempts to broaden this relationship to include investment in other areas. There are consultations between the two countries on many matters concerned with international economic governance. This book seeks to explore the complex economic relationship between China and India. It also seeks to analyse the many common problems that the two countries face and to isolate similarities and differences in their approaches to common problems.

The first section of the book deals with aspects of the system of international governance. The establishment of the NDB and the AIIB was in response to certain trends in aid from the developed countries and also from the multilateral development banks (MDBs) that seem to have been driven by the developed countries. Agarwal in his paper argues that these trends do not support development in developing countries as aid has been declining, whether as a share of GDP or of imports or of investment. Aid to countries in Latin America and East Asia is negligible. Aid to South Asia though still considerable is declining, rapidly in importance. Even aid to Sub-Saharan Africa (SSA) where it is mostly concentrated is declining, even for the least developed countries. The sector distribution of aid has also shifted away from productive sectors such as agriculture and manufacturing or even infrastructure or supporting expenditures in education and health. Aid is particularly important for infrastructure because of the long gestation lags, difficulties in private investors appropriating the benefits accruing from such investments and the need to often coordinate investments in different sub-sectors of infrastructure. The scale of operations of the two banks that were set up to provide finance for infrastructure is not yet clear. Both institutions will face the dilemma that the existing MDBs have faced; the limited capacity of developing countries to service loans at market rates of interest that forced MDBs to set up soft loan windows. Another aspect of their operations that will be important for the future aid architecture is whether the banks will adopt the "no conditionality rule" that many developing countries follow in their bilateral programmes. If the operations of these banks can be successful without conditionality, then the older MDBs will be forced to change their method of operations.

The chapter by Mehra and Pandey (MP) analyses the experience of selected countries on the effectiveness of different policy instruments that have been used for development of renewable energy technologies (RETs). They argue that strong political will is needed to enable countries to comply with international agreements. Policy design and implementation can also be linked to the market structures in the economy. MP analyse three sets of support schemes in detail: price-based market instruments such as feed-in-tariffs (FITs) and feed-in-premiums (FITPs), quantity-based market instruments called renewable portfolio standards (RPSs) or quota obligations and tendering/competitive bidding. They focus on stimulus to RETs and their cost-efficiency.

They stress the role of the regulatory, institutional and the political environment, especially as the level and structure of the instrument will have to be benchmarked against the prices of conventional energy, besides other advantages that conventional energy sources enjoy.

A significant impact on innovation could not be found for a large set of countries. The exception is Denmark. Also, government R&D support has had a very significant and positive impact on innovation in RETs in Germany, Spain and US (especially California and Minnesota).

In general, price-based instruments have worked better when compared to quantity-based instruments. Furthermore, tendering and/or green certificates reveal better the true costs. However, market-based instruments may circumscribe producers from reaping sufficient rents that can otherwise help spur innovation. Thus, incentives for dynamic efficiency for less mature technologies (in particular) should not be ignored. Since the costs of RETs tend to decline over time, a smooth phasing out/exit policy for the RE technology is also needed.

The average impact of both FITs and certificate schemes has risen over time, though the former is more effective, in spite of the lack of conclusive evidence on the link between energy support measures and innovation. However, in terms of static efficiency, competitive bidding and transferable green certificates (TGCs) are more effective. However, TGCs are beset with the risk of over-rewarding some technologies. Competitive bidding/tenders offer high security to project investors once the bid has been won. In the initial phase of project development, however, tenders are uncertain for investors, which could pose a hindrance, especially for smaller developers. The advantage of bidding is that it permits competitive price discovery.

China's record of RET D&D is unparalleled. Clear political resolve, supported by aggressive price incentives and a strong manufacturing base, has enabled China to emerge as a world leader in the deployment of RETs. India has a well-diversified portfolio of regulatory policies as well as fiscal incentives and public financing for RE development and deployment. As in South Africa, in India also, civil society plays a pivotal role in bridging the information gap regarding cost of various RETs. India continues to face challenges because of the lack of transparency, accountability and grid infrastructure facilities. Insufficient trained manpower, weak transmission networks, delays in payment by distributing companies also pose a challenge to the growth of RETs.

Electricity auctions tailored to individual technology features have occupied centre-stage in the regulatory framework adopted by Brazil. The RE auctions have been immensely successful attracting large amounts of investments, and allowing consumers to benefit from cheaper and cleaner energy. However, the contracts were too generous for investors and reserve auctions have usually been relatively better than technology-specific auction.

A number of countries that have relied on FITs/FITPs have witnessed larger than expected amounts of installation of solar PV capacities, thereby posing difficulties for policy makers and stakeholders in terms of the cost support policies. MP show that Germany has better tackled the resulting situation than Spain. The use of price to control volume rather than putting hard caps on volume turned out to be a successful strategy for Germany.

USA has one of the largest Production Tax Credit Program (PTC) programs. The performance-based incentive that rewards producer on the basis of actual energy produced, helped the US wind industry to lead the clean energy market. The main issue with the USPTC for wind energy has been that it has been allowed to expire several times intermittently, leading to cycles of boom and bust in the market, which in turn has led to suspension of projects, worker lay-offs, and loss of momentum in the industry.

The key lesson to be learnt from Denmark is that its current position as a front-runner in innovation in RE can be ascribed to the bold political decisions to transform the energy system, the early mover advantage in wind energy, and a favourable climate for innovative start-ups. The relatively low costs of patent applications and the opportunity to apply for patents in English language may have also played a favourable role in this regard.

The chapter by Whalley and Yin (WY) analyses the strategies that China may adopt to maintain a high rate of growth. China's integration into the world economy is seen as being central to both China's emergence as, for now, the global manufacturing centre, and the primary mechanism for arbitraging globally the advantages of China's high quality, low wage labour pool restrained globally by OECD immigration restrictions. WY ask the question whether the current regime can continue to underpin China's growth strategy in the post-crisis world, as, even before the crisis, questions were being asked about the sustainability of the pre-crisis (in 2005–2007) growth of exports. Sustainability was questioned on the basis that China at some point must run out of markets, face increasing competitive pressures from even lower wage countries, slower growth of the world economy, increased volatility and adjusting to anti-dumping and other actions being adopted by many countries. However, sharply elevated educational attainment since 1999, and accelerated innovation and patenting point the way to continued export growth led by new products and ideas.

WY provide a disaggregated period and commodity wise analysis of China's trade since 1990. The authors conclude their analysis of China's post-crisis performance by noting that there is slower but persistent growth of both exports and GDP; demand shifted from shrinking industrial economies to the expanding South. Furthermore, there is a very slow increase in product variety and quality/value-added, partly in response to rapidly rising wage rates in manufacturing.

The authors analyse six alternative growth strategies ranging from measures to maintain export momentum to concentrating on domestic markets/consumption to concentration on innovation building on the rapid increase in patenting in China.

The chapter by Chen and Whalley (CW) examines the likely effect of China's accession to the government procurement agreement (GPA) of the WYO on its trade. The GPA is a plurilateral agreement covering both goods and services dating from 1996 and covering 41 (mainly OECD) countries/areas. It mutually extends commitments only to signatories. Government procurement entities were obliged to follow core multilateral trade rules, i.e. non-discrimination and transparency rules. However, now the commitments go beyond those in the earlier GATT procurement code embodying deeper commitments both in terms of items covered and thresholds for competitive bidding. Government service markets are large, and trade in these also has spillover effects on trade in services and goods.

CW first estimate the effect of the GPA on trade in both goods and services among members using a gravity model applied to a panel data set covering 20 OECD countries over the period 1996–2008 for trade in goods and 1999–2008 for trade in services.

Results obtained by CW suggest that GPA membership has a positive impact on trade in both goods and services between parties as well as on outward foreign affiliate services sales. GPA membership plays a more important role in promoting bilateral trade in services than in goods as the coefficients on service imports and exports via cross-border supply mode are higher than for goods imports and exports. The authors argue that this may be because service suppliers gain more business opportunities in the government procurement market with non-discriminatory and transparent policies than manufacturing suppliers, since services are more important than goods in the government procurement market for most GPA parties. Results also suggest that exports are influenced more by GPA membership than is the case for imports. The number of GPA parties has a small marginal negative effect on trade in goods. Service exports increase slightly with more parties participating in the GPA. The growth of government procurement contracts above the threshold under the GPA also fosters service imports, exports and outward foreign affiliate sales.

The second section treats international trade relations and negotiations particularly for preferential trading arrangements (PTAs). The chapter by Yao and Whalley (YW) focuses on the economic relationship between China and India after the 2008 financial crisis. YW find that China was more negatively affected by the crisis than India, and India is recovering more rapidly in economic performance. The slower recovery in China may be because the crisis has required more deep seated changes in the Chinese economy. Before the crisis, growth in both economies was accelerating and the growth rate was higher for China than for India. Since the crisis, the growth rate has slowed and is more equal between the two countries. But both GDP and per capita GDP remain substantially higher in China. They also find that the demand structures are very different in the two countries. Consumption is much higher in India, while investment is lower. Also YW note that net exports are positive in China and negative in India. Production structures are also very different in the two economies. Agriculture and services hold a much larger share of GDP in India than in China, whereas, manufacturing is much more important in China.

The trade ratio is considerably higher for China than for India, but again the gap has been narrowing since the crisis. China exports much more to India than it imports. Though trade between the two countries has continued to increase since the crisis, the importance of the Chinese market for India has decreased. In services trade India has a surplus. China's imports of services have grown much more rapidly than its exports so the deficit with India on services trade has grown. The trade costs between China and India are still high, which means that the bilateral trade volume lags the potential.

In other economic relations, YW find that China has more inward and outward FDI than India, but lack of data prevented them from conducting a bilateral analysis. They argue in favour of a possible PTA between China and India. The two countries also coordinate in the WTO and on global climate issues. Although their bilateral relationship is mainly dual, to the rest of the world China and India are duelling in the competition for exports market and imports of natural resource. The chapter by Agarwal and Chakravarty in this volume finds that the structure of India's export basket to the world has become similar to that of China during the period 1995–2011.

The next chapter by Wang and Whalley (WW) compares the trade performance of the major Asian economies, China, India, Thailand, Malaysia, South Korea, Japan, Singapore and Chinese Taiwan, both during and following the 2008 financial crisis. They compare the size, speed and acceleration of trade compression with the onset of the crisis, and the reverse effects on recovery both in aggregate and by product and bilateral trading partner.

Pre-crisis, the fastest growth of imports occurred in India and Korea, whereas the lowest growth rates in 2008 were for Malaysia and Japan. Imports of all these economies declined in the first 10 months of 2009, and Korean imports declined the least among these economies. The worst performer was Japan; exports shrank by over 30% for 10 months, and they were almost half of that the previous year in the first quarter of 2009. Taiwan's exports declined by over 40% in two months starting from November 2008; exports from Malaysia showed a similar but milder trend. China's 2009 performance was slightly better than that of India, Malaysia and Taiwan.

The authors note, as have others, that the rate of trade compression occurred at a much greater rate than GDP growth during the crises, especially in the early stages, and the equally high rate of rebound is a puzzle that remains largely unexplained.

Asian countries' exports to the US fell sharply from January 2009 to August 2009, with high monthly declines. Thailand and China's exports to the US rebounded at the end of 2009, and other countries followed with a significant rebound in 2010. On the import side, the imports by India, Korea, Thailand and Taiwan of US products declined more than their exports to the US. China's exports to and imports from the US are similar in trend, but imports show a stronger rebound in 2010 than exports.

As far as trade with China is concerned, exports by India, Korea, Thailand and Taiwan fell sharply in the last quarter of 2008, and declined more than exports to the US in terms of percentage. Japan's exports to China declined less than those to the US during the crisis, which is slightly better than Japan's total export performance. All countries' exports to China rebounded strongly from the end of 2009. These countries' imports from China fell sharply in the first quarter of 2009, lagged a couple of months more than exports to China, and started to rebound from the end of 2009, almost synchronously with exports.

The trade of China, India and Thailand with the EU began to fall from the end of 2008 (imports of Thailand from the EU fell from January 2009) and declined sharply during the first half of 2009. From the end of 2009, trade between China and the EU showed a strong rebound. Similarly to trade with the US, Japan's trade with the EU shrank the most among the Asian economies during the financial crisis.

As far as commodity composition of trade is concerned WW find that China saw a major decline in manufacturing exports trade with a slow recovery, whereas Korea experienced a smaller initial impact but a quick rebound. Export impacts are mildest for India and commodity exporters including Malaysia. On the import side, the falls in world oil prices impact sharply on import values. When WW compare these trade effects with those in some earlier crises they find that percentage impacts on trade in the first year were similar, but of much longer duration in the 1930s. In the 1998 Asian crisis, trade impacts were much smaller since export markets in the OECD were not affected, but negative growth impacts on affected countries were greater. WW find that US, Germany, France and China experienced a significantly deeper trade compression in the Great Depression than China and Japan in this financial crisis. During the Asian financial crisis, growth of exports by China and Vietnam was positive between 1996 and 2003 whereas others experienced a fall, but at most for two years.

Both China and India have been increasingly active on the regional trade agreement front. There seems to be a trade war brewing in terms of PTAs. The Trans-Pacific Partnership and the Trans-Atlantic one would exclude China, and, incidentally, India also, and isolate China. But Chinese policy makers have been negotiating their own mega PTA, the Regional Economic Cooperation Partnership. The two papers by Li, Wang and Whalley (LWW) and Agarwal and Ghosh (AG) analyse the agreements that the two countries have negotiated. LWW say that China's agreements, unlike the US and EU cases, follow no template form of agreement but vary substantially one among the others and are in part an attempt to customise agreements to partner's preferences including their prior agreements. China presently has 12 concluded agreements, 6 under negotiation, and four others under consideration. Those concluded are in the main with smaller countries. Those in prospect are with major trading areas (US, Japan, Korea and India).

LYY argue that China clearly sees both Regional and Bilateral Trade Agreements (RTAs) as an increasingly key element of its integration into the global economy, a broad strategy which still underpins her overall growth strategy. The current focus of such agreements is mainly on Asia, and to a further degree the Pacific. All are driven in part by China's needs for export access to fuel continuing export lead growth. The basic idea is to use RTAs to further open up the economy to the outside world and speed up domestic reforms. However, other elements enter including using regional agreements to offset unwelcome elements of multilateral arrangements (such as the non-market economy labelling), and attempting to put in place via RTA building blocks an Asian trading hub. Outstanding issues not centrally addressed by these agreements include anti-dumping duties, and investment and competition issues. YWW point out that a feature of China's FTAs has been their linkage to bilateral investment treaties (BITs).

YWW's analysis suggests that by including all of China's major trading partners in RTAs and with an average current tariff of 10% to be reduced to zero, the medium term impact of the RTA strategy could be substantial.

India has entered into a number of trading arrangements. Some are free trade areas (FTAs), some are FTAs and Economic Integration Agreements (EIAs), whereas others are Preferential Scope Agreements (PSAs). Out of the 13 agreements at the end of 2015, four were EIAs, another four were FTAs and five were PSAs. These agreements have almost all been signed since 2003.

AG find that trade with the future partners actually started increasing in 2002. Both India's exports to the future RTA partners and imports from them increased rapidly more than the increase in overall exports and imports. The share of the partners in India's trade has continued to grow. India usually experienced a trade deficit with its RTA partners, having a surplus for only a few years in the early 1990s. Usually the deficits were not very large. Indian policy makers ascribe the deficits to the agreements and are chary about entering into more such agreements. AG find that there is no uniform pattern of surpluses and deficits. The deficit is mainly because of India's deficit with China. The deficits are also because of the overall trade deficits that India has run through most of this period.

AG did not find any significant intra-industry trade in India's trade with her RTA partners unlike India's trade with the world. They also found that most of the commodities exported by India to the RTA partners are those in which India has a Revealed Comparative Advantage with respect to the world. This would suggest that the RTAs are trade creating and not trade diverting and so prima facie may be considered welfare enhancing.

The third section deals with rural development. The chapter by Wan studies the impact of the Agricultural Tax Abolishment program (ATA) on agricultural labour time in rural China. As part of its tax reforms, the government launched a program in 2001 to abolish all agricultural taxation (including agricultural tax, special agriculture products tax and agricultural tax surcharges). Agricultural taxation has been important in China for over 2600 years. But with its abolition on January 1, 2006, total agricultural taxation was reduced from CNY 51.7 billion (about US $6.2 billion)[1] in 2003 to CNY 1.62 billion in 2005.

The chapter employs difference in difference method with the microeconomic panel data to find the effect of abolition on on-farm working time. Wan finds that the policy exerts a significant effect on on-farm working. The program promoted 6.19% more of farmers to engage in agriculture in 2004. Meanwhile, for the peasants that were already in agriculture, the program increased agriculture labour time by 24 hours in 2004. Furthermore, the program impacts more the educated, young males working in the garden produce field, while the effect is not significant in the farm and livestock segments. These results are stable and robust in different sub-group datasets, which implies a strong and significant on-farm working effect of the ATA program.

Li and Guo (LG) analyse the working of the land transfer system in China. Rural welfare is at the top of the Chinese government's priority list today, while rural land is at the heart of most rural issues and disputes. Agricultural output has grown rapidly since the adoption of the Household Responsibility System (HRS) in the late 1970s. This growth has been accompanied by significantly higher living standards for farmers. Despite this, farmers' incomes have been lagging far behind their urban counterparts. Secure, long-term, and marketable land rights is one of the fundamental prerequisites for the assurance of a basic rural livelihood, sustainable investments in land by farmers, the orderly development of a rural land transfer market and the continuing growth of rural income.

In 2002, a specific law governing rural land contracts granted farmers' inheritance rights to their land and the ability to transfer out and transfer in land, was enacted. However, LG find that not many farmers actually possess any written documentation that confirms their legal rights to land. The vast majority of the already issued Certificates or Contracts do not comply with law and lack legal validity. Further, the insecurity of farmers' land rights is demonstrated by frequent illegal land expropriations, administrative readjustments, or re-contracting to outside developers against farmers' wishes. Finally, the level of land transactions has

[1] The exchange rate of the Chinese Renminbi Yuan (CNY) against the US dollar was 8.28 CNY per USD in 2003 and 2004.

been relatively low due to the insecurity of rights, the lack of institutional safeguards, and high transaction costs.

The ownership rights and contracting rights of rural land registered by two Ministries are incomplete, inconsistent or even contradictory. Secondly, there are no clear laws on how land rights should be registered. The utility of the current registration system is minimal and serious reform is required.

A rural land registration pilot project was undertaken in two villages of Feidong County of Anhui Province, during the period July 2005 to January 2009. It was followed by another agricultural land registration pilot project in 2009 covering eight provinces. The invaluable experiences will be used in formulating recommendations for further larger-scale pilot projects which will in turn eventually lead to a national roll-out strategy.

LG find in an analysis of 244 completed questionnaires that the land-transfer rate appears to be relatively high in provinces covered by the survey, whether considering the number of transfers or the area of land transferred. The land transfer ratio in Anhui is significantly higher than in Shandong. 64.79% of land parcel transfers are due to labour shortages; 23.94% are due to farmers' unwillingness to cultivate (due to age, low benefit level, etc.); while 5.63% are due to having no time to cultivate and the remaining 5.63% transferred their lands for other reasons.

The most popular types of land transactions are leasing and subcontracting. Taking Anhui and Shandong provinces together, it was reported that, 52.11% of cultivated land was transferred by sub-lease, and 28.17% by subcontract, together accounting for 80.28% of the transactions. The bulk of transfers were to farmers' relatives and neighbours (local villagers) which accounted for 81.70% of the transfers. Only 14.08% of the transfers were to non-local farmers and a mere 4.22% were to enterprises. There were no transfers to Land Cooperatives and few cases of entrusting to Village Committees. Most land transfers were made by oral agreement. Only farmers who transferred their lands to non-local farming households and enterprises signed formal contracts. 'Floating' rents, where the rent is agreed, for example, annually were rare. According to the survey results, the income before land transfers was much higher than the rent received under the transfer agreements.

The increasing income gap between rural livers and those in cities observed by LG for China is also true for India. Furthermore, because growth of agricultural production and productivity has been lower in India than in China, poverty levels in Indian rural areas are much higher than in urban areas. In India, the Mahatma Gandhi National Rural Employment Guarantee Act (MGNREGA) was passed to tackle unemployment and poverty. The act guarantees unskilled employment on public works to all rural households at the statutory minimum wage for at least 100 days every year. Initially implemented in a limited number of rural districts, in 2008, the programme was extended to the entire country.

The chapter by Das and Singh (DS) reviews the implementation of the programme in the state of West Bengal and compares it with the rest of the country. It evaluates the programme in terms of number of person-days generated and its inclusiveness in reaching out to the poorest and deprived households. They consider evaluation of MGNREGA in West Bengal especially important for two reasons. Firstly, the Left Front led by the Communist Party of India (Marxist) (CPIM) ruled in the state for 34 years from 1977 to 2011 These parties were part of the government at the centre, the United Progressive Alliance (UPA) and were instrumental in its enactment. It is, therefore, interesting to compare the implementation of the programme in West Bengal in comparison to other parts of the country that were ruled mostly by non-Left political parties. Secondly, the state of West Bengal is among the poorest in the country.

The chapter highlights three aspects of the programme — inclusiveness, guarantee of 100 days employment and works expenditure at the India level and also in West Bengal for the time period 2011–2012 to 2014–2015. To examine inclusiveness, the fulfilment of the guarantee of 100 days' work for marginalised groups has been analysed. West Bengal is performing better than other states. Per capita availability of person-days work for scheduled castes is higher in WB than the all India average. In addition, West Bengal's performance is better than that of the neighbouring states, e.g., Bihar, Jharkhand, Odisha and Assam. Though West Bengal lags behind the participation rate for scheduled tribes in all of India, it performs better than the neighbouring states with a higher proportion of ST population; e.g., Jharkhand (with ST population share of 26%) and Assam (a share of 12.4% ST population), In terms of women participation rate, West Bengal's performance is usually below the all-India average. However, the performance is better than in the neighbouring states of Bihar, Jharkhand and Assam. Broadly speaking, West Bengal has higher participation than the all-India average. However, in terms of participation of the ST population and women, the performance of West Bengal has been poorer though it is better than in the neighbouring states.

West Bengal has fared well in terms of sustainable inclusiveness. A higher proportion of SC households worked for more than 100 days in West Bengal than the India average overall and all neighbouring states except Assam. On the other hand, West Bengal is lagging behind in the participation of STs compared to the national average. Also high ST populated states, Assam, Chhattisgarh and Odisha, performed better than West Bengal.

As far as the share of labour payments to material expenditure is concerned, the share is higher in West Bengal than in Bihar, Odisha, Jharkhand, and Assam; but lower than the all India average.

The broad conclusion is that that the WB programme has been able to reach the vulnerable and deprived population more than that in other parts of the country except for tribals.

The fourth section discusses a number of sectoral issues. The chapter by Agarwal and Chakravarty (AC) analyses the performance of manufacturing in developing countries especially in the BRICS. Despite the unprecedented growth of GDP in developing countries during 2001–2007 the manufacturing sector lagged so that the share of manufacturing in GDP fell in many regions and countries. AC then used the data in the World Input–Output to analyse the performance of the manufacturing sector in Brazil, China, India and Russia. The share of the manufacturing sector in GDP has declined in China, Brazil and Russia, very drastically in the last two where it has almost halved. The share has increased slightly in India.

In line with trends in many other countries and the spread of value chains they find that the share of value added in gross value of output fell and the use of imported inputs increased in Brazil, China, India and Russia. Also, the share of manufacturing output exported has increased in Brazil, China and India but decreased in Russia. AC then compared the sectoral composition of the output of the manufacturing sector and also the structure of exports. The latter was analysed in two different ways, the sector composition of the exports and the share of output of each sector that is exported. The correlations between the structures in 1995 and in 2011 are usually very high for Brazil, China and Russia. Only in the case of India do they find a significant change in the structure of the manufacturing sector. There has been considerable transformation of the manufacturing sector during this period only in India. This could be because of the very large decrease in the import duties levied by India and the elimination of import quotas after it lost a dispute with the US at the WTO.

AC find that the share of the manufacturing sector exported has increased for all the countries. But in recent years it has been decreasing; the peak share for Russia was achieved in 1999, for China in 2005 and for Brazil in 2004. For India, the share has continuously increased over the 1995–2011 period though with some fluctuations, so that by 2011 India among the four countries was exporting the highest share of its manufacturing output. Brazil has experienced the greatest variation. It exported the lowest share of its output in 1995, but increased the share so that by 2002 it was exporting the largest share of its output. However, the share then decreased so that by the end of the period in 2011 it was again exporting the smallest share of its manufacturing output.

Manufacturers of these countries do not compete in the world market as their export baskets are very different. The only exception is that the export baskets of China and India are very similar and have become more similar over the period.

AC then decomposed the sources of growth for the manufacturing sector. Employment in manufacturing declined in Russia though it increased in the other three countries. The hours worked per worker increased in China, India and Russia but declined in Brazil. Labour productivity has grown most rapidly in China followed by Russia and India; it has been stagnant in Brazil. The chapter goes on to argue that there is a shortage of sources of long term finance for the sector and this needs to be rectified for improved performance by the manufacturing sector. The New Development Bank could have a role here.

The chapter by Agarwal on BRICS and MDGs (A2) looks at the progress made towards achieving the Millennium Development Goals (MDGs). The analysis is conducted at the aggregate regional level and also at the individual country level for the BRICS in order to see how their performance is compared to other countries in the region. The MDGs were accepted at the UN in 2000 following extensive discussions at various UN conferences and among bilateral aid donors. Developing countries had almost no role in their development. A2 finds that East Asia, Latin America and the Middle East and North Africa regions are well on the way to reaching their MDG goals for most of the indicators. The laggards are South Asia and Sub-Saharan Africa, though South Asia will meet its goal of reducing poverty by half.

A2 then calculates the responsiveness of improvement of social indicators to economic growth. These elasticities are less than 1 for Asia, both East and South Asia, and substantially higher for the other regions. The acceptance of the MDGs had a positive impact on social progress. There was faster progress after the acceptance of the MDGs not merely because growth was faster but the elasticities were higher. The higher elasticities could be because the nature of the growth process had changed or that it was now accompanied by more or better special social programmes.

The BRICS countries have already reached the goal of reducing poverty by half. The elasticity of reduction is lower in China than for other countries in its region, whereas for the other BRICS countries the elasticities are greater than for other countries in their region. As far as reduction in mortality rates is concerned China is likely to achieve all three goals, whereas Brazil is likely to meet the goals of reducing infant and child mortality. India might achieve the goal of reducing maternal mortality.

In contrast to the goal of reducing poverty and malnutrition, there is no acceleration of progress after acceptance of the goals.

The chapter then compares the performance of the BRICS countries with a group of 31 large developing economies. The rank correlation between the ranks in 1990 and 2009 is very high. In general, countries in Latin America have the highest ranks and those in Africa the lowest ranks. Among the BRICS, China improved its rank from 13 in 1990 to 7 in 2009. India improved its rank by a mere 2 positions from 24 to 22. Brazil maintained its rank. However, South Africa saw its rank fall from 14 to 20, much closer to the level of achievement by other African countries.

The author then tries to relate social progress to economic performance. He finds that a higher growth in per capita GDP is usually associated with a better social index in a later year. But a better index in a year does not always translate itself into higher growth in the subsequent period. Causality is seemingly running from economic growth to social progress rather from social progress to economic growth.

The chapter then tries to examine what could explain the differential progress in reducing mortality rates. The chapter finds that health expenditures by the government seem to explain the difference, with higher expenditures leading to better health outcomes.

The chapter by Shen, Wang and Whalley (SWW) assesses changes in China's technology gaps both with the US and India between 1979 and 2008, comparing the technology level of these economies using a CES production framework in which the technology gap is reflected in the change of technology parameters. Their measure is related to but differs from the Malmquist index. The parameter values for a country's technology are determined using calibration procedures. The calculations suggest that the technology gap between China and the US is significantly larger than that between India and the US for the period before 2008. The pair wise gaps between the US and China, and the US and India remain large while narrowing at a slower rate than GDP per worker. This narrowing of the gap is supported by other measures. Although China has a higher growth rate of total factor productivity than India over the period, the bilateral technology gap between China and India is still in India's favour. India had a higher income per worker than China in the 1970s, and China's much more rapid physical and human capital accumulation has allowed China to move ahead, but a bilateral technology gap remains.

The chapter by Gao and Whalley (GW) analyses the ways in which product fragmentation (producing part of a product in one country, and a part elsewhere) is part of the strategies adopted by firms along the spectrum of where to produce and whether to produce in a country or to export to the country, and if it is decided to produce in the country what should be the mode of production adopted. GW find that the strategy adopted by a multinational firm depends critically on its productivity in areas where product chains can be internationally and arbitrarily fragmented. Besides exporting and horizontal FDI, firms face another choice which is to supply abroad through international fragmentation. Product fragmentation is thus an additional option to serving markets abroad by either horizontal or vertical FDI.

Upon opening a market to trade, firms with the lowest productivity will exit, those with intermediate productivity will export, and those with higher productivity will choose fragmentation. Among the latter, the more productive a firm is, the more product chains are allocated abroad. Firms with the highest productivity will choose horizontal FDI. At a sector level, the more prone to fragmentation a sector is, the lower will be the ratio of exports to FDI sales.

The chapters in the volume point to the importance of exports to the economic performance of both China and India. With the slowdown in the world economy both have embraced a strategy of using preferential trading arrangements to provide a fillip to their exports. Both have also collaborated in creating new international economic institutions. Apart from maintaining a high rate of growth of the overall economy they face specific problems in the rural areas. The rural–urban income disparity has been growing. Also there is scarcity of land which is also needed by the high rates of urbanisation and by industry. So the governments face the challenge of reforming the market for land, particularly rural land. The problems are however different. Migration to urban areas is much higher in China sometimes creating a problem of how the land can be best utilised. In India, employment creation in the manufacturing sector has been slower so that there is considerable pressure on land and the need to implement income maintenance schemes. Technology will obviously play a major role in tackling these issues and both governments are changing their education systems and policies regarding technology to spur innovations.

Part I

International Governance

Chapter 1

The New Development Bank, the Asian Infrastructure Investment Bank: A New Aid Architecture

Manmohan Agarwal

Centre for Development Studies
Thiruvananthapuram, Kerala, India
Adjunct Fellow,
RIS, India
manmohan@cds.ac.in

Abstract: This chapter analyses the performance of developing countries and the role of aid in this. This chapter argues that the New Development Bank (NDB) and the Asian Infrastructure Investment Bank (AIIB) have the potential to increase substantially aid flows to developing countries, though in the initial stages they will likely make only a small contribution to the increased flow of financial resources. They would fill a lacuna in the current financial architecture, particularly if their mandate is extended to provide finance for all long gestation projects including manufacturing.

They are as yet no challenge to the hegemony of the current multilateral aid institutions. They however, are a small beginning and may be a pointer of things to come. It is like a swimmer on the seashore who gingerly puts a toe in the water to test the temperature.

1 Introduction

In this chapter we examine the implications of the establishment of the NDB and the AIIB for the international aid architecture. We first analyse in Section 2, the developments in the international aid situation, both in terms of the trends in aid flows and the current debate on the future of two of the major multilateral aid agencies, the International Development Association (IDA) and the World Bank (WB). We then discuss in Section 3, the needs of developing countries by examining their economic performance paying particular attention to the savings investment balance and the state of their current account balance.

In Section 4, we discuss the importance of the NDB for the international aid architecture in the context of the current aid institutions and the needs of developing countries. We conclude that the NDB has the potential to become an important component of the international aid architecture not only in terms of increasing the quantity of funds but also in terms of the practices that accompany aid flows, the conditionality. We end by making some concluding observations in Section 5.

2 The Regional Distribution of Aid and Its Diminishing Importance

The importance of aid as a share of GDP has been declining, particularly for the regions of East Asia and Pacific (EAP) and for Latin America and the Caribbean (LAC) (Table 1).[1] But it is still very important for the poorest countries, the low income group and the least developed countries (LDCs).

Table 1. Regional distribution of aid (% of GNI).

	1960–1973	1974–1982	1983–1990	1991–2000	2001–2007	2008–2010	2011–2012
LDCs	7.5	9.2	9.8	9.0	7.6	6.5	
Low income	3.5	5.2	8.4	8.8	9.2	9.2	8.1
Land M income	1.2	1.4	1.5	1.2	1.0	0.8	0.6
Lower M income	2.2	2.5	2.1	2.0	1.4	1.0	0.8
Upper M income	0.3	0.3	0.4	0.3	0.3	0.1	0.1
EAP	1.1	0.9	1.0	0.8	0.3	0.2	0.1
LAC	0.5	0.3	0.5	0.3	0.3	0.2	0.2
SA	1.6	2.0	1.5	1.2	0.8	0.8	0.7
SSA	2.0	2.6	4.6	5.2	5.2	4.2	3.3

Note: These regions are as defined by the WB. LDCs are LDCs.
Source: http://databank.worldbank.org/data/databases.aspx. World Development Indicators, WB, Washington DC.

[1] It has also been declining as a share of GFCF and of imports. For a fuller discussion see Agarwal (2009).

Aid in recent years supports about a third of investment in low income countries, but surprisingly a smaller portion in the LDCs, though till 2000 aid was a larger share of investment in the LDCs than in the low income countries. As far as the regional distribution of aid is concerned it is still quite significant for SSA; it continues to play an important role in South Asia also.

Examination of the absolute amounts of bilateral aid (Table 2) to the different regions and the distribution between the regions (Table 3) reveals the following trends:

1. There was a slow increase in the amount of nominal aid between 1983 and 1992. It then tended to decline till 2001.
2. There was a very substantial increase in aid between 2001 and 2005 (134%).
3. Since 2005 the nominal amount of aid has fluctuated with overall a small increase.
4. The share of Africa declined substantially between the period 1983–1990 and the period 1991–2000. But has been constant since. The share of Asia and America has shown an almost steady decline throughout.
5. The share of other has increased. This is mainly the aid given through multilateral agencies, either through direct contributions to the capital of these agencies or through earmarked funds. The latter have increased particularly sharply. For instance, whereas multilateral aid grew by 31% between 2007 and 2012 earmarked resources grew by 79% (OECD, 2014). Earmarked funds have the advantage that they can help meet specific needs and evolving development challenges, and can make tracking easier. But they also have several disadvantages. Earmarked funds can make coordination and coherence of the international development cooperation system more difficult and undermine the strategic and coherent allocation of resources for individual multilateral organisations.[2]
6. Use of trust funds help donors reduce the cost of managing the programme, while achieving the donor's objectives. The utilisation of earmarked funds is more driven by the objectives of the donor than of the recipient. It leads to essentially a bilateralisation of multilateral aid.

[2] The Report of the IEG of the WB (2011) comes to similar conclusions. Among other observations it notes "Trust funds do not demonstrably provide additional resources at the global level. Donor countries generally allocate money to trust funds from within a fixed aid budget". It goes on to say "Trust funds have not been a consistently effective way of providing financing. They do not necessarily integrate well with countries' own programs, nor do they foster coordination on the ground with other sources of aid. …Notably, many trust funds of global scope involve insufficient recipient participation in the design of their objectives and modalities and lack clear outcome objectives".

Table 2. Net disbursements by regions (Billions of US$).

	Africa	America	Asia	Europe	Oceania	Other	Total
1983	6.5	2.1	6.2	0.4	0.9	1.7	17.8
1984	7.2	2.2	6.0	0.3	0.9	2.5	19.0
1985	8.1	2.6	6.9	0.3	0.8	2.5	21.2
1986	9.3	2.9	8.6	0.4	1.1	2.9	25.2
1987	10.7	3.4	8.9	0.5	1.2	4.1	28.9
1988	12.0	3.3	10.4	0.5	1.3	4.5	31.9
1989	12.1	3.8	10.6	0.4	1.3	4.7	32.9
1990	15.8	4.2	11.3	0.8	1.2	5.1	38.5
1991	16.5	4.8	13.2	1.5	1.2	5.6	43.0
1992	16.2	4.3	13.4	1.4	1.3	6.1	42.8
1993	13.4	4.3	12.0	1.8	1.4	6.1	39.0
1994	14.4	4.6	13.7	1.1	1.6	5.5	41.0
1995	13.2	4.8	12.4	1.3	1.7	7.0	40.5
1996	12.8	5.8	11.9	1.2	1.7	5.7	39.1
1997	11.4	3.9	8.1	1.0	1.4	6.5	32.4
1998	11.2	4.0	10.3	1.2	1.5	6.9	35.2
1999	10.3	4.3	12.6	2.5	1.4	6.8	37.8
2000	10.4	3.8	11.0	2.1	0.7	8.1	36.1
2001	10.1	4.4	10.6	1.7	0.7	7.4	35.1
2002	13.4	3.9	11.3	3.4	0.7	8.2	40.8
2003	19.1	4.6	13.7	2.3	0.7	9.3	49.7
2004	19.3	5.1	15.4	1.9	0.8	11.7	54.3
2005	24.6	4.8	37.8	2.4	0.9	11.9	82.4
2006	31.5	5.2	22.3	3.1	1.1	13.7	76.9
2007	24.5	4.7	24.3	2.1	1.2	15.9	72.9
2008	27.2	6.9	28.9	3.0	1.3	19.1	86.4
2009	28.2	6.6	23.6	3.0	1.4	21.1	83.9
2010	29.4	7.6	24.8	3.1	1.8	24.3	91.0
2011	32.7	7.8	23.8	2.7	2.0	25.5	94.4
2012	30.5	6.6	22.9	2.1	1.8	24.6	88.6

Source: OECD Data Base Access date 27/10/014.

Table 3. Net disbursements by region by DAC donors (Share of total net disbursements).

	Africa	America	Asia	Europe	Oceania	Other
1983–1990	0.43	0.13	0.36	0.02	0.05	0.15
1991–2000	0.34	0.12	0.31	0.04	0.04	0.17
2001–2005	0.33	0.09	0.34	0.04	0.01	0.18
2006–2008	0.35	0.07	0.32	0.03	0.02	0.21
2009–2012	0.34	0.08	0.27	0.03	0.02	0.27

Source: OECDE Data Base Access date 27/10/014.

3 The Sector Distribution of Aid

Over the years, the sector distribution of aid has varied. What is significant is that productive investment, whether directly productive in agriculture or industry or indirectly assisting production through better infrastructure tended to decline. (Table 4). However, investment in infrastructure has been increasing substantially since the turn of the century. Its share of total aid has increased from 12.6% in the years 2001–2005 to 15.0% during 2010–2012. Investment in agriculture has also increased from 3.9% of the total during 2001–2008 to 5.3% in the years 2010–2012. At the same time aid for multi-sector projects, including for environment, has increased consistently over the years from merely 3.1% during 1983–1990 to 11.1% during 2010–2012.

Table 4. Sector distribution of aid.

	1983–1990	1991–2000	2001–2005	2006–2008	2010–2012
Social sectors	24.8	27.7	32.9	38.2	42.1
Infrastructure	18.8	20.1	12.6	13.5	15.0
Production	17.2	10.8	6.2	5.8	7.5
Of which agriculture	10.5	7.3	3.9	3.9	5.3
Multi sector	3.1	5.4	6.9	6.3	11.1
Of which environment		1.2	1.9	2.5	4.3
Commodity assistance	5.6	2.6	1.7	5.2	4.8
Humanitarian aid	1.8	5.0	6.8	7.4	8.5
Debt relief	6.6	8.8	18.2	14.3	3.2
Administrative costs	3.4	4.7	5.1	4.8	5.6[1]
Support to NGOs		1.8	1.4	2.7	2.6
Refugees in donor countries		1.2	2.2	2.4	4.4

Source: DOECD Development Cooperation report various years.

There has been a substantial increase in aid to social sectors; but the increase is not to education or even much to health, It is to other social sectors, particularly to civil society organisations.

4 The Future Role of the WB and IDA

The main issues before the WB and its soft loan window, the IDA, are how to maintain their level of activities. Many of the large borrowers from IDA, e.g., Bangladesh, India and Vietnam, will graduate in the next decade or so. A number of options about the operations of IDA are being discussed (Moss and Leo, 2011).[3] One of the options is a reduction in the size of IDA.[4] But another option that should be explored is to increase lending to low income countries and LDCs thereby reversing the declining share of aid for these groups of countries that has been occurring in recent years.

The lending capacity of the WB which depends on its capital will soon hit a ceiling unless the capital is increased; the developed countries do not seem inclined to do that. Furthermore, an increasing share of resources made available to the WB come through earmarked funds which increases the role of donors in determining the priorities for the lending program. Borrowing countries have a greater say in the use of the WB's own funds, whether owned or borrowed, namely, there is greater country ownership in the case of the WB's own funds.

In addition, there are single borrower limits (SBL) that apply to the largest borrowers. These limits apply to three of the BRICS countries. In FY 2014 (the fiscal year runs from July to June) the SBL was raised for India to US$ 20 billion and for the other four, Brazil, China, Indonesia and Mexico, to US$ 19 billion (World Bank, 2014).[5,6] A country can borrow beyond its SBL under special agreements that essentially mean no increase in net availability of resources to the borrowing country because the country must either prematurely pay off previous loans or subscribe to the resources of the WB in other ways.

---

[3] The options being discussed are (i) loans to middle income countries for poverty reduction as most of the poverty would be concentrated in these middle income countries, (ii) decrease the amounts lent by IDA, (iii) increase the amounts lent to the remaining IDA eligible countries. These would be mainly in SSA and the issue whether these countries would have the absorptive capacity, and (iv) lend for projects that supply global or regional public goods. These would be mainly in the areas of either public health or infrastructure.

[4] The options that are being explored in the current, 17th round of replenishment range from maintaining the real value of the replenishment to an 11% decrease.

[5] These countries will have to pay an additional 50 basis points if they borrow more than their previous SBL limit, US$ 17.5 billion for India and US$ 16.5 billion for the others.

[6] India has a larger amount because of its greater need as levels of poverty are much higher.

Major issues before the international aid system is devising a new aid program for IDA and an agreement on its size, increasing aid programmes for large borrowers who are approaching their single country borrowing limits and, perhaps, increased capitalisation of the WB. The resolution of these issues will influence the possibilities available to the NDB and what role it can play in the international aid architecture.

4.1 Economic performance of developing countries

In this section, we look at the differential economic performance among developing countries.

Since 1991 developing countries particularly the low income countries have grown faster than the high income countries (Table 5). Furthermore, per capita GDP in the developing world did not fall after the 2008 financial crisis unlike in high income countries. But there has undoubtedly been a slowing down of the growth rate in developing countries.

However, the low income countries actually have grown faster since the crisis so that though they continue to grow slower than the middle income countries the gap in growth rates has narrowed. But within the middle income countries the lower middle income group has faced a greater slowdown than the upper middle income group. Similarly among low income countries, the LDCs which were growing

Table 5. Growth of per capita GDP (annual average %).

	1991–2000	2001–2007	2008–2010	2011–2013
High income	2.0	1.9	−0.7	1.2
Middle income	2.4	5.0	4.2	4.0
Upper middle income	3.0	5.3	4.5	4.5
Lower middle income	1.4	4.7	4.1	3.5
Low Income	−0.2	3.0	3.5	3.5
Least developed	0.3	4.3	3.2	2.0
Brazil	1.0	2.2	3.2	1.2
China	8.8	10.1	9.2	7.7
India	3.7	5.9	6.1	4.1
Russia	−3.5	7.2	0.6	2.7
S. Africa	−0.4	2.8	0.4	1.3

Source: http://databank.worldbank.org/data/databases.aspx. World Development Indicators, WB, Washington DC.

faster than other low income countries before the crisis have experienced a greater slowdown after the crisis than other low income countries.

There are considerable variations in the growth achieved by the different BRICS countries and also over time. In general, China has grown much faster than the other countries by a very large margin. Per capita income in China increased more than seven times between 1991 and 2013; almost tripled in India. But per capita income increased by only 50% in Brazil and barely grew in each of Russia and S. Africa (20% over 23 years). Growth in the period 2011–2013 as compared to that in the pre-crisis period 2001–2007, has decreased the most in Russia and the least in Brazil and South Africa.

We next examine whether there has been convergence.

4.2 GDP and GDP per capita relative to that in the US

We next look at per capita GDP and the GDP of the large economies relative to that in the US. We find three phases in the evolution of relative per capita incomes. In the first phase, till the early 1980s, countries and regions raised their per capita incomes relative to that in the US. In the second phase of the later 1980s and 1990s per capita income in most other parts of the world remained constant as a share of US per capita income or declined. In the third phase, the years of this century, the relative share of per capita incomes in most countries is again increasing. Only in EAP does relative per capita income rise fairly steadily and among the large economies this is true for China, India, Indonesia and Korea. Turkey's relative size has also increased.

Table 6. GDP per capita in constant 2000 US$ (% of US GDP per capita).

	1965	1973	1982	1990	2000	2007	2011
High income countries	62.5	69.1	73.0	73.5	71.8	72.8	73.5
Canada	71.3	73.7	69.1	67.2	67.8	68.5	68.8
France	65.0	71.8	66.2	62.1	60.7	61.0	61.1
Germany	65.1	70.9	69.3	65.4	65.3	68.1	69.5
Italy	51.8	59.6	58.7	55.3	52.4	50.7	50.3
Japan	96.7	109.6	121.0	106.3	105.5	107.1	105.0
UK	71.9	70.5	71.0	71.4	76.9	75.6	74.9
Average	70.3	76.0	75.9	71.3	71.4	71.8	71.6
Other developed	67.0	79.5	75.5	74.1	75.7	77.0	77.1
o.w Australia	64.6	67.4	62.0	61.9	64.1	68.2	68.0

(Continued)

Table 6. (*Continued*)

	1965	1973	1982	1990	2000	2007	2011
Austria	62.6	71.1	67.8	68.3	69.8	71.4	72.3
Belgium	64.3	69.8	66.2	64.7	64.7	65.8	72.3
Netherlands	68.7	69.4	66.6	68.9	69.7	71.0	70.7
Norway	83.0	101.0	97.5	106.8	108.2	107.1	106.2
Spain	39.7	39.4	40.1	41.1	42.2	41.3	41.0
Sweden	86.2	88.0	83.0	79.4	85.9	87.4	89.3
Switzerland		129.7	120.9	101.6	100.7	104.0	103.9
Developing countries	3.3	3.4	3.8	3.3	3.3	4.2	4.9
EAP	0.9	1.0	1.3	1.7	2.7	4.3	5.6
ECA				7.6	5.1	7.0	7.4
LAC	14.4	15.0	15.9	12.1	11.1	12.6	12.7
MNA	5.0	5.7	6.0	4.6	4.5	4.9	5.4
SA	1.3	1.1	1.1	1.1	1.3	1.7	2.0
SSA	2.9	2.7	2.5	1.8	1.4	1.5	1.7
Brazil	12.9	14.5	11.8	10.5	11.1	12.6	12.7
China	0.7	0.9	1.4	2.7	4.8	6.5	7.0
India	1.0	1.1	1.1	1.3	1.7	2.2	2.2
Mexico	18.9	23.3	17.3	16.6	16.4	16.4	16.7
Russia			9.2	5.1	7.5	7.8	8.0
South Africa	15.8	15.5	11.1	8.6	9.6	10.1	10.1
Argentina	34.0	29.4	19.7	21.9			
Indonesia	1.3	1.8	2.1	2.2	2.6	3.1	3.2
Korea	11.6	16.6	24.4	32.	39.0	43.4	44.3
Saudi Arabia	60.7	57.6	31.6	26.8	24.2	25.4	26.3
Turkey	11.4	11.8	12.2	11.9	13.8	14.3	15.2

Source: http://databank.worldbank.org/data/databases.aspx. World Development Indicators, WB, Washington DC.

When we compare the GDP of other countries with that of the US, we find a similar pattern. Initially till the 1990s, GDP of other countries increases relative to that of the US; then it decreases and finally, in recent years, it again increases (Table 7).

However, the behaviour of total GDP and per capita GDP differs between the developed economies and the developing economies. The GDP of more developed economies had declined relatively to the US between 1965 and 2011 than had

Table 7. GDP in constant 2000 US$ (% of US GDP).

	1965	1973	1982	1990	2000	2007	2011
Canada	7.0	7.5	8.0	7.7	7.3	7.4	7.6
France	14.6	16.3	17.3	15.5	13.4	12.9	12.8
Germany		24.2	24.0	22.0	19.1	17.8	18.2
Italy	12.0	13.4	14.6	13.3	11.2	10.3	9.8
Japan	35.6	49.3	56.0	59.9	47.8	44.7	43.1
UK	19.4	19.1	17.1	16.3	14.9	15.6	15.1
Average	17.7	21.6	22.8	22.4	18.9	18.1	17.8
Other developed							
o.w Australia	3.8	4.1	4.4	4.2	4.2	4.5	4.9
Austria	2.1	2.2	2.3	2.1	1.9	1.9	2.0
Belgium	2.8	3.0	3.0	2.6	2.4	2.3	2.3
Netherlands	4.1	4.4	4.3	4.0	3.9	3.8	3.8
Norway	1.5	1.6	1.8	1.7	1.7	1.7	1.7
Spain	5.4	6.5	6.5	6.2	5.9	6.3	6.1
Sweden	3.5	3.3	3.2	2.8	2.5	2.6	2.7
Switzerland			3.6	3.3	2.6	2.5	2.6
Developing countries	3.3	3.4	3.8	3.3	3.3	4.2	4.9
EAP	4.6	5.6	8.2	11.0	17.4	27.6	38.0
ECA				11.9	7.2	9.4	10.1
LAC	18.3	21.5	25.5	21.2	20.8	22.5	25.5
MNA	2.9	3.7	4.6	4.2	4.4	5.1	5.7
SA	4.1	3.9	4.7	5.3	6.3	8.6	11.1
SSA	3.9	4.1	4.4	3.8	3.4	4.0	4.7
Brazil	4.2	6.3	8.0	7.1	6.5	7.0	8.0
China	2.3	2.8	4.1	6.3	12.1	21.1	30.2
India	3.0	2.9	3.4	3.9	4.8	6.8	8.9
Mexico	4.2	5.1	7.2	5.9	5.9	5.9	6.1
Russia				5.5	2.6	3.5	3.7
South Africa	1.7	1.8	1.9	1.6	1.3	1.5	1.6
Argentina	4.1	4.1	3.7	2.6	2.9		
Indonesia	0.6	0.8	1.2	1.5	1.7	2.0	2.5
Korea	1.2	1.9	2.8	4.2	5.4	6.3	7.1
Saudi Arabia	1.9	2.8	2.0	1.9	2.0	2.4	
Turkey	1.8	2.0	2.4	2.6	2.7	3.2	3.6

Source: http://databank.worldbank.org/data/databases.aspx. World Development Indicators, WB, Washington DC.

increased (Table 5) whereas more developing countries gained on the US than lost ground. But in terms of per capita GDP, most developed economies gained relatively to the US and only some lost ground. But more developing economies lost ground than caught up to the US. Most of the countries catching up to the US are in Asia.

That the developed economies are catching up to the US in terms of per capita income, but not in terms of total GDP is mainly a reflection of their slower growth of population, nine of the advanced economies in our group saw population grow slower than in the US. On the other hand, population in developing countries usually grew faster than in the US and this enabled their GDP to catch up to that in the US. But productivity in many of them is not growing very rapidly so there is less of a narrowing of the gap in per capita income.

There is very limited convergence. *Per capita* incomes in developing countries are by and large not catching up with that in the US and since most other developed countries are catching up to the US, this implies that the gap between developing countries and most developed countries is increasing. It is only the countries in Asia, particularly those in East Asia that are catching up with the developed countries.

4.3 The changing role of aid

After the Second World War, when analysis of development issues commenced, stress was placed on the inadequate savings (Lewis,1954; Nurkse,1953). Some analysts combined this with an inadequate incentive to invest because of shortage of purchasing power (Rosenstein–Rodan,1943; Nurkse,1953). The role of foreign aid was to augment domestic savings and permit the larger investment needed to raise the rate of growth of GDP.

Many developing countries raised savings and investment rates in the 1950s and 1960s which enabled them to achieve faster rates of growth of their GDP. But the economies did not grow smoothly; there were considerable fluctuations. These fluctuations were caused by the large current account deficits that these economies often ran and the necessity to adopt policies to rectify these large deficits. The current account deficits were caused by the inability of their earnings from exports, mainly primary exports, to keep pace with their import payments as imports of capital goods for investment and intermediate goods for the new industries grew rapidly. Development economists then argued that developing economies faced two gaps, a savings investment gap and a foreign exchange gap that was the difference between their exports and imports. Aid should equal the larger of the two gaps (Chenery and Bruno, 1962; Chenery and Strout, 1966).

Developing countries were able to further raise their savings rates which together with aid enabled them to achieve higher growth rates in the 60s and 70s. However, there was considerable concern about the slow increase in employment and the consequent slow decrease in poverty.[7] Consequently, there was a shift in the aid supported development strategy. Greater stress was laid on poverty reduction in the WB's aid allocations (McNamara, 1973).

However, the debt crisis of the eighties had serious consequences. Aid was geared towards restoring macro stability which it was believed required reduced government involvement in the economy (Williamson, 1990). So the balance of payments loans from the IMF and loans from the WB were accompanied by conditions that reduced government involvement in the economy. They were less aimed at project financing as had been the case earlier. It is difficult to evaluate the effects of these conditions, known as structural adjustment programmes (SAP). They have, however, been criticised for their social effects (Cornia *et al.*, 1988) as well as their efficacy in restoring macro stability (Mosley *et al.*, 1991). Others attribute their lack of success to organisational weaknesses in developing countries.

As a consequence, aid has been geared towards improving the efficiency of the delivery of government services; the goal is to achieve the Millennium Development Goal (MDGs), and now the Sustainable Development (SDGs).

4.4 Trends in investment and savings

An important positive feature of recent developments in developing countries is the maintenance of high rates of investment despite the growth slowdown; and these investments have been financed largely by higher rates of domestic savings (Table 8). The share of gross capital formation (GCF) in GDP has increased in all the developing regions despite the economic slowdown and in all the BRICS countries except Russia. Also gross domestic savings (GDS) as a share of GDP has usually continued to increase. However, the savings investment gap has tended to worsen, and so correspondingly the current account balance. Though the gap has remained manageable, partly because of accumulated foreign exchange reserves, and growth reducing measures have not had to be implemented, this is a

[7] International Labour Office (1972), Employment, Incomes and Equality: A Strategy for Increasing Productive Employment in Kenya, January, 1972, ILO, Geneva.

Also see International Labour Organisation (1973), Strategies for employment promotion: An evaluation of four inter-agency employment missions. ILO pub-WEP pub. Conference report on the evaluation of the four pilot ILO Missions conducted under the WEP in Colombia, Kenya, Iran, Islamic Republic and Sri Lanka.

Table 8. GCF and GDS (% of GDP).

		1965–1973	1974–1982	1983–1990	1991–2000	2001–2007	2008–2013
EAP	(i)	26.7	32.7	34.4	36.4	36.7	42.7
	(ii)		32.9	33.9	38.2	41.4	46.5
LAC	(i)	21.1	24.2	20.2	19.6	19.6	21.2
	(ii)	20.4	23.1	23.6	18.6	20.3	20.1
SA	(i)	15.3	18.9	22.1	23.0	28.9	33.0
	(ii)	13.6	16.0	18.9	21.4	26.2	27.0
SSA	(i)	24.6	25.5	18.1	16.7	17.6	20.6
	(ii)	22.5	23.2	20.4	16.8	17.1	18.8
Low income	(i)	12.4	15.1	16.9	18.2	21.3	25.1
	(ii)	8.2	6.7	8.7	9.8	10.8	11.7
Low middle income	(i)	15.8	22.0	22.8	22.7	25.5	29.1
	(ii)	14.0	19.2	20.3	21.0	23.9	24.5
Brazil	(i)	20.5	23.4	20.4	18.6	16.9	19.0
	(ii)	20.2	21.2	24.0	18.0	19.1	18.0
China	(i)	29.2	34.8	36.8	39.0	40.8	42.8
	(ii)		35.2	36.1	41.0	45.3	51.9
India	(i)	15.8	19.6	23.0	23.8	31.0	36.0
	(ii)	14.9	18.4	21.4	22.9	29.0	30.9
Russia	(i)				24.3	29.0	23.2
	(ii)				32.3	33.0	30.9
S.Africa	(i)	26.4	28.4	20.5	17.1	18.2	20.4
	(ii)	26.7	30.9	26.8	9.6	19.1	20.0

Note: Row (i) is GCF as percent of GDP and row (ii) is GDS as percent of GDP.
Source: WB, World Development Indicators.

worrisome factor for the future. In the past large current account deficits have called for corrective measures that have reduced the rate of growth.[8] Historically this gap has been large in low income countries and has worsened as the investment share in GDP increased without a concomitant increase in the share of domestic savings.

[8] The Contingent Reserve Arrangement that was also agreed upon could provide an additional source of balance of payment financing. But it does not provide for a new model for the operation of the international monetary system and so is not a solution for the ills of the current international monetary system (Agarwal *et al.*, 2015).

The above data on investment and savings shows that investment levels have been maintained in all the regions and income groups listed above after the financial crisis. The maintenance of GFCF despite the fall in growth rates of GDP suggests that capital is being invested in more capital intensive sectors as could happen if developing countries are seeking to reduce imports in line with the diminished export prospects.[9] Another possibility along somewhat similar lines is that domestic investment is being concentrated in the infrastructure sector and that tends to be capital intensive.

Furthermore, domestic savings rates have also increased. However, the difference has increased implying that the current account balance has worsened. This raises two concerns. One is whether the investment levels can be maintained in the face of the current account situation. Though the levels of foreign exchange reserves have cushioned the impact of the deficit, the reserve position is no longer as comfortable as it was earlier. Second, despite higher investment levels the rate of growth of GDP has fallen in many countries and regions (Table 4) reflecting perhaps the worsening investment climate and therefore again raising questions about the sustainability of investment levels.

What can the AIIB and the NDB contribute in this situation?

5 The NDB and the Aid Architecture

5.1 Governance and resources of the NDB

The NDB has been established to mobilise resources for infrastructure and SD projects. It will do so through "loans for public or private projects, guarantees, equity participation and other financial instruments".[10] It will also provide technical assistance to projects supported by the Bank. Membership to the NDB is open to all members of the UN. But the presidency will rotate among the original members. The subscriptions of the other members and thus their voting power will be determined by the Governing Council (GC). However, the voting power of the original members will not be allowed to fall below 55% and those of non-borrowing members to exceed 20%.[11] Furthermore, the voting power of a non-founding member cannot exceed 7% of the total. These rules may lead to the founding

---

[9] In line with the Heckscher–Ohlin trade theory developing countries being capital scarce would import capital intensive products so any import substitution would raise the capital output ratio in the economy.

[10] The details are contained in the agreement that can be accessed at http://brics6.itamaraty.gov.br/media2/press-releases/219-agreement-on-the-new-development-bank-fortaleza-july-15.

[11] In essence this limits the voting power of the developed countries if they become members of NDB.

members being charged with running a non-democratic organisation just as the governance of the WB is criticised.

The first two subscriptions would be due in 18 months after the coming into force of the agreement and would amount to merely US$ 2 billion. After the rest of the capital is paid in over a period of five years the total paid in amount would be US$ 10 billion. The WB had started in 1945 with an authorised capital of 10 billion of which 20% was paid in. Only about 6% or about US$ 12 billion of the total authorised capital of US$ 191 billion at the end of 2010 was subscribed, the rest was callable. Similarly of the US$ 81 billion increase agreed in 2010 only 6% was subscribed. More important than the subscribed capital are the accumulated reserves which are almost twice the size of the subscribed capital. The WB's loan portfolio of about US$ 200 billion is mainly supported by its borrowings from the market, which are supported by its large callable capital.

The 10 billion paid in capital of the NDB at the end of the seventh instalment would compare very favourably with the US$ 18 billion paid in capital of the WB. However, the resources of the NDB would have two shortcomings in comparison to the WB. The NDB would not have any significant reserves and these are very large at the WB. Furthermore, the WB is able to leverage its own resources by considerable borrowings from capital markets. Initially its bonds were given only an "A" rating. Prudent financial management, its large callable capital and the developed countries being its main shareholders ultimately resulted in its bonds getting a "triple A" rating in 1959. Initially the NDB may not have a high rating and so may not be able to borrow cheaply and so similarly leverage its own resources. This would limit its lending capacity. The GC might be faced with a dilemma. A high rate of interest may be needed to win the confidence of private bond markets. But a high rate of interest would not only limit the demand for loans, and may also lead to debt servicing problems later.[12]

A further development has occurred in the aid architecture. On October 24, 2014, a signing ceremony held in Beijing, formally recognised the establishment of the AIIB. 21 countries, all Asian, participated at the meeting and signed the bill. Subsequently more countries joined as founding members, all countries that join by March 31, 2015 would be considered founding members. There are 31 members as of March 17, 2015 and this includes European countries such as the UK, France, Germany and Italy who had earlier held off. Australia and South Korea who had also refrained from becoming members at US insistence are expected to also become members soon.

[12] For instance, India started borrowing from the WB and other bilateral donors only in 1958–1959. But this debt was restructured six times between 1968 and 1976 (Rieffel, 2003).

The AIIB would also have an authorised capital of US$ 100 billion. But clearly the AIIB is making headway in attracting members in contrast to the NDB which has not yet attracted any new members. The Chinese who are contributing 50 billion to the AIIB are obviously going to dominate it. The obvious point is that China is more interested in the AIIB which is a Chinese initiative and is pushing to get countries to join. No similar push is being made to get countries to join the NDB. Countries may have come to the conclusion that the AIIB is a more serious endeavour.

Questions have been raised about the possible functioning of the AIIB. There are suspicions it is a vehicle for Chinese infrastructure investment and for expanding Chinese influence. However, econometric analysis of the factors that influence countries' aid allocation decision do not support the hypotheses the Chinese aid is more mercatilistic or goes to countries that have large reserves of natural resources.

Of course, the AIIB and the NDB may have separate spheres of operation. The AIIB is restricted to Asia. It may then be likely that the NDB will operate mainly in LA and SSA.

5.2 Lending strategies of the new institutions

The new institutions have been set up to lend mainly for infrastructure. Investment in infrastructure has always been considered crucial for accelerating economic growth. However, a major issue has been whether to build infrastructure ahead of the demand, so that it acts as a pull factor for other investments or that might be wasteful, as the inadequate initial usage would lower the returns to the investment. Returns to infrastructure can also be delayed because of the long gestation lags in completing the investments. Consequently, investment in infrastructure requires sources of long-term finance. However, this is not unique to infrastructure. Manufacturing also requires producers to have access to long-term finance. Gerchenkron analysing European growth examines the innovative policies adopted by late comers to provide such long-term finance.

Developing countries in the post Second World War period established development finance companies (DFCs) to provide such long-term finance. Few DFCs have been successful. Many, particularly in Latin America, have depended FCs such as aid to provide long-term finance, and have used their own resources for short term loans. Even successful DFCs such as Brazil's BNDES have lent mainly to natural resource companies and to large companies which could have accessed financial markets on their own. The Indian financial structure as it developed in the 1980s was able to successfully intermediate household savings into private investments. But inadequate regulation of the newly liberalised markets in the 1990s resulted in households losing confidence in financial markets, and increasingly investing in bank deposits or gold and land.

Lack of long-term finance may be an important factor in the lack luster performance of the manufacturing sector BRICS countries (Table 9).

The share of manufacturing in GDP has declined in Brazil and South Africa (Table 9). There are indications that it has also declined in Russia.[13] In India also it has been declining in recent years.

The integration of developing countries particularly the low income countries, into the world FDI system has resulted in a dramatic increase in inflows (Table 10).

But these inward inflows have not been able to boost manufacturing growth. A successful investment strategy for the AIIB and the NDB, even for its infrastructure investments to be fruitful requires a more broad based investment strategy.

Concentration on infrastructure also has the danger of creating structural imbalances.

Table 9. Share of manufacturing in GDP (%).

	1991–2000	2001–2007	2008–2010	2010–2012
Brazil	16.1	15.4	14.3	13.2
China	29.6	32.6	32.8	n.a
India	14.0	14.3	15.1	14.9
S. Africa	17.0	16.6	15.6	15.3

Source: http://databank.worldbank.org/data/databases.aspx. World Development Indicators, WB, Washington DC.

Table 10. Inward flows of FDI (% of GDP).

	1990–2000	2001–2005	2006–2007	2008–2011
World	1.6	2.1	3.9	2.5
High income	1.5	1.9	4.0	2.4
Middle income	2.0	2.6	3.7	3.0
Low income	0.9	2.2	2.6	3.4
Brazil	1.8	2.7	2.5	2.6
China	3.8	3.4	4.5	3.4
India	0.4	0.9	2.1	2.4
Russia	0.8	1.6	3.6	3.3
S. Africa	0.6	2.2	1.0	1.8

Source: http://databank.worldbank.org/data/databases.aspx. World Development Indicators, WB, Washington DC.

[13] The available data for Russia is for the industry sector of which manufacturing is usually a substantial part. Share of industry in GDP has declined in Russia.

For instance, in the case of India, the concentration on infrastructure and on housing resulted in the share of construction in total gross fixed capital increasing from about 45%in the early 1990s to almost 60% in recent years (Agarwal *et al.*, 2015). The lack of investment in machinery and equipment reduced the rate of growth of the economy from over 9% to under 5%. Furthermore, the increased demand emanating from the construction activity was for both tradeable and non-tradable. The former resulted in larger current account deficits and the latter in higher inflation.[14]

5.3 Lending policies of the institutions: the role of conditionalities

The NDB can make a significant contribution in the management of aid and projects. Preparation of projects by the WB is time consuming and uses scarce administrative talent intensively. Furthermore, the projects are accompanied by many conditions. The BRICS countries do not put any conditions on the amounts they make available through their development cooperation programmes. They might continue with this policy in the NDB. There is the danger that lack of conditionality may endanger the viability of the projects. On the other hand it has been argued that what is important is ownership of the project by the country. If there is ownership, conditionality may not be required. If the projects of the NDB are successful even with no conditionality, the multilateral development banks may be forced to change their practices. So the NDB has the potential to change the international aid architecture.

6 Conclusions

The NDB and the AIIB have the potential to substantially increase aid flows to developing countries, though in the initial stages they will likely make only a small contribution to the increased flow of financial resources. They can fill a useful lacuna in the international financial architecture. However, the mandate of the two institutions should be extended to provide finance for all long gestation projects including manufacturing.[15]

---

[14] This state of affairs is predicted in the choice of techniques literature of the 1950s and 1960s. Choice of too labour intensive a technique would reduce the savings and so the investment and lower the growth rate. So higher employment today would be at the expense of lower employment tomorrow (Sen, 1960).

[15] Finance for manufacturing has been an important issue historically. Banks provided long-term finance and to protect their investments they were involved in the management of enterprises (Gerschenkron, 1962). This pattern seems to have been replicated in Korea and Taiwan (Amsden, 1989; Wade, 1990). In the case of Russia, the state had to step in to provide the finance (Gerschenkron, 1962).

They are as yet no challenges to the hegemony of the current multilateral aid institutions. These small beginnings may be a pointer of things to come.[16] It is like a swimmer on the seashore who gingerly puts a toe in the water to test the temperature.

References

Agarwal, M. (2009), Shrinking Aid paper presented at a conference on Rising states Rising Donors and the Global Aid Regime, held at York University Toronto Canada, 20–21 Nov 2009.

Agarwal M., S. Mitra and J. Whalley (2015), Indian Economic Growth: Its Ups and Downs, in Manmohan Agarwal and John Whalley (Eds.), *Asia and The World Economy Vol. 1 Sustainability of Growth: The Role of Economic, Technological and Environmental Factors*, World Scientific, Singapore.

Amsden, A. (1989), *Asia's Next Giant: South Korea and Late Industrialization*, Oxford University Press: Oxford.

Chenery, H. and M. Bruno (1962), Development Alternatives in an Open Economy: The case of Israel, *Economic Journal*, 72 (1), 79–93.

Chenery, H. and A. Strout (1966), Foreign Assistance and Economic Development, *American Economic Review*, 61(4), 679–733.

Cornia, A., R. Jolly and F. Stewart (1988), *Adjustment with a Human Face*, Clarendon Press.

Gerschenkron, A. (1962), *Economic Backwardness in Historical Perspective*, Preager: New York.

Independent Evaluation Group (IEG) (2011), *Trust Fund Support for Development: An Evaluation of the World Bank's Trust Fund Portfolio*, Independent Evaluation Group, The World Bank Group: Washington, DC.

Lewis, W.A. (1954), Economic Development with Unlimited Supplies of Labour, *Manchester School of Economic and Social Studies*, 22, 1–31.

Mosley, P., J. Hartigan and J. Toye (1991), *Aid and Power: The World bank and Policy Based Lending*, Routledge: London.

Moss, T. and B. Leo (2011), IDA at 65: Heading Toward Retirement or a. Fragile Lease on Life? CGD Working Paper 246, Center for Global Development: Washington, DC.

Nurkse, R. (1953), *Problems of Capital Formation in Underdeveloped Countries*, Oxford: Basil Blackwell.

Rosenstein-Rodan, P. (1943), Problems of Industrialisation of Eastern and South Eastern Europe, *Economic Journal*, 53, 202–211.

Sen, A. (1960), *Choice of Techniques: An Aspect of the Theory of Planned Economic Development*, Oxford: Basil Blackwell.

Tortora, P. and S. Steensen (2014), Making earmarked funding more effective:
Current practices and a way forward OECD Development Co-operation Directorate
Report No. 1 2014, Paris.

[16] Already the BRICS are thinking of setting up their own credit rating agency.

Wade, R. (1990), *Governing the Market, Economic Theory and the role of the Government in East Asian Industrialization*, Princeton University Press: Princeton.

Williamson, J. (1990), *Latin American Adjustment: How Much has Happened?* Institute for International Economics: Washington DC.

World Bank (2014), Information Statement International Bank for Reconstruction and Development.

Chapter 2

Emerging Experience with Design and Implementation of Policy Instruments for Renewal Energy Technologies Development and Deployment across Countries

Meeta Keswani Mehra
Jawaharlal Nehru University, New Delhi, India
meetakm@mail.jnu.ac.in

Rita Pandey
National Institute of Public Finance and Policy, New Delhi, India
rita.pandey@nipfp.org.in

Abstract: The deployment of policy instruments for renewal energy (RE) programs requires choice of instruments based on many criteria — policy effectiveness in terms of stimulation of RE deployment, cost effectiveness indicators for the economy, incentives to reduce costs and prices and incentives to innovate/technological learning or market maturation. We analyse the experience of selected countries on how the deployment policy instruments for RE technologies have performed in order to derive important lessons. In this respect, this chapter complements the chapter, "Choice and Design of Policy Instruments towards Promoting Renewable Energy Technologies: Conceptual Framework and Guiding Principles" by Mehra and Pandey (2016) from Volume 3 of this book, with an analysis of country experiences from a broad set of emerging economies, such as China, India and Brazil on the one hand, and OECD countries such as Germany, Spain, USA and Denmark on the other.

The chapter focuses on identification and discussion of the best practices associated with the design of the instruments as well as the main lessons learned of the implementation of RE policy tools. In what follows immediately, the regulatory and policy environment for RE development and deployment is presented.

1 Policy Context in which RE Technology (RET) D&D Incentives have Emerged

It is important to understand the policy environment in which measures towards promoting renewal energy technology (RET) development and deployment have emerged in developed and developing countries. This helps identify the context in which specific factors have proved conducive to or barriers to effective dissemination of RETs. On the one hand, a strong political will and compliance with international treaty/agreement has favoured the development of RETs, while on the other hand, planning and bureaucratic hurdles and grid connection issues have hindered their effective deployment. Policy design and implementation can also be linked to the market structures in the economy. The tabulation below is elucidatory (Table 1).

Against this backdrop, we discuss the country experiences with use of incentives and support measures for RE development and deployment and allude to the lessons learnt there from.

2 Effectiveness and Efficiency of Support Schemes for Development and Deployment of RETs: Lessons Learnt from Country Experiences

Designing policy for RE programs requires choice of instruments based on many criteria — policy effectiveness in terms of stimulation of RE deployment, cost effectiveness indicators for the economy, incentives to reduce costs and prices and incentives to innovate/technological learning or market maturation (Menanteau *et al.*, 2003). A discussion is now presented on how the deployment policy instruments for RE technologies have performed on these accounts in terms of select country experiences (IEA, 2008, 2011; EEA, 2014). The discussion forms the basis for the dos and don'ts for future policy design and implementation. Broadly, three sets of support schemes have been taken up for analysis, namely,

- Price based market instruments such as feed-in-tariffs (FITs) and feed-in-premiums (FITPs);
- Quantity based market instruments called RPSs or RPO;
- Tendering/competitive bidding.

Table 1. Policy context within which RET development and deployment incentives are placed.

Policy impacts	Policy context	Country-wise analysis
Policy supports	Presence of a clear political resolve	*China*: Presence of a definitive political resolve has led to the successful design and implementation of policies and support measures for encouraging RETs in China. China is now a world leader in non-hydropower RE capacity (at 70 GW at the national level by 2011), and has installed more wind turbines and manufactured more solar PV panels than any other country in the world. The impressive growth of RE capacity (from 27.8 GW in 2001 to 183 GW in 2013, with share of RE to account for 20% of aggregate electricity generation in the country by 2020) can be ascribed to a clear political will, combined with an aggressive pricing mechanism and a strong manufacturing base to back this process. Chinese RE law of 2006 had specified time-bound goals and objectives for RE development and deployment. These were aided by complementary measures toward diversification of the energy mix, development of a strong indigenous manufacturing base, and putting in place aggressive incentives mechanism. Support instruments instituted by the National Development and Reform Commission (NDRC) of China included reliance on competitive bidding system. Subsequently, in 2009, a move to FITs differentiated by type of wind energy resources were instituted. Companies that won the bid were provided guaranteed grid access through a power purchase agreement, coupled with a range of complementary measures such as preferential loan and tax conditions, and financial support for road and grid extension (WWF and WRI, 2013). *Germany*: Germany too exhibits a strong and steady rising share of RE in electricity, heat and biofuel sectors. In 2012, RE generation, including hydropower, accounted for 23.5% (140,000 GWh) of total power consumption in the country, up from 11% in 2005 and a mere 4.3% (19.000 GWh) of total power consumption in 1990. In 2000, the Erneuerbare–Energien–Gesetz (EEG) (Renewable Energy Sources Act) was made effective, which has been the primary instrument for promoting RE in the electricity sector of Germany. The EEG received immense support from parties across the entire political spectrum of the country. RE development was also incorporated as an integral part of the industrial development policy, complemented by Germany's commitment to shift from nuclear and fossil fuels to RE. The other key policies driving RE dissemination have been the market incentive program for renewable heat generation and the tax exemptions in the biofuel sector. The success of the EEG can be attributed to a stable flow of investment, priority grid access and sufficiently high FITs for renewables (Jager and Rathmann, 2008).

(Continued)

Table 1. (*Continued*)

Policy impacts	Policy context	Country-wise analysis
		Japan: In Japan as well, it was the National Energy Law (1997) that specified the target for RE in aggregate primary energy supply. This was supported by RE promotion rules on how the costs of grid reinforcement were to be financed, and how the transmission networks were to be improved and maintained (Jager and Rathmann, 2008). Renewable Energy Sources for Electricity (RES-E) has generally relied on support from a Renewables Portfolio Standard (RPS) scheme that was launched in 2003. RPSs have been implemented for a range of technologies, namely, offshore wind, onshore wind, solar Photovoltaic (PV), solar thermal electric, Countrating Solar Power (CSP), biomass, small hydropower and geothermal. Besides RPS, voluntary agreements between government and energy suppliers to buy electricity generated from RE at the residential retail price (suitable FITs) that were introduced in 1992 have also been a significant determinant of power generation from RE until 2002. Solar PV plays an important role in the Japanese power system. The financial support for PV has been mainly aimed at RD&D schemes. In the past, the thrust on the development of PV cell technology was achieved mainly through the Moonlight and Sunshine Projects in the 1970s and 1980s.
	Countries' compliance with international environmental treaties	*Canada*: So far, the development and deployment of RES in Canada is largely confined to hydropower and some biomass. Since the late 1990s, a number of support policies and measures were instituted by the federal and provincial governments, but these were not adequate to stimulate significant RE development. It is after the adoption of the Kyoto Protocol in December 1997 that a fresh thrust on policy and measures supporting RE investment and deployment were introduced in Canada. Prior to this, efforts were concentrated on competitive technologies such as large hydropower and biomass for application in paper and forest product industries. Recently, the key support instruments that have been put in place at the federal government are a FITPs for almost all RES-E technologies and flexible depreciation on investment cost. Conditional on the specific project, complementary instruments have been used, such as investment subsidies and low interest loans (Jager and Rathmann, 2008).
	Mix of domestic policy resolve and compliance with international environmental treaties	*India*: Presently, the RE development and deployment in India is guided by the targets laid down in the various national Five Year Plans (FYPs), the National Action Plan on Climate Change (NAPCC) and the Jawaharlal Nehru National Solar Mission (JNNSM). Thus, the driving factors in India have been a mix of national policy resolve and requirements placed by the international treaties. The 11th FYP (2007–2012)

		set a target of additional 12.4 GW of grid connected RE that was exceeded with actual installation being over 14 GW during this period (ABPS Infra, 2009). The target set for the 12th FYP (2012–2017) is 30 GW of RES-E with the following mix of technology: 15 GW wind, 10 GW solar and 2.1 GW of small hydro (Government of India, 2013). The NAPCC was launched in 2008 and envisages around 15% electricity consumption from RES by 2020. Under the umbrella of NAPCC, the Jawaharlal Nehru National Solar Mission (JNNSM) was initiated that sets out a target of 22 GW of solar capacity by 2022 in both grid- and off-grid modes. It also proposes an integrated approach to policy support, including support toward R&D, manufacturing development and market deployment (EPIA, 2012; WWF and WRI, 2013). So far, in India, reliance has been placed on both quantity and price based measures, namely Renewable Purchase Obligations (RPO) scheme with tradable renewable energy certificate scheme and FITs. Despite the impressive growth, India continues to face the challenge of broad basing RE development and deployment as, so far, this has been restricted to select states.
Policy barriers	Complex administrative and planning procedures and grid connectivity constraints	*China*: The absence of accountability has discouraged full realisation of grid connection potential, as grid companies face no burden to achieve their quotas. While the Renewable Energy Law deems that grid companies connect renewable energy projects, and while the 11th FYP of 2008 stipulated that from 2015 and 2020 the power companies would have to achieve a 1% and 3% portfolio of renewable energy generation in their output, these provisions have not been followed. In addition, disincentives exist as the compensation for accepting wind power is not enough to encourage grid companies, even though a cost sharing mechanism has been implemented. That is, the pricing policies for wind power do not fairly reflect the difficulties encountered in terms of grid connections. *France*: Due to these barriers, there has been only modest development of RE in France in the recent past. Currently, the dominating RES-E technology in France is hydropower, although, there exists large potential for wind and biomass based energy. The French feed-in-laws are beset with complicated administrative and planning procedures that diminish the realised potential of the incentives put in place. RES support in France has been mainly provided through three instruments: FIT for RES-E, multiple tax reductions for RES in all the sectors and different subsidy programs run by the French Environment and Energy Management Agency (ADEME). The specific structure of the scheme has varied across regions and tends to be subject to frequent changes. Despite relatively high FITs, RES-E and especially wind energy development, has been hindered

(*Continued*)

Table 1. (*Continued*)

Policy impacts	Policy context	Country-wise analysis
		by bureaucratic planning regulations. The change of regulatory procedures in 2005 has somewhat improved the situation, in that, in 2006, with newly installed capacity of 810 MW, France managed to more than double its market for wind power (Jager and Rathmann, 2008).
		Italy: Similar constraints can be observed in case of Italy, where the production of RES-E from wind and biogas sources has displayed some increase, but this has not been commensurate with the growth of aggregate electricity consumption. The incentive and support measures instituted by the Italian authorities have been generally unstable. Moreover, the administrative procedures for grid connection have been long and complicated, entailing high transactions costs. During the 1990s, the most important incentive for penetration of RES-E was FIT. Since 2001, there has been a move towards a quota obligation with tradable green certificates. In 2005, a separate FIT for solar PV was put into practice. A switch back to FITs for most technologies is imminent, which will replace the quota obligations. In spite of these measures, the development and deployment of RES-E has been disappointing — mainly due to political, administrative and financial reasons. Further, no specific national support instruments have been implemented for RES-H (Jager and Rathmann, 2008).
Policy performance linkages	Size of the economy and the market structures therein.	*Select emerging economies*: Azuela and Barroso (2011) find a clear distinction between large and medium-size countries (defined in terms of gross national income and size of power sector) in the variety of instruments found in the policy package. In general, Brazil, India and Turkey have implemented a more diverse set of mechanisms to promote RE than Indonesia, Nicaragua and Sri Lanka. Also, BRICS countries Brazil and India have been relying on more evolved types of instruments (well-developed FIT design, REC market and auctions). Furthermore, the policies to support RE have been more effectual in the higher-income countries (Brazil, India and Turkey). This could also be due to other complementary factors, such as the domestic investment climate, economic and political stability, and governance and institutional issues. In comparison, low RE market growth has been exhibited in both Indonesia and Nicaragua for reasons related to policy or contract design in combination with select external or background factors (such as regional financial crises, governance constraints or regulatory uncertainty).

Source: Authors' compilation.

Next, the discussion focuses on the impact of support measures on stimulus to RES-E based on the policy impact indicator (PII) and the cost-efficiency of the support scheme by relying on the total cost indicator (TCI). Both the indicators have been harmonised by the International Energy Agency (IEA) to allow cross-country comparisons (IEA, 2011). In addition, the other impacts studied pertain to incentives toward technology cost reduction and technology market maturation based on Jager and Rathmann (2008), which indirectly point towards incentive to innovate.

3 Stimulus to RES-E

The level of market deployment of a technology can be measured by the stimulus provided to RES-E. IEA has been relying on the PII for the OECD and BRICS countries, with focus on wind power and solar PV. PII measures the progress toward a defined goal and provides a measure of the impact of policies on stimulating RE deployment. It calculates the percentage of gap between the 2005 generation and the World Energy Outlook (WEO) 2030 target that was achieved in a given year. The indicator helps in comparing policy effectiveness across countries in stimulating the deployment for different technologies. The sample included 35 countries, of which 17 were using FITs, 6 were relying on certificate schemes and 5 were without any policies.

PII for onshore wind: Observably, for the entire period 2001–2009, the average PII in countries with reliance on FITs was 3.23%, 1.5 times the level for countries using certificate schemes (at 2.1%). Of the 10 countries with the highest PII, the top eight were using FITs (namely, Denmark, Germany, Spain, Portugal, Ireland, Canada and Netherlands), with New Zealand ranking fifth albeit in the absence of a dedicated policy support. The only country amongst the top 10 that exhibited reliance on certificate schemes was Italy (Figure 1).

Interestingly, however, the difference in PII values has decreased between FITs and certificate schemes: the country average being 4% for FITs and 3.6% for certificate schemes in 2008–2009. Of the top 10 countries in 2008/2009, six utilised an FIT (namely, Denmark, Portugal, Spain, Hungary, Germany and Korea) and two a certificate scheme (Italy and Sweden). New Zealand ranked third, and the US ranked ninth (with relying on federal tax credits and state-level quota obligations, some of them combined with a certificate system).

In general, the average impact of both FITs and certificate schemes has risen over time, but certificate schemes have displayed a stronger relative increase. Based on the 2009 data alone, TGCs systems fared even better than FITs (4.75% vs. 4.36%). The reasons for this development could be traced to a number of

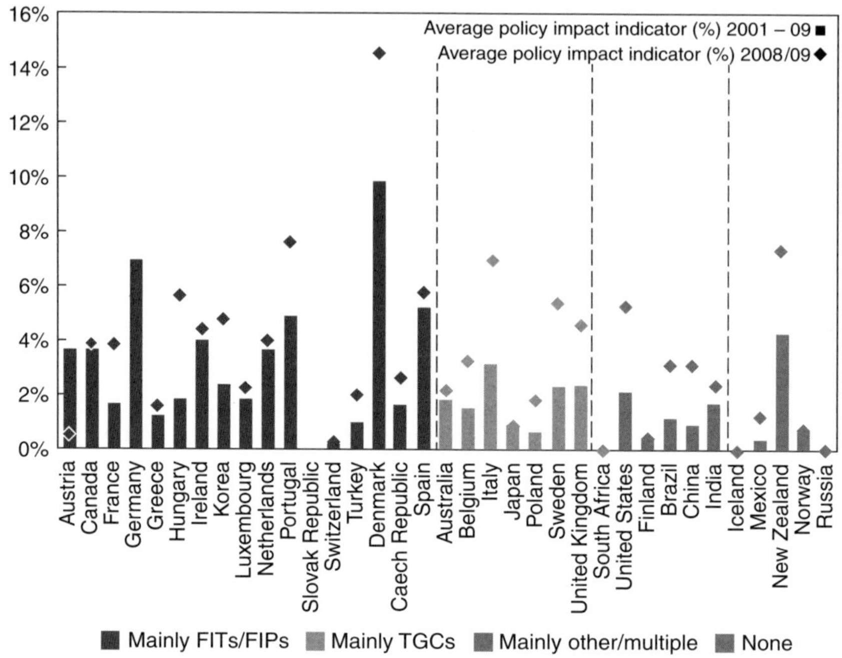

Figure 1. PII for wind support policies in OECD and BRICS countries, 2001–2009.
Source: IEA, 2011.

factors. First, the RE systems may have encountered strong learning effects, more so in recent years. Another reason may be the low baseline effectiveness level of certificate systems to start out with, and deployment on select sites rendered easier after some level of learning is attained. This conclusion is corroborated by the observation that two countries using an FIT and with high past effectiveness are now demonstrating lower levels (namely, Germany and Austria).

Policy impact indicator for solar PV: The comparative analysis of PII is now presented for 35 countries of which 18 countries have been using FITs, five are relying on certificate schemes and the rest have various other support policies in place. The average PII for countries using FITs is much higher (at 0.83 for the overall time period 2001–2009 and 2.13 in 2008–2009) as compared to those relying on certificate schemes (which are found to be at 0.43 for 2001–2009 and 0.42 for 2008–2009). Moreover, countries that succeeded in deploying solar PV (with the exception of Belgium) used FITs to do so. This is due to the fact that certificate schemes' objective was to use the least-cost options, implying that more expensive options (such as solar PV) did not witness any marked deployment (Figure 2).

In general terms, the policy effectiveness of solar PV deployment has risen overtime, as PV markets have evolved and matured. Moreover, FITs and FITPs

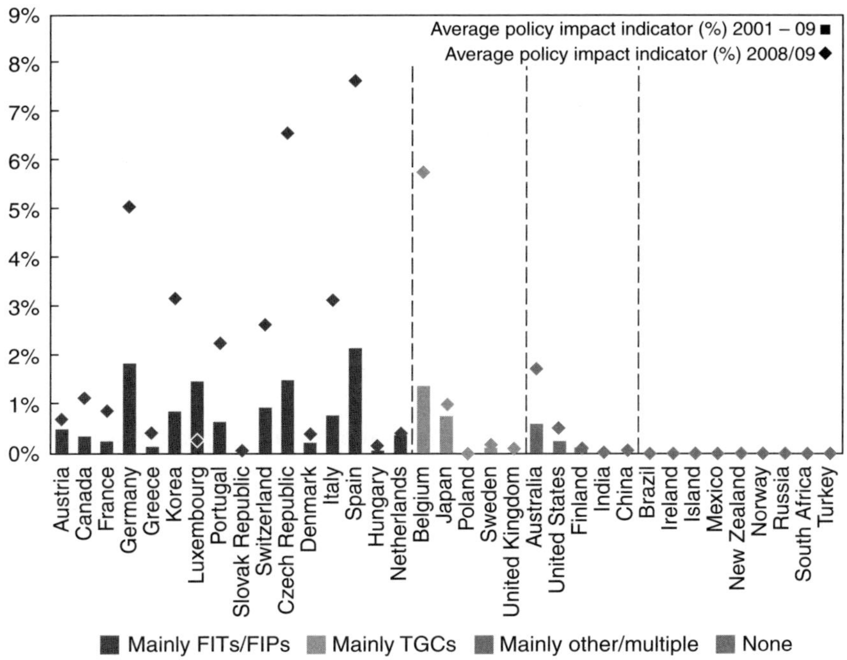

Figure 2. PII for solar PV support policies in OECD and BRICS, 2001–2009.

Source: IEA, 2011.

have been most effective in stimulating PV deployment. According to IEA, in terms of country-wise impacts, five distinct categories can be identified. The first group comprises countries that display little or no noticeable rise in PV deployment and have very low domestic policy support levels (namely, Brazil, China, South Africa, Mexico, Russia, Norway, Iceland, New Zealand, Turkey, Ireland, Hungary and Denmark). The second group exhibits very low levels of deployment, even though the policies provide for substantial financial support (as in India and, to a lesser extent, Greece with 2010 effectiveness of 3.3%). Evidently, non-economic barriers are inhibiting larger levels of deployment in these countries. The third group displays a steady and smooth increase in policy effectiveness over time (as in case of US, Japan, Switzerland and Canada) or an established effective policy environment (Germany). In contrast, the fourth group includes countries that have seen a sudden jump in policy effectiveness (namely, Australia, Belgium, Italy, Austria, Slovakia, France and the Czech Republic). The last group witnessed a peak in effectiveness but thereafter very low levels of deployment. This consists of Spain (where there was a boom in 2008, followed by a phase of market constraining in 2009 and 2010) and, to a lesser extent, Portugal and Korea (Figure 2).

4 Cost Effectiveness

As deployment volumes reach a large scale, a concern that has arisen relates to the overall cost of the policy to the economy in the form of support tariffs, premiums and subsidies. The varied types of power market structures render it problematic to assess the additional premiums that are paid in excess of the market price. Thus, IEA has attempted to quantify the total cost of policy support across the same group of countries, the TCI. The TCI is defined as the amount of additional annual premiums paid for an additional unit of generation per year. For normalisation across countries, the annual premiums are expressed as a percentage of the total wholesale value of all the electricity generated.

Cost effectiveness indicator for onshore wind: On a broader spectrum, countries show very large dispersion of total premium payments as measured by TCI, and a generally positive correlation between TCI and deployment of wind power. The lowest values have been exhibited by New Zealand, where no incremental premiums were required to be paid for the 1.5% of electricity that was covered by new wind generation in 2009. This is followed by India and Australia. Ireland too paid relatively smaller premiums and displays low TCI in comparison to the extent of stimulus to wind power. The premiums were comparably large in Sweden, taking into account the smaller contribution of new wind generation. Portugal paid the highest total premiums for wind power capacity that was deployed in 2009, which is why it also reaped a large amount of additional generation from wind power. Similar results can be observed for Spain and Denmark (Figure 3). It can also be seen that FIT and FITP exhibit a better trade-off than TGCs between wind's additional deployment and total premium costs.

Cost effectiveness indicator for solar PV: As the diffusion of some RE technologies such as solar PV are still in nascent stage of the learning curve, at large volumes of deployment, the total support cost indicators have come under policy review. In general, solar PV support deems it necessary to have payment of comparably high premiums. To evaluate the aggregate burden that support policies put on the national energy economy, the TCI was worked for the incremental generation produced in 2010 (Figure 4). Due to its relatively small size, combined with very high tariffs, the Czech Republic displays the largest burden with respect to its overall power system: the share being almost double of that for Germany. Also, compared to onshore wind, much larger premiums need to be paid.

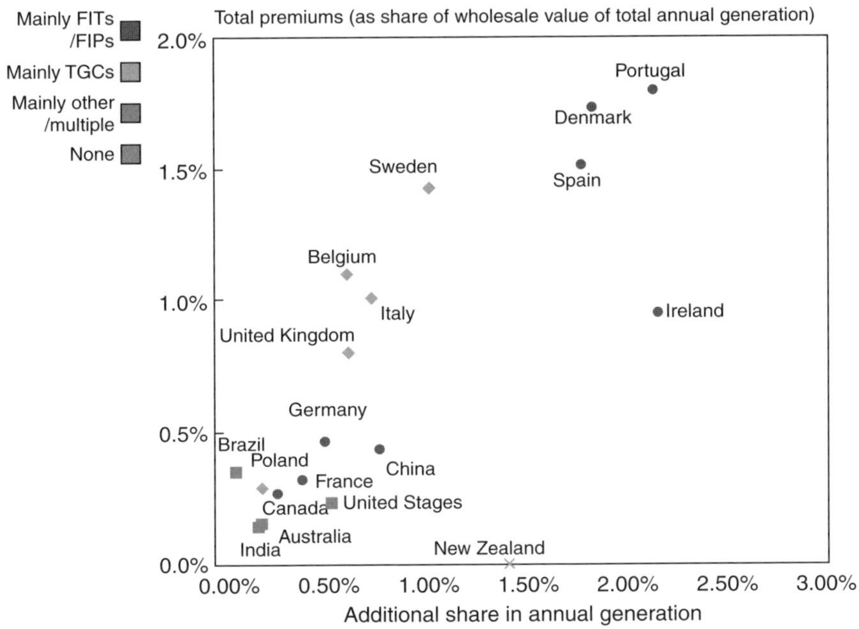

Figure 3. Total cost indicator for onshore wind, 2009.

Source: IEA, 2011.

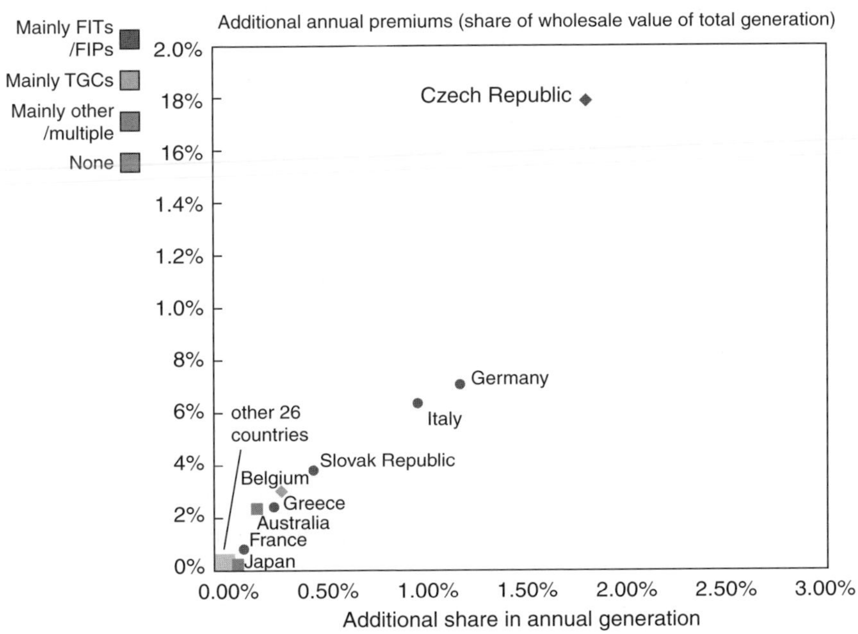

Figure 4. Total cost indicator for solar PV in major markets, 2010.

Source: IEA, 2011.

5 Contribution of Scheme Toward Cost Reduction for Technologies and Level of Market Maturation

In terms of static efficiency, the incentive to reduce costs is mainly experienced in the case of competitive bidding and TGCs (as the producers tend to be price takers). In comparison, the FITs/ FITPs do not provide the same level of incentive for cost reduction. However, once the dynamic effects are internalised in relation to the stimulus to RES capacities (these largely operating through the effects of learning curves on cumulative production) FIT is likely to perform relatively better in terms of the overall installation than competitive bidding or TGC systems. That the system that performs better dynamically is the one that stimulates RE market is corroborated by the data below (Table 2).

As can be seen from the 2006 data for select OECD countries where the RE support policies have been in place for some time (Jager and Rathmann, 2008), price instruments FITs and FITPs have generally performed better in reducing the cost of technology (significantly or moderately significantly) than quota obligation (with TGCs), competitive bidding, production and other fiscal incentives. Moreover, wind (both on-shore and off-shore) technologies exhibit the highest possibility of cost reduction, followed by combined biomass power and heat, with the lowest cost reduction experienced in case of solar PV. Notably, however, the cost reduction trends here have been reported only for the most dominant instrument used in a country and not available for all the others. Further, evidence is weak as to whether FITs or FITPs are associated with mature markets for technologies in comparison with quota obligations or tendering schemes.

6 Impact on Innovation

There is lack of conclusive evidence on the link between energy support measures and innovation (EEA, 2014). It depends critically on the original goal of the energy support measure: attaining social equity and access, achieving energy security, correcting for externalities, supplementing domestic production and spurring employment. The data from EEA for the EU-27 group of countries for the period 2005–2011 demonstrates a weak relationship between per capita RE production (wind, solar and geothermal) and per capita patent applications granted in (Figure 5). Denmark is the only exception: it exhibits a much larger share of patents compared to the other countries. This is followed by Luxembourg, Norway and Switzerland, which too display a relatively high number of patents compared to their RE generation from these specific technologies. In comparison, Italy, Portugal, and Spain have much fewer patents applications as compared to RE generation. This leads to the conclusion that a mere strong focus on deployment

Table 2. Contribution of the support scheme to cost reduction of RES and level of market maturity.

Country	Instrument characterisation	Contribution of the scheme towards reducing the costs of RES				Market maturity level
		Wind-onshore	Wind-offshore	Combined heat and power biomass combustion	Solar PV	
Canada and Canadian Provinces	Production incentive	Insignificant	Insignificant	Insignificant	Insignificant	Moderately mature
Ontario	FIT	Significant			Moderately significant	Moderately mature
	Tax incentives					
	Competitive bidding: Tender (contract price)					
Quebec	Competitive bidding: Tender (contract price)	Significant				Moderately mature
France	FITs	Significant	Significant	Significant	Significant	Emerging
	Competitive bidding:/tendering					
	Tax measures					
Germany	FITs	Significant	Significant	Significant	Significant	Fully mature
Italy	RPS (Quota obligation)	Significant	Significant	Significant	Significant	Emerging
	FITs	Significant	Significant	Significant	Significant	Emerging
Japan	RPS (Quota obligation)	Insignificant		Insignificant	Insignificant	Moderately mature
Netherlands	FITP	Significant	Significant	Moderately significant	Insignificant	Moderately mature
Norway	Investment subsidy	Moderately significant	Insignificant	Moderately significant		Emerging

(*Continued*)

Table 2. *(Continued)*

Country	Instrument characterisation	Contribution of the scheme towards reducing the costs of RES				Market maturity level
Spain	FIT FITP Tax deduction Low interest loan	Significant	Insignificant	Moderately significant	Significant	Fully mature
UK	RPS (Quota obligation)	Significant	Moderately significant	Moderately significant	Insignificant	Moderately mature
	Tax deduction	Significant	Moderately significant	Moderately significant	Insignificant	Moderately mature
	Investment subsidy	Significant	Moderately significant	Moderately significant	Insignificant	Moderately mature
US & US States	Production tax credit	Insignificant		Insignificant	Insignificant	Fully mature
California	RPS (Quota obligation)/ production incentive	Significant		Significant	Significant	Fully mature
Minnesota	RPS (Quota obligation)	Moderately significant		Moderately significant	Moderately significant	Moderately mature

Source: Adapted from Jager and Rathmann, 2008.

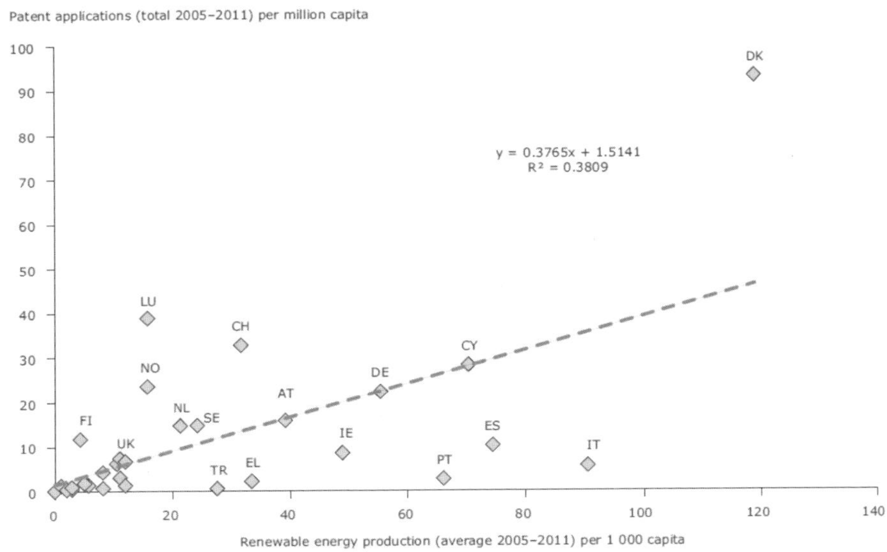

Figure 5. Patent application vs. renewable energy production per capita in select countries.

Note: These technologies were selected as relatively new renewables technologies, and production was calculated as an average over the period from 2005 to 2011. In addition, an analysis for the total renewable energy production would be heavily influenced by hydro electricity production, and would show less clear linkages with patent applications.

Country codes: AT (Austria), BE (Belgium), BG (Bulgaria), CH (Switzerland), CY (Cyprus), CZ (the Czech Republic), DE (Germany), DK (Denmark), EE (Estonia), ES (Spain), FI (Finland), FR (France), GR (Greece), HU (Hungary), IE (Ireland), IS (Iceland), IT (Italy), LI (Liechtenstein), LT (Lithuania), LU (Luxembourg), LV (Latvia), MT (Malta), NL (The Netherlands), NO (Norway, PL (Poland), PT (Portugal), RO (Romania), SE (Sweden), SI (Slovenia), SK (Slovakia), TR (Turkey), UK (the United Kingdom).

Source: EEA, 2014.

(demand-pull) does not necessarily lead to accelerated innovation in the renewable sector. In contrast to the above findings, there is clear evidence that public support for R&D have proved to be an important driving factor for innovation. Figure 6 demonstrates that there exists a strong positive correlation between R&D expenditure by the government and patents applications.

The case of four countries (of the EU-27), namely Czech Republic, Netherlands, Switzerland and Spain, are illustrative. For these four countries, Figure 7 depicts the data on share of RET patent applications in the total patent applications in EU-27 and Switzerland between 2006 and 2010 (the years being different due to data limitations). As can be seen, for Spain RE deployment had led to substantial R&D activity. Spain demonstrated a very high share in patent applications for wind, and a relatively high share for solar PV as well. There was a rapid increase in the number of patents for both these technologies between 2006 and 2010. In comparison, however, for concentrated solar power (CSP), Spain had a relatively low share in patent applications during this period, despite CSP being acknowledged as an important technology. By contrast, Switzerland demonstrated the highest share in CSP and solar PV patent applications, despite very low deployment rates. The same holds true for Netherlands.

In all the four countries the key driver for innovation in the RES sector has been the availability of targeted budgetary funding for R&D (Figure 6). In the Netherlands, for example, funding allocation can be ascribed to the specific demands of (mostly larger) private industry players that worked through innovation contracts. In addition, in the Netherlands, the existence of a strong PV cluster in the south-east of the Netherlands (Limburg and Noord-Brabant), comprising producers, suppliers and equipment factories, has spurred successful R&D in solar PV. In comparison, Switzerland's strong point in solar technology could be linked to its existing technological capabilities in this area, while its forte in geothermal stems from its relatively high domestic potential for geothermal energy. Spain's leading position in wind and solar thermal may be related to its early mover status in these technologies. By comparison, in the Czech Republic, a number of sectors already exist where skilled labour force and innovation activities has helped spur further innovation in the RES sector, such as electrical and electronics engineering, mechanical engineering, wood processing and information and communication

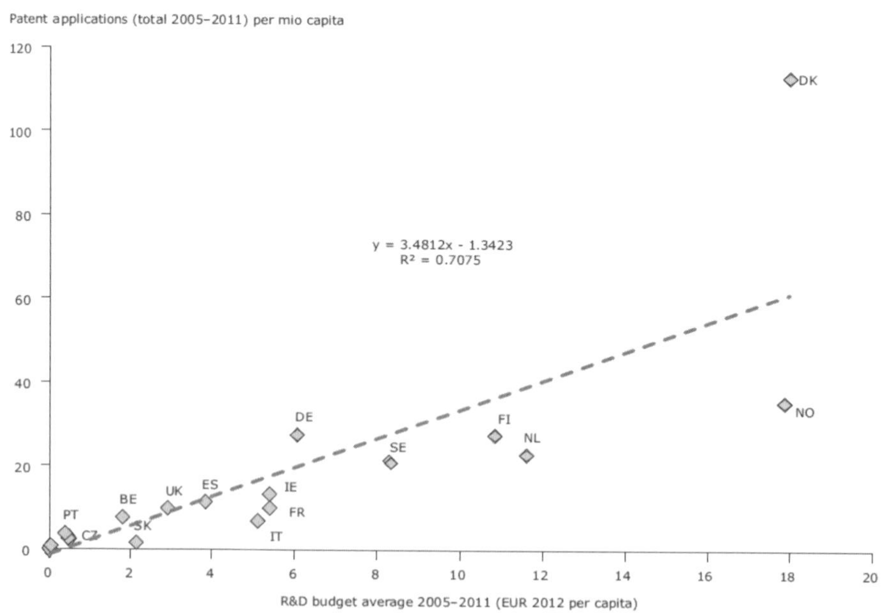

Figure 6. Patent applications per capita vs. R&D budgets per capita in select countries.

Note: For country codes, please refer to note attached to Figure 5.

Source: EEA, 2014.

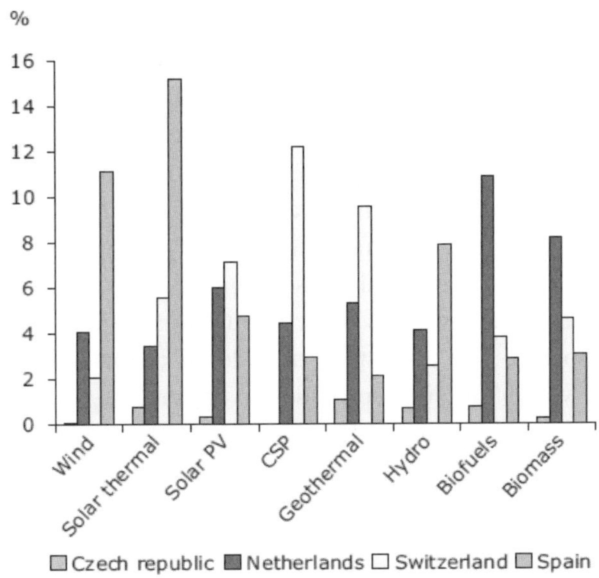

Figure 7. Share of RETs patent applications in the total patent applications of EU-27 and Switzerland between 2006 and 2010.

Source: EEA, 2014.

technologies. Further, environmental awareness has been high in the Czech Republic, leading to the setting up of technological parks and business incubators for eco-friendly technologies (Figure 7).

7 Key Lessons Learnt

According to IEA (2008) and IEA (2011), some key points need to be bornc in mind in the overall choice and design of support instruments for effective and efficient RE deployment. That is,

- FITs/FITPs have observably had their impact on RE deployment in varied situations. For FITs, support levels can be customised, and combined with regular built-in tariff reviews to avoid over-compensating investors as costs reduce over time. This is especially true for modular technologies with short development times and high learning rates (such as solar PV), for which built in mechanisms to avoid explosive growth (via a capacity or expenditure cap) becomes necessary. FITs do not expose the technologies to the direct competitive market with other technologies. They are, therefore, well suited to technologies that are somewhat away from being competitive. Implementing a feed-in system in the form of a premium on top of electricity market prices can be used to expose technologies to competition.

- TGCs are also known for being effective in stimulating RE deployment. In this case, deployment volumes and prices can be regulated via caps, buy-out fees, and price floors and banding. These regulations, however, are beset with the risk of over-rewarding some technologies. In general, given the overall nature of support, TGCs are most suitable for the more mature technologies that are approaching competitiveness and as a market-based mechanism.
- Competitive bidding/tenders offer high security to project investors once the bid has been won. In the initial phase of project development, however, tenders are uncertain for investors, which could pose a hindrance, especially for smaller developers. The advantage of bidding is that it permits competitive price discovery and, therefore, provides an opportunity to bring forward quantified levels of deployment at a low cost in the context of the local market. It is believed to be best suited for mature technologies that are on the verge of being competitive.
- Grants provide a less complex instrument to stimulate RE deployment, but it is perhaps most appropriate for technologies at or just leaving the demonstration stage, and for deployments at a limited scale. Grant schemes are often constrained by budgetary changes, and thus fail to provide the long-term market certainty needed to develop an established supply chain capability.
- Tax incentives measures provide poor management of deployment volumes and prices, and wield little or no pressure on developers to control or reduce costs. They too are sensitive to budgetary constraints and may cause a stop-go deployment pattern that is not conducive to sustained growth in RE deployment.
- Evidently, a high level of RE deployment encouraged by public support measures does not necessarily result in a sound and steady innovation process. On the contrary, too effective (and too generous) policy support may not stimulate cost reduction via technological innovation, but rather culminate in high levels of deployment at high costs, as witnessed in the case of Czech Republic and Spain. Factors such as R&D budgets coupled with a strong national innovation policy and industrial base to support technology development and deployment are equally important for innovation in the renewable sector.

8 Country Case Studies

8.1 China: A global leader in deploying RETs

China's record of RET D&D is unparalleled. Its clear political resolve, supported by aggressive price incentives and a strong manufacturing base, have been the main driving force behind the country's success with RE. With rapid progress in installation of RE in the last decade or so, China has emerged as a world leader in the deployment of RETs. Over the last decade, the country has made huge investments in generation and transmission, more than doubled its installed capacity in just six years (from 519 GW in 2005 to 1,073 GW in 2011) and significantly expanded access to grid-connected electricity to its populace. Although China still relies heavily on coal base electricity, programs to promote RE have gained momentum, to an extent that the country is currently the world leader in total wind power capacity (75 GW at the end of 2013) and ranks third in total solar PV capacity (18 GW at the end of 2013) (REN21 2013).

The rapid strides taken by RET deployment in China follows most significantly from the promulgation of its 2005 Renewable Energy Law, one of the first in the developing world. The law, which was made effective in 2006, established a solid base for accomplishing the firm goal of increasing the share of non-fossil fuel generation (including both renewable and nuclear energy) to 15% of primary energy supply by 2020. Although the law was initially intended to support the use of a FIT, key stakeholders could not agree on the tariff level, and an auction-based concession scheme was adopted to establish market-based tariffs. Subsequently, the stead-fast scale-up of RETs continued under the 12th FYP (2011–2015), with special focus on increasing the competitiveness of the renewables industry through a combination of regulatory policies and market-based approaches and increasing reliance on FITs (Azuela *et al.*, 2014).

In the initial phases, to spur the growth of wind energy, a competitive bidding process was implemented in 2003 in a number of select locations. Companies who won the bids were approved for project development and assured grid connectivity. These companies were also granted a power purchase agreement (PPA) for the initial batch of 30,000 h of generation, preferential loan and tax arrangements, and financial support for road and grid extension (WWF and WRI, 2013).

In its strife to drive down costs the National Development and Reform Commission (NDRC) of China moved the focus of support mechanisms from competitive bidding system to a FITs with variations based on regions and wind resource base. The FITs composed of four possible price levels ranging from 8 to 9.6 US cents/kWh (Yang, 2011). In 2009, wind power capacity grew by over 40%, 10% higher than the average over the previous 10 years (Junfeng *et al.*, 2010). In August 2011, the government implemented policies to encourage domestic PV generation through the implementation of a solar FIT. The FIT has been designed to decline overtime (to avoid excessive subsidy burden and formation of a PV bubble) and has been originally set at about \$0.18/kWh (Montgomery, 2011). This program has met with an overwhelming success in stimulating installation and generation, with PV capacity growing in 2011 by 500% over the 2010 level. Thus, in general, the introduction of the FITs has led to positive developments in wind and solar power generation capacity in the country (WWF and WRI, 2013).

Like most other countries, China RE D&D program also faces infrastructure constraints. In light of the staggering growth of RETs, China is now facing grid integration issues. This has become the biggest drawback for the future development of wind power in the country. It is claimed that a quarter of all wind-generated electricity is yet to get grid inter-connection (Ernst and Young, 2012). The root cause of this constraint can be traced back to a lack of accountability of the grid companies in the country, which are under no pressure to achieve their targets. While the Renewable Energy Law requires grid companies to connect RE projects (more specifically, the 11th FYP of 2008 has declared that from 2015 and 2020 there would be requirements for the power companies to achieve a 1% and 3% portfolio of RE generation in their output), the follow up of these provisions has been abysmal.

However, some measures are underway to address these constraints. In May 2012, the Chinese Ministry of Science and Technology (MOST) released the Special Planning of 12th FYP (2011–2015) on Smart Grid Major Science and Technology Industrialization Projects. The Plan lays down the overall objectives for smart grid construction during the 12th FYP period as well as the industries that China will mainly focus on supporting (WWF and WRI, 2013).

8.2 Renewable energy in India

India has a well-diversified portfolio of regulatory policies as well as fiscal incentives and public financing for RE development and deployment. These include FITs, renewable energy portfolio, tradable RECs, production tax credit, tendering, net metering and capital subsidies among others. It represents the world's sixth largest RE market (REN 21, 2012). According to the Global Status Report, 2014, India is among the top five countries investing in hydropower, concentrated solar power, wind power and solar water heating capacity. It is also among the top nations for total capacity or generation of renewable power (excluding hydropower) as at the end of 2013. The country plans to double its RE capacity from 25 GW in 2012 to 55 GW in 2017. The national targets for RE are set in consonance with the National FYP as well as the NAPCC. In order to overcome the cost barriers, fiscal incentives are being provided like the Generation Based Incentive (GBI) scheme which pays USD 0.01/kWh to producers (REN21, 2014).

Most of the states are complementing reverse bidding program with a FIT as a ceiling cap for tariff rate for solar PV. For wind projects, FITs are taken up without bidding programs. These are facilitated with the help of Jawaharlal Nehru

National Solar Mission (JNNSM) laid by NAPCC and state government policies. Due to the efforts of JNNSM, the solar PV power capacity has risen from 8 MW in 2010 to 1,200 MW in 2013. In addition to this, prices fell from 35 c/kWh to less than 17 c/kWh due to reverse bidding process making the renewable sources in comparison with fossil fuel based energy (EEW and NRDC, 2012). As in South Africa, here as well, civil society plays a pivotal role in bridging the information gap regarding cost of various RETs (WRI, 2013). In solar PV industry, manufacturing units operate at low or idle capacity because of less competition reason being lack of scale, low cost financing and underdeveloped supply chains. With regard to the weak enforcement and on-compliance issues in implementing RPOs amongst states, the Ministry of New and Renewable Energy plays an active role to check any misconduct (Parihar, 2012).

JNNSM is considered to be the most successful policy toward the deployment of RE but the domestic content regulation in solar manufacturing industry attracted strong criticism because of its ineffectiveness. Also the facilitation of RETs is limited to a few states, which restricts the scope for their expansion. Policies and targets vary across states and the Central Electricity Regulatory Commission plays a key role in deciding where the projects should be based. Despite the rapid growth in the RE deployment, India continues to face challenges because of the lack of transparency, accountability and grid infrastructure facilities (WWF and WRI, 2013). Insufficient trained manpower, weak transmission networks; delays in payment by DISCOMS also pose challenge to the growth of RETs (Government of India, 2006; MNRE, 2012). Improvements on these fronts can increase investor confidence and governance, thereby enhancing scope of RE in the country.

8.3 The experience with auctions in Brazil

Electricity auctions have occupied centre-stage in the regulatory framework adopted by Brazil when it embarked on reforming its electricity sector in 2004. Since then, regular operation of energy auctions has resulted in construction of 58 GW of new generation capacity (of which 46% is hydropower and another 29% is RE based), through about US $350 billion in long-term contracts. Wind energy auctions have, in particular, progressed in two phases. The first stage was marked by a strong policy determination to promote the development of non-conventional RE sources, in the pre-2013 period, in order to diversify the primary energy supply mix in favour of small hydro, wind and biomass energy. In this stage, contracts were tailored to individual technology features, so that more investment could be attracted while insulating the investors from risks — such as inflation and uncertainty of variable generation. Consequently, the result was a humongous success with RE auctions that managed to attract large amounts of investments from both the public and private sectors, and allowed consumers to benefit from cleaner energy at cheaper costs. However, this was criticised on the ground that the terms offered in contracts were too generous for investors and that, as a result, generators had an incentive to bid aggressively and to give unworkable guarantees about their plants' anticipated performance. With security of supply in mind, the second stage of wind power development with auctions was ushered in 2013 with much needed revisions of some key aspects of the auction design now seeking an optimal allocation of risk in the contracts offered to wind producers.

So far, Brazil has adopted two types of auctions schemes for deployment of RE: technology-specific auctions and reserve energy auctions. Technology-specific or project-specific auctions are used to deploy new capacity and supply the regulated market, when the auction has been targeted to support specific energy policy decisions or the introduction of special projects (such as large hydroelectric plants). In this case, contracts have to procure Firm Energy Certificates (FECs) to ensure that new power production is added to maintain minimum adequacy and reliability levels at the system level. Reserve energy auctions, by contrast, are carried out to directly increase the system's reserve margin, and contracts need not be covered by FECs.

Several points are noteworthy about the Brazilian experience with auctions for RE. The performance of RE procurement through reserve auctions has been relatively better than through technology-specific auction. The lackluster performance of the latter can be attributed to: ability of RE developers to obtain higher prices in the free market on account of the attractiveness of the T&D discount, general difficulty for RE to comply with FEC coverage obligation, since intermittent generation tends to face the risk of penalisation, finally, the upper limit for the remuneration level in the auction was set at a rate lower than that allowable under the PROINFA (the early policy framework on RE promotion). In comparison, the reserve auctions have emerged as a more promising option, as these carry lower risks for the investor. As of today, three rounds of reserve energy auctions for RE have been initiated (August 2008, December 2009 and August 2010), providing a total capacity of about 6.2 GW in small hydro power, sugarcane bagasse cogeneration, and wind-based generation for delivery during 2008 and 2015, and with contract terms ranging from 15 to 30 years (Azuela and Barroso, 2011).

Secondly, auctions have resulted in huge price reductions on account of competition between national and international companies. As compared to the PROINFA period, prices fell by nearly 45% in the 2009 auction alone, and then they fell by almost a further 40% in 2009–2011. Thus, wind farms' participation in the regular new energy auctions over the past few years has contributed to bring down the price of new generation in Brazil as a whole. From the history of all the auctions in Brazil since 2004 it can be inferred that, between 2005 and 2009, auctioned prices that had been stable at around 80 US$/MWh, after 2011 fell and stabilised around a lower value of 50 US$/MWh. Thus, Brazilian wind energy auctions contributed to enhanced competition in conventional energy auctions, driving down investors' profits and allowing consumers to capture the benefits of lower energy prices (Azuela *et al.*, 2014).

Thirdly, however, concerns have been raised with regard to the impact of competitiveness of the bids on the sustainability of the Brazilian wind auction mechanism in the future. Given the regular financing conditions and given investment and operation costs, bids in the most recent auctions have been below the level that could sustain the wind power supply chain, thus compounding the risk of construction delays or defaults by the winners that placed unrealistic or adventurous bids.

Fourthly, a phenomenon associated with the wind energy based auctions is Brazil is that these have prompted the participation of new equipment suppliers in the wind energy market. In addition to Wobben Wind Power, which has been present in the market for many years (a subsidiary of German company Enercon), IMPSA (Argentinean), Suzlon (Indian), Vestas (Danish), Siemens (German) and GE (United States) are now operating or in the process of commencing operations in Brazil (Azuela and Barroso, 2011).

Lastly, the Brazilian government's recent strategy of adopting tight ceiling prices seems opposed to the country's past experience, since in the earlier auctions competition among suppliers was the most important factor that led to price reductions below the ceiling. Recently, this strategy has brought in a risk of compromising security of supply if auctioned demand is not met. In fact, the prevailing observable trend of having a marginal price very close to the ceiling price points implies that there has been hardly any competition encountered, with many suppliers dropping out immediately and others simply offering the ceiling price.

In general, auctions appear as an effective market-based instrument for stimulating competition among investors, providing price disclosure while eliciting the optimal amount of investment in RE. The key lessons learnt from the Brazilian experience are (Azuela *et al.*, 2014):

- Auctions tend to make available stable guarantees to both investors and consumers. Auction winners are assured a steady, long-term revenue stream, while consumers benefit from the security that the optimal amount of renewable energy capacity will be installed.
- Well-conceived auction schemes could spur a country's RE program. By attracting attention from national and international players, well-organised auctions provide an interesting alternative for countries in which the energy

market lacks a mature RE segment. In fact, this is why auctions have been popular in emerging economies, such as India and Brazil, where the risk of a few firms exerting too much market power has been a barrier to RPS schemes.

- To allow policy consistency and compatibility, auction mechanisms should be fully integrated with other regulatory, planning and economic strategies of the country.
- Evidently, auction mechanisms have proved to be very effective in lowering energy prices in Brazil, China and India, when compared with the levelised cost benchmarks calculated on the basis of "reasonable" assumptions (which are generally used to ascertain an auction's ceiling price and price levels for FIT programs).
- Discouraging overoptimistic behaviour has been a major challenge of past implementation of auctions. Commonly, delays in construction and underperformance have been identified as key systemic problems with auctions. Although these problems can be dealt with to some extent by stiffening penalties for failing to meet the original objectives, it does seem that more often than not, winning the bid represents a best-case scenario rather than a most probable one. Policy makers should be aware of this risk seek to build mechanisms that would provide early warning of potential problems, so that mitigation measures can be taken at the earliest possible stage.

8.4 The case of FITs and emergence of PV bubbles in Germany and Spain

A number of countries that have relied on FITs/FITPs as the dominant measure of support for RE deployment have witnessed larger than expected amounts of installation of solar PV capacities. These unexpectedly large and booming PV markets have posed a difficulty for policy makers and stakeholders in terms of the cost support policies. The case of the PV boom in Germany and Spain is illustrative (see also Table 3).

Germany has been supporting solar PV growth at the regional and national level since the early 1990s by relying on a range of policy mechanisms. Germany managed PV volumes for much of the last decade by utilizing predetermined rate decreases. The most recent breakthrough in policy space has been the introduction of PV rates that decline progressively based on the amount of capacity installed in the prior periods. That is, the price paid for PV per unit is now linked to the PV market volume. As observed by Fulton and Mellquist (2011), from an investor's perspective time triggered automatic rate adjustments based on volumes, whose circulation formulae are transparent and methodically grounded, best deliver the triple features of transparency, longevity and certainty (TLC).

Table 3. Experience with FITs in Germany and Spain: A comparison.

What Germany did	What Spain did
Used price to control volume (**no hard caps**)	**Overcompensated** solar PV
Increase in solar PV delivery with a **fall in FIT costs**	**Exponential** growth in solar PV deployment with a corresponding **growth in costs of FIT**
FIT degression options — Degression was automatic and transparent	**No subsidy degression** options — transition period between revisions of FITs were too long
Initially a fixed degression followed by a flexible degression schedule	Rise in prices of Solar PV subsidies
Active policy makers and **political consensus** in tune with investor's needs	**Slow reaction** by the government in turn hurting investor confidence
Adopted **triggers, adjustments** and most important **review** concepts and how it impacts TLC	Should design a policy that **avoids cost crisis**, develop tracking methods so that government can **detect and react** to problems promptly and try to **limit damage** in case of crisis
Increased employment and trade in international market of solar PV	Domestic **job losses** and contraction in international market
Merit Order Effect (MOE) took place	No MOE took place
Germany is world's dominant solar energy market	The solar energy market failed in Spain

Source: Authors' construction based on Fulton and Mellquist, 2011.

When combined with transparent, periodic reviews, such adjustments can render the flexibility deemed to support policy longevity. Thus, after relying on the hard caps for its PV FIT policies of 1990s and early 2000, the German government has since relied on strategies for limiting (enabling) market growth by regulating the FIT price levels. For instance, there was only a single rate available for PV technology during 2000–2003. Starting with 2004, Germany introduced PV rates that were differentiated by size (e.g., capacity) and by application (e.g., façade integrated or free standing).

Germany managed to consistently exert a downward pressure on solar PV prices through degression during the past decade, in response to significant acceleration in market growth. During 2000–2009, degression was set as a fixed annual amount. During 2009–2011, however, the German government introduced a volume response "corridor" or "flexible" degression schedules. During 2010 and 2011, the government also implemented the concept of "non-scheduled adjustments" as a result of unforeseen developments in the prices of PV systems. It was observed that since 2008, PV component prices declined sharply, with panel prices falling around 40% in 2009 alone.

Due to the well managed price degression followed by Germany, the scale of the PV sector transactions costs — including grid connection fees and installation — were significantly lower compared to the other European countries. Thus, the use of price to control volume rather than putting hard caps on volume was a strategy which really nailed the success of FIT for PV in Germany.

Spain's FIT policy was kick-started with the Electricity Sector Law of 1997 (Law 54/1997) with the very first amendments ushered in 2004, when a target of 150 MW for solar PV was established. It was envisaged that once the target is attained, the support levels would be adjusted. This policy change came under criticism from the RES generators, who argued that the annually revised support levels were not transparent and raised the risk for investors, thus causing high risk premiums being charged from them by the lending institutions. In 2007, post detailed negotiations with investors and developers; the Royal Decree 661/2007 was promulgated leading to a marked impact on Spain's solar PV sector, which delinked the FIT rate from the Average Electricity Tariff (AET). This is because, as the AET rose between 2005 and 2006, the cost of RES-E support also rose, forcing the government to undertake policy reforms. The other main features of RD 661/2007 were: revision of FIT rates scheduled for every four years, establishment of mandatory guarantees to prevent speculation, RE to receive priority access to the electricity grid, evolving a long term energy plan (2011–2020) and putting in place a cap-and-floor price system.

An immediate fall out of this policy change was a sudden massive spike in PV delivery in 2007 and 2008, due to the generous FIT. Initially, there was a steady but low rate of installation up until 2006, followed by a sudden spike in deployment in 2008. However, later a reduction in support led to a subsequent plummeting of installations to zero in the following year. By 2009, the total annual cost of subsidizing solar PV was US$2.6 billion per year. At this level of expenditure, solar PV subsidies represented over 50% of all RE spending, despite producing a mere 12% of all renewable electricity generation, and only 2.45% of total electricity generation. This was ruined as the government stepped in to reduce the costs of the FIT. This angered the investors, and the failure on part of the government to control costs damaged the future prospects of taxpayer-funded solar PV delivery in Spain and lost the faith of the investors.

The poor design of FIT was one of the main reasons for its failure in Spain that included:

- An over-generous rate structure of FIT, especially in 2007.
- No subsidy degression initiation with the falling cots of the solar PV projects.

- Extremely long period of transition to policy schemes when tariff reduction was expected.
- A lag in the reporting of investments by regional government.

The government basically failed to lower the compensation in response to the rapidly declining costs on account of technical change and learning. Additionally, the investors were able to install the solar PV, which is a modular technology, in a short time span while the policy makers were not able to react to the changing conditions at the same rate. The slower internal communication within the government machinery caused delays in communication to the national government to make them aware of the scale of regional investments, and the crisis had already hit.

The final outcome was lose–lose situation for all stakeholders. The electricity system was burdened with costly solar PV generation. The policy changes had repercussions for the ongoing viability of the industry, with solar PV developers losing faith in government's retroactive tariff changes. Numerous companies associated with solar PV manufacture either had to close down or undergo a merger, and employment in the sector fell from a high of 41,700 reported jobs to fewer than 10,000 in 2012. In fact, the recurrent policy changes had far reaching implications for RE sector as a whole, damaging the investor confidence in the reliability of Spanish policy framework.

8.5 United States' (US') production tax credit program

US has one of the largest Production Tax Credit (PTC) programs. The need for a secure, supply of homegrown energy source to power the nation led to introduction of PTC in US. A PTC aims at incentivizing RE production and provides tax benefit against the amount of RE actually produced and fed into the grid. According to the American Wind Energy Association, this performance-based incentive has helped the US wind industry to lead the clean energy market. It rewards producer on the basis of actual energy produced, increases the rate of return to the investor and reduces the payback period as well. PTC has often been preferred over investment incentives because the latter cannot promise installation at optimal level, whereas production incentives encourage optimality as well as sustainability in the industry (Sawin, 2003).

PTC was first implemented in US as a component of the Energy Policy Act of 1992 and, in combination with the renewable electricity standards, has been the main driver of wind power development in US since then. PTC covered wind and bio energy resources. PTC provides a 2.2% per kilowatt hour benefit for the first

10 years of RE facility's operation. In order to avail this, the wind energy equipment should be located in US and energy produced should be sold to an unrelated party only. The unused credits can be carried forward for up to 20 years following generation[1]. The installation of wind capacity at large scale in Texas along with introduction of US Federal PTC has made wind energy competitive. The US department of Energy quotes that US wind capacity has more than tripled during 2007–2012, and the costs of generating electricity from wind have fallen during this period. But lapses in the policy have led to a dramatic slowdown in the planned wind projects, which affect the further growth of industry. While short term PTCs are less likely to induce adequate R&D, long term policy of PTC can spur positive growth in R&D and innovation. Short-term PTCs expiring soon lead to hurried investments with small installation capacities and thus, high electricity costs.

The main issue with the USPTC for wind energy has been that it has been allowed to expire several times intermittently, leading to cycles of boom and bust in the market, which in turn have led to suspension of projects, worker lay-offs, and loss of momentum in the industry. This approach of halting and then restarting of policy has posed a challenge for the US industries (Sawin, 2003). The long term extension of PTC could help development of RE capacity by bringing stability in the wind energy sector. This would also aid in bringing wind energy at par with fossil fuel and nuclear power industries which have enjoyed incentives for long periods.[2]

The American Wind Energy Association reports that PTC fosters economic security as the price of wind power has dropped by around 43% over the past four years (2008–2012) benefitting the consumers as well as utilities (AWEA, 2013). According to the US Dept. of Energy, there are over 550 US wind equipment manufacturing facilities across 43 states and for the past five years, this industry has been driving $15 billion of private investment on annually.

The lesson learnt from the US experience in respect of PTC is that frequent expiration of the policy have created uncertainty in the industry, which has posed a challenge to development of renewable energy and this could be corrected by appropriately timing the extension of PTCs which can cater to the issue and provide for continued expansion and economies of scale to persist.

[1] Renewable Electricity Production Tax credit, Database of State Incentives for Renewables and Efficiency, DSIRE, North Carolina State University, 2011.

[2] Union of Concerned Scientists (Based on data from US Dept. of Energy and American Wind Energy Association).

8.6 Denmark: The case of a leader in innovation in RETs

The patent activity is a significant measure of a country's level of specialisation in certain technologies and of future potential for market share growth. From the analysis presented in Section 4.2.4, it is evident that Denmark is a clear leader as far as the number of patents filed in RETs as compared to other countries is concerned.

Denmark (besides Germany and Japan) can be termed an established RE market leader that has long placed its industrial and economic development objectives at the heart of its support for RETs (IEA, 2011; Jochem *et al.*, 2008; Mizuno, 2010). Denmark has promoted the creation of effective industrial clusters and developed vibrant home markets by instituting stable, enabling policy frameworks along the innovation chain, besides creating favourable investment conditions for innovative RETs, including solar PV and wind. It has specialised at an early stage in the supply of new RETs that were embodied with high knowledge intensity and learning potential, and thus the country has emerged a front-runner in terms of RE innovation (IEA, 2011).

On March 22, 2012, Denmark witnessed the signing of an agreement amongst the major political parties, which set the institutional structure for a changeover to a green and sustainable energy economy in the country. One of the provisions of the framework was large investments in RE and energy efficiency up to the year 2020 (in the range of DKK 90 million to DKK 150 billion). In addition, the energy agreement also set the stage for the need for a continued intensive RD&D of new green energy technologies. However, this is not a new development. Denmark has been consistent in implementing sustainable energy concepts over the years, and it is now very advanced in achieving a sustainable energy system through increased energy efficiency and the share of renewable energy as well as the integration of energy networks (electricity and heat but gas as well is being considered). Furthermore, Denmark has had a very favourable environment for innovative clean-technology start-ups (EEA, 2014).

A closer look at patent applications in Denmark shows that most of the patents are in wind energy technologies. Wind power made available over 30% of electricity production in Denmark in 2012, and this is expected to rise to around 50% by 2020. Moreover, historically, Denmark has been a pioneer in developing commercial wind power during the 1970s, and today a substantial share of the wind turbines around the world are produced by Danish manufacturers such as Vestas and Siemens Wind Power along with many component suppliers (EEA, 2014).

The key lesson to be learnt from Denmark is that its current position as a front-runner in innovation in RE can be ascribed to the bold political decisions to transform the energy system, the early mover advantage in wind energy, and a favourable climate for innovative start-ups. The relatively low costs of patent applications and the opportunity to apply for patents in English language may have also played a favourable role in this regard (EEA, 2014).

9 Conclusion

The issue of design and implementation of support measures for RETs is complicated and requires a nuanced, case by case approach. However, some broad conclusions can be drawn from a review of conceptual underpinnings and country case studies as regards design and implementation of such measures discussed in the chapter.

Foremost, the design of the support instrument needs to be placed in a specific policy context (e.g., energy and climate policies), with clear identification of drivers and barriers to its design and deployment. The role of the regulatory, institutional and political environment needs to be emphasised, especially as the level and structure of the instrument will have to be benchmarked against the prices of conventional energy, besides other advantages that conventional energy sources enjoy (e.g., supporting infrastructure, consumer acceptability, established technology and such like).

A clear political resolve and incorporation of RE targets in the national policy framework are important to introduce and effectively implement policies on RET dissemination. China with its strong manufacturing base and aggressive incentive mechanism has clearly emerged as a world leader. Time bound objectives along with complementary policies towards diversification have been the mainstay of policy in China. In Germany as well, policies concerning RETs have been an integral part of the industrial development policy. For India, both political resolve and need to comply with international treaties were the driving force. The French FITs suffered because of complicated administrative and planning procedures.

Policy support measures have been affecting the cost effectiveness of technologies by giving stimulus to RES. A significant impact on innovation could not be found for a large set of countries. The exception being the case of Denmark, in which a large number of patents were filed in accordance with the policy support. Government R&D support, however, has had a very significant and positive impact on the innovation in RETs, for instance, in Germany, Spain, US (especially California and Minnesota).

In general, it has been found that price-based instruments have worked better as compared to quantity-based instruments, and amongst various RES, wind technology has had the maximum potential for cost reduction and dissemination. It is also commonly suggested that incentives/support measures need to rely, as much as possible, on market based instruments, e.g., quota obligations coupled with tendering and/or green certificates, such that the true costs get revealed. A caveat that is put forward in this regard is that reliance on market forces will circumscribe the ability of the producers to reap the sufficient rent that can otherwise help spur innovation. Thus, incentives for dynamic efficiency for less mature technologies (in particular) should not be ignored.

The costs of RETs tend to decline over time as there is learning-by-doing and market maturation. Thus, the instrument design needs to have in-built flexibility in the price or quantity domain so as to adapt to the changing market situation. In this regard, a smooth phasing out/exit policy for the RET is also prescribed as the levelised cost of the technology is lowered to approach that of conventional energy in the limit. With respect to the best practices for specific instruments, FIPs help in achieving low costs and innovation. CB, being a self-regulating instrument has a built-in phasing out mechanism. It can be concluded that an instrument is appropriate when it is able to adjust flexibly according to technology learning, and has built-in revision mechanisms with respect to the global market scenario. A suitably designed phase-out plan for the support scheme would alleviate the need for authorities making *ad hoc* administrative revisions of the existing scheme in terms of its scope, level and the time frame and avoid undue burden on government budgets.

References

AWEA (2013), Federal Production Tax Credit for Wind Energy. American Wind Energy Association.

Azuela, G.E. and L.A. Barroso (2011), Design and Performance of Policy Instruments to Promote the Development of Renewable Energy: Emerging Experience in Selected Developing Countries. *Energy and Mining Sector Board Discussion Paper No.22*. Washington DC: The World Bank.

Azuela, G.E., L. Barroso, A. Khanna, X. Wang, Y. Wu and G. Cunha (2014), Performance of Renewable Energy Auctions: Experience in Brazil, China and India. Energy and Extractives Global Practice Group, *World Bank Policy Research Working Paper 7062*, Washington DC: World Bank.

Council on Energy, Environment and Water (EEW) and Natural Resources Defense Council (NRDC) (2012), Laying the Foundation for a Bright Future: Assessing Progress under Phase 1 of India's National Solar Mission. EEW & NRDC. (Online) Available from: http://www.nrdc.org/international/india/files/layingthefoundation.pdf.

EEA (2014), Energy Support Measures and their Impact on Innovation in the Renewable Energy Sector in Europe. *EEA Technical Report No 21/2014*, Copenhagen, Denmark: EEA.

European Photovoltaic Industry Association (EPIA) (2012), Global Market Outlook for Photovoltaics until 2016. EPIA.

Ernst and Young (2012), Renewable Energy Country Attractiveness Indices. E&Y. (Online) Available from: http://www.ey.com/Publication/vwLUAssets/Renewable_energy_country_attractiveness_indices_-_Issue_33/$FILE/EY_RECAI_issue_33.pdf.

Fulton, M. and N. Mellquist (2011), The German Feed-in Tariff for PV: Managing Volume Success with Price Response. DB Climate Change Advisors, Deutsche Bank Group.

Government of India (2006), Report of the Working Group on R&D for the energy sector for the formulation of the Eleventh Five Year Plan (2007–2012). (Online) Available from: http://www.psa.gov.in/sites/default/files/11913296631_energy.pdf.

Government of India, Ministry of New and Renewable Energy (MNRE). Mission. (Online) Available from: http://www.mnre.gov.in/mission-and-vision-2/mission-and-vision/mission-2/.

Government of India (2013), Twelfth Five Year Plan (2012–2017) Economic Sectors, Volume II. New Delhi: SAGE Publications India Pvt Ltd. (Online) Available from: http://planningcommission.gov.in/plans/planrel/12thplan/pdf/12fyp_vol2.pdf.

IEA (2008), Deploying Renewables, Principles for Effective Policies. IEA, Paris, France. Available from: https://www.iea.org/publications/freepublications/publication/DeployingRenewables2008.pdf.

IEA (2011), Deploying Renewables, Best and Future Policy Practice. IEA, Paris, France.

Jager, D. and M. Rathman (2008), Policy Instrument Design to Reduce Financing Costs in Renewable Energy Technology Projects. ECOFYS and IEA.

Jochem, E., C. Jaeger, A. Battaglini, H. Bradke, C. Cremer, W. Eichhammer, H. Förster, A. Haas, E. Henning, F. Idrissova, B. Kasper, J. Köhler, D. Köwener, J. Krause, W. Lass, J. Lilliestam, W. Mannsbart, M. Müller, F. Meißner, B. Pflüger, P. Radgen, M. Ragwitz, M. Rauschen, F. Reitze, L. Riffeser, K. Saure, W. Schade, F. Sensfuß, F. Toro, R. Walz and M. Wietschel* (2008), Investitionenfüreinklimafreundliches Deutschland (Investments for a Climate-Friendly Germany), Synthesis report of study commissioned by the German Federal Ministry for the Environment, Nature Protection and Nuclear Safety (BMU), Potsdam Institute for Climate Impact Research (PIK), European Climate Forum (ECF), Fraunhofer Institute for Systems and Innovation Research (Fh- ISI), BSR-Sustainability, Öko-Zentrum NRW, Potsdam.

Junfeng, L., S. Pengfei and G. Hu (2010), China Wind Power Outlook 2010. Beijing: CREIA, GWEC, Greenpeace.

Mehra, M. and Pandey, R. (2016), Choice and Design of Policy Instruments towards Promoting Renewable Energy Technologies: Conceptual Framework and Guiding Principles. In *The Economics of China and India: Cooperation and Conflict. Volume 3: Economic Growth, Employment and Inclusivity: The International Environment.* Agarwal, Manmohan, Wang, Jing and Whalley, John (Eds.), World Scientific.

Menanteau, P., D. Finon and M.L. Lamy (2003), Price versus Quantities: Choosing Policies for Promoting the Development of Renewable Energy. *Energy Policy*, 31(8), 799–812.

Ministry of New and Renewable Energy (MNRE) (2012), Generation of Power under JNNSM. (Online) Available from: http://pib.nic.in/newsite/pmreleases.aspx?mincode=28.

Mizuno, E. (2010), Renewable Energy Technology Innovation and Commercialization Analysis. *Report Prepared for the IEA Energy Divisio*n, Cambridge: Cambridge Centre for Energy Studies (CCES), Judge Business School, University of Cambridge.

Montgomery, J. (2011), China Stamps Solar Feed-in tariff, But What Does it Mean? Renewable Energy World.com. (Online) Available from: http://www.renewableenergyworld.com/rea/news/article/2011/08/china-stamps-solar-fit-but-what-does-it-mean.

Parihar, R. (2012), Congress gets burned by the sun: Rajasthan government issue fraud certificates to Cong MP for solar projects. *India Today* (march 26) (Online) Available from: http://indiatoday.intoday.in/story/.

REN21 (2013), Renewables 2013 Global Status Report. Paris: REN21 Secretariat.

REN21 (2014), Renewables 2014 Global Status Report. Paris: REN 21 Secretariat.

Sawin, J.L. (2004), National Policy Instruments: Policy Lessons for the Advancement and Diffusion of Renewable Energy Technologies Around the World. *Thematic Background Paper in Proceedings of the International Conference for Renewables*, Bonn.

Sawin, J.L. (2003), Charting a New Energy Future in Starke, L. (Ed.), *State of the World: Progress Towards a Sustainable Society*, 20th Edition. Washington DC: World Watch Institute, 85–109.

World Wildlife Fund (WWF) and World Resources Institute (WRI) (2013), Meeting Renewable Energy Targets: Global Lessons from the Road to Implementation. Available from: http://awsassets.panda.org/downloads/meeting_renewable_energy_targets__low_res_.pdf.

Chapter 3

China's Trade Performance and Deepening International Engagement: Evaluating Post-Crisis Options to Maintain Growth

John Whalley*,†,‡ and Xiaopeng Yin†,§

**Western University, Canada*

†University of International Business and Economics (UIBE), China

‡jwhalley@uwo.ca

§xyin@uibe.edu.cn

Abstract: After surveying China's trade performance between 1980 and 2010 as China's trade by total values (1980–2010), by products and by trade types like goods trade and service trade, we find that the growth rates of China's imports and exports have shown a kind of "co-movement" situation during 1980–2010. Moreover, the category of China's changing main trading goods and trade types can reveal several special characteristics of China's economy, e.g., the enriched different consumption goods trading, bad health habits like increasing tobacco consumption, and important but externally-affected machinery equipment. Service trade in China is much stronger than expected. Moreover, China's trade by geographical regions with her major trade partners shows that while crises from 1997 to 2008 brought in some negative effects on China's economy with lower growth rates, the general trade structure in world trade system does not seem to be changed too much by different levels among trading countries including China. Therefore, we suggest six options to solve seven questions we conclude in the chapter to support China's future sustainable growth as the way of deepening her international engagement. Our results indicate that tariffs/taxes reduction, involving/engaging trading blocks, expanding more trade with the South, revaluating Chinese RMB, encouraging domestic private consumption and innovation seem to be important policy options for China. The empirical evidences in the chapter also support our analysis and suggestions.

1 Introduction

China's trade growth is widely seen as central to China's spectacular growth performance in recent decades and especially so since the 1990s. Trade (exports and imports together) climbed from below 3% of GDP in 1978 to nearly 70% recently. Contemporaneous to this trade growth have come large FDI inflows fuelling the growth of processing trade, growing from under $2 billion/year in the 1990s to over $100 billion in 2010. Moreover, China's integration into the world economy is seen today as being central both to China's emergence as, for now, the global centre of manufacturing activity, and the primary mechanism for arbitraging globally the advantages of China's high quality, low wage labour pool restrained globally by OECD immigration restrictions. (Harrigan and Deng, 2008) It is a very important factor people need to think about. Based on these facts, we evaluate China's performance and explore her potential and ongoing engagement from discussing her trade performance and focus it in this chapter.

In this chapter, we look into the future and ask whether current regime can continue to underpin China's growth strategy in the post-subprime crisis (the Crisis thereafter) world we are entering. Even before the Crisis, questions were being asked about whether China's near 30% exports growth annually that existed during pre-Crisis (in 2005–2007) could continue. Even with sharp growth of IT exports relative to the 1990s, new products would be needed to add to China's exports. Autos would be one component and other high technology products including electric, machinery and electronic products would be another. But at some point, as the argument goes, China must run out of markets. China is also a country under increasing competitive pressures from even lower wage countries such as India, Indonesia, Cambodia and others, especially in early stage for labour intensive products such as clothing. Outsourcing from China (and exports reduction) is emerging to Vietnam and elsewhere in Asia (Ministry of Commerce, National Bureau of Statistics, and State Administration of Foreign Exchange, 2010). China still faces the potential problem of adjustment resisting measures being introduced in large exporting markets (in the US and the EU) through anti-dumping and other actions, which in turn have been spreading to other developing countries, such as India, Brazil, Turkey and others. Already pre-Crisis, continued 30% exports growth seemed like an increasingly hard road to travel.

The Crisis has added new elements to these pressures, while in general it has some different and negative impacts to global trade and countries including China. (see Amiti and Weinstein, 2009; Anderton and Tewolde, 2011; Baldwin, 2009;

Bems, Johnson and Yi, 2010; 2011; Berkmen, Gaston, Rennhack and Walsh, 2009; Blanchard, Das and Faruqee, 2010; Chor and Manova, 2010; Claessens, Dell'Ariccia, Igan and Laeven, 2010; Ferrantino and Larsen, 2009; Fukuchi, 2010; Haddad, Harrison and Hausman, 2010; Lane and Milesi-Ferretti, 2011; Levchenko, Lewis and Tesar, 2010; Milberg and Winkler, 2010; Naude, 2009; OECD, 2009; TeVelde, 2009, etc.). Slower and anaemic growth in Europe and possibly North America means large exporting markets will grow even more slowly than before. Also, the risk of future financial volatility on a scale comparable to or more extreme than in 2008, and again possibly geographically centred in Europe and North America also suggests a more balanced approach. Growing exports to markets that may again experience financial turmoil, with costs of adjustment, becomes a less attractive global integration led growth strategy. And the prospect of even more rapid growth in Brazil and India, for want of a better term, the larger South, suggests policy reorientation towards their markets. China has the products to penetrate these growing markets with less R&D and new product development needed.

The picture that emerges contains conflicting elements of pessimism and optimism. China's global integration growth strategy of the past is seemingly now coming under pressure from a range of factors. There is the seeming inconsistency of the arithmetic of 30% export growth and world GDP growth of around 4.5%. There is pressure on China from Chinese Renminbi (i.e. RMB) revaluation, other lower wage economies, adjustment resisting trade measures in exporting markets, and increasing wage rates at home. Environment constraints at home also enter, and added to this is the Crisis originating of a larger growth rate gap relative to Europe and North America, and how to respond to financial instability risk. And with this have also come G20 rebalancing pressures, and a world seemingly united against China's trade surplus. It thus appears that the Chinese pre-Crisis growth process must inevitably evolve and change.

But there are also rays of hope for sustained strong trade growth as part of a high growth regime. Sharply elevated educational attainment since 1999, and accelerated innovation and patenting point the way to export growth led by new products and ideas. Relatively small and lagging service trade growth, resulting in a service to goods exports ratio well below comparable economies suggests new exports opportunities. And the very rapid growth over 10 years (from a small initial base) of India–China and China–Brazil trade along with continued high growth in the larger South suggests growing Southern orientation in trade may help (see Agarwal and Whalley, 2013; Medianu and Whalley, 2010; and Shekhar and Whalley, 2010).

China's problem for the next 10 years on the trade front, we suggest, may as oriented toward how to get through the next 5–10 years with reasonably strong trade growth and allow new markets and products to develop. Key to this is how best to counter adjustment resisting measures in today's large exporting markets while the new and more rapidly growing markets come on stream. How best to manage the slow transition to innovation and service led exports growth? How to respond to the changing world of rebalances, climate change policy, and rapid growth in the even lower wage world elsewhere?

We do not claim to be able to provide a precise road map for all of this, and many of the premises for our discussion may prove false (such as continued high growth in China). But the elements we identify do seem to centrally enter post-Crisis policy design in the trade area for China, and we hope our discussion can contribute to further debate.

In what follows, we first document China's trade performance since the 1990s in detail and assess its links and contribution to China's high growth from the 1990s on. We also assess China's trade performance during the Crisis, when GDP growth held up remarkably well as trade compression and dislocation occurred. We then discuss in more detail the residue that the 2008 financial crisis may leave as far as trade and the sustainability of China's growth in the future go. We finally conclude with a discussion in general of China's possible policies options both globally and in supporting domestic policy towards continued integration into the world economy.

2 China's Trade Performance since the 1980s

Following our discussions on the relationship between China's trade, especially her exports, and her GDP growth above, let us see China's trade performance since the 1990s first.

During the past period, there are several critical time points that are needed to be considered. China's reform has been started from the late 1970s, say, 1978, which is called formally as "Reform and Opening-up" period. In 1988, Chinese government has challenged her planned economy system by attempting to ease all price controls but failed, which heavily affects domestic macroeconomic situation but with little effects on her international trade. In 1989, China incurred political turmoil and suffered by the Western countries' imposition of economic sanctions to restrict China's imports of high-tech goods (high-valued goods as well). In 1994, China carried out her foreign exchange market reform by unifying the "dual-track system" of exchange rates, which was expected to affect her imports and exports, and China formally transited to the new market-driven economic system from the existing planned economic system. In 1998, the Asian financial crisis swapped the East Asia except China, while exchange rates of East Asian currencies depreciated with "non-depreciation" policy implemented by Chinese government. It was expected influence China's trade. In 2001 after the event of "9/11" attack, the US economy stepped into short-time recession in the second half of 2001 that brought some negative impact on its trade as expected. China is the largest trade partner to the US. The more important event was in 2001 when

China gained access to the World Trade Organization (i.e. WTO), the only multilateral cooperation organisation in the world focusing on trade liberalisation. It was presumed the trade volume/value will be increased dramatically in the following year(s). The year 2004 is another remarkable year since the central Bank of China, i.e. the People's bank of China, resumed the further once of its foreign exchange market to allow expanding the floating band of Chinese RMB. We all suffered the US subprime (loan) financial crisis in 2008 that continued for at least two years until its significant recovery.

2.1 China's trade: Total growth on value

One can see that China's trade growth rate is more than 30% annually between 1980 and 2010. The interesting thing here is that the annual growth rate of imports is more than 20% while that of exports is about 20% over three decades, which is different from what people imagine that China's growth for past three decades was heavily dependent on its import restrictions to create some kind of manipulation in her trade surplus to support her high growth of GDP/economy. Well, the initial difference between her imports and exports at the beginning of China's "Reform and Opening-up" at the end of 1970s has been kept and been persistent for a long time, which also leaves increasing trade surplus over time along with rapidly increasing trade size/value.

If one can explore the change in China's trade more precisely (see Figure 1), it can be found that during 1982–1983, both imports and exports were decreasing, which should that the initial effect of China's reform on trade diminished soon. It reveals

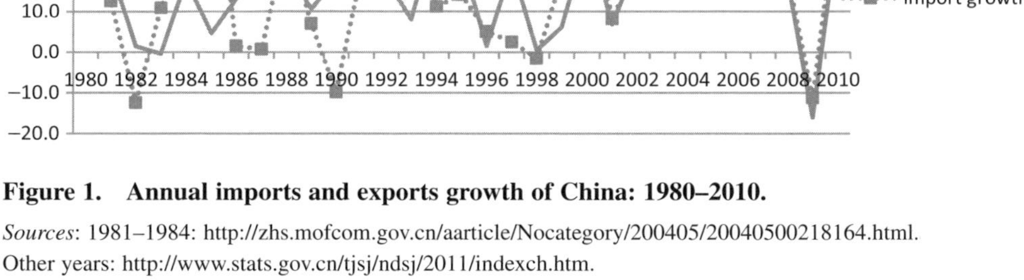

Figure 1. Annual imports and exports growth of China: 1980–2010.

Sources: 1981–1984: http://zhs.mofcom.gov.cn/aarticle/Nocategory/200405/20040500218164.html.
Other years: http://www.stats.gov.cn/tjsj/ndsj/2011/indexch.htm.
Authors calculate by themselves.

the China's government policies about "Reform and Opening-up" have no large "growth effect" for her kind of institutional reform, even though they still have some.

From the period of 1986–1987, exports seem to have a lagged response to imports change. That is, when imports decrease in this year, exports slowdown in the next year. It seems to mean that China's exports could largely be the "processing trade" and/or "tasked trade", which depend on imports of intermediates mainly.

Between 1989 and 1990, imports growth reduced significantly, while exports did not change as much as expected due to the possible impact of the very severe political crisis.

The year 1994 was the time that Chinese government unified the existing "dual-track" exchange rates into a single rate, and also the market-driven economic system was confirmed formally. For the RMB value, it seemed to have depreciated. So the China's trade's situation was the same as people expected: the exports were raised and imports reduced. The interesting thing is, however, it seems from this period, the relationship between exports and imports, which we called as a kind of lagged effect, has been changed and both go separately.

Asian financial crisis that occurred in 1997–1998 really damaged China's trade as expected China's "non-depreciation" policy enhanced such damage as it raised her imports and decreased the exports.

From the data in 2001, one can find that the effect of China's access to WTO is larger than that of the US recession due to the "9/11" attack on the US in 2001 and the US stock market collapsing in 2000. It looks quite significant and interesting needs further exploration.

The further exchange rate reform resumed in 2004 focusing on broadening the floating band for RMB showing its effects on both exports and imports are same. The increasing risk of foreign exchange market makes both exports and imports reduced.

Now we come to our focus, the US subprime financial crisis in 2008, which had a significant effect on both China's exports and imports negatively.

In general, when we document the detailed change in China's trade due to important changes that occurred at each critical time point, we can figure out that all of such changes are similar with our expectations and the general trend in China's trade is increasing positively and significantly.

2.2 China's trade: Analysis by products

We extend our analysis from various aspects. First of all, we try to explore China's trade performance by analysing the category of commodities, i.e. SITC category, in details.

Figure 2 shows China's exports. There are two categories, "Animal and Vegetable Oils, Fats and Wax" and "Machinery and Transport Equipment" which are most fluctuating over time with highest growth rates. It can be understood in

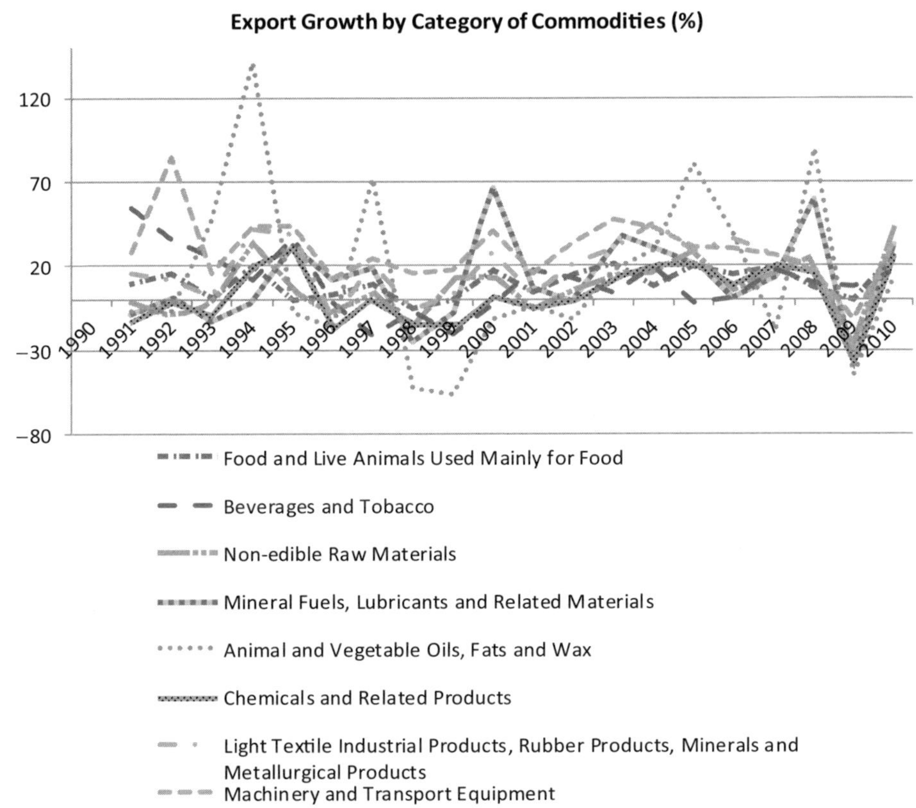

Figure 2. Exports growth by goods category (%).

Sources: 1981–1984: http://zhs.mofcom.gov.cn/aarticle/Nocategory/200405/20040500218164.html.
Other years: http://www.stats.gov.cn/tjsj/ndsj/2011/indexch.htm.
Authors calculate by themselves.

some way that the latter is the new focus for China's exports, and also belongs to the so-called "business cycles" commodities.

For the aspect of imports (see Figure 3), there are also two categories, "Beverages and Tobacco" and "Animal and Vegetable Oils, Fats and Wax" which are most fluctuating over time with highest growth rates. The former indicates the bad news in China that China has become the largest country in the world in terms of tobacco/cigarettes consumption with little limitation on them. The latter shows that "Animal and Vegetable Oils, Fats and Wax" could be the differential goods that indicate huge consumption demand for heterogeneous goods in a rapides growing domestic market in China. It could indicate the domestic consumption growth accompanying rapid economic growth, while it could consume more different/differential goods to adopt more desirable life style that will be more costly. It does not show, however, the trend of significant change on manufacturing goods in both imports and exports for China, which is very interesting.

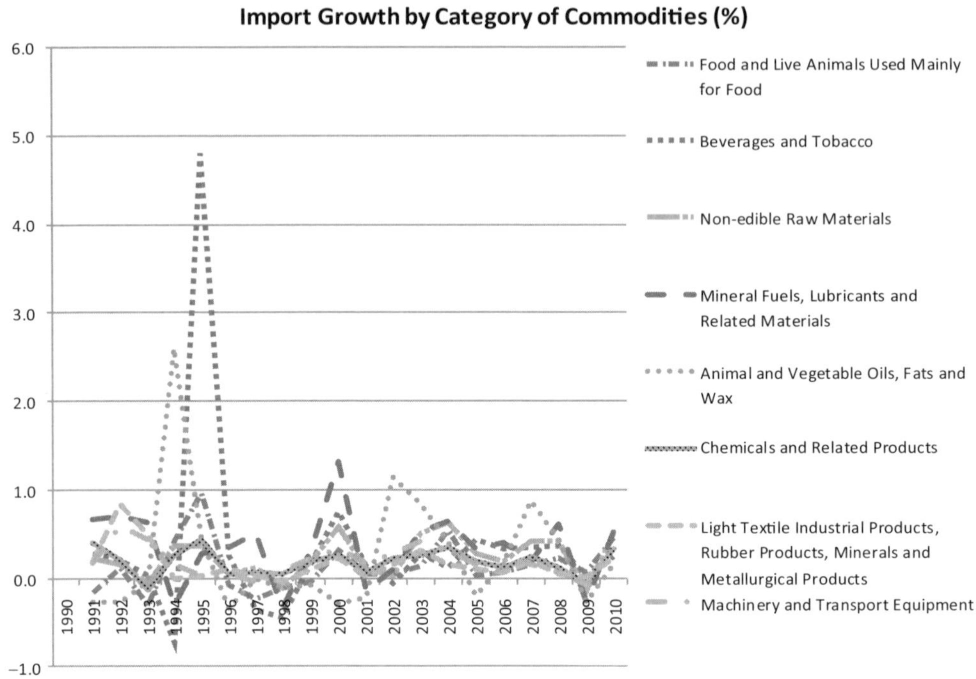

Figure 3. Imports growth by goods category (%).

Source: The original data is on http://www.stats.gov.cn/tjsj/ndsj/2011/indexch.htm. Authors calculate by themselves.

In general, except the kind of "institutional reform" in 1994–1995, all other events seem to bring some "level effect" on growth, while such effect could be decreased quickly. On the other hand, there should be a kind of "growth effect" occurring on at least categories such as "Non-edible Raw Material", "Mineral Fuels, etc.", "Animal and Vegetable Oils, etc.", due to rapid and continuous growth of Chinese economy, which could be the excuse for domestic demand (both industrial and consumers' demand) rising rapidly, while we could not provide deeper reasons for such "growth effects".

2.3 China's trade: Analysis by trade types

There is another angle to examine China's trade performance: good trade and service trade. As long as goods/commodities trade is discussed largely, this section could focus on service trade to provide a complete picture on China's trade.

Merchandised goods/commodities trade is always the main focus among majority of existing international trade across countries for centuries. It is obviously for people to know and understand the whole picture of world trade and economy, same as of China's trade. However, for trade measurement, since 1990s, or even since 1980s, until 2000s, all trade measure includes almost the merchandised goods trade because of China's long time manufacturing-focus thinking/plan and much lagged service supply (perhaps also demand). Therefore, as long as one can distinguish trade into merchandised goods trade and service trade, one could examine service trade, this seemingly "unknown" trade, and her performance in China.

As service trade has been playing a more important role in international trade recently (see Mattoo, Stern and Zanini, 2007; Borchert and Mattoo, 2009; Francois and Hoekman, 2010), more and more countries show more interest in service trade in order to increase their trade value by catching up the developing trends in world trade and increasing their potential/opportunity for sustainable trade in the current and future world. As service trade contains too many aspects that are hard to find, developing a simple united model to describe all of them, with great different characteristics for their activities, does not seem to be an easy task especially integrating aspects of service trade that cannot be separated them from goods trade. On the other hand, China, which is in similar position as other leading developing countries such as India, etc., has been rapidly expanding her trade in service in recent decades.

China's service trade has developed very quickly (see Figures 4 and 5), while its total value of service trade is ranked as number two in Asia after Japan (see Ministry of Commerce, 2008; 2009; 2010, etc.). It is also different from what people anticipated, while India's service trade, especially its computer software and office service has attracted much attention in the world and gained relatively large profits and reputation compared to its commodity trade value.

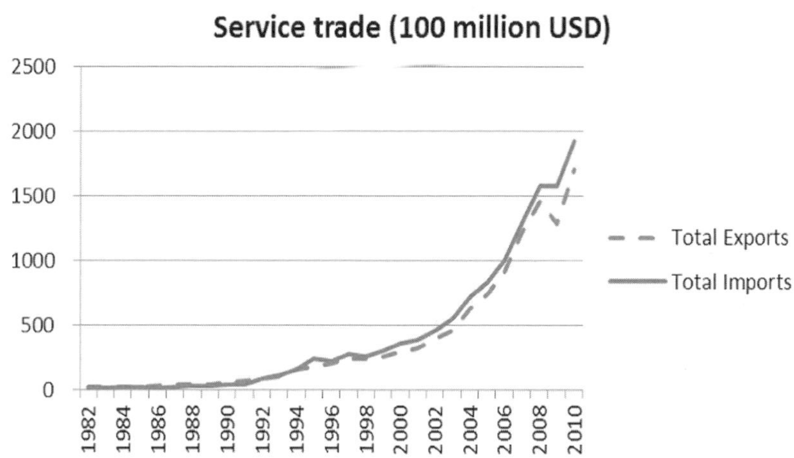

Figure 4. Service trade growth by value.

Source: http://www.stats.gov.cn/tjsj/ndsj/2011/indexch.htm.

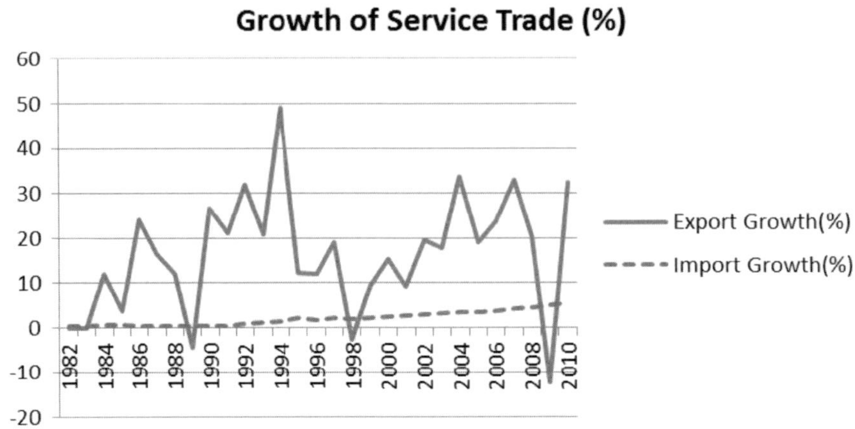

Figure 5. Service trade growth by percentage (%).

Source: The original data is on http://www.stats.gov.cn/tjsj/ndsj/2011/indexch.htm. The growth is calculated by authors.

China's exports are significantly larger than her imports in her service trade that shows there is much room for China's imports, which is similar to the goods trade. Precisely, Asia financial crisis in 1998 and the subprime financial crisis in 2008 are the two largest affecting factors in China's exports in her service trade ones recent decades.

3 China's Potential Trade Growth During and After the Crisis

To understand the entire process of change and/or China's trade potential with other countries, it is better to examine the related data pre-crisis, during and post- Crisis (i.e. post-2008 financial crisis) to see how much change has taken place 4.

From 2000, for example, one could find how weak and unstable the Western (or developed) economies are. Let us treat the world economy as the background for studying China's trade. The world economy, represented by some industrial countries, suffered during and post-9/11 and post-US subprime crisis, while their GDP growth rates were less than 1% between 2001 and 2012, as the detailed quarterly data shows in (Figure 6). Certainly, the subprime financial crisis are a big negative shock. China's growth rate of GDP, however, is shown above 8% every year with an average above 10% per year.

Now one can have a clear view about China's performance during the Crisis by analysing China's trade with her major trading partners in this period in the following sections.

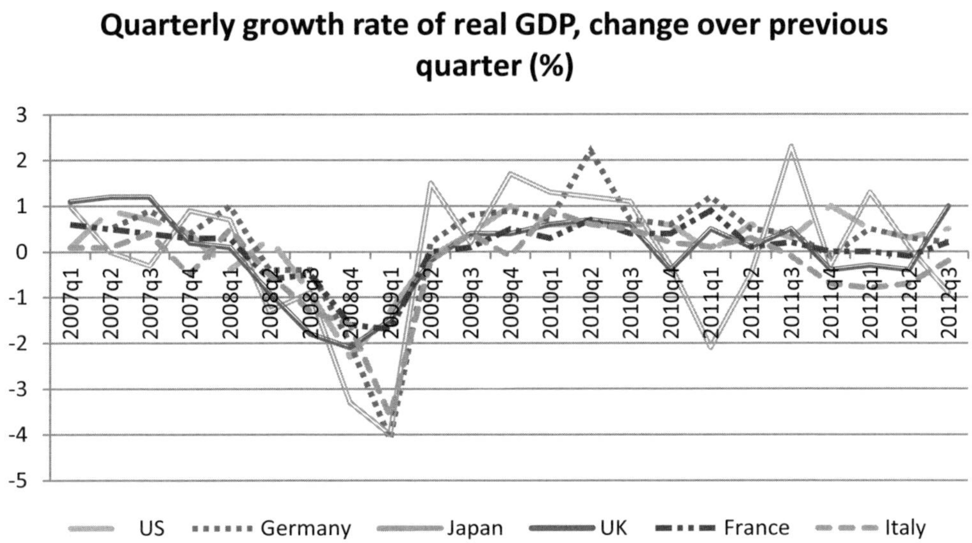

Figure 6. Quarterly growth rates of real GDP for industrial countries: 2001–2012.

Source: http://stats.oecd.org/index.aspx?queryid=350#. Authors calculate them by themselves.

3.1 China's trade: Analysis by geographical regions

One could change the angle to analyse China's trade by geographical regions, say, by some representative trading partners, who are China's major trading partners. One observes that there are surprising results (see Figure 7): there exist some consistent behaviours from following important events since 2000: the positive effect resulting from China's access to WTO (2001), and the negative impact resulting from subprime crisis, i.e. the Crisis (2008), and Euro financial crisis (two lagged shocks in 2009 and 2012).

Having faced the severe situation after the Crisis in 2008, for her exports, however, China still has more than 10% annual growth rate on them. It shows that China's very strong ability/potential to adapt to the quick changing market even though the external/outside markets became so bad for her exports. This ability could also indicate China's potential to continue her exporting value/volume though her exports growth rate will not be that high in the future.

In the exporting market, one can see there are several levels among the major trade partners, which are also the major economies in world trade, when one can divide trading countries into these different levels. Figure 8 shows China has a very high level of exports among those major trade partners. One could divide these levels as follows: the top level, i.e. Level 1, as the highest exporting value, and that is EU. China and US belong to the second highest level, i.e. Level 2, Level 3 is South Korea, Brazil, and India as depicted in Figure 9. It shows that there is steady and significant growth for China as well.

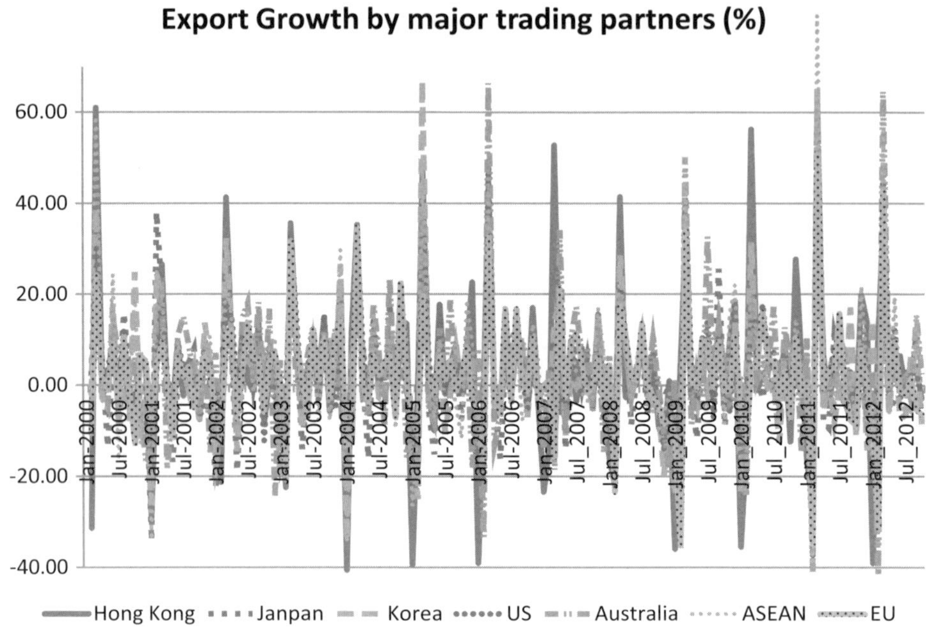

Figure 7. Export growth by major trading partners.

Source: http:/edu.macrochina.com.cn. Authors calculate the above data by themselves.

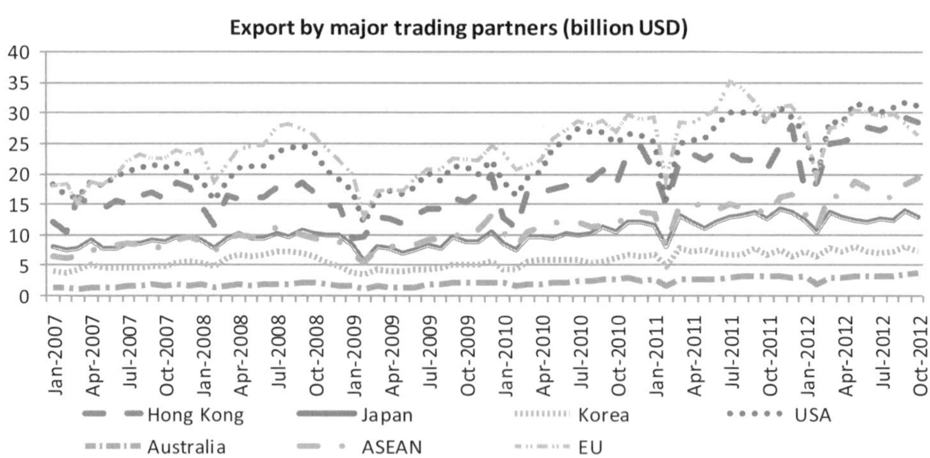

Figure 8. Export by major trade partners.

Source: http:/edu.macrochina.com.cn. Authors calculate the above data by themselves.

For such trade measures against China, Figures 9 and 10 show monthly data about merchandise trade with a clear division.

There is a strange phenomenon: China's exports seem to keep increasing during the subprime financial crisis! It is very surprising. Does it result from the

Figure 9. Monthly merchandise exports of selected economies.

Source: http://www.wto.org/english/res_e/statis_e/quarterly_world_exp_e.htm. Authors calculate the above data by themselves.

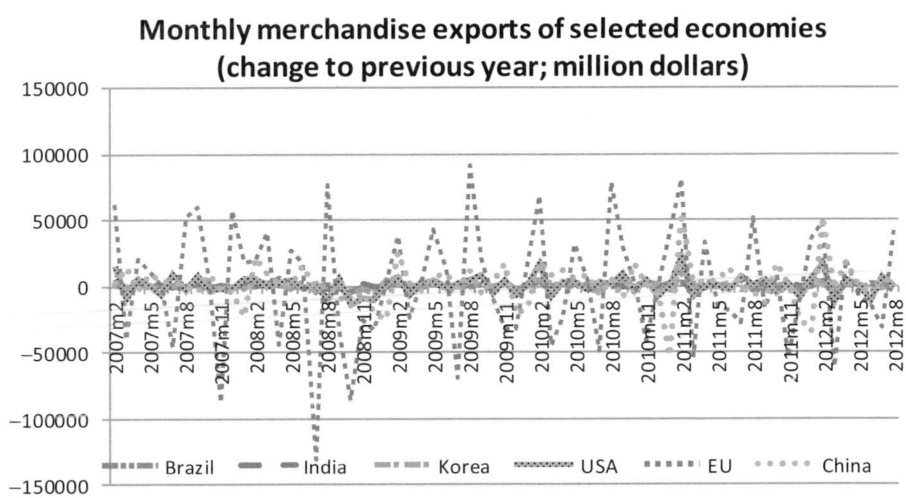

Figure 10. Monthly merchandise exports of selected economies (Change to previous year).

Source: http://www.wto.org/english/res_e/statis_e/quarterly_world_exp_e.htm. Authors calculate the above data by themselves.

growing internal demand that more imports create more exports? Or does it result from the firms' own effort that Chinese exporters do well in searching for new exporting markets?

For China's imports, one could see the same argument discussed above, i.e. the trend of China's rapid growth on her trade and her trade surplus could slow down considering the severe world economy that is still held.

Furthermore, the value of imports could indicate the same trend one discusses for exports.

Figures 11 and 12 show such trends clearly using monthly data. That is, for such trade measures against China, the trend of her imports is very similar, or consistent with that of her exports. So, one can observe that the highest levels of exports, i.e. Level 1, is still EU, and Level 2 is still US and China, and the lowest level/value of imports, i.e. Level 3 is still South Korea, Brazil and India. The country with more exports has more imports. It implies that trade for major economies in the world seems to be balanced mainly. The only different and relatively significant thing from our data is at Level 2, imports of US are clearly higher than that of China, which could not be found in corresponding figure of exports above. Certainly, China's imports are still steady and significantly growing, while she has more potential for her imports.

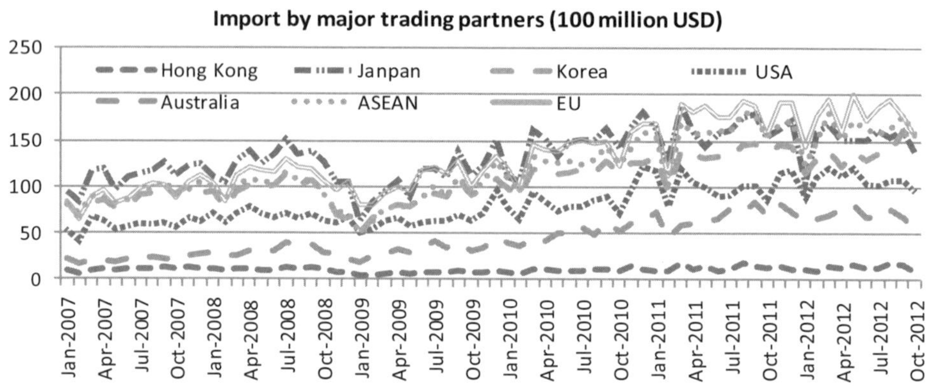

Figure 11. Import by major trading partners.

Source: http:/edu.macrochina.com.cn. Authors calculate the above data by themselves.

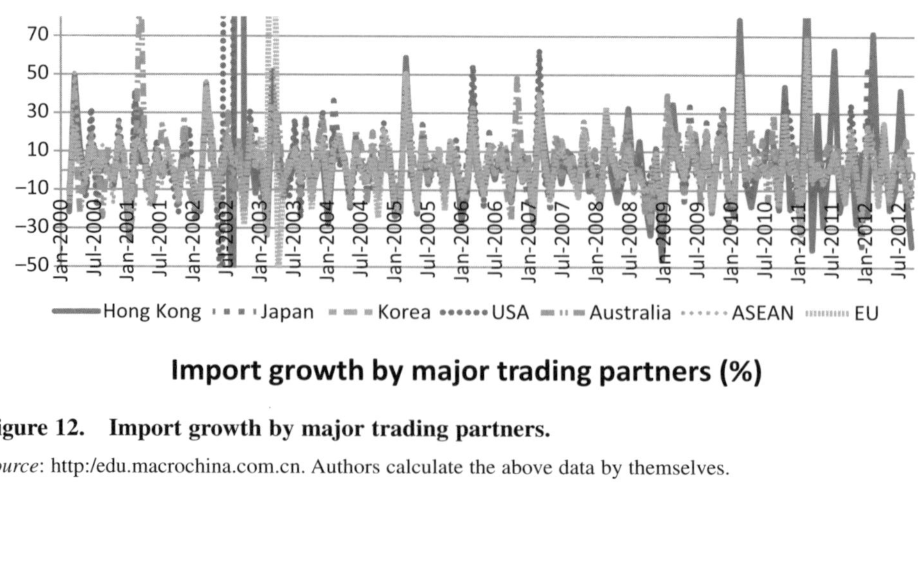

Figure 12. Import growth by major trading partners.

Source: http:/edu.macrochina.com.cn. Authors calculate the above data by themselves.

Precisely, as the pattern of imports is same as that of exports above for all selected economies, one can also find something more (see Figures 13 and 14). For example, when EU is at the highest level, i.e. Level 1, in both exporting and importing, its growth rate is fluctuating more. Thus, such highest level shows something more than one could expect: the average rate of trade growth of EU over this period is similar to all others', that is, as close to 0%. It shows the actual

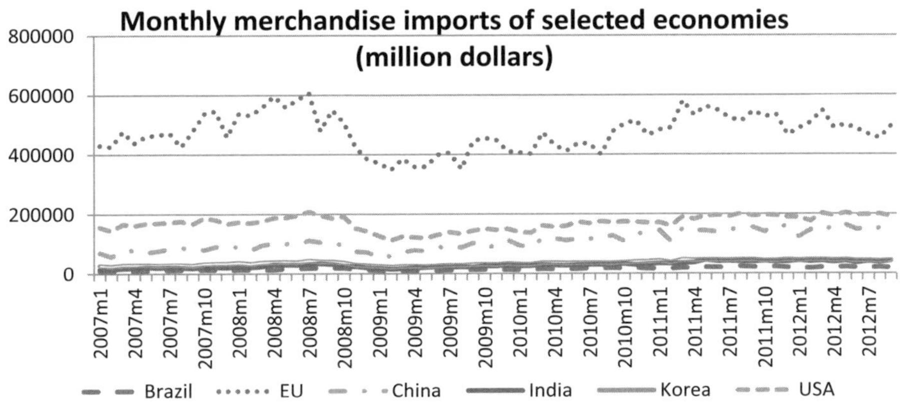

Figure 13. Monthly merchandise imports of selected economies.

Source: http://www.wto.org/english/res_e/statis_e/quarterly_world_exp_e.htm. Authors calculate the above data by themselves.

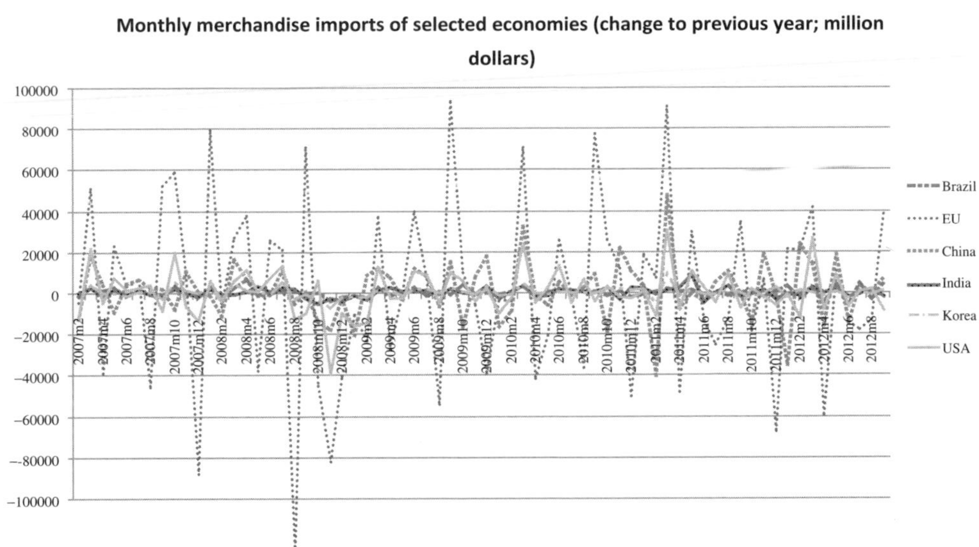

Figure 14. Monthly merchandise imports of selected economies (change to previous year).

Source: http://www.wto.org/english/res_e/statis_e/quarterly_world_exp_e.htm. Authors calculate the above data by themselves.

impact of the Crisis: it offsets the possible growth of trade for most representative economies just because of this Crisis.

In general, if we can conclude something about China's potential trade growth in the post-Crisis period, we can examine China's growth scenarios as follows: (1) there is slower but persistent growth in both exports and GDP; (2) there are unexpected external demands for China's exports: from shrunk and gloomy industrial economies, especially the large exporting markets (with more restrictions), and expanded demands from the South; (3) there is slow but persistent growth of domestic (private) consumption/market due to same economic fluctuation; (4) there is very slow increase in product variety and quality/value-added and markets; and (5) one faces rapid increase in wage rates in manufacturing in China.

In addition, there are some facts that provide some reasonable explanations. First of all, there is the slow-growing European and North American markets. Secondly, there is financial turbulence risk bothering China and industrial economies during this Crisis period. Thirdly, there exists trade adjustment resistance abroad: G20 rebalancing pressures, investment restrictions and various regional integration pressures. Fourthly and finally, there also exist internal wage pressures at home and in low wage economies, which challenge China's current production possessing the comparative advantage in her trade/exports.

4 A Balance Sheet of Prospects: For China's Future Growth and Trade Performance

One is always looking for a balanced sheet for China's future growth of trade and consequently, her GDP/economy. Let us see the existing circumstances indicating the potential problems (see Tong and Zhang, 2009; Wang and Whalley, 2010): (1) There are arithmetic inconsistencies of 30% export growth and 4.5% gross world product growth. (2) There are pressures to resist global adjustments driven by China's continued growth (trade measures, antidumping), G20 imbalances, Renminbi revaluation. (3) There is competition from elsewhere; India and other lower wage economies. (4) There exist financial turbulence risk and trade performance. (5) There are opportunities from continued high growth in the larger South. (6) There is product upgrading from innovation/ideas. (7) There is exports diversification to services. All of these are general reflections from our detailed analysis discussed so far.

4.1 Options for China international engagement

Our main purpose is to attempt to figure out the post-Crisis options for China at post-Crisis era in this chapter. There are many discussions and suggestions. Here, we summarise six possible options we think that are most reasonable and feasible for China's near future, corresponding to problems China faces before and after the global financial crisis resulting from the US subprime financial crisis in 2008.

Proposed Option 1: *To attempt to ream up/revive trade and FDI growth with tariff/tax deal to maintain high growth.*

The problems that occur now and can be expected in the near future for China are: (1) world economy slump and/or no growth in exports (see Yi, 2009, etc.); (2) FDI falls; (3) severe competition from low wage countries; (4) closing/dumping duties; and (5) energy prices fluctuating.

There is some hope, however, appearing for solving corresponding problems and as possible support for solutions. There was observable revival of world economy growth, and it seemed to return to normality in 1980s. The following Table 1 and Figures 15–17 for the Year 2004, 2007 and 2011 (i.e. before and after the Crisis) demonstrate this situation, even though the manufacturing industry has always attracted most of foreign direct investment (i.e. FDI) to support the title of "World Factory" for China, while one can observe the decreased number of investment projects and increased values of such investments.

The importance of tariffs/duties, including the export VAT rebate (see Chen, Mai and Yu, 2006; Chi-Chur and Chou, 2001; Li and Whalley 2012c), is under debate, while most economists agree tariffs/duties play inevitable role in international trade in general, which also concern the trade cost (e.g. Jacks, Christopher and Novy, 2009). While some researchers think the tariff/subsidy should significantly affect the trade performance in China (e.g., Yu, 2015), and some disagree to it while they focus on the role of fixed costs in international trade (e.g., Maskus *et al.*, 2013; Gao *et al.*, 2016).

We will discuss the possible solution for this in the following text.

Proposed Option 2: *To involve/engage the expanded trading blocks with the rapidly reorganised world.*

With the formation of global supply/value chain and closer regional economic integration/cooperation, there is eagerness to sign some kind of FTAs for both China and her trading partners.

There is an increasing regional integration in Asia, especially in East Asia. Figure 18 shows quick and increased regional FTAs in Asia in the recent two decades, even though Asia also experiences global financial crisis from the US subprime crisis in 2008.

Moreover, this trend has become more significant in East Asia (see Figure 19). For China, there are several trade agreements to form various levels of trading blocks as different types of regional integration to meet trading partners' requirements.

Table 1. Foreign Direct Investment by sector for selected years.

	Number of projects (unit)			Actually utilised value (USD 10000)		
Sector	**2004**	**2007**	**2011**	**2004**	**2007**	**2011**
Total	43664	37871	27712	6062998	7476789	11601100
1 Agriculture, Forestry, Animal Husbandry and Fishing	1130	1048	865	111434	92407	200888
2 Mining	279	234	87	53800	48944	61279
3 Manufacturing	30386	19193	11114	4301724	4086482	5210054
4 Production and Distribution of Electricity, Gas and Water	4555	352	214	113624	107255	211843
5 Construction	411	308	215	77158	43424	91694
6 Transport, Storage and Post	638	658	413	127285	200676	319079
7 Information Transmission, Computer Services and Software	1622	1392	993	91609	148524	269918
8 Wholesale and Retail Trade	1700	6338	7259	73959	267652	842455
9 Hotel and Restaurants	1174	938	513	84094	104165	84289
10 Financial Intermediation	43	51	156	25248	25729	190970
11 Real Estate	1767	1444	466	595015	1708873	2688152
12 Leasing and Business Services	2661	3539	3518	282423	401881	838247
13 Scientific Research, Technical Service	629	1716	1357	29384	91668	245781
14 Management of Water Conservancy, Environment	164	154	151	22911	27283	86427
15 Services to Households and Other Services	251	270	212	15795	72270	188357
16 Education	59	15	15	3841	3246	395
17 Health, Social Security and Social Welfare	21	13	11	8738	1157	7751
18 Culture, Sports and Entertainment	272	207	152	44776	45109	63455
19 Public Management and Social Organization	2		1	180	44	66

Source: *China Statistical Yearbook*: 1984–2012.

There are four levels for China to deal with her FTA style regional integration, beyond WTO (e.g. Li and Whalley, 2012b). The first level is to build the China-centred FTAs, such as (a) ECFA (Mainland vs. Taiwan), (b) CEPA ("Closer Economic Partnership Arrangement") (Mainland vs. Hong Kong), (c) China-oriented bilateral agreements with other countries (12 countries/regions up to 2012). The

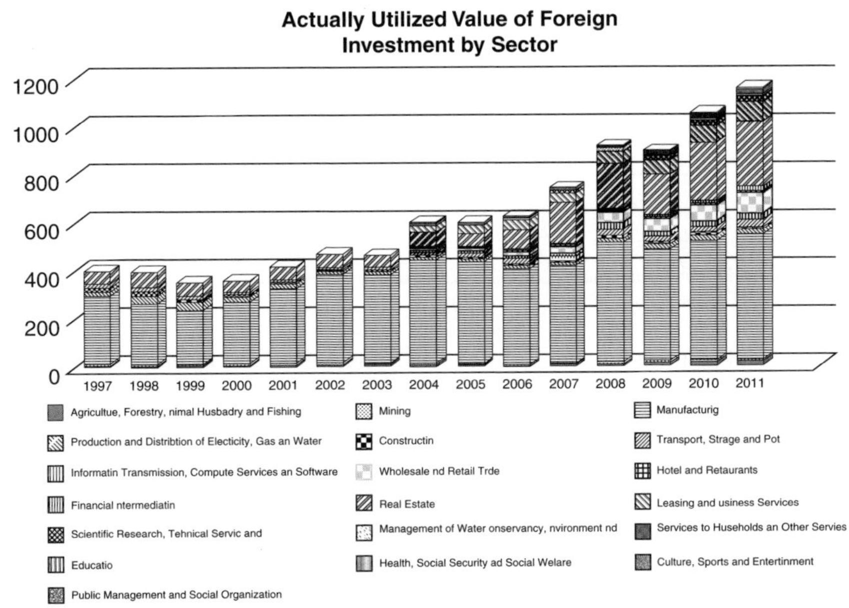

Figure 15. Actually utilised value of foreign direct investment by sector.

Source: http:/edu.macrochina.com.cn.

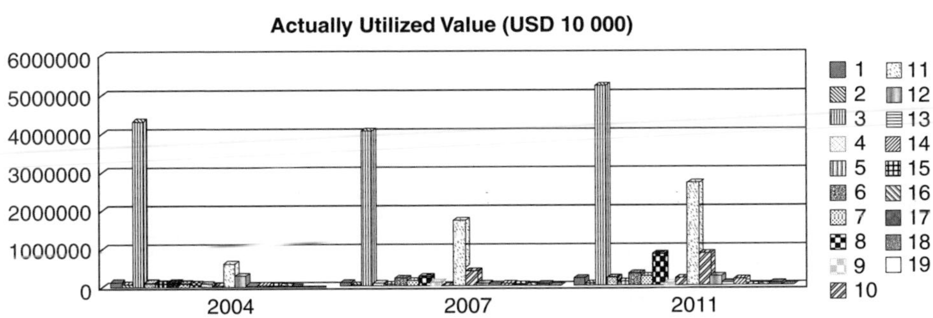

Figure 16. Foreign direct investment by sector for selected years: by actual used value.

Source: 1984–2012 *China Statistical Yearbook*.

1. Agriculture, Forestry, Animal Husbandry and Fishing. 2. Mining. 3. Manufacturing. 4. Production and Distribution of Electricity, Gas and Water. 5. Construction. 6. Transport, Storage and Post. 7. Information Transmission, Computer Services and Software. 8. Wholesale and Retail Trade. 9. Hotel and Restaurants. 10. Financial Intermediation. 11. Real Estate. 12. Leasing and Business Services. 13. Scientific Research, Technical Service. 14. Management of Water Conservancy, Environment. 15. Services to Households and Other Services. 16. Education. 17. Health, Social Security and Social Welfare. 18. Culture, Sports and Entertainment. 19. Public Management and Social Organization.

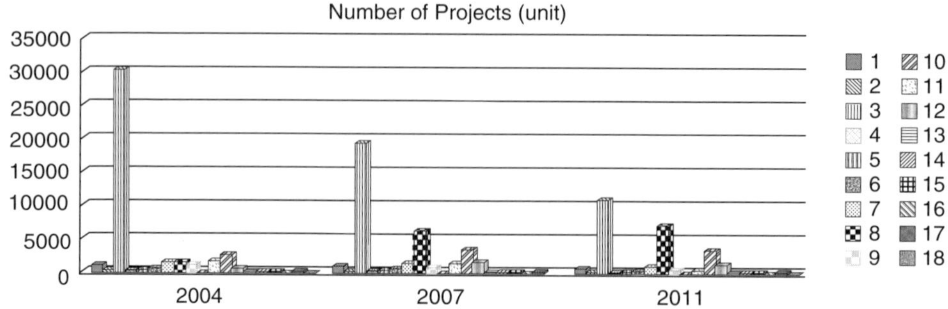

Figure 17. Foreign direct investment by sector for selected years: by numbers.

Source: 1984–2012 *China Statistical Yearbook*.

1. Agriculture, Forestry, Animal Husbandry and Fishing. 2. Mining. 3. Manufacturing. 4. Production and Distribution of Electricity, Gas and Water. 5. Construction. 6. Transport, Storage and Post. 7. Information Transmission, Computer Services and Software. 8. Wholesale and Retail Trade. 9. Hotel and Restaurants. 10. Financial Intermediation. 11. Real Estate 12. Leasing and Business Services. 13. Scientific Research, Technical Service. 14. Management of Water Conservancy, Environment. 15. Services to Households and Other Services. 16. Education. 17. Health, Social Security and Social Welfare. 18. Culture, Sports and Entertainment. 19. Public Management and Social Organization.

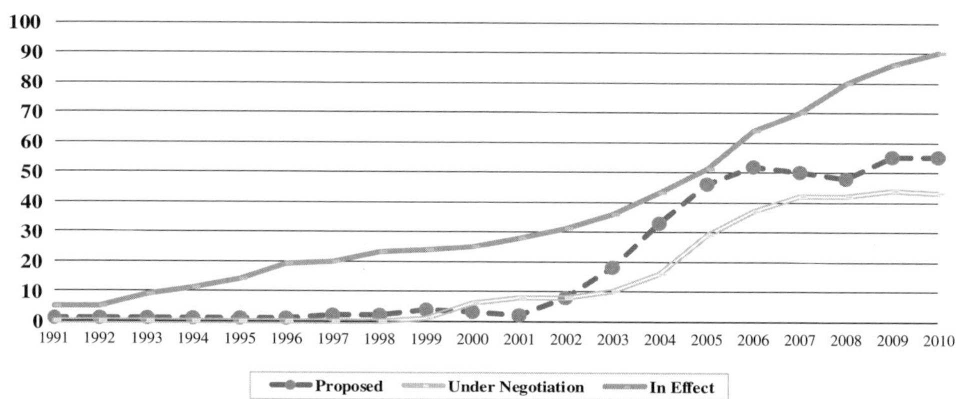

Figure 18. Accumulated number of FTAs in Asia: 1991–2010.

Source: Asia regional Integration Center, ADB.

second level is for China good relationship to build with her neighbouring countries, which is being done accomplished now, such as (a) ASEAN 10 countries with China (10+1), ASEAN with Northeast Asia (China, Japan, South Korea three countries) (10+3), and ASEAN with six neighbour countries (China, Japan, South Korea, India, Australia and New Zealand) (10+6); (b) APEC and (c) RCEP (i.e. Regional Comprehensive Economic Partnership, same countries as 10+6 but initialised by ASEAN). The third level is to propose to join/negotiate some important regional integration, that is, TPP (Trans-Pacific Partnership Agreement), which is led by US

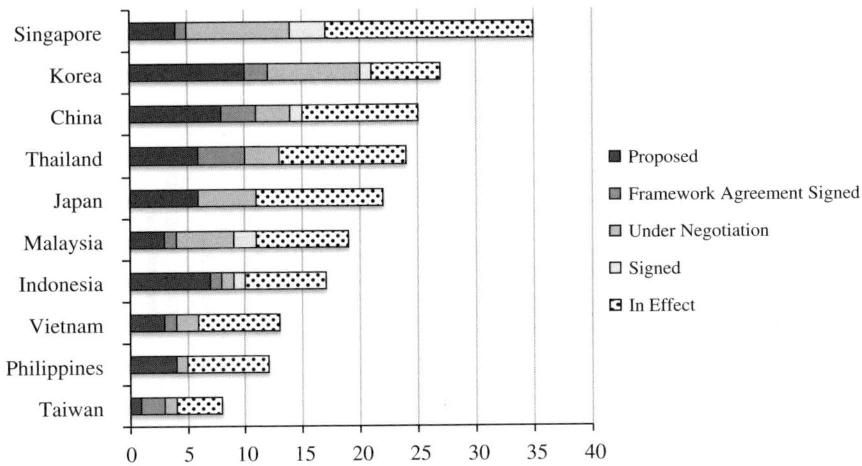

Figure 19. FTA Status for major economies in East Asia: 2010.
Source: Asia regional Integration Center, ADB.

and would gather some important economies like Canada, Japan, South Korea, Australia and Mexico, since it is very important for China's future (e.g. Li and Whalley, 2012a). There is one more possible change for world trade. That is, the US dominating the two important trade negotiations, TPP and TTIP (i.e. "Transatlantic Trade and Investment Partnership") could challenge the existing global trade organisation, WTO, if both TPP and TTIP can be successfully researched.

There is more evidence to show such FTAs do occur in East Asia to increase the internal integration within East Asia, which does not mean more outside connection with non-Asian countries instead.

We could see such detailed distribution in the world as three major trading blocks, East Asia (here, East Asia = ASEAN+3+Taiwan+Hong Kong), NAFTA, and EU, in Figures 20 and 21, as the goods (divided as intermediate goods, final goods and value-added exports) sell within the same block (i.e. internally) or outside this block (i.e. externally). We find that there is very high intra-regional dependence on intermediate trade in manufacturing sectors in East Asia. However, recent research from USITC (US International Trade Commission, hereafter) indicates that roughly 70% of final manufacturing goods exports in East Asia depends on external demand from the other two blocks and/or rest of world.

Proposed Option 3: *To attempt to have more trade with the South.*

Considering the gloomy existing markets for exporting and rapidly increasing trade disputes, China should expand her exporting markets, especially the South, since most of the existing markets for China's exports are developed countries, such as North America, EU, Japan, etc. Figure 22 shows that there is

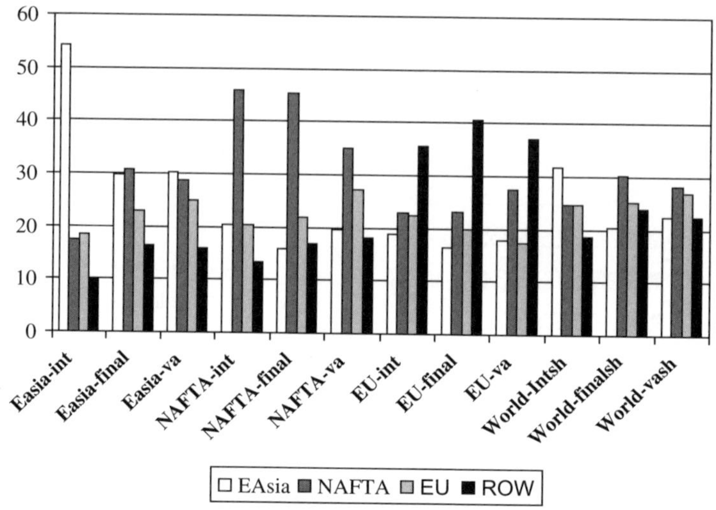

Figure 20. Manufacturing export destination of the three trading blocks — *intermediates, final goods and value-added exports, 2004 (%).*

Source: Value-added trade estimate by Zhi Wang's calculation (USITC).

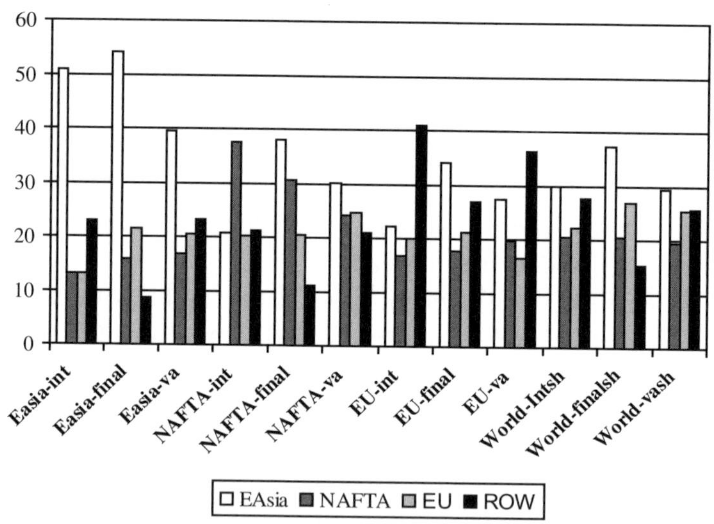

Figure 21. Manufacturing import destination of the three trading blocks — *intermediates, final goods and value-added exports, 2004 (%).*

Source: Value-added trade estimate by Zhi Wang's calculation (USITC).

much room to adopt new entrants from ASEAN countries, BRICs to general South, including Africa, Asia (including Middle East) and Latin America (including the Caribbean countries) (see Medianu and Whalley, 2010; Shekhar and Whalley 2010).

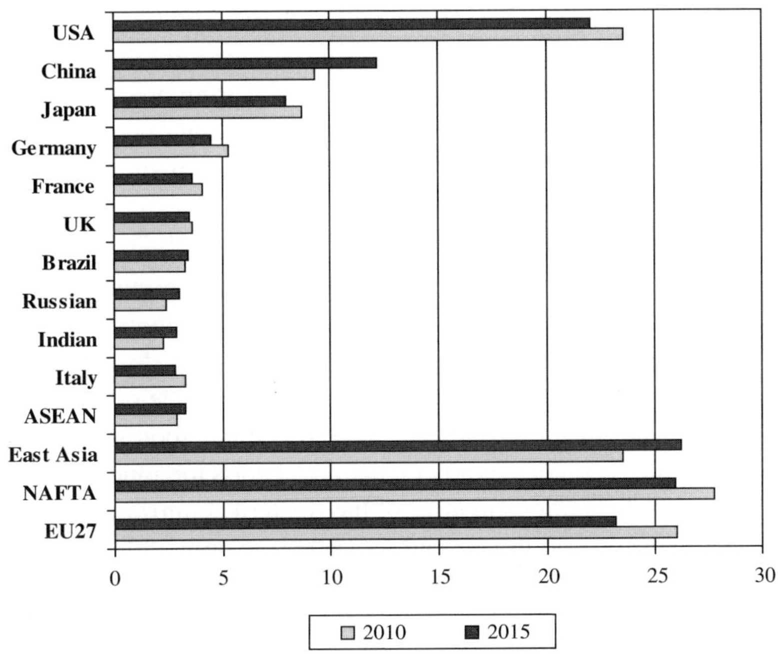

Figure 22. Three trading blocks and top ten export markets by 2015 — *share of world nominal GDP, 2010 and 2015.*

Source: IMF, World Economic Outlook Database, October 2010.

For example, East Asian countries are quite diversifying in general. Most East Asian countries are deeply involved in the vertical specialised global production chain and stay at the low end of such production chain. In this chain, Japan and China seem to be the major hubs staying at high and low ends, which show different stages of economic development.

Proposed Option 4: *To revaluate Chinese RMB to obtain the persistent trade.*

The valuation of Chinese currency Renminbi (i.e. RMB) is always a sensitive and key dispute between China and her trade partners, which causes large uncertainty for China's trade growth. The Chinese economic growth itself will lead to Chinese RMB's revaluation, which also reduces pressure from her trading partners for the possible dumping and dramatically increases exports on some products. The revaluation of Chinese RMB could result in temporary decrease in China's exports, which is one of the major sources of China's growth. Besides the external pressure indicated above, however, the internal reasons, such as releasing the pressure of Chinese firms' high interest costs and internationalising Chinese RMB to integrate Chinese domestic monetary policy and exchange rate policy, etc. will also force the Chinese government to revaluate her exchange rate soon. Other important and necessary measures China will undertake in the near future such as RMB's effort to enter the basket of IMF's SDR (i.e. special drawing rights) will also push China to revaluate her RMB, which should bring persistent trade for her sustainable growth. The question is, when should the Chinese government attempt this? We think she should pick up a "suitable" time to do it soon.

Proposed Option 5: *To go for domestic markets/consumption.*

It is a very possible solution to support China's future growth. See Figure 23.

From 1978 to 2010, Chinese economy grew rapidly at more than 10% annual rate. The growth rate of domestic consumption has been decreasing averagely from about 65% to 50% of national GDP, although the value of consumption has been increasing due to the domestic GDP rise. It is not a good signal that China's national economy has been depending on her net exports too much. It is also found that in such abnormal situations in most of the western countries, the consumption will take about two-thirds to three-quarters of their national GDP. It shows China still has large room to increase her domestic consumption.

There are three possible ways to boost China's consumption: (1) Raising the trade flow by increasing her infrastructure expenditure (e.g., moving out of recession-debt in local governments). (2) Promoting consumption, which needs big change in the institution forms that would be a change-slowly adjust experience. (3) Attracting more PDI based on experience growth and improved infrastructure and enough well-trained skilled labour, which has already 50% of large companies going for domestic market of China.

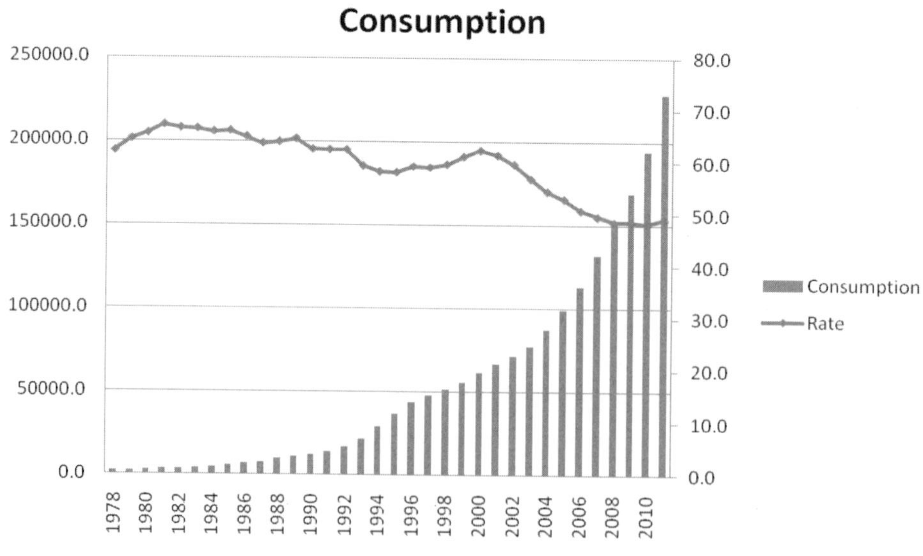

Figure 23. Consumption and its growth.

Source: 1984–2012 *China Statistical Yearbook*.

Proposed Option 6: *To Innovate.*

There should be an ideas-led sustainable growth in China, which is sustainable over time. There could be (1) innovation that the world/China leads, (2) education (e.g., patents), and/or (3) innovation increasing at least in the form of international initiatives China undertakes for US, which could support China's future, either trade/exports or national economy.

Figures 24 and 25 indicate the quick growth of patents applied and/or examined/certified at more than 20% growth rate for the past two decades (1994–2010). It shows that there is great future for China's innovation/R&D activities.

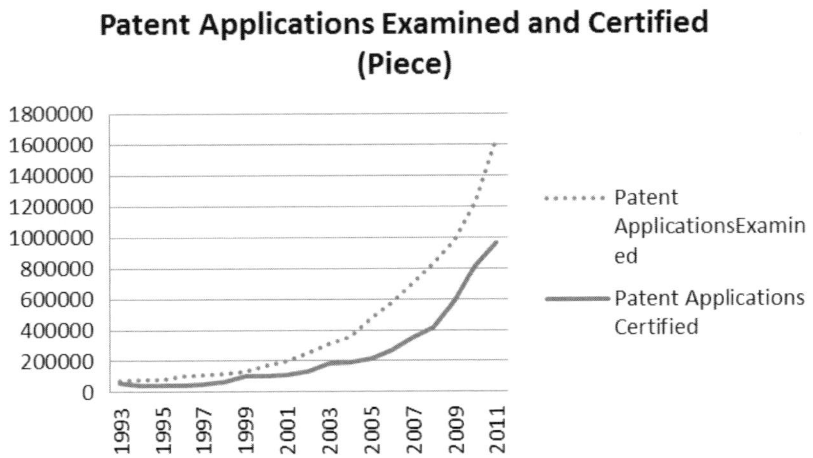

Figure 24. Patent applications examined and certified.

Source: 1984–2012 *China Statistical Yearbook.*

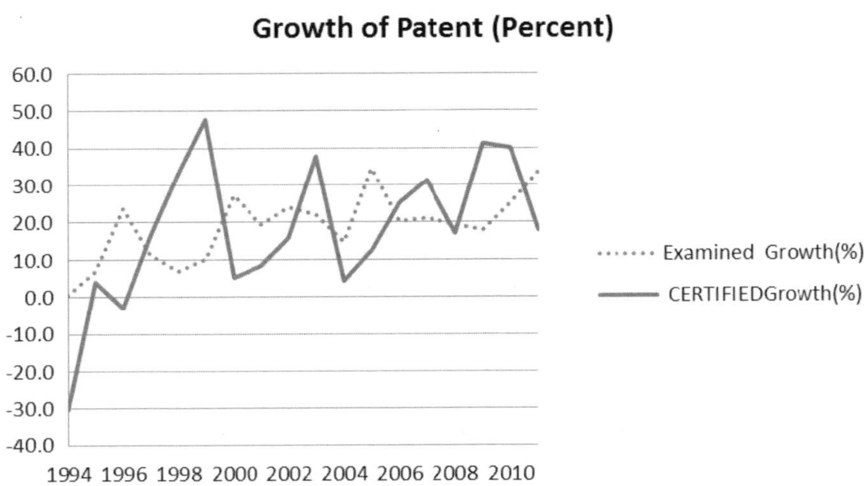

Figure 25. Growth of patent.

Source: 1984–2012 *China Statistical Yearbook.*

5 Concluding Remarks

Starting from the analysis of China's trade performance, we preliminarily evaluate the current scenarios China faces for her past/current success thus far, problems she incurs, and discuss six possible post-Crisis options, as her future roles/tasks to engage the international society, as we suggest and discuss in general.

We assess impacts of the Crisis on China's growth performance, represented mainly by her trade (with some discussion on FDI) and of ways of China's international engagement, and some problems/difficulties China incur/incurred by comparing her performance before, during and after the Crisis, focusing on patterns, values and growth rates of imports/exports with selected economies.

We find, from various aspects, that China's past/current success does not mean her current ways/patterns through trade/exports can hold for her future potential growth/international engagement as the international society needs.

This world needs a strong, stable China to play a positive role for her future and China herself needs the same. China has changed for herself and the rest of the world reasonable and constructive, and will be changed further on the correct way, we hope.

Appendix

Table A.1. Table for Figure 8.

(Country/Region)	Hong Kong	Japan	Korea	USA	Australia	ASEAN	EU
Feb-2007	−13.48	−5.99	−5.95	−10.23	3.63	−5.76	0.97
Mar-2007	52.74	2.88	14.28	−0.91	−18.56	7.47	−15.72
Apr-2007	−5.95	17.48	18.50	16.35	34.15	16.02	21.14
May-2007	−5.66	−13.99	−10.96	−4.48	−10.79	−0.33	−2.58
Jun-2007	9.76	−0.28	1.66	9.67	9.73	9.97	8.77
Jul-2007	−3.44	9.21	−0.32	3.51	17.36	2.65	11.52
Aug-2007	8.11	−0.44	1.55	2.62	5.91	−1.58	4.87
Sep-2007	2.93	6.18	1.76	2.06	8.15	−3.40	−1.60
Oct-2007	−5.16	−2.69	−0.22	−1.68	−5.82	−3.64	0.01
Nov-2007	15.60	9.72	14.60	3.11	14.68	16.86	5.94
Dec-2007	−4.62	1.28	3.38	−7.81	−14.60	7.38	−4.15
Jan-2008	−16.14	−6.95	−6.37	−4.16	6.53	−9.59	4.43
Feb-2008	−21.75	−14.60	−9.82	−19.22	−23.34	−16.97	−23.38
Mar-2008	41.46	20.28	28.59	21.56	19.95	27.82	17.21

(Continued)

Table A.1. ***(Continued)***

(Country/Region)	Hong Kong	Japan	Korea	USA	Australia	ASEAN	EU
Apr-2008	−2.65	10.19	8.62	10.85	8.54	6.45	10.95
May-2008	0.58	−8.67	−2.59	1.71	−2.76	−3.40	1.99
Jun-2008	0.16	1.40	2.37	0.44	3.78	4.01	1.05
Jul-2008	10.62	8.55	10.72	10.76	11.26	10.86	13.56
Aug-2008	−2.35	−6.16	−0.82	1.96	0.28	−4.21	0.24
Sep-2008	6.99	10.96	−5.54	2.59	10.33	−5.79	−2.53
Oct-2008	−8.70	−4.25	−4.28	−4.21	−0.04	−5.67	−4.20
Nov-2008	−12.84	−2.73	−19.87	−13.91	−10.24	−6.11	−8.48
Dec-2008	0.98	−0.26	−6.59	−5.85	−19.10	−1.71	−7.50
Jan-2009	−36.00	−17.46	−24.03	−9.78	1.46	−21.12	−10.67
Feb-2009	2.81	−31.79	−7.42	−31.88	−36.31	−23.03	−35.20
Mar-2009	31.09	43.16	21.33	39.69	50.12	44.94	33.91
Apr-2009	−2.57	−2.42	−1.02	4.41	−8.53	3.64	0.83
May-2009	−4.77	−11.69	−4.54	−2.74	2.42	2.29	−0.45
Jun-2009	10.41	7.02	10.46	6.17	−4.97	2.51	9.97
Jul-2009	9.21	11.10	−1.50	14.25	32.70	10.00	9.12
Aug-2009	−0.61	−5.63	4.34	−7.14	0.14	1.24	−0.49
Sep-2009	12.53	25.59	13.26	12.43	13.33	9.16	9.62
Oct-2009	−5.14	−8.91	0.38	0.70	3.74	−8.53	−1.31
Nov-2009	9.67	−0.97	−1.22	−6.09	−3.92	15.58	−1.07
Dec-2009	18.57	19.13	13.85	11.02	−2.40	22.14	10.82
Jan-2010	−35.50	−18.05	−23.28	−15.70	2.16	−19.73	−4.57
Feb-2010	−13.89	−12.18	−0.28	−12.44	−23.99	−22.87	−11.85
Mar-2010	56.24	26.61	31.40	17.90	20.49	29.53	4.22
Apr-2010	−1.03	2.29	1.16	5.88	1.36	8.06	3.95
May-2010	2.48	−2.87	3.07	17.78	5.61	6.12	15.97
Jun-2010	3.61	7.06	−0.26	5.82	3.32	−1.52	5.21
Jul-2010	5.10	−1.20	0.59	7.21	17.24	2.00	5.40
Aug-2010	0.57	1.36	−12.61	−2.25	−7.67	−6.44	−2.60
Sep-2010	8.71	9.86	8.84	0.91	12.72	1.08	3.12
Oct-2010	−12.36	−5.49	8.44	−6.92	4.42	1.14	−7.21
Nov-2010	27.74	13.88	7.47	5.35	10.53	14.62	10.51
Dec-2010	5.36	−0.64	−5.01	−0.94	−14.93	3.43	−2.02
Jan-2011	−16.52	−3.31	6.28	−3.79	10.35	−2.96	0.80

(Continued)

Table A.1. (*Continued*)

(Country/Region)	Hong Kong	Japan	Korea	USA	Australia	ASEAN	EU
Feb-2011	−26.15	−29.19	−30.07	−37.37	−40.92	−38.76	−35.10
Mar-2011	46.08	60.35	65.20	58.94	63.69	81.25	50.50
Apr-2011	6.35	−7.72	−5.72	1.90	−1.38	0.92	−0.61
May-2011	−4.48	−9.30	1.39	1.02	2.05	−1.71	3.40
Jun-2011	5.21	10.96	−8.09	8.37	−2.08	−4.43	3.48
Jul-2011	−1.47	4.79	−0.20	7.00	11.52	6.65	15.72
Aug-2011	−4.11	3.42	−3.88	0.43	5.79	−3.94	−2.56
Sep-2011	−0.26	2.93	17.15	0.08	−0.29	1.50	−7.48
Oct-2011	−7.47	−7.07	−11.34	−5.04	−0.18	−9.17	−9.09
Nov-2011	19.90	12.05	9.98	8.22	6.25	21.77	7.86
Dec-2011	13.65	−2.69	−14.23	−5.20	−9.15	2.61	0.08
Jan-2012	−39.02	−11.02	14.42	−9.33	2.76	−18.61	−9.00
Feb-2012	8.28	−15.02	−11.38	−27.22	−41.45	−20.26	−31.44
Mar-2012	35.55	30.21	17.54	47.85	64.51	56.73	42.61
Apr-2012	0.18	−5.88	−6.02	−1.69	−1.07	−6.54	0.15
May-2012	3.38	−2.76	9.80	12.93	6.53	19.43	9.55
Jun-2012	6.48	−1.72	−7.15	−2.55	0.31	−5.64	−1.07
Jul-2012	−1.47	3.64	−6.57	−2.71	2.00	−4.47	−1.98
Aug-2012	3.91	−2.51	6.86	2.83	−3.05	−6.44	1.59
Sep-2012	3.37	12.70	8.45	2.54	15.34	15.46	−5.38
Oct-2012	−2.80	−8.09	−8.56	−1.88	2.48	4.84	−6.39

Table A.2. Table for Figure 12.

(Country/Region)	Hong Kong	Japan	Korea	USA	Australia	ASEAN	EU
Jan-2007							
Feb-2007	−27.17	−11.06	−18.61	−21.78	−23.99	−10.85	−23.74
Mar-2007	38.75	38.26	21.85	63.16	25.79	24.58	39.71
Apr-2007	12.82	1.30	5.43	−5.46	0.75	−0.07	7.26
May-2007	−5.97	−19.08	−11.01	−15.31	−9.89	−8.00	−14.98
Jun-2007	10.43	14.92	2.25	5.82	19.46	3.83	7.48
Jul-2007	−6.32	3.49	15.78	6.53	−2.50	8.02	11.07
Aug-2007	10.32	3.70	1.78	−1.26	5.55	6.78	4.79
Sep-2007	7.40	7.52	7.12	1.52	−4.11	7.13	−1.15
Oct-2007	−9.89	−12.02	−8.00	−6.93	−9.50	−12.26	−13.71

(*Continued*)

Table A.2. *(Continued)*

(Country/Region)	Hong Kong	Japan	Korea	USA	Australia	ASEAN	EU
Nov-2007	16.69	9.63	10.89	15.98	25.43	5.29	20.23
Dec-2007	−10.51	1.69	−7.75	−2.88	7.76	7.71	6.00
Jan-2008	−6.43	−10.81	0.73	11.50	10.65	−4.84	−7.11
Feb-2008	−14.81	−4.75	−17.97	−14.35	−16.93	−14.13	−18.96
Mar-2008	30.21	20.25	23.40	17.31	2.76	21.14	33.38
Apr-2008	−2.80	9.52	7.08	9.93	22.09	3.88	7.40
May-2008	−16.37	−10.49	−3.04	−11.32	−8.35	−0.15	−2.39
Jun-2008	−2.91	8.64	2.01	−5.18	10.99	−5.50	−1.78
Jul-2008	32.51	10.98	13.52	9.91	26.71	14.55	12.82
Aug-2008	−6.81	−10.12	−10.83	−9.45	−8.00	−8.08	−6.73
Sep-2008	15.34	3.07	5.33	9.14	2.29	0.94	−2.29
Oct-2008	−15.20	−7.56	−10.95	−13.04	−21.32	−14.54	−10.20
Nov-2008	−33.51	−19.01	−26.26	−0.54	−8.12	−21.40	−9.66
Dec-2008	11.72	1.04	−7.48	9.43	−19.44	−0.91	9.01
Jan-2009	−46.43	−40.58	−22.89	−26.57	−14.13	−30.24	−22.64
Feb-2009	9.97	34.54	31.58	9.24	39.33	25.76	−1.50
Mar-2009	34.68	12.45	15.76	14.50	4.35	22.40	15.80
Apr-2009	1.64	11.82	4.77	6.22	19.24	3.05	7.69
May-2009	−3.06	−15.61	−2.97	−12.82	−10.99	−1.48	−3.86
Jun-2009	6.04	33.48	11.15	6.93	20.33	12.78	22.87
Jul-2009	18.90	0.01	7.07	2.96	19.46	14.77	2.39
Aug-2009	−8.96	−7.79	−3.60	−0.49	−18.03	−11.03	−6.06
Sep-2009	18.53	25.30	21.01	10.11	15.78	21.65	12.73
Oct-2009	−21.72	−18.64	−16.69	−10.68	−22.88	−13.78	−21.10
Nov-2009	9.19	8.86	8.94	16.40	11.62	11.20	17.18
Dec-2009	24.91	23.08	11.39	32.48	30.57	22.10	13.39
Jan-2010	−11.89	−26.56	−10.48	−18.64	−12.38	−14.67	−11.43
Feb-2010	−23.72	−2.59	−7.52	−16.96	−9.05	−13.12	−18.04
Mar-2010	78.75	49.53	31.63	46.90	24.83	39.47	49.42
Apr-2010	−4.39	−5.06	−0.81	−9.03	−5.61	−3.33	−3.31
May-2010	−18.67	−12.22	−3.18	−14.02	22.28	−1.73	−1.11
Jun-2010	−2.30	10.67	0.68	5.56	−3.17	1.56	6.34
Jul-2010	−0.40	2.18	3.34	1.38	16.17	−3.23	2.56
Aug-2010	20.90	−0.96	−2.47	9.08	−15.83	5.35	−2.44

(Continued)

Table A.2. (*Continued*)

(Country/Region)	Hong Kong	Japan	Korea	USA	Australia	ASEAN	EU
Sep-2010	13.56	9.01	9.98	4.01	29.86	11.05	1.04
Oct-2010	−19.88	−12.82	−9.93	−21.23	−17.79	−13.37	−17.86
Nov-2010	43.79	15.50	9.99	37.51	17.56	13.58	30.18
Dec-2010	−20.06	9.37	−0.67	25.60	3.79	12.41	6.11
Jan-2011	−9.72	−9.73	6.12	−4.65	15.23	−2.93	−0.63
Feb-2011	−9.58	−21.29	−27.69	−32.77	−37.94	−33.29	−32.83
Mar-2011	105.29	46.52	46.42	54.07	29.82	64.58	68.44
Apr-2011	−40.88	−14.82	−4.50	−13.08	5.29	−6.84	−5.24
May-2011	29.37	−9.57	−1.93	−4.80	1.23	−0.17	3.93
Jun-2011	−28.27	9.78	0.67	−10.90	6.45	2.22	−6.05
Jul-2011	5.99	1.93	0.39	1.92	14.87	−1.41	0.35
Aug-2011	63.00	8.15	9.19	11.04	−2.61	13.27	9.79
Sep-2011	−21.31	2.26	1.65	0.69	12.87	−1.45	−3.35
Oct-2011	−6.08	−13.30	−6.21	−15.89	−15.74	−12.93	−16.21
Nov-2011	12.22	4.76	5.22	34.69	17.34	8.80	22.53
Dec-2011	−27.57	5.76	−1.87	3.47	−11.81	2.38	−0.58
Jan-2012	8.91	−39.14	−19.96	−25.50	−13.41	−28.42	−24.43
Feb-2012	−23.67	52.12	14.11	26.82	5.01	22.54	22.93
Mar-2012	71.45	5.45	7.50	7.36	5.10	18.80	9.62
Apr-2012	−8.31	−10.55	−12.62	−6.68	9.56	−16.26	−17.65
May-2012	24.61	0.66	12.56	7.50	7.00	14.05	24.78
Jun-2012	−20.20	0.01	−6.12	−14.92	−17.55	−5.37	−14.17
Jul-2012	−10.52	7.46	5.01	−1.23	2.04	−2.55	8.26
Aug-2012	41.88	−4.54	1.73	4.26	10.91	3.32	4.73
Sep-2012	−9.64	4.36	16.21	0.97	−10.03	8.04	−8.74
Oct-2012	−39.29	−13.87	−8.03	−11.11	−19.60	−11.25	−12.40

Table A.3. Table for Figure 15.

Change to previous year	Brazil	EU	China	India	Korea	USA
2007m2	−1276.21	−4778.72652	−12368	37.8	−2153.949	−11628.1
2007m3	2399.96	51203.0868	18328	2651.9	3889.308	22133.3
2007m4	−1324.68	−38828.807	4074	1234.4	301.422	−4734.9
2007m5	1613.44	23103.08029	−9116	2779	260.055	6978.6

(*Continued*)

Table A.3. (*Continued*)

Change to previous year	Brazil	EU	China	India	Korea	USA
2007m6	–514.62	3618.32155	4825	–1134	–1348.839	1045.2
2007m7	1522.92	6851.79756	6878	1113	715.103	2470.2
2007m8	843.6	–45854.0996	2877	–763	418.849	3951.3
2007m9	–924.5	52607.36412	2039	–2149	–2448.468	–8292.7
2007m10	1778	58743.29576	–7716	3616	5547.65	19632.7
2007m11	–328.1	9246.83332	10656	271	1184.892	–6633
2007m12	–1512.8	–88003.1225	520	–1987	–30.209	–13399.8
2008m1	1914.8	79384.1312	–1442	2727	2422.085	6150.8
2008m2	–427	–6412	–11135	–2040	–3694	–3508
2008m3	–437	26917	16719	2770	4487	6071
2008m4	754	38028	6529	6743	1149	11338
2008m5	3012	–37698	–1613	–873	444	808
2008m6	690	25558	–335	–493	–876	7218
2008m7	1377	21518	10966	2674	5124	12983
2008m8	354	–126814	–5413	1898	–2532	–12816
2008m9	–174	70727	793	–2387	–892	–9899
2008m10	–101	–44809	–14044	–5267	–3429	5974
2008m11	–4067	–81952	–18091	–2381	–7245	–39374
2008m12	–1946	–40644	–2611	–4032	–2278	–9954
2009m1	–1240	–10880	–20674	–1228	–1677	–15580
2009m2	–2650	–22862	8687	–3166	–2301	–14427
2009m3	2341	37073	11792	1535	1323	12723
2009m4	–1514	–26931	7132	2726	953	–2622
2009m5	747	578	–3318	714	–1467	–2804
2009m6	501	40013	11846	2976	2282	10896
2009m7	1427	6608	7640	–1289	1991	8600
2009m8	–452	–54624	–6908	716	–272	–4524
2009m9	1833	93564	14956	–976	2349	9957
2009m10	255	9919	–16351	3926	640	6161
2009m11	–708	–6167	7843	–603	–862	–3838
2009m12	251	–38764	17658	3404	3385	2883
2010m1	–811	–3312	–16846	–2946	–1408	–10112
2010m2	350	–3980	–8487	735	–464	–2029

(*Continued*)

Table A.3. (*Continued*)

Change to previous year	Brazil	EU	China	India	Korea	USA
2010m3	3402	71035	32445	3411	4511	23986
2010m4	−1213	−41809	−1107	−1722	−54	−4316
2010m5	428	−20467	−6144	−1088	−606	2924
2010m6	577	25888	5021	1718	497	13438
2010m7	1591	−1044	−434	871	26	−4781
2010m8	512	−36589	2469	509	−166	6942
2010m9	979.4	77364.86662	9094	−167	−254.22	−3868.4
2010m10	−1250.6	25667.80534	−19249	2950	1999.315	3044.6
2010m11	873.5	11657.25459	21874	−3620	1668.209	−1695.2
2010m12	−1901.3	−50442.3718	10508	2669	1387.696	−2710.7
2011m1	−817.8	18413.2196	3422	1843	1929	949.1
2011m2	719.5	7556.81094	−40361	−381	−5583	−11224.2
2011m3	2266	90404.77996	47770	1294	9113	30259.1
2011m4	569	−48330.0741	−7954	2329	−1333	−7775.7
2011m5	1459.2	29888.20647	−248	8658	1102	10906.5
2011m6	−477.7	−13842.4172	−4420	−4404	−465	2665.3
2011m7	−140.9	−25246.5102	5313	256	−527	−4379.5
2011m8	3280.1	−12448.378	10369	−1121	1090	9245.8
2011m9	−2133.5	34752.98202	−390	−229	−134	−7007.8
2011m10	−488.4	−18811.2251	−14776	1419.06	−2517	2311.7
2011m11	1526	6852.02772	19504	−2060.06	276	−1694.1
2011m12	−2991.3	−67877.6307	−1559	548	2480	−5967.1
2012m1	−957.8	21384.10049	−35375	3311	−2012	−827
2012m2	−1185.3	20206.85026	23599	−2791	1566	−12181.9
2012m3	2681.4	41408.73761	14011	2143	−3	26201.3
2012m4	−259.4	−59407.1997	−15786	−4541	−1056	−7701
2012m5	1704.5	10915.1396	18300	3782	559	8904.5
2012m6	−1813.3	−14534.3626	−14679	−5820	−2495	−6718.8
2012m7	−399.4	−18060.1325	3388	4840	−96	837.9
2012m8	1071.1	−13007.6074	−205	−3175	−915	2233.3
2012m9	−1790	40306.7672	7303	4367	1480	−8620.9

References

Agarwal, M. and J. Whalley (2013), China and India: Reforms and the Response: How Differently have the Economies Behaved. *NBER Working Paper 19006.*

Amiti, M. and D.E. Weinstein (2009), Exports and Financial Shocks. *CEPR Discussion Papers No. 7590.*

Anderton, R. and T. Tewolde (2011), The Global Financial Crisis: Understanding the Global Trade Downturn and Recovery, *The World Economy*, 34(5), 741–763.

Baldwin, R. (2009), The Great Trade Collapse: What Caused It and What Does it Mean? in Baldwin, R. (Ed.), *The Great Trade Collapse: Causes, Consequences, and Prospects* (VoxEU.org).

Bems, R., R. C. Johnson, and K.-M. Yi (2011), Vertical Linkages and the Collapse of Global Trade. *American Economic Review*, 101(3), 308–312.

Bems, R., R.C. Johnson and K.-M. Yi (2010), Demand Spillovers and the Collapse of Trade in the Global Recession. *IMF Working Paper No. 142.*

Berkmen, P., G. Gaston, R. Rennhack and J.P. Walsh (2009), The Global Financial Crisis: Explaining Cross-Country Differences in the Output Impact. *IMF Working Paper WP09/280.*

Blanchard, O.J., M. Das and H. Faruqee (2010), The Initial Impact of the Crisis on Emerging Market Countries. *Brookings Papers on Economic Activity*, 263–307.

Borchert, I. and A. Mattoo (2009), The Crisis-Resilience of Services Trade. *World Bank, Policy Research Working Paper No. WPS 4917.*

Chen, Mai and Yu (2006), The Effect of Export Tax Rebates on Export Performance: Theory and Evidence from China. *China Economic Review*, 17, 226–235.

Chi-Chur, C. and W.L. Chou (2001), Export Duty Rebates and Export Performance: Theory and China's Experience. *Journal of Comparative Economics*, 29, 314–326.

Chor, D. and K. Manova (2010), Off the Cliff and Back? Credit Conditions and International Trade During the Global Financial Crisis. *NBER Working Paper 16174.*

Claessens, S., G. Dell'Ariccia, D. Igan and L. Laeven (2010), Cross-country Experiences and Policy Implications from the Global Financial Crisis. *Economic Policy*, 25(62), 267–293.

Ferrantino, M. and A. Larsen (2009), Transmission of the Global Recession Through US Trade, in Baldwin R. (Ed.), *The Great Trade Collapse: Causes, Consequences and Prospects*, CEPR, The Graduate Institute, Geneva, a VoxEU.org Publication, 173–182.

Francois, J. and B. Hoekman (2010), Services Trade and Policy, *Journal of Economic Literature*, 48(3), 642–692.

Fukuchi, A. (2010). South Korea's Export Competitiveness: Critical to Overcoming the Global Crisis and Issues Going Forward, *Economic Review*, 5(2).

Gao, Y., Y. He and X. Yin (2016), Fixed Export Costs and Trade Patterns: The Case of China forthcoming, World Economy.

Haddad, M., A. Harrison and C. Hausman (2010), Decomposing the Great Trade Collapse: Products, Prices, and Quantities in the 2008–2009. *NBER Working Paper No. 16253.*

Harrigan, J. and H. Deng (2008), China's Local Comparative Advantage. *NBER Working Paper No. 13963*.

Jacks, D.S., M.M. Christopher and D. Novy (2009), The Role of Trade Costs in the Great Trade Collapse, in Baldwin, R. (Ed.), *The Great Trade Collapse: Causes, Consequences, and Prospects* (VoxEU.org).

Lane, P.R. and G.M. Milesi-Ferretti (2011), The Cross-Country Incidence of the Global Crisis. *IMF Economic Review*, 59, 77–110.

Levchenko, A.A., L.T. Lewis and L.L. Tesar (2010), The Collapse of International Trade During the 2008–2009 Crisis: In Search of the Smoking Gun. *NBER Working Paper No. 16006*.

Li, C. and J. Whalley (2012a), China and the TPP: A Numerical Simulation Assessment of the Effects Involved. *NBER Working Paper 18090*.

Li, C. and J. Whalley (2012b), China's Potential Future Growth and Gains from Trade Policy Bargaining: Some Numerical Simulation Results. *NBER Working Paper 17826*.

Li, C. and J. Whalley (2012c), Indirect Tax Initiatives and Global Rebalancing. *NBER Working Paper 17919*.

Maskus, K.E., T. Otsuki and J.S. Wilson (2013), Do Foreign Product Standards Matter? Impacts on Costs for Developing Country Exporters, *Asia-Pacific Journal of Accounting and Economics*, 20(1), 37–57.

Mattoo, A., R.M. Stern and G. Zanini (2007), *A Handbook of International Trade in Services*. Oxford University Press: Oxford.

Medianu, D. and J. Whalley (2010), The Deepening China–Brazil Economic Relationship. *CESifo Working Paper 3289*.

Milberg, W. and D. Winkler (2010), Trade Crisis and Recovery: Restructuring of Global Value Chains. *World Bank, Policy Research Working Paper WPS5294*.

Ministry of Commerce of the People's Republic of China (2008), China Trade in Services Report 2008, Beijing, China Commerce and Trade Press.

Ministry of Commerce of the People's Republic of China (2009), China Trade in Services Report 2009. Beijing, China Commerce and Trade Press.

Ministry of Commerce of the People's Republic of China (2010), China Trade in Services Report 2010. Beijing, China Commerce and Trade Press.

Ministry of Commerce, National Bureau of Statistics, State Administration of Foreign Exchange, P.R. China (2010), 2009 Statistical Bulletin of China's Outward Foreign Direct Investment.

Naude, W. (2009). The Financial Crisis of 2008 and the Developing Countries. *WIDER Discussion Paper2009/01*.

OECD (2009), Review of Sector Specific Stimulus Package and Policy Responses to The Global Economic Crisis, International Labor Organization Sectoral Activities Programme. *OECD Economic Outlook*, 1(85).

Shekhar, T. and J. Whalley (2010), The Rapidly Deepening India–China Economic Relationship. *CESifo Working Paper 3183*.

TeVelde, D.W. (2009), Effects of the Global Financial Crisis on Developing Countries and Emerging Markets — Policy Responses to The Crisis, *ODI Background Working Paper*.

Tong, S.Y. and Y. Zhang (2009), China's Responses to the Economic Csrisis. *EAI Background Brief No. 438.*

Wang, J. and J. Whalley (2010), The Trade Performance of Asian Economies During and Following the 2008 Financial Crisis. *Working Paper 16142.*

Yi, K.-M. (2009), The collapse of global trade: The Role of Vertical Specialisation, in Baldwin, R. and S. Evenett (Eds.), The Collapse of Global Trade, Murky Protectionism, and The Crisis: Recommendations for the G20, VoxEU Publication.

Yu, M. (2015), Processing Trade, Tariff Reductions and Firm Productivity: Evidence from Chinese Firms. *Economic Journal*, 125(585), 943–988.

Chapter 4

The WTO Government Procurement Agreement and Its Impacts on Trade

Hejing Chen
Department of Economics, Western University, Canada
hjchen.xmu@gmail.com

John Whalley
Department of Economics, Western University, Canada
Center for International Governance Innovation (CIGI) and NBER
jwhalley@uwo.ca

Abstract: This paper assesses the impacts of the WTO Government Procurement Agreement (GPA) on trade in both goods and services among members using a gravity model applied to a panel dataset covering 20 OECD countries over the period 1996–2008 for trade in goods and 1999–2008 for trade in services. The agreement dates from 1996 and covers 41 (mainly OECD) countries (/areas). China is now negotiating possible membership. Little has been written on the GPA which is a plurilateral agreement covering both goods and services. It mutually extends commitments only to signatories, but has commitments going beyond those in the earlier GATT procurement code. Government service markets are large, and trade in these also has spillover effects on trade in services and goods.

Results suggest that GPA membership has a positive impact on trade in both goods and services between parties as well as on outward foreign affiliate service sales. The number of GPA parties has a small marginal negative effect on trade in goods. Service exports also increase slightly with more parties participating in the GPA. The growth of government procurement contracts above the threshold under the GPA also fosters service imports, exports, and outward foreign affiliate sales.

1 Introduction

Governments at central and sub-central levels as well as other public entities play an important role in world trade. But it was not until the Tokyo Round that efforts began to bring government procurement under international trade rules. The belief was that discriminatory government procurement practices were a significant non-tariff barrier and retarded the growth of world trade. Under the GATT Government Procurement Agreement signed in 1979 (GATT GPA 1979), government procurement entities were obliged to follow core multilateral trade rules, i.e. non-discrimination and transparency rules. But since the conclusion of the Uruguay Round in 1994, ongoing negotiated procurement liberalisation has been focused on the WTO GPA 1994. It is not a condition of WTO membership that countries join the GPA, since the GPA superseded the 1994 single undertaking when the WTO evolved from the GATT. The agreement is a plurilateral agreement only involving signatories and embodies deeper commitments than the GATT GPA 1979 both in terms of itemised coverage and thresholds for competitive bidding. It began in 1996 as an arrangement to which 21 countries initially committed themselves, including US, Japan, and the EU; Other countries have subsequentially joined, and currently around 41 countries are parties to the agreement. As with other trade agreements, with non-discriminatory and transparency among parties as key rules, parties are entitled to impartial (thus enhanced) access rights to foreign member markets, but simultaneously agree to grant those rights to other member countries.

Despite its potential significance for world trade, there are few papers which empirically evaluate its impacts on trade flows, and especially on trade in services. We evaluate its impacts in ways which take advantage of the sequential addition of countries to GPA membership. We first outline the evolution of the GPA and also highlight the gap between its nominal and real coverage. We use data on notifications to the WTO GPA committee of procurement contract awards under the GPA over time to assess the government procurement market size for the main GPA parties. We then use a gravity model to estimate the GPA's impacts on trade flows using the panel data for 20 OECD countries from 1996 to 2008.

Our results show that the WTO GPA has had a positive influence on inter-OECD trade in goods and services as well as on outward foreign affiliate service sales. Simple data analysis of contracts awarded under the GPA overestimates the extent of trade and impacts of the GPA since not all GPA covered international transactions would not have occurred without the GPA. Hence our use of a gravity model. Additional, restrictions in GPA articles and regulations also imply that enhanced market access by foreign suppliers will not be automatically achieved through membership of the GPA.

2 The Origins of the WTO PA

2.1 The GPA from 1979 to 2010

Buy national policies in government purchasing (government procurement) were omitted from the original GATT in Article III "National Treatment on Internal Taxation and Regulation" and Article XVII "State Trading Enterprises" in 1947. The first GATT Agreement on GPA was signed only in 1979 and entered into force in 1981. It contained obligations of non-discrimination (national treatment and most-favoured-nation treatment (MFN)) and transparency rules for procurement of goods by central government entities of its signatories, and a purchasing contract threshold set at SDR 150,000.

In 1987, the GATT GPA 1979 was amended by adding a limited number of services (such as construction services), reducing the threshold for contracts involving goods for central government entities to SDR 130,000 and setting the threshold for construction contracts at a higher level of SDR 5,000,000. The amended GATT GPA entered into force in 1988.

But during the Uruguay Round, parties to the Agreement also held negotiations trying to extend the scope and coverage of the Agreement to sub-central government and quasi-governmental bodies, and also to services and construction services as well as incorporating a bid-challenge system. As a result, a new GPA (WTO GPA) was signed at the end of the Uruguay Round in 1994, and entered into force on January 1, 1996. A new revised text was agreed in December 2006 and updated in December 2010.

Table 1 summarises the evolution of these Agreements. This history embodies two major milestones. One was the introduction of GATT GPA in 1979 which brought government procurement under GATT. The other was the WTO GPA of 1994 which broadened the coverage of the GPA under WTO.

Table 1. The evolution of GATT and WTO agreements on government procurement.

Date	GPA version
1947	Government procurement excluded under GATT Article III:8 and XVII:2
April 1979	GPA 1979 signed
January 1981	GPA 1979 enters into force
November 1983	Negotiations based on Article IX:6(b) of GPA 1979 commence
November 1986	Protocol to the Agreement include amendments to Articles I, II, IV, V and VI of GPA 1979
January 1988	Amended GPA 79 enters into force
April 1994	GPA 1994 signed in Marrakesh
January 1996	GPA 1994 enters into force
February 1997–ongoing	Preparatory work for negotiations under Article XXIV:7 of GPA 1994
December 2006	Provisionally agreed revised GPA text (GPA/W/297)
December 2010	Provisionally agreed revised GPA text (GPA/W/313)

Source: WTO, http://www.wto.org/english/tratop_e/gproc_e/overview_e.htm.

2.2 GPA parties and observers

As a plurilateral agreement, the WTO GPA (hereafter GPA) only regulates government procurement practices on a voluntary basis of those WTO members who choose to bind in the GPA. The GPA itself has no enforcement mechanism for commitments going beyond WTO obligations. So far, the membership of GPA is still limited. Most of the 41 parties[1] are developed countries (areas) and NICs,[2] while the majority of developing countries have not joined. There are also 27 observers[3] in the GPA Committee who approve accession to the GPA. Nine countries are currently in ongoing negotiation for accession.

The smaller number of GPA members than of the WTO, reflects the reluctance of most developing countries to join the GPA. Current GPA members have

[1] Current GPA members (with effect from January 1, 2010) include Canada, European Communities (including its 27 member States: Austria, Belgium, Bulgaria, Cyprus, Czech Republic, Denmark, Estonia, Finland, France, Germany, Greece, Hungary, Ireland, Italy, Latvia, Lithuania, Luxemburg, Malta, Netherlands, Poland, Portugal, Romania, Slovak Republic, Slovenia, Spain, Sweden and United Kingdom), Hong Kong China, Iceland, Israel, Japan, Korea, Liechtenstein, Netherlands with respect to Aruba, Norway, Singapore, Switzerland, Chinese Taipei, United States.

[2] Korea, Singapore, Hong Kong, and Israel participated in the Uruguay Round as developing countries, however, they are so called new industrialised countries not typical developing countries.

[3] Current GPA observers (with effect from July 1, 2010) include 23 countries and four international intergovernmental organisations, among which Albania, Armenia, China, Georgia, Jordan, Kyrgyz Republic, Moldova, Oman, Panama are undergoing acceding negotiation.

Table 2. Entry and acceptance date of GPA parties and observers.

Parties	Date of entry into force/ accession (dd/mm/yyyy)	Observer government	Date of acceptance by committee as observers (dd/mm/yyyy)
Canada, United States, Japan, Norway, Switzerland, Israel	01/01/1996	Albania*	02/10/2001
European Communities with regard to		Argentina	24/02/1997
its 27 member States:		Armenia*	16/07/2004
Austria, Belgium, Denmark,	01/01/1996	Australia	04/06/1996
Finland, France, Germany,		Bahrain	09/12/2008
Greece, Ireland, Italy,		Cameroon	03/05/2001
Luxemburg, the Netherlands,		Chile	29/09/1997
Portugal, Spain,		China*	21/02/2002
Sweden, and the United Kingdom	01/05/2004	Colombia	27/02/1996
Cyprus, Czech Republic,		Croatia	05/10/1999
Estonia, Hungary, Latvia,		Georgia*	05/10/1999
Lithuania, Malta, Poland,		India	10/02/2010
Slovak Republic and Slovenia		Jordan*	08/03/2000
Bulgaria, and Romania	01/01/2007	Kyrgyz Republic*	05/10/1999
Hong Kong, China	19/06/1997	Moldova*	29/09/2000
Iceland Korea	28/04/2001	Mongolia	23/02/1999
Liechtenstein	01/01/1997	New Zealand	09/12/2008
the Netherlands with respect to Aruba	18/09/1997	Oman*	03/05/2001
Singapore	25/10/1996	Panama*	29/09/1997
Chinese Taipei	20/10/1997	Saudi Arabia	13/12/2007
	15/07/2009	Sri Lanka	23/04/2003
		Turkey	04/06/1996
		Ukraine	25/02/2009

Note: * means the observer is undergoing negotiating accession.
Source: WTO, http://www.wto.org/english/tratop_e/gproc_e/memobs_e.htm.

frequently tried to persuade countries seeking to join the WTO (especially those with a large state sector) to commit to joining the GPA upon WTO accession, although GPA membership is not a prerequisite for WTO accession (Wang, 2007).

Table 2 lists the entry date of GPA parties and observers. EU members make up more than half of the parties, and the rest are in North America and Asia. All 27 observers are developing countries in Asia, South America and Africa, except Australia and New Zealand, which are OECD members in Oceania. Among observers who have started negotiating accession, China is the prime concern of the current GPA parties; not only because of its high growth rate and large size of its economy, but also due to the historically dominant role and large size of different level of governments.

2.3 The difference between the GPA's nominal and real coverage

The impact of GPA membership on its members' trade is qualified in various ways since the effective coverage of commitment to the GPA is ambiguous due to a four step procedure of accession negotiations covering membership, entity coverage, product coverage, and threshold. Countries have to first choose whether to join the GPA when they become WTO members. After the accession procedure to the GPA starts, observers can then determine which entities are bound under their GPA commitments. Under the Annexes 1–3 of Appendix I of the GPA, each party notifies lists of central level government, sub-central government and other public entities covered. Only those entities in the list undertake GPA commitments. For example, many parties exclude the department of defense from their central government list.

Product coverage is also typically selective for GPA members. As a general rule, all goods are covered by the GPA, while Annexes 4 and 5 to Appendix I specify each Party's covered services and construction services.[4] Services deemed sensitive, for instance dredging, transportation, R&D, and printing services, are often excluded from GPA parties' Annex 4. Finally, the threshold value above which the public procurement contract is obliged to follow GPA rules can provide a fourth element of weakened coverage. For each party of the GPA, there are 9 (3 times 3) thresholds to be determined for three categories of products (goods, services and construction services) and entities (central government, sub-central government and other entities); though generally there are ranges set for thresholds.

Table 3 reports the GPA threshold commitments of the EU, Japan and USA. These thresholds differ among the three categories, with a much higher threshold for construction services. Due to different financial regimes across countries, the thresholds for three types of entities vary among members, while sub-central government and other social entities apply higher thresholds than central government entities.

The GPA text (article XV in the GPA 1994, article III and XIII in the GPA 2006 and 2010) also provides exceptions to its general non-discriminatory rules and open or selective tendering procedures which can also potentially provide extra coverage for own country preferential government procurement activities. Although negotiations on government procurement in the Tokyo and Uruguay Round achieved substantial expansion of coverage by extending rules to the

[4]The newly provisionally agreed revised GPA text 2010 differ from preceding version in one way that one new Annex is added to list the goods covered by each party, therefore the coverage of goods becomes selective, and there are altogether 7 Annexes in Appendix I, with Annexes 1–3 for entity list, Annexes 4–6 for product list and Annex 7 as General Notes.

Table 3. Threshold commitment of main GPA parties.

unit: thousand SDRs

	Annex 1			Annex 2			Annex 3		
Country	**Goods**	**Services except construction services**	**Construction services**	**Goods**	**Services except construction services**	**Construction services**	**Goods**	**Services except construction services**	**Construction services**
EU members	130	130	5,000	200	200	5,000	400	400	5,000
Japan	130	130	4,500 Architectural services: 450	200	200	15,000 Architectural services: 1,500	130	130	4,500 or 15,000 Architectural services: 450
United States	130	130	5,000	355	355	5,000	250,000 (USD) or 400,000 SDRs	250,000 (USD) or 400,000 SDRS	5,000

Source: WTO, http://www.wto.org/english/tratop_e/gproc_e/thresh_e.htm.

procurement of goods and services (including construction services) by national and sub-central level government as well as public entities, the selection of membership, entity coverage, product coverage and threshold along with the exception option for non-discriminatory and transparency rules once again make the GPA's real coverage unclear.

3 The Government Procurement Market under the GPA

3.1 The government procurement market for main GPA parties

3.1.1 *Market size*

A critical element in assessing the impact of the GPA on inter-party trade flows is the size of the GPA covered procurement market. There are two different methods for calculating the size of the government procurement market for GPA countries, reflecting two different sources of available data. One uses the SNA (System of National Accounts) to estimate the size of the government procurement market based on government receipts and payments.,This method yields an upper based in estimate of the possible scale of government procurement since not all government expenditure other than compensation of employees and defense can be treated as government procurement. EC (1997, 1998), Francois *et al.* (1996), Trionfetti (2000) and OECD (2001) use this method using the 1968 version of the SNA to yield consistent data across countries.

The other method uses a bottom-up approach based directly on data on procurement expenditure by national entities responsible for procurement decisions and forming their WTO notifications. This approach yields a direct estimate of the size of government procurement market since government procurement values are based on a contract by contract basis. It is however not ideal because of a lack of consistency across countries subject in notification requirements. The data source for this bottom-up method is annual data submit by the GPA parties to the WTO on their procurement covered by the GPA; and periodic surveys of the *Tenders Electronic Daily* (TED) and notices published in the *Official Journal of European Union* (OJEU) with respect to the requirement of the EU members (through EU Directives) to publish procurement tender and contract award notices.

Table 4 reports literature estimates of the size of procurement markets using both SNA-based and bottom-up approaches. The estimates for the ratio of public procurement to GDP lie in a wide range between 0.42% and 19.96%, illustrating the disparity among studies. Using a bottom-up approach, our estimates on a aggregate basis are similar to those of EC (2000), while the estimate on an above threshold basis is significantly higher than that of Hoekman (1997) which only takes procurement of goods by central governments into consideration. This

Table 4. Estimates of the size of government procurement markets.

Studies				For general government			
					Exclude non-tradable		
Authors	Sources	Countries	Period	Total expenditure % of GDP	Compensation of employees	Compensation of employees & defense	For sub-central levels
SNA-based							
EC (1988)	SNA-OECD	EU-12	1987			11.7%	Yes
EC (1997)	SNA-OECD	EU-15	1994			11.2–11.8%	Yes
Francois *et al.*	SNA-OECD	USA	1992–1993	18.3%			Yes
Trionfetti	SNA-UN	9 OECD	1983–1990		7–9%		
Trionfetti	IMF data	8 OECD	1984–1990		10–18%		
OECD	SNA-OECD	28 OECD	1990–1997	19.96%*	9.17%*	7.75%*	Table A1
OECD	SNA-OECD	13 OECD	1990–1997		9.02%*	7.79%*	Table A3
OECD	SNA-UN	106 non-OECD	1990–1994	14.48%*	6.89%*	5.10%*	Table A2
Bottom-up							
Hoekman	WTO	20	1983–1992	0.42%			
EC (2000)	*Official Journal*	EU-15	1993–1998			13.9–14.6%	

Note: *= weighted average; In the reported EC studies, the ratios measure public procurement.
Source: OECD (2001).

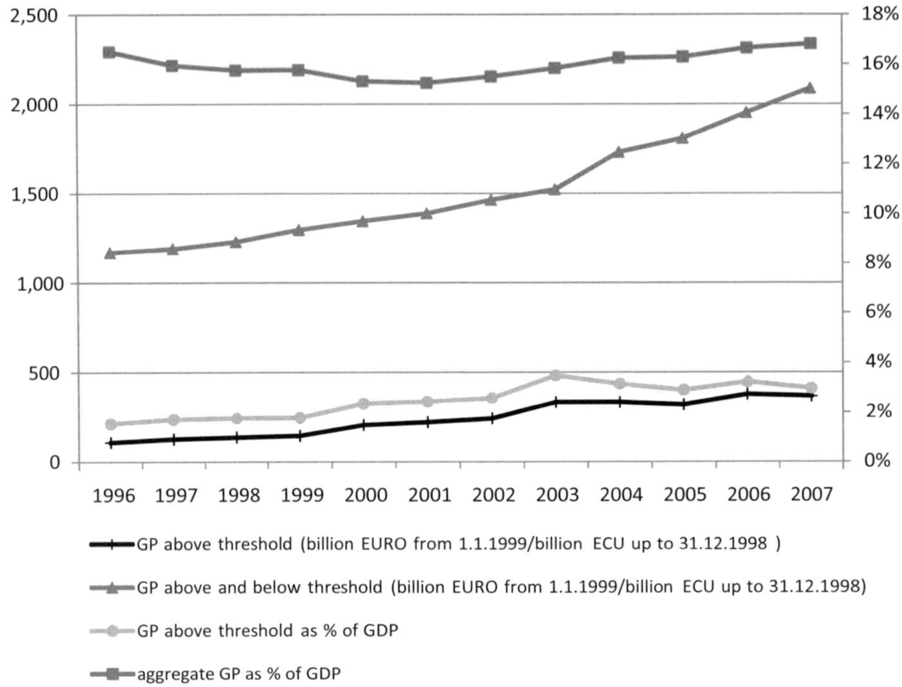

Figure 1. Estimates of the size of the EU government procurement market: 1996–2008.

Note: EU (15 members, EU Institutions excluded) 1996–2003.
EU (25 members, EU Institutions excluded) 2004–2006.
EU (27 members, EU Institutions excluded) 2007.
GP means Government Procurement.
Source: World Bank Indicators, European Central Bank statistic data warehouse, EU's GPA notification to the WTO.

difference is, to some extent, a reflection of the evolution of the GPA from the Tokyo Round to the Uruguay Round.

Figure 1 displays EU government procurement to GDP as a proportion of GDP, as an example of a large region situation, with added detail among above threshold and aggregate (above and below threshold). In the figure the ratio of the government procurement to GDP is roughly constant over time, and government procurement above threshold is only one-tenth to one-fifth of aggregate procurement, suggesting space and opportunity for the GPA to play a role in the future. There is a trend of growth in the absolute value of government procurement on either basis of above threshold or aggregate.

US notifications to the WTO on government procurement under the GPA are not as detailed as those for the EU, and data on government procurement below threshold are available only at federal government level. Table 5 reports estimates of the size of government procurement markets in the US and the ratio to GDP.

Table 5. Estimates of the size of the US government procurement market: 1996–2008.

Unit: billion US$

Year	Annex 1 above threshold	Annex 1 below threshold	Total government procurement*	GDP (current price)	Total government procurement as % of GDP (%)
1996	216.130	9.101	485.900	7783.9	6.24
1997	195.742	9.671	477.871	8278.9	5.77
1998	197.899	9.286	496.531	8741	5.68
1999	205.408	9.857	525.675	9301	5.65
2000	63.503	5.692	414.226	9898.8	4.18
2001	133.268	4.638	528.632	10233.9	5.17
2002	180.878	5.146	610.245	10590.2	5.76
2003	320.834	5.809	767.006	11089.2	6.92
2004	250.677	5.956	722.179	11812.3	6.11
2005	380.502	9.519	890.221	12579.7	7.08
2006	431.328	7.122	964.041	13336.2	7.38
2007	760.510	7.328	1316.993	14061.8	9.37
2008	384.945	8.082	1150.161	14369.1	8.00

Note: *total government procurement is added up across the contract awards of entities in Annex1 (both above and below threshold), Annexes 2 and 3.

Source: GDP data are from World Development Indicators, World Bank, 2010. Data on the government procurement are calculated by the authors using US' GPA notification to the WTO.

The proportion of the US federal government procurement above threshold is high, amounting to more than 90% of total procurement for Annex 1 commitments. Also, the absolute value of government procurement in the US increases nearly three times from 1996 to 2008, while the ratio to GDP ranges from 5% to 9%

Based on these estimates of the size of government procurement markets in the EU and the US, if government procurement below threshold is excluded, government procurement markets covered by the GPA are about 3% of GDP for the EU and 7–8% for the US. These estimates are lower than most earlier OECD studies based on SNA data source.

3.2 The composition of government procurement markets under the GPA for the main GPA parties

3.2.1 *By entity*

The central, sub-central government and other entities are the three categories covered by the GPA, and their relative importance in the government procurement market varies between different countries. However, with thresholds set for most parties of the GPA, the threshold for Annex 3 (other entities) is generally higher

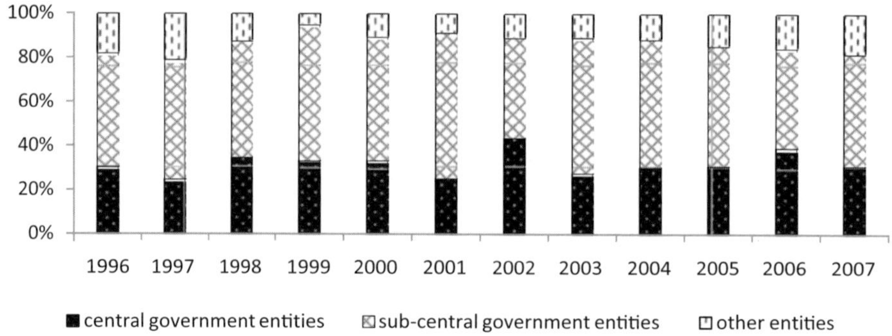

Figure 2. Entity composition of the EU government procurement market under the GPA: 1996–2008.

Source: Calculated by the authors using data on EU GPA notifications to the WTO.

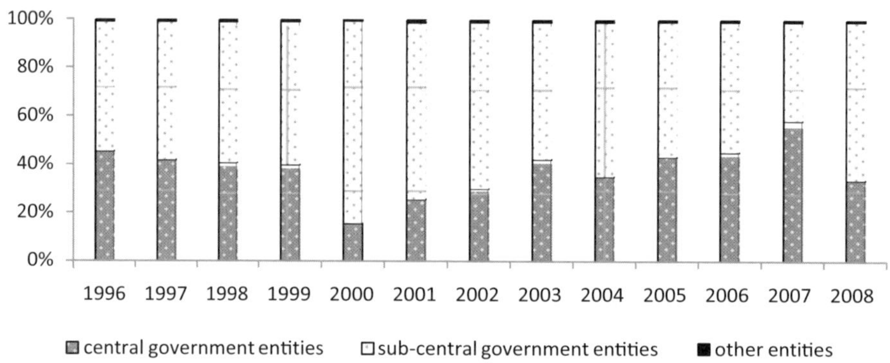

Figure 3. Entity composition of the US government procurement market under the GPA: 1996–2008.

Source: Calculated by the authors using data on US GPA notifications to the WTO.

than that for Annex 1, and also sometimes Annex 2. The entity composition for EU and US government procurement markets reflect threshold levels for different entities (see Figures 2 and 3). In the EU government procurement market under the GPA,[5] other entities with the highest threshold are the smallest portion. These relative share account for about 10–15%, while the sub-central government is the largest with a 50% share. The share for the central government is nearly 30–35%.

As with the US case, the relative ranking across the three categories are the same as for the EU, except that the share for Annex 3 is minor. The share for central governments is roughly 40%.

[5] The government procurement market under the GPA means that only those contracts belonging to product list in Annexes 4–6 with awards above threshold for the entities in Annexes 1–3 are considered.

3.2.2 *By product*

Products covered by the GPA are divided into two categories, goods and services. When we analyse the product composition of the government procurement market under the GPA, we include construction services in the services category. Within the two major categories, services occupy the dominate position, with 60–65% of government procurement above threshold. This is the case for the EU, US, and Japan. According to the WTO Universal List of Services in WTO document code of MTN.GNS/W/120, construction services belong to the services category. In the GPA, the threshold for construction service is individually listed. This is because construction services purchased by governments and other entities (especially state-owned enterprises) are often connected to other infrastructure construction with large contracts.

3.2.3 *By origin of suppliers*

Under GPA Article III, the principles of non-discrimination apply to both foreign affiliates and ownership (Article III:2(a)) and country of origin (Article III:2(b)).[6] This means that foreign suppliers can compete against domestic suppliers and meet procurement bids either through cross-border supply or foreign affiliation sales. Based on the notifications of GPA parties, government procurement markets seem far from being internationally integrated. Figure 4 shows the relative shares of Japan's government procurement above threshold for goods and services by domestic suppliers and foreign suppliers. Even compared with the low share of

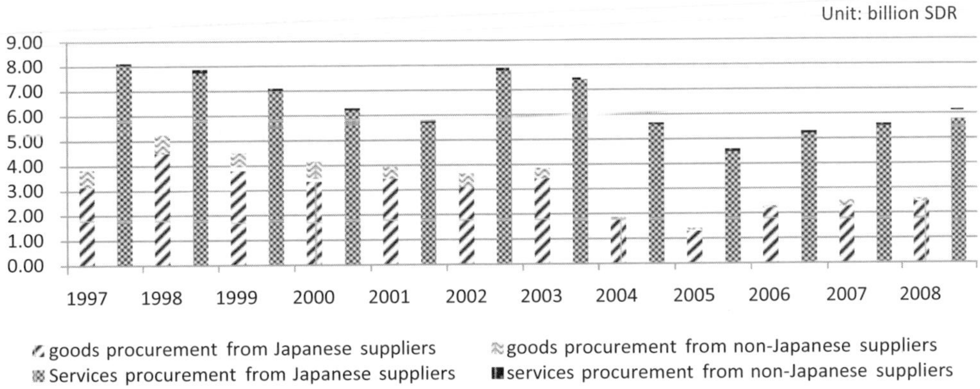

Figure 4. Origin composition of Japan's government procurement on goods and services under the GPA: 1997–2008.

Source: Calculated by the authors using data on Japan's GPA notifications to the WTO.

[6] In GPA 2006 and 2010 version, these regulation are in Article V:2(a)(b) and Article IV:2(a)(b), respectively.

procurement for goods by non-Japan suppliers, the situation of market access is even lower in the service sector, which suggests a strong home bias in government procurement markets.

4 Assess the Impact of the GPA Using a Gravity Model

The gravity model has been widely applied in empirical trade analysis, following Tinbergen (1962) and Pöyhönen (1963). More recent developments (e.g., Anderson, 1979; Helpman and Krugman, 1985; Deardorff, 1995; Feenstra *et al.*, 2001; Eaton and Kortum, 2002; Anderson and Wincoop, 2003) also support the use of gravity models from a trade theoretic view point. Gravity models have previously been used to analyse the impact of barriers to services trade by comparing predicted and actual levels of services trade flows (see Francois, 2001; Park, 2002; Grunfeld and Moxnes, 2003; etc) and to compare differences in determinants of trade in services and goods (see Kimura and Lee, 2006; Lennon, 2006). Here we use a standard gravity model augmented with GPA variables to assess the GPA's impact on bilateral trade flows in both goods and services among GPA parties.

Academic research on the impact of government procurement on international trade flows started in the 1970s. Baldwin (1970) argued that discriminatory procurement policy may have inconsequential impacts on trade flows under assumptions of perfect substitution between domestic and foreign products, a relative small size of government procurement and unique market price for private and public demand. His proposition was further examined by Mattoo (1996). McAfee and McMillan (1989), Trionfetti (2000), Evenett and Hoekman (2005) analyse the welfare effect of different discriminatory form of government procurement practices.

Empirical studies including Baldwin and Richardson (1972) and Trionfetti (2001) show that the discriminatory government procurement exists and has a negative impact on import.

4.1 Empirical specifications and data

A standard gravity model takes the following form:

$$\text{LnT}_{ij} = \beta_0 + \beta_1 \text{LnGDP}_i + \beta_2 \text{LnGDP}_j + \beta_3 \text{LnDIST}_{ij} + \text{E}_{ij}, \tag{1}$$

where T_{ij} = bilateral trade flows (exports or/and imports) between country i and country j, GDP_i = economic mass of country i, GDP_j = economic mass of country j, DIST_{ij} = geographical distance between the capitals of country i and country j, E_{ij} = error term.

In order to capture the impacts of the GPA on bilateral trade in goods and services, we introduce three additional variables on the right side. One is a dummy variable GPA, which takes the value 1 if the two countries *i* and *j* are both members of the GPA. A positive effect on bilateral trade is expected from the dummy variable GPA. The second is NGPA, an interactive variable obtained by multiplying the dummy variable GPA by the total number of GPA parties in year *t* (represented as "gpan"). We use this interactive variable to capture the effect of the number of GPA parties on bilateral trade in goods and services. The expected effect of the NGPA on bilateral trade is negative since bilateral trade may be switched to new or other members of the GPA. The third variable is CLNGVI (CLNGVJ), also an interactive variable, obtained by multiplying the dummy variable GPA by the log of an index of government procurement values above threshold (with the government procurement value under GPA in year 2000 equalling 1 in the base period) for country *i* or country *j* (represented as "gvii" or "gvij"). The government procurement value above threshold under the GPA by different members is provided in different local currency units, hence, we use this indexing method to control for this influence. This interactive variable captures variation in government procurement values on bilateral trade in goods and services.

A final dummy variables RTA is included to reflect the impact of trading bloc membership. As a plurilateral agreement only applicable to signatories, the GPA is similar to a RTA. We use dummy variable RTA to control for the influence of other trade-related arrangements. RTA takes the value 1 if the two countries *i* and *j* signed a free trade agreement with each other.

In existing gravity model literature, there is no consensus on whether the dependent variable should be exports, imports or total trade flows (i.e. the sum of export and import). We use both exports and imports as dependent variables, since home biased government purchasing will reduce imports while GPA membership will potentially yield enhanced access rights to foreign member markets. Since members simultaneously agree to grant rights to other member countries both exports and imports should increase.

Our estimation equations are

$$\begin{aligned}\text{LnIM}_{ijt} &= \beta_0 + \beta_1\text{LnGDP}_{it} + \beta_2\text{LnGDP}_{jt} + \beta_3\text{LnDIST}_{ij} + \beta_4\text{GPA}_{ijt} \\ &\quad + \beta_5\text{NGPA}_t + \beta_6\text{CLNGVI}_t + \beta_7\text{RTA}_{ijt} + \gamma_i + \gamma_j + \delta_t + \varepsilon_{ijt},\end{aligned} \tag{2}$$

$$\begin{aligned}\text{LnEX}_{ijt} &= \beta_0 + \beta_1\text{LnGDP}_{it} + \beta_2\text{LnGDP}_{jt} + \beta_3\text{LnDIST}_{ij} + \beta_4\text{GPA}_{ijt} \\ &\quad + \beta_5\text{NGPA}_t + \beta_6\text{CLNGVJ}_t + \beta_7\text{RTA}_{ijt} + \gamma_i + \gamma_j + \delta_t + \varepsilon_{ijt},\end{aligned} \tag{3}$$

where NGPA = GPA*gpan and gpan = the number of GPA parties in year *t*; CLNGVI = GPA*Lngvii and Lngvii = log of index of government procurement value above threshold in country *i* (with the year 2000 as the base period);

CLNGVJ = GPA*Lngvij and Lngvij = log of index of government procurement value above threshold in country *j* (with the year 2000 as the base period).

Equations (2) and (3) are similar to each other, except that when the dependent variable is imports of country *i* from country *j*, only procurement values above threshold for country *i* matter, while procurement values above threshold of country *j* affect the opposite trade flow, i.e. export of country *i* to country *j*.

4.1.1 *Data and methodology*

The data we use is from OECD statistics on international trade in services, and is available for both service exports and imports, broken down by partner country, and for 20 OECD member countries from the years 1999–2008. Data are on a balance-of-payments basis, and mainly reflect GATS supply mode 1 (cross-border supply) and mode 2 (consumption abroad) of trade in services. Supply mode 3 (commercial presence) of trade in services is of special importance in competing for government procurement contract for foreign suppliers.

Service imports and exports *via* foreign affiliates are likely the most affected when countries enter the GPA. Data on bilateral trade in service for foreign affiliate trade in services among OECD members is not directly available. We use inward and outward foreign affiliate turnover data with industry sector division specified within services on the UN international standard industrial classification basis code (ISIC Rev. 3) as proxies of service exports and imports *via* mode 3. To check the robustness of results, we compare results when service exports and imports are on a BOP basis (SE/SI) and service exports and imports are on a FATS basis (FAE/FAI) as dependent variables. For trade in goods, we also compare the impact of the GPA on exports (GE) and imports (GI).

Our data covers 20 OECD members.[7] For trade in goods, the period starts from 1996 and ends in 2008, since the GPA came into effect under the WTO in 1996. For trade in services, the period is 1999–2008, since the earliest available data on bilateral services trade released by the OECD starts from 1999.

Bilateral exports and imports data on trade in goods are obtained from the UN COMTRADE database. Bilateral exports and imports data on trade in services (BOP and Foreign Affiliate Sales) are from OECD Statistics. GDP data are from World Development Indicators, and the distance in kilometres between capitals are from COW database Version 2.0. RTA data are from RTA database of WTO. GPA, NGPAN, CLNGVI/CLNGVJ data are calculated by the authors based on WTO notifications.

[7]The full list of countries included in the sample: Australia, Austria, Canada, France, Germany, Hungary, Ireland, Italy, Japan, Korea, Luxembourg, Mexico, Netherlands, New Zealand, Norway, Spain, Sweden, Switzerland, UK, US.

We first use an ordinary least squares regression with pooled data, and then use fixed country and time effect regressions using panel data following the arguments of Egger (2000) and Feenstra (2003) that the proper specification of the gravity model in most applications would be one of fixed country and time effects, which reflect both the time-invariant export- and import-country effects and the common business cycle or globalisation process over the sample period. The Hausman test also supports using fixed effect rather than random effects models.

4.2 Results

Table 6 presents the summary statistics for the variable used in the estimations. Definitions are provided in the text and S.D., Min, Max and N denote standard deviation, minimum, maximum and number of observation, respectively. The mean of NGPA, Lngvii and Lngvij are used to calculate the net effect of the dummy variable GPA on bilateral trade flow. In a similar way, the mean of dummy variable GPA is used to calculate the net impact of number of the GPA parties and

Table 6. Summary statistics.

Trade in goods						Trade in services (BoP and foreign affiliate sales)					
Variable	**Mean**	**S.D.**	**Min**	**Max**	**N**	**Variable**	**Mean**	**S.D.**	**Min**	**Max**	**N**
LnGI	7.411	2.133	–5.498	12.734	4820	LnSI	6.737	1.926	–0.061	10.760	2626
LnGE	7.328	2.162	–2.500	12.776	4820	LnSE	6.814	1.872	0.000	11.051	2671
LnGDPi	13.208	1.450	9.826	16.481	4940	LnFAI	9.016	2.487	0.000	15.233	1124
LnGDPj	13.208	1.450	9.826	16.481	4940	LnFAE	9.423	2.886	0.385	17.388	706
LnDIST[a]	8.230	1.225	5.438	9.896	4940	LnGDPi[b]	13.289	1.430	9.913	16.481	3800
GPA	0.659	0.474	0	1	4940	GPA	0.682	0.466	0	1	3800
NGPA	20.380	15.439	0	39	4937	NGPA	22.183	15.864	0	39	3800
CLNGVI	0.144	0.568	–1.067	2.483	3420	CLNGVI	0.263	0.526	–0.678	2.483	2622
CLNGVJ	0.142	0.565	–1.067	2.483	3420	CLNGVJ	0.263	0.525	–0.678	2.483	2622
RTA	0.447	0.497	0	1	4940	RTA	0.468	0.499	0	1	3800
gpan	30.465	5.957	22	39	4937	gpan	32.200	5.654	26	39	3800
Lngvii	0.165	0.624	–1.067	2.483	3420	Lngvii	0.316	0.562	–0.678	2.483	2622
Lngvij	0.165	0.624	–1.067	2.483	3420	Lngvij	0.316	0.562	–0.678	2.483	2622

Note: (a) applicable to LnDIST for trade in services. The only difference between this explanatory for trade in goods and trade in services is the length of time period, which has no effect for the time-invariant variable of bilateral distance.

(b) applicable to LnGDPj for trade in services. The summary statistics for LnGDPi and LnGDPj for trade in services are the same.

Table 7. OLS regression results.

	Dependent variables					
	LnGI (1)	**LnGE (2)**	**LnSI (3)**	**LnSE (4)**	**LnFAI (5)**	**LnFAE (6)**
LnGDPi	1.040***	0.843***	0.815***	0.728***	0.344***	1.549***
	(0.0133)	(0.0125)	(0.0142)	(0.0171)	(0.0621)	(0.0943)
LnGDPj	0.846***	1.009***	0.804***	0.806***	0.295***	0.778***
	(0.0131)	(0.0121)	(0.0145)	(0.0159)	(0.0572)	(0.0561)
LnDIST	–0.955***	–1.032***	–1.003***	–0.714***	–0.416***	–0.254
	(0.0308)	(0.0272)	(0.0329)	(0.0371)	(0.118)	(0.299)
GPA	1.038***	1.065***	0.337***	0.665***	0.667	dropped
	(0.101)	(0.0951)	(0.124)	(0.148)	(0.477)	
NGPA	–0.0330***	–0.0311***	–0.0177***	–0.0191***	–0.0500***	–0.0159
	(0.00310)	(0.00283)	(0.00354)	(0.00388)	(0.0136)	(0.0201)
CLNGVI	–0.00598		0.112***		0.292**	
	(0.0317)		(0.0349)		(0.147)	
CLNGVJ		0.00696		0.159***		0.670***
		(0.0311)		(0.0417)		(0.205)
RTA	0.164**	0.172***	0.302***	0.312***	0.158***	0.269
	(0.0649)	(0.0599)	(0.0706)	(0.0841)	(0.274)	(0.689)
Constant	–9.818***	–8.868***	–6.648***	–8.311***	2.056	–21.13***
	(0.325)	(0.296)	(0.394)	(0.484)	(1.530)	(3.386)
Observations	3320	3318	2115	1822	1,099	528
R-squared	0.843	0.854	0.815	0.752	0.235	0.580

Note: *,** and *** indicate statistical significance at 90%, 95% and 99% level, respectively.
Robust standard errors in parentheses.

government procurement valued bounded to the GPA of each member on bilateral trade flow.

Table 7 reports pooled regression results for these specifications, with six dependent variables (Log of GI, GE, SI, SE, FAI and FAE) corresponding to columns (1)–(6) respectively. Focusing on the explanatory variables related to the GPA, the coefficients β_4 for the dummy variable GPA are positive and significant at % level in columns (1)–(4), which indicate a positive impact for the GPA on bilateral trade in goods and bilateral trade in services *via* cross-border supply mode.

For trade in services *via* the commercial presence mode, the dummy variable GPA is not significant for inward foreign affiliates sales. It is dropped in the regression for outward foreign affiliates sales.[8] The interactive variable NGPA has a minor negative coefficient β_5 as expected and is significant in most equations. The coefficients β_5 for NGPA in columns (1) and (2) are larger than those in columns (3) and (4). This suggests that GPA bilateral trade in goods may be switched more easily between suppliers than bilateral trade in services. The intangibility of services makes the switching costs higher for buyers and bilateral trade in services tends to repeat between current partners.

The interactive variable CLNGVI/CLNGVJ has a positive and significant coefficient β_6 in columns (3)–(6), but we find no significant coefficient for this explanatory variable for trade in goods. Meanwhile within the two different supply modes for trade in services, exports and imports *via* foreign affiliate sales are more affected than trade flows involving cross-border supply. We attribute the difference in the impact of this explanatory variable on trade in goods and in services, as well as the different effects between the two supply modes of trade in services to the high share of services in product composition and high preference for local presence of suppliers by procuring entities in the government procurement market.

All the traditional gravity control variables, such as the log of GDP of importers and exporters and the log of distance are of the right sign and statistically significant, except that distance and RTA are not significant in column (6) for FAE. Generally, the magnitudes of the coefficients are also in line with previous literature. Distance has more negative effects on trade in goods than on trade in services regardless of the different supply modes of services, while RTAs are more important for trade in services than trade in goods. This indicates the relative importance of transportation cost for trade in goods and institutional cost for trade in services.

Table 8 presents results from the regressions for country and time fixed effects models using panel data, with six dependent variables (Log of GI, GE, SI, SE, FAI and FAE) corresponding to columns (1)–(6). The coefficients of log of GDP of exporter and importer also have correct signs and are statistically significant, consistent with the previous pooled regression results. The log of geographical distance are dropped in the country and time fixed effect regressions since they are time-invariant. Based on statistical significance, the dummy variable RTA only shows a positive impact on service export *via* cross-border supply and inward foreign affiliate sales.

Focusing on the three explanatory variables used to reflect the impact of the GPA on bilateral trade, the coefficient β_4 for dummy variable GPA is positive and significant at 1% level in columns (1)–(4), similar to the pooled regression results.

---

[8] The possible reason lies in the correlation between the dummy variable GPA and the other two interactive variables.

Table 8. Fixed effects results.

	Dependent variables					
	LnGI (1)	**LnGE** (2)	**LnSI** (3)	**LnSE** (4)	**LnFAI** (5)	**LnFAE** (6)
LnGDPi	0.454***	0.491***	1.115***	0.680***	0.506**	1.227***
	(0.0592)	(0.0418)	(0.0756)	(0.0777)	(0.198)	(0.247)
LnGDPj	0.526***	0.558***	0.616***	0.901***	0.333*	0.757***
	(0.0597)	(0.0415)	(0.0713)	(0.0674)	(0.199)	(0.222)
LnDIST	dropped	dropped	dropped	dropped	dropped	dropped
GPA	0.295***	0.569***	0.301**	0.858***	0.121	dropped
	(0.114)	(0.0797)	(0.153)	(0.158)	(0.489)	
NGPA	–0.00674**	–0.00853***	–0.00119	0.0177***	–0.00458	–0.00605
	(0.00325)	(0.00229)	(0.00331)	(0.00451)	(0.0105)	(0.0261)
CLNGVI	0.0133		0.0564***		-0.0800	
	(0.0213)		(0.0213)		(0.0559)	
CLNGVJ		0.00939		0.0792***		0.153**
		(0.0149)		(0.0208)		(0.0628)
RTA	0.0390	0.0204	0.00539	0.265***	0.795***	dropped
	(0.0541)	(0.0373)	(0.0849)	(0.0878)	(0.290)	
Constant	–5.634***	–6.829***	–16.70***	–15.32***	–2.625	–18.76***
	(1.126)	(0.789)	(1.410)	(1.419)	(3.825)	(4.528)
Exporting country fixed effect	Yes	Yes	Yes	Yes	Yes	Yes
Importing country fixed effect	Yes	Yes	Yes	Yes	Yes	Yes
Year fixed effect	Yes	Yes	Yes	Yes	Yes	Yes
Observations	3320	3318	2115	1822	1,099	528
R-squared	0.410	0.619	0.588	0.715	0.382	0.489

Note: *,** and *** indicate statistical significance at 90%, 95% and 99% level, respectively. Robust standard errors in parentheses.

These indicate a positive impact of the GPA on bilateral trade in goods and bilateral trade in services *via* cross-border supply mode. For trade in service *via* commercial presence mode, β_4 is not significant for inward foreign affiliates sales and is dropped in the regression for outward foreign affiliates sales partly because there are too many empty cells to use fixed effects defined over the sample unit as the choice set. However, the higher β_4 in columns (3) and (4) suggests that bilateral trade in services is affected more than for bilateral trade in goods by GPA membership.

The interactive variable NGPA has a negative coefficient β_5 , and is highly significant in columns (1) and (2), while when the dependent variables involves trade in services, regression estimates suggest that the GPA has only a small marginal positive effect on service exports *via* cross-border supply. We attribute the difference in the sign of the coefficient for NGPA in goods and services to the characteristics of services. This suggests the adverse switching effect on bilateral trade in goods can be ignored when assessing GPA impacts on bilateral trade in services.

The sign and the statistical significance of the coefficient β_6 , for interactive variable CLNGVI/CLNGVJ in Table 9 are almost the same as in the pooled regression, except that the magnitude of coefficients in fixed effects regressions becomes smaller. We find no significant coefficients for this explanatory variable in trade in goods and inward foreign affiliate sales. The positive coefficients in columns (3), (4) and (6) indicate that with government procurement values above threshold under the GPA, bilateral trade in services and outward foreign affiliate service sales increase. Due to the high proportion of services possess in the government procurement market, any increase in government procurement value above threshold will be largely attributed to services and in turn stimulate bilateral trade in services.

The net effects of GPA membership, number of the GPA members and the growth rate of government procurement values above bound thresholds for the GPA on bilateral trade flow are reported in Table 9. Except for service imports *via* foreign affiliate sales, GPA membership is positive factor for bilateral trade between the included OECD countries during the sample period. The coefficients on service imports and exports *via* cross-border supply mode are higher than for goods imports and exports. This indicates that GPA membership plays more important role in promoting bilateral trade in services than for trade in goods. A possible reason may be that service suppliers gain more potential business opportunities in the government procurement market with non-discriminatory and transparent policies than manufacturing suppliers since services account for the majority of the government procurement market for most GPA parties. Results also suggest that exports are influenced more by GPA membership than is the case

Table 9. The net effect of variables relating to the GPA on bilateral trade flows.

	Dependent variables					
	LnGI (1)	**LnGE (2)**	**LnSI (3)**	**LnSE (4)**	**LnFAI (5)**	**LnFAE (6)**
Fixed effect regression						
	1.038***	1.065***	0.337***	0.665***	0.667	n.a.
	–0.0067***	–0.0085***	–0.00119	0.0177***	–0.00458	–0.00605
	–0.0133	0.00939	0.0564***	0.0792***	–0.0800	0.153***
Mean of gpan	30.465	30.465	32.2	32.2	32.2	32.2
Mean of Lngvii	0.165		0.316		0.316	
Mean of Lngvij		0.165		0.316		0.316
Mean of GPA	0.659	0.659	0.682	0.682	0.682	0.682
GPA membership	0.0897	0.3091	0.3188	1.4529		0.0483
Number of the GPA members	–0.0044	–0.0056		0.0121		
Lngvii			0.0384			
Lngvij				0.0540		0.1043

for imports. The value of the coefficient for exports (both trade in goods and services) is almost three times of that of imports.

The number of GPA parties has small marginal negative effects on trade in goods. For service exports it has the opposite sign. Service transactions tend to be repeated and based on reciprocal trust and satisfaction attained in previous deals. Switching costs for either service consumer or service producer are typically higher than for tangible goods consumer and producer. With more members participating in the GPA, bilateral trade in goods between pairs of countries may thus decrease slightly due to switching effects, while existing service trade partners tend to intensify. The log of index of government procurement values for importers or exporters is a positive determinant of bilateral trade in service, but has no effect on bilateral trade in goods, resulting from the high service share in the growth of government procurement value above threshold under the GPA.

From our results we suggest following policy implications. First, trade in services is likely to be fostered by joining the GPA. Country with competitiveness in services will gain from being the GPA party and enlargement of service trade, and may have strong incentive to increase the number of GPA parties and the degree of openness in government procurement market. Second, the high level threshold for the GPA makes foreign affiliate sales the most important supply mode in government service procurement market. Procuring entities will prefer suppliers with local commercial presence to lower supervision costs when open bidding for large procurement contract occurs. This preference for foreign affiliate sales will also deter developing countries from entering the GPA since their suppliers are not bidding with large amounts compared to rivals from developed countries.

Some caveats apply to these results. First the share of government procurement above threshold from foreign suppliers for each GPA party is not included in the explanatory variables due to the unavailability of data in WTO notifications. We use the dummy variable GPA, the interactive variables NGPA and CLNGVI/CLNGVJ to measure the possible impacts the GPA may have on bilateral trade. These proxies need not reflect the real changes in market access in government procurement market. Second, the effective enforcement of non-discriminatory and transparency rules under the GPA is a precondition for the enhanced market access and degree of competition in government procurement market, which generates a two-way interaction between the GPA and bilateral trade in goods and services. On one hand, only when the enhanced market access is achieved will the GPA promote bilateral trade between the GPA parities. On the other hand, market access for the government procurement market is determined by both bilateral and multilateral trade arrangements concerning goods, services and investment.

5 Concluding Remarks

In this paper we both discuss the operation of the GPA and the size of markets it covers, and also assess the potential impacts of the GPA on trade among contracting parties using a gravity model. We extend the simple gravity model by adding three explanatory variables relevant to the GPA. These are the GPA membership, the number of the GPA parties and the government procurement value above threshold under the GPA. Our panel data covers 20 OECD countries among which 17 are GPA members and three are non-members. The sample period is 1996–2008 for bilateral trade in goods, and 1999–2008 for bilateral trade in services.

Our results suggest that for most parties the GPA has a positive impact on bilateral trade in goods and services, though the magnitude of the impact may varies between trade in goods and services (with different supply modes). An implication would seem to be that improvements for the GPA should focus on the market access rights for foreign suppliers and should consider the characteristics of services from goods in order to promote international trade. The WTO could also require GPA members to fulfil their obligation in submitting detailed data on government procurement above threshold by origins so as to provide a clear cognition of the openness of the government procurement market under the GPA.

References

Anderson, J.E. (1979), A theoretical foundation for the gravity equation, *American Economic Review,* 69, 106–116.

Anderson, J.E. and E. van Wincoop (2003), Gravity with gravitas: A solution to the border puzzle, *American Economic Review*, 93, 170–192.

Baldwin, R. (1970), *Nontariff Distortions of International Trade*. Brookings Institution, Washington, DC.

Baldwin, R. and J.D. Richardson (1972), Government purchasing policies, other NTBs, and the international monetary crisis, In English, H. and K. Hay (Eds.): Obstacles to Trade in the Pacific Area. Carleton School of International Affairs, Ottawa.

Deardorff, A.V. (1995), Determinants of bilateral trade: does gravity work in a neoclassical world?, *NBER Working Papers No. 5377*. Massachusetts: NBER.

Eaton, J. and S. Kort (2002), Technology, geography, and trade. *Econometrica*, 70, 1741–1779.

Egger, P. (2000), A note on the proper econometric specification of the gravity equation, *Economics Letters*, 66, 25–31.

European Commission (1988), The cost of non-Europe in public-sector procurement, commission of the European communities, Luxembourg.

European Commission (1997), The single market review, subseries III: dismantling of barriers, vol. 2: public procurement, Commission of the European Communities, Luxembourg.

European Commission (2000), Measuring the impact of public procurement policy: first indicators, Single Market News, March.

Evenett, S. (2002), Multilateral disciplines and government procurement, in Hoekman, B.M., A. Mattoo and P. English (Eds): Development, Trade and the WTO: A Handbook, Washington DC : The World Bank, 2002, 417–427. ISBN 0-8213-4997-X.

Evenett, S. and B. Hoekman (2005), Government procurement: Market access, transparency, and multilateral trade rules, *European Journal of Political Economy*, 21,163–183.

Feenstra, R.C., J.A. Markusen and A.K. Rose (2001), Using the gravity equation to differentiate among alternative theories of trade, *Canadian Journal of Economics*, 34, 430–447.

Feenstra, R.C. (2003), *Advanced International Trade: Theory and Evidence*, Princeton University Press: Princeton, NJ.

Francois, J.F., D.R. Nelson and D.N. Palmeter (1996), Public Procurement: A post-Uruguay round perspective, centre for economic policy research, Discussion Paper No. 1412, London.

Francois, J. (2001), The next WTO round: north–south stakes in new market access negotiations, CIES Adelaide and the Tinbergen Institute, CIES: Adelaide, ISBN: 0 86396 474 5.

Grünfeld, L.A. and A. Moxnes (2003), The intangible globalization: explaining the patterns of international trade in services. Discussion Paper 657. Norwegian Institute of International Affairs, Oslo.

Helpman, E. and P. Krugman (1985), *Market Structure and Foreign Trade: Increasing Returns, Imperfect Competition and the International Economy*. Cambridge, Mass.: MIT Press.

Hoekman, B. (1997), *Operation of the Agreement on Government Procurement, 1983–1992*, in Hoekman and Mavroidis (Eds.), Law and Policy in Public Purchasing, Ann Arbor, Michigan: University of Michigan Press.

Kimura, F. and H. Lee (2006), The gravity equation in international trade in services, *Review of World Economics*, 142, 92–121.

Lennon, C. (2006), Trade in services and trade in goods: differences and complementarities, paper presented at the 8th annual conference of the European trade study group, 7th–9th September, 2006, Vienna.

Mattoo, A. (1996), The government procurement agreement: implication of economic Theory, *The World Economy*, 19, 695–720.

McAfee, R.P. and J. McMillan (1989), Government procurement and international trade, *Journal of International Economics*, 26, 291–308.

OECD (2001), Organisation of economic cooperation and development. The Size of Government Procurement Markets, *Journal of Budgeting*, 1(4).

Park, S.-C. (2002), Measuring tariff equivalents in cross-border trade in services, Korea institute for international economic Policy Working Paper, No. 02–15.

Pöyhönen, P. (1963), A tentative model for the volume of trade between countries, *Weltwirtschaftliches Archiv*, 90, 92–100.

Tinbergen, J. (1962), *Shaping the World Economy — Suggestions for an International Economic Policy*, New York: The Twentieth Century Fund.

Trionfetti, F. (2000), Discriminatory public procurement and international trade, *The World Economy*, 23, 57–76.

Trionfetti, F. (2001), Public procurement, market integration, and income inequalities, *Review of International Economics*, 9, 29–41.

Wang, P. (2007), Coverage of the WTO's agreement on government procurement: challenges of integrating china and other countries with a large state sector into the global trading system, *Journal of International Economic Law*, 10, 887–920.

Part II

International Trade and Negotiations

Chapter 5

Dual or Duelling? The China–India Economic Relations After the 2008 Financial Crisis

Daqing Yao
Institute of World Economy,
Shanghai Academy of Social Sciences, China
Telyaodaqing@sass.org.cn

John Whalley
Department of Economics, Western University,
Centre for International Governance Innovation (CIGI), Canada
National Bureau of Economic Research (NBER), USA
jwhalley@uwo.ca

Abstract: This chapter focuses on the economic relationship between China and India after the 2008 financial crisis. China was more negatively affected by the crisis than India, and India is recovering more rapidly in economic performance. China and India's bilateral trade volume grows steadily after the crisis, but India has diversified its exports and China's share has dropped. The commodity structure in their bilateral trade has also changed. In services trade India has more competitive advantage than China and its services surplus is increasing. The two countries are deepening their cooperation in bilateral Foreign Direct Investment (FDI), possible China–India Regional Trade Agreements (RTA), negotiation in the World Trade Organisation (WTO), and partnership in Climate change policy. Although their bilateral relationship are mainly dual, to the rest of the world China and India are duelling in the competition for exports market and imports of natural resource. The trade costs between China and India are increasing after the financial crisis, which means the two largest developing countries have more potential to enhance their economic relations.

1 Introduction

China and India are the two largest developing countries in the world and comprise together 36% of the world's population in 2014. Although both integrated into the world economy gradually, China and India paid more attention to economic relations with the western developed countries than the economic relations between themselves. Shocked by the 2008 financial crisis, China and India are recovering with different strategies. How have the economic relations between them changed after the financial crisis, and what is the prospect in the future?

This chapter aims to shed light on the change of China–India economic relations after the 2008 global crisis. We come to the following arguments: (1) The financial crisis affected more negatively on China than on India. India is recovering more rapidly in economic performance. (2) With bilateral trade growing rapidly, China and India are more integrated than before. (3) In other economic relations, China has more inward and outward FDI than India, there is a possible RTA between China and India, and they co-ordinate in the WTO and on global climate issues. (4) China and India have a dual bilateral relation, but they are duelling to the rest of the world. (5) The trade costs between China and India are still high, which means that the bilateral trade volume lags the potential.

2 Economic Growth of China and India since 2008

(a) GDP Growth

China and India are the largest and among the most dynamic developing economies in the world. From Figure 1, we can see that the GDP of both countries have grown rapidly since 2001. If evaluated in 2005 constant US$, China's GDP in 2001 was 1.54 trillion and accounted for 3.71% of the world's total, while that of India was US$ 0.63 trillion and had a world share of 1.52%. In 2014, China's GDP was US$ 5.27 trillion and 9.08% of the world's total, while India's GDP was US$ 1.60 trillion and 2.76% of the world's total.

The 2008 financial crisis was a big shock to both China and India's economy. As shown in Figure 2, the increasing trend of GDP growth rate of both countries was interrupted in 2008. China's growth rate fell from 14.2% in 2007 to 9.6% in

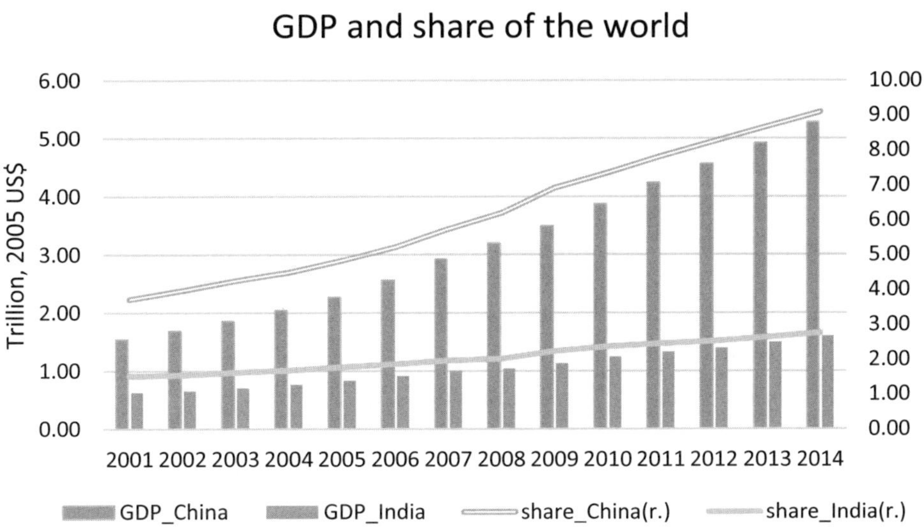

Figure 1. GDP and share of the World, China and India, 2001–2014.

Source: The World Bank's World Development Indicators, 2015.

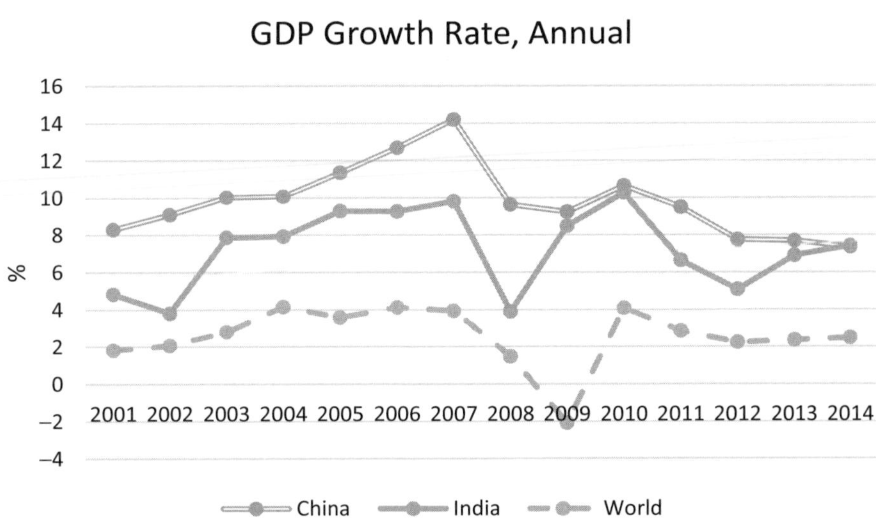

Figure 2. Annual GDP growth rate of China, India and the World, 2001–2014.

Source: The World Bank's World Development Indicators, 2015.

2008, and India's GDP growth rate dropped from 9.8% to 3.9% in the same period. After the crisis, China and India showed different trends in economic growth. Although its growth rate recovered slightly in 2010 to 10.6%, China's economy showed a tendency of slowing down since 2008, and the growth rate fall to 7.35% in 2014. On the other hand, India recovered rapidly after the 2008 slump. In 2010, India's growth rate was higher than the peak before the 2008 crisis. India's growth rate fell again to 5.1% in 2012, but then returned to 7.42% in 2014, which was higher than China for the first time in the past 15 years. The average GDP growth rate of China and India between 2001 and 2007 were 10.82% and 7.54% respectively. Since 2008, the gap between each year's growth rate and such an average has widened to more than 3% for China, but for India this gap is narrowing to a 0.12% in 2014.

Although India is catching up in its growth rate of GDP, its GDP per capita is still far behind than that of China. As Figure 3 shows, in 2001 China's GDP per capita was 1212 (in constant 2005 US$), almost the double of that of India. Since then, China's GDP per capita has grown in an average annual rate of 9.3%, and reached 3,866 US$ in 2014. The GDP per capita of India has grown in a slower average rate of 5.9% during the same period, and in 2014 it was 1,263 US$, almost the same as China in 2001. Now, China's GDP per capita is three times as high as that of India. This enlarged gap is not only because of China's higher GDP growth rate, but also because of the higher population growth rate of India. In the period between 2001 and 2014, China's population grew from 1.27 billion to

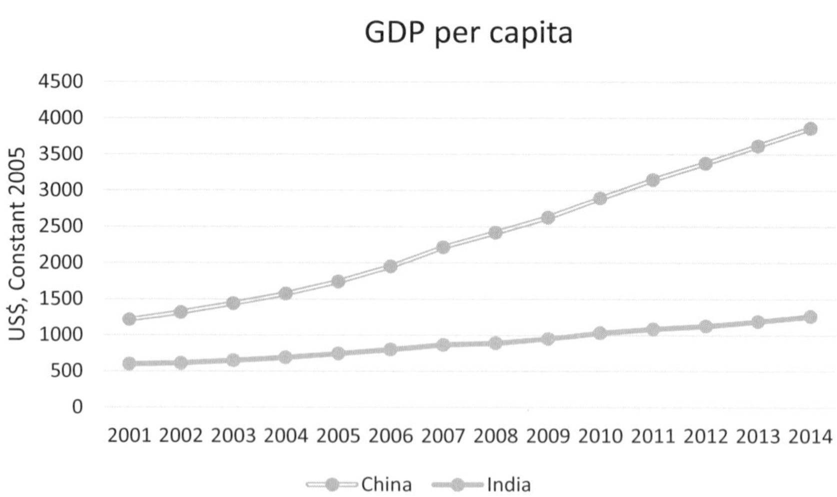

Figure 3. GDP per capita of China and India, 2001–2014.

Source: The World Bank's World Development Indicators, 2015.

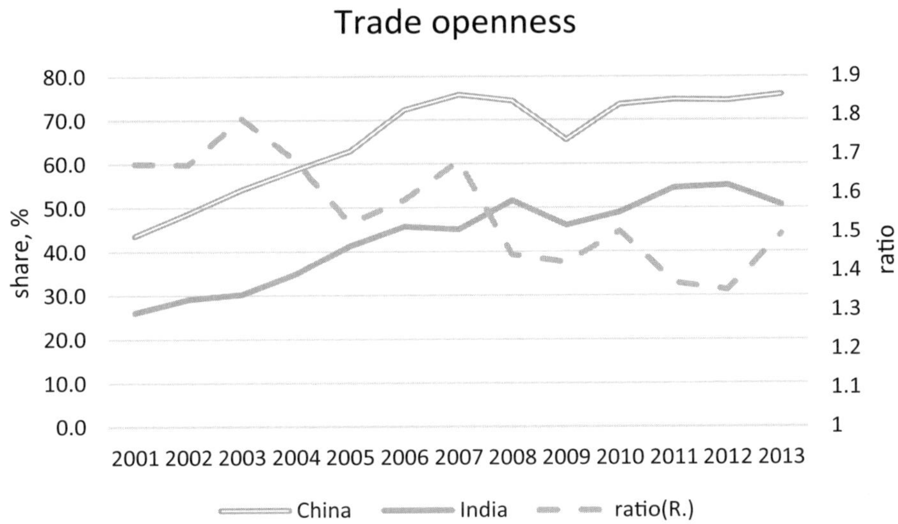

Figure 4. Trade as share of GDP, China and India, 2001–2013.

Notes: The Ratio in the right axis is China's share to India's share.

Source: The World Bank's World Development Indicators, 2015.

1.36 billion, with an annual growth rate of only 0.54%, while India's population increased more quickly, from 1.06 billion to 1.27 billion, with an annual growth rate of 1.39%.

The share of trade to GDP, computed as the sum of a country's exports and imports divided by its GDP, is called as trade openness ratio. From Figure 4, we can see that this trade openness ratio index for China is much higher than that for India. After the 2008 crisis, this ratio dropped significantly for China, from 74.4% to 65.5% in 2009. The ratio for India also dropped from 51.6% to 46.0%, but dropped less than that of China did. This means that China's economy is more opened and more dependent on the foreign market. The trade openness ratio of China quickly restored to its pre-Crisis peak of 75.8% in 2013. The trade openness ratios for India peaked in 2012 at 55.1%, and then show a tendency to decrease. The ratio of these two countries' trade openness ratios (China's ratio/India's ratio) shows a tendency to decrease from its peak of 1.79 in 2003 to 1.35 in 2012, although recovered to 1.49 in the following year. Therefore, the Indian economy is more domestic depended than China. China is more integrated with the world economy, but India shows a more rapid opening tendency.

(b) Changes in GDP Components (C, I and X-M)

The three components of China and India's GDP also changed after the 2008 crisis with a different tendency. As shown in Figure 5 China's gross final consumption

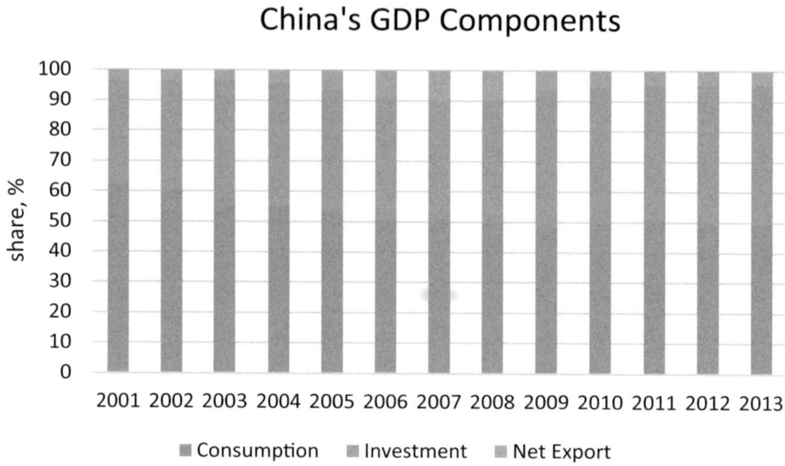

Figure 5. The four components of China's GDP, 2001–2013.
Source: The World Bank's World Development Indicators, 2015.

expenditure as percent of GDP kept decreasing before the crisis, from 62.2% in 2001 to 49.7% in 2008, and reached a bottom of 48.5% in 2009. After that the consumption ratios remain in the range between 49% and 51%. The shares of gross capital formation (investment), which were stable around 40% before the crisis, jumped to 45% in 2009 and remained in such level for five years. The ratios of net export of goods and services, which equal to exports minus imports, fell from its peak of 10.2% in 2007 to 4.6% in 2013. With the consumption already low and net exports diminishing caused by the sluggish world economy, China had to increase investment to maintain stable economic growth.

Figure 6 shows that the components of India's GDP is quite different from that of China. The consumption ratios were much higher, 76% in 2002 and decreased to 66% in 2007. After the crisis, the consumption ratios recovered to around 70%. The investment ratios increased from 25% in 2001 to 33% in 2007, and then remained within 30–33%. The contribution of net exports to India's GDP can be neglected since it usually around plus or minus 2%. Again we can see the China economy is investment driven, while the India economy relies more on domestic consumption.

(c) GDP Sector Composition

The GDP sector composition of China and India also shows different trends over time. As in Figure 7, the value added in China's agriculture sector as a share of GDP, which had decreased from 14.1% in 2001 to 10.3% in 2008, fell further to below 10% after the crisis. The share of industry remained around 46% before the crisis, and then fell to 42% in 2014. On the other side, the share of services sector, which had remained below 42% for many years, increased after the global crisis

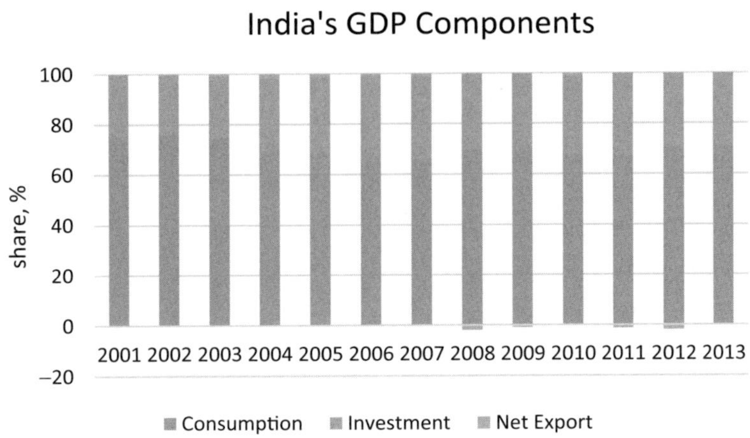

Figure 6. The three components of India's GDP, 2001–2013.

Source: The World Bank's World Development Indicators, 2015.

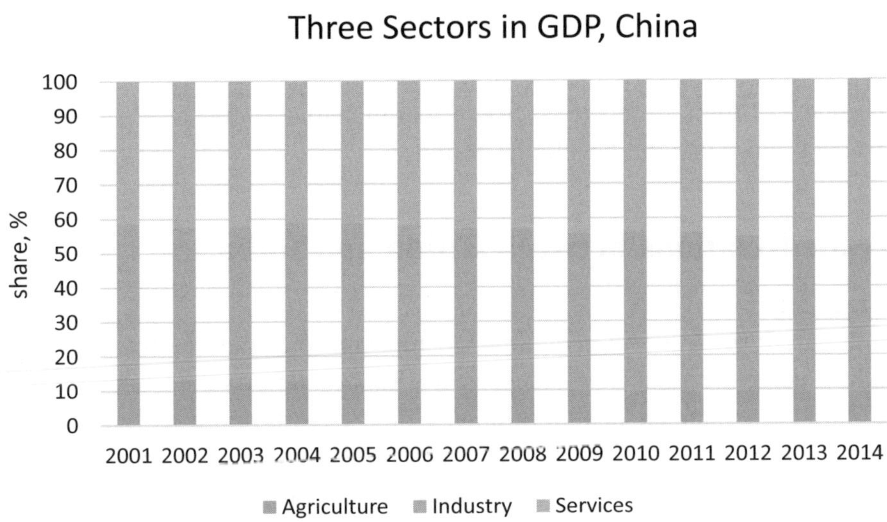

Figure 7. The sector composition of China's GDP, 2001–2014.

Source: The World Bank's World Development Indicators, 2015.

and reached 48.2% in 2014. This shows that China has begun the transition from traditional industrial economy to modern service economy.

The picture of India is quite different, as Figure 8 shows. Agriculture's share, although decreasing continuously since 2001, still accounts for 17% of India's GDP in 2014. The share of industry sector shows a tendency of increase, but in 2014 it only accounted 30.1%. The share of services sector remains the largest sector in India's GDP, which was 53% in 2014. This is because of the under

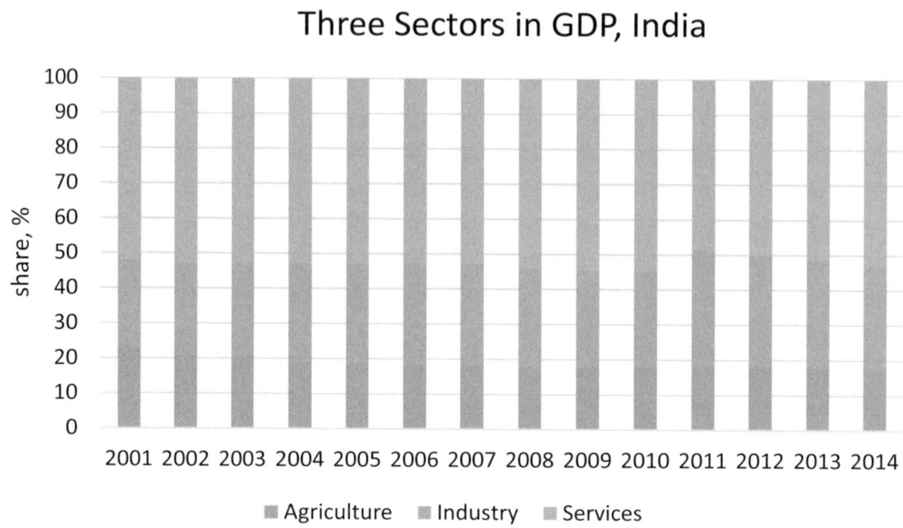

Figure 8. The sector composition of India's GDP, 2001–2014.

Source: The World Bank's World Development Indicators, 2015.

development of India's industry sector, rather than that, India has entered the stage of service society like the developed countries.

3 Trade Relations between China and India

(a) Trade relations

With the GDP growth and economic opening up, the trade between China and India has increased quickly in recent years. Table 1 reports their bilateral exports since 2007. If evaluated in the volume, China exports more to India than *vice versa*, usually with two to three times. In 2014, China's exports to India was four times as large as India's exports to China. Therefore, India maintains a large trade deficit with China.

If evaluated in the share of total exports, Chinese market is more important to India than India' market to China. India's exports to China accounted for over 8% of its total exports before the crisis, and dropped to 4.2% in 2014. On the other hand, China's exports to India as a share of its total is only 2.31% in 2014, though it increased rapidly from a small base of 1% in 2004. Therefore, the 2008 crisis brought a break point in China and India's bilateral trade. Before the crisis, China was one of the most important export markets of India, usually accounted for more than 10% of the total. But since the crisis, India has diversified its exports and China's share dropped to under 5%. On the other hand, China's export to India keeps a stable increasing trend after the 2008 crisis, with the export volume almost

Table 1. Comparison of bilateral exports as a share of the total.

Year	China's exports to India ($billion)	China's exports to India (% of total exports)	India's exports to China ($billion)	India's exports to China (% of total exports)
2004	5.94	1	7.68	10.16
2005	8.93	1.172	9.77	10.15
2006	14.58	1.505	10.28	8.49
2007	24.05	1.97	14.62	9.94
2008	31.59	2.21	20.26	11.3
2009	29.67	2.47	10.37	5.87
2010	40.91	2.59	17.44	7.91
2011	50.54	2.66	16.72	5.55
2012	47.68	2.33	14.73	5.09
2013	48.43	2.19	16.42	4.88
2014	54.22	2.31	13.43	4.23

Source: WDI Database, and Whalley (2015) for data before 2007.

doubled and the share increased from below 2% to about 2.5%. In 2014, India was China's ninth largest export market, after the USA, Hong Kong, Japan, Korea, Germany, Netherland, Vietnam and Britain, while China was India's third largest export market, only after the USA and United Arab Emirates.

In order to analyse the causes of such a pattern change after 2008, we compare the countries structure of China and India's exports in selected years. Since the earliest year of detailed export data in the United Nation's Comtrade Database is 2007 for China and 2009 for India, we use these two years respectively, and the latest year is 2014.

From Table 2 we can see, while India's share as an export market of China becomes higher, the US, Japan and Korea see their shares become lower, and Singapore is no longer in the top 10 list. For India's export markets in 2009 and 2014, the US and the United Arab Emirates switched their place as the top two markets, China remained the third with a lower share and Saudi Arabia witnessed the most rapid share increase and became the fifth largest export market of India. Both China and India are diversifying their export markets, with the Others' share in the table increasing more than 5% over these years.

(b) Goods (services) categories structure

From Table 1, we can see in 2005 India had a trade surplus to China of 0.84 billion. Why this surplus became deficit and huge unbalance between China and India's bilateral trade? We attempted to find out the reasons by analysing the commodity category structure change since the 2008 global crisis.

Table 2. China and India's Top 10 export markets in selected years.

% of total

	China 2007		China 2014		India 2009		India 2014	
1	USA	19.11	USA	16.95	ARE	14.38	USA	13.44
2	HKG	15.12	HKG	15.50	USA	10.82	ARE	10.37
3	JPN	8.37	JPN	6.38	CHN	5.87	CHN	4.23
4	KOR	4.63	KOR	4.28	HKG	4.05	HKG	4.22
5	DEU	4.00	DEU	3.10	Areas, n	3.88	SAU	4.11
6	NLD	3.40	NLD	2.77	SGP	3.86	SGP	3.05
7	GBR	2.60	VNM	2.72	GBR	3.69	GBR	3.04
8	SGP	2.45	GBR	2.44	NLD	3.66	DEU	2.44
9	RUS	2.34	IND	2.31	DEU	3.31	BRA	2.25
10	IND	1.97	RUS	2.29	SAU	2.19	NLD	2.13
	Others	36.03	Others	41.24	Others	44.29	Others	50.71

Source: UN's Comtrade Database.

Table 3. The commodity category structure of China and India's bilateral exports.

Share of total, and growth rate, %

		China's export to India			India's export to China		
	Commodity category	2007	2014	Annual growth	2009	2014	Annual growth
0	Food and live animals	0.43	0.50	14.88	2.15	1.59	−0.82
1	Beverages and tobacco	0.01	0.01	11.67	0.05	0.01	−16.30
2	Crude materials, except fuels	1.59	1.04	5.72	54.80	24.96	−10.01
3	Mineral fuels, and related materials	1.27	1.44	14.42	0.53	11.95	96.67
4	Animal and vegetable oils	0.01	0.01	6.67	1.59	2.08	11.13
5	Chemicals and related products	18.16	22.15	15.55	8.52	12.90	14.44
6	Manufactured goods by material	24.75	21.42	10.02	19.69	33.60	17.19
7	Machinery and transport equipment	48.96	40.86	9.45	6.35	9.92	15.14
8	Miscellaneous manufactured articles	4.76	12.57	29.05	5.56	2.92	−7.43
9	Commodities not classified elsewhere	0.08	0.00	−55.97	0.78	0.06	−37.33

Source: UN's Comtrade Database, categories are in SITC, Rev.4.

Table 3 depicts a detailed picture of China and India's bilateral trade in different commodity categories. China's exports to India are concentrated on categories 5–8, all of which are manufactured products. On the other hand, India's exports to China are mainly in categories 2, 3, 5 and 6. In 2009, category 2 crude materials, except fuels, even accounted for more than a half of India's total exports to China. In the following five years, mineral fuels exports increased very quickly, with an annual growth rate of 96.67%, and now accounts for 12% of India's exports to China. Crude materials except fuels, which accounted for 54.8% in 2009, have decreased at an annual rate of 10%, but in 2014 crude materials except fuels still accounted one quarter of India's exports to China. The category 6, manufactured goods by material, has become the largest category in India's exports to China and accounts for one-third of the total. The category that contributes the most of India's trade deficit to China is category 7, machinery and transport equipment. In 2014, about 41% of China's exports to India was in this category, while only 10% of India's exports to China fell in here. The category 8, miscellaneous manufactured articles, is another main source of India's deficit, in which China's exports increased at an annual rate of 12.57%, but India's exports decreased at an annual rate of 7.43%.

There are two categories in India's exports to China which deserved more analysis, categories 2 and 3. Category 2 once accounted one-half of India's total export to China in 2009, but in 2014 it only accounted one-fourth. As a comparison, category 3 in 2009 was less than 1% of India's total export to China, but in 2014 it accounted for 12%, almost doubled in the following each year. We analyse the sub-category data in these two categories.

As Table 4 shows, three sub-categories made up more than 90% of category 2, crude materials except fuels, which are 26 (textile fibres), 27 (Crude fertilizers, and crude minerals), 28 (Metalliferous ores and metal scrap). Although sub-categories 26 and 27 have kept increasing over 2009–2014, it is the sub-category 28 which decreased four-fifth brought the drop of category 2. In category 3, the sub-category 33 (Petroleum, petroleum products and related materials) increased

Table 4. The details of India's export to China in selected sub-categories.

US$, million and share

Category	2	26	27	28	share 26–28	3	32	33	share 32–33
2009	5682.5	557.0	272.3	4782.9	0.988	54.6	3.9	50.7	1.000
2010	8908.1	1925.3	396.4	6453.9	0.985	372.1	0.0	372.1	1.000
2011	7684.5	2510.4	605.3	4208.3	0.953	1618.7	150.7	1468.1	1.000
2012	6392.8	2751.4	713.1	2522.8	0.937	341.6	15.6	325.9	1.000
2013	5880.6	2956.7	848.9	1694.7	0.935	739.7	4.9	734.8	1.000
2014	3353.8	1437.2	723.0	906.0	0.914	1605.5	0.0	1605.5	1.000
increase rate	−0.410	1.580	1.656	−0.811	n.a.	28.422	−0.999	30.663	n.a.

Source: UN's Comtrade Database, categories are in SITC, Rev.4.

rapidly and in 2014, it was 51 times more than in 2009. Therefore, after the 2008 crisis, India exported more petroleum related materials to China, but exported less Metalliferous ores and metal scrap, which caused the stagnation of India's total export to China.

(c) Services Trade of China and India

Services trade is increasingly important in both China and India's foreign trades. A distinguished difference in services trade is that India is more advanced than China, which is in contrast to the goods trade.

Table 5 reports the overall service trade of China and India. We can see that in terms of trade volume, China is significantly larger than India. In 2014, China's services import was US$ 383.48 billion, more than two times higher than that of India. China's services exports are also larger than that of India, at US$ 223.48 billion in 2014, but with a factor of only 44%. Therefore, China has continuing and enlarging deficit in services trade, while India has large trade surplus in service. During 2005–2014, China's service imports increased at an average annual rate of 18.4%, and its service exports increased at an average annual rate of 10.8%. Such a gap in growth rate caused the service trade deficit increasing at an average annual rate of 47.1%, from surplus 4.5 billion in 2005 to deficit 160.0 billion in 2014. The services trade of India is more steady and balanced, with the exports increased at an average annual rate of 12.8%, and imports increased at an average annual rate of 11.4%. The service trade surplus of India in 2014 is six times large as that of 2005, with an average annual increase rate of 21.9%.

Table 5. The service trade of China and India.

billion US$

	China			India		
Year	**Import**	**Export**	**Balance**	**Import**	**Export**	**Balance**
2005	84.18	89.15	4.97	47.17	52.18	5.01
2006	101.04	113.85	12.81	58.51	69.44	10.93
2007	130.29	147.51	17.22	70.17	86.55	16.38
2008	159.02	165.99	6.97	87.74	106.05	18.31
2009	159.23	144.19	−15.05	80.35	92.89	12.54
2010	194.01	171.49	−22.52	114.74	117.07	2.33
2011	238.91	184.76	−54.15	125.04	138.53	13.49
2012	282.06	216.15	−65.90	129.66	145.53	15.87
2013	331.19	207.69	−123.50	126.26	148.65	22.39
2014	383.48	223.48	−160.00	124.97	154.64	29.67

Source: WTO's Trade in Services Database.

Table 6. The service import and export of China in detailed categories.

billion US$

	Service import				Service export			
Category of service	**2005**	**2008**	**2010**	**2012**	**2005**	**2008**	**2010**	**2012**
Goods S.	0.22	0.09	0.68	0.88	18.15	26.02	18.36	40.23
Transport	28.5	50.3	63.3	85.9	15.4	38.4	34.2	38.9
Travel	21.8	36.2	54.9	102.0	29.3	40.8	45.8	50.0
Construction	1.6	4.4	5.1	3.6	2.6	10.3	14.5	12.2
Insurance	7.2	12.7	15.8	20.6	0.5	1.4	1.7	3.3
Financial S.	0.2	0.6	1.4	1.9	0.1	0.3	1.3	1.9
Intel. property.	5.3	10.3	13.0	17.7	0.2	0.6	0.8	1.0
Info services	2.2	4.7	4.1	5.5	2.3	7.8	10.5	16.2
Other bus. S.	16.5	38.6	34.3	42.4	19.9	39.2	43.2	51.1
Personal S.	0.2	0.3	0.4	0.6	0.1	0.4	0.1	0.1
Government S.	0.6	0.9	1.1	1.0	0.5	0.7	1.0	1.0
Total	84.2	159.0	194.0	282.1	89.1	166.0	171.5	216.2

Note: Goods-related Service (Goods S. in the table) consists of two parts, Manufacturing services on physical inputs owned by others, and Maintenance and repair services, n.i.e.

Source: WTO' Trade in Service Database.

Table 6 sets out the detailed service trade data of China in selected years. We can see that four categories made up to the largest share of China's deficit in services trade: transport, travel, insurance, intellectual property and commercial services. In 2012, these four categories added up to a trade deficit of US$, –133 billion larger than China's total service deficit in that year. On the other hand, Goods-related services contributed the largest service trade surplus.

Table 7 reports the detailed service trade data of India in selected years. We can see that three categories made up to the largest share of India's surplus in services trade: travel, info services, other business services. In 2014, these three categories added up to a trade surplus of US$ 77.9 billion, which was larger than India's total services surplus in 2014 of US$ 29.6 billion. Transport contributed the most deficit to India's services trade, in 2014 it equalled US$ 38 billion.

(d) Projections of the next 10–15 years

We conduct projections on China and India's bilateral exports. There are many methods to project on the future, we employ the simplest one: time trend. We first compute the five-year rolling annual growth rate of China and India's bilateral exports using the data from 2001 to 2014 (20.8% and 6.6% respectively for China and India), and then project out the trade volume based on such growth rate for

Table 7. The service import and export of India in detailed categories.

billion US$

	Service import				Service export			
Category of service	**2005**	**2008**	**2011**	**2014**	**2005**	**2008**	**2011**	**2014**
Goods S.	NA	NA	NA	0.32	NA	NA	NA	0.29
Transport	20.9	43.2	57.9	56.0	6.5	12.8	17.7	18.0
Travel	6.2	9.6	13.7	12.7	7.5	11.8	17.7	18.6
Construction	0.6	0.7	1.1	1.2	0.3	0.8	0.8	1.5
Insurance	2.3	4.3	6.2	5.7	0.9	1.6	2.6	2.2
Financial S.	0.9	3.5	8.3	4.8	1.1	4.3	6.2	6.5
Intel. property.	0.7	1.5	2.8	4.3	0.2	0.1	0.3	0.7
Info services	1.5	4.3	3.2	3.9	16.9	37.1	47.1	55.4
Other bus. S.	13.6	19.7	25.1	26.8	18.2	36.4	38.5	47.3
Personal S.	0.1	0.3	0.3	1.4	0.1	0.7	0.3	1.3
Government S.	0.5	0.5	0.8	1.0	0.3	0.4	0.6	0.6
Total	47.2	87.7	125.0	125.0	52.2	106.1	138.5	154.6

Notes: Goods-related Service (Goods S. in the table) consists of two parts, Manufacturing services on physical inputs owned by others, and Maintenance and repair services, n.i.e.

Source: WTO's Trade in Service Database.

2015–2030. In Figure 9, we can see that such a difference in growth rate would bring huge gap after one and a half decades. In 2014, the bilateral exports for China and India are 54.2 and US$ 13.4 billion, and in 2030 these would be 1116.6 and US$ 37.1 billion, respectively.

4 Other Economic Relations between China and India

(a) FDI relations

FDI is another important economic relation between China and India, but the FDI data is not as easy to access as the trade data. The UNCTAD provides basic FDI data of the world and most countries, but the data is yearly at an aggregate level. As Figure 10 shows, we can see that China and India experienced quite different FDI flows after the 2008 global crisis. China's FDI, both inwards and outwards, recovered shortly after the crisis. But India's inwards FDI volume fluctuated with a down trend, and outwards FDI of India kept decreasing since the crisis.

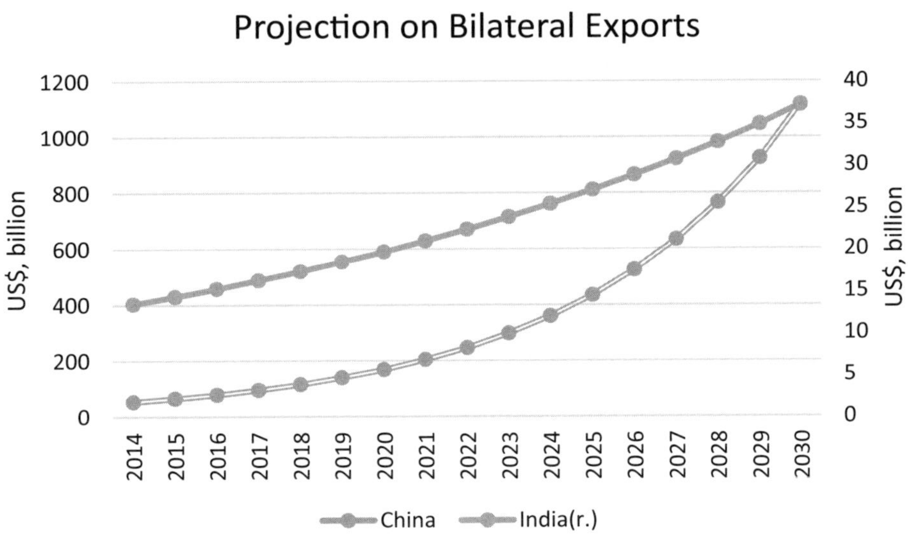

Figure 9. The projection of China and India's bilateral exports, 2015–2030.

Source: Authors' Computation.

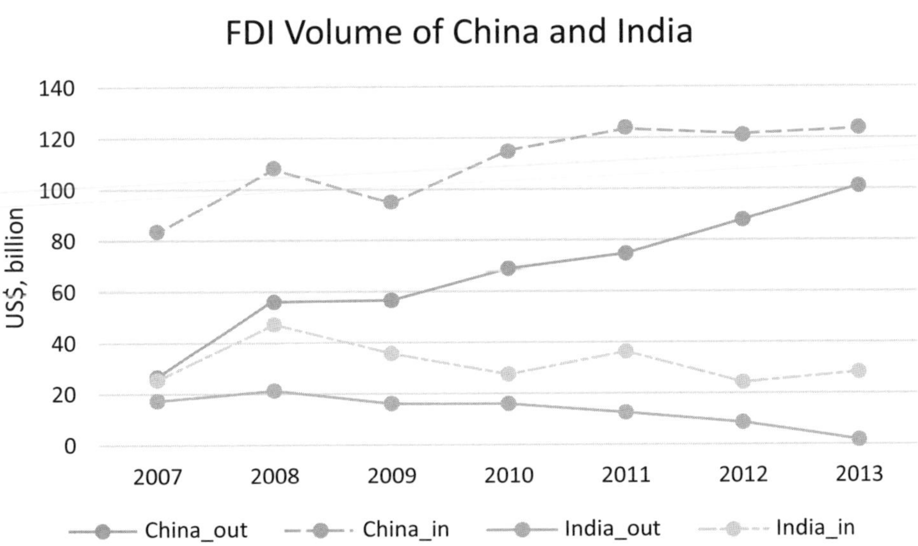

Figure 10. The FDI volume of China and India, 2007–2013.

Source: The UNCTAD Database.

Without detailed data on China and India's bilateral FDI, we cannot make further analysis on the FDI relation. We can reason that India's FDI to China should be diminishing, because the total volume of India's outwards FDI dropped from 17.2 billion in 2007 to 1.7 billion in 2013. Similarly, China's FDI to India may be increased after the crisis, but the volume is unknown.

(b) Possible RTA between China and India

In 2003, China and India established a Joint Study Group to examine the potential of economic engagement between the two countries. In October 2007, the Joint Task Force finalised its report on the feasibility of a China–India RTA. According to the feasibility report, a China–India RTA will be mutually advantageous. Both sides welcomed the conclusion of the feasibility study on the RTA between the two countries, and agreed to explore the possibility of commencing discussions on a RTA that meets the common aspirations of both countries and will also benefit the region. But the China–India RTA is still in proposed stage and not yet notified to the WTO.

In May 2013, Chinese Premier Li Keqiang visited India and expressed the willingness to start the negotiation on RTA between China and India. A major issue between bilateral trade is the deficit of India to China, which exceed US$ 40 billion in 2014. In order to balance this deficit, India is pushing its progress in information technology and services sector to China. During Chinese President Xi Jinping's visit to India in September 2014, more than 20 Chinese companies signed purchase agreements with India companies to buy copper cathodes, seafood, polypropylene, oil and cotton yarn among other items, worth $650 million. China also announced investments of more than $7 billion in industrial parks in Maharashtra and Gujarat. During Indian Prime Minister Narendra Modi's visit to China in May 2015, China committed to enlarge the investment to $20 billion in the next five years.

(c) On the WTO negotiations

China and India also showed evidence of coordinating positions in WTO's negotiating forums. The current Doha Round negotiation was launched in November 2001 and its aimed to achieve major reform of the international trading system through the introduction of lower trade barriers and revised trade rules. For more than 12 years, the Doha Round was hampered by the frequent disagreements between the developed countries led by the US and EU, and the developing countries led by Brazil, China, India and South Africa. Since the Doha Round covers about 20 areas of trade, it is difficult to reach an agreement at one time. Therefore, a Bali Package aimed on trade facilitation, agriculture, cotton, development and least development countries (LDCs) issues, was discussed separately and adopted at the Bali Ministerial Conference on December 7, 2013, and subsequent decisions related to the Bali ministerial outcomes were adopted by the General Council on November 27, 2014. The Bali Package was planned to be adopted in July 2014, and was postponed owing to objection, raised by India, Cuba, South Africa and others. As before, China supported India's stand in these topics.

(d) On the Climate Change policy
China and India are the two largest developing countries in the world and face the same situation on balancing economic development and environment issues. On May 15, 2015, China and India governments published a Joint Statement on Climate Change. In this joint statement, they recall the Agreement on Cooperation on Addressing Climate Change between them signed in 2009, and the Memorandum of Understanding (MoU) between them on Green Technologies signed in 2010. They decided to further promote bilateral partnership on climate change. They emphasise that the United Nations Framework Convention on Climate Change (UNFCCC) and its Kyoto Protocol are the most appropriate framework for international cooperation for addressing climate change. They reaffirmed the principles of equity and common but differentiated responsibilities and call for the leadership of developed countries in reducing greenhouse gas emissions and providing finance, technology and capacity building support to developing countries. They are also undertaking ambitious actions domestically on combating climate change.

5 Dual or Duelling? Relations of China and India, and to the Rest of the World

(a) Relations of China and India is dual, for market integration
India and China have different comparative advantages in different sectors, there fore the potential economic cooperation is huge.

First is the service sector. As we analyse in Table 5, since 2005 (the first year of data available) China has kept an enlarging deficit in service trade, while India maintains a surplus in services trade. China and India can use the comparative advantage of each other to trade more in services sector. As to the different categories of service, general service and commercial service are two categories that China has the most deficit, while India has the most surplus. China can import more service from India in these categories, and can also invite Indian service companies to invest in China.

Second is in different commodity categories. There are 10 categories in UN's Comtrade data, and in Table 2 we compare China and India's bilateral trade in different categories. Instead of bilateral trade, here we use the Comtrade data to

Table 8. RCA index of China and India, 2014.

Exports in US$, billion

Category	China's exports	India's exports	World export	RCA_cn	RCA_in	cn/in
0	58.9	32.0	1052.2	0.378	1.512	0.250
1	2.9	1.2	136.7	0.142	0.433	0.329
2	15.8	12.8	641.1	0.167	0.991	0.168
3	34.4	62.3	1743.4	0.133	1.779	0.075
4	0.6	0.9	83.5	0.050	0.537	0.094
5	134.5	37.3	1793.9	0.506	1.035	0.489
6	401.8	76.8	2040.0	1.329	1.874	0.709
7	1070.5	48.5	5570.4	1.296	0.433	2.994
8	620.5	42.3	1973.5	2.121	1.067	1.989
9	2.3	3.4	766.2	0.020	0.223	0.090

Source: UN's Comtrade Database, categories are in SITC, Rev.4.

compute China and India's RCA index in these categories. A country *i*'s RCA in industry *j* is defined as:

$$\mathrm{RCA}_{ij} = \frac{X_{ij}/X_i}{W_j/W},$$

where X_{ij} is the country *i*'s export to the world in sector *j*, X_i is country *i*'s total export to the world, W_j is the world's total trade in industry *j* and *W* is the world's total trade volume in the same year. China and India's RCA index in 2014 is listed in Table 8, while the last column is the ratio of the two countries' RCA.

From Table 8, we can see that China's RCA is larger than 1 in categories 6, 7 and 8, while India's RCA is larger than 1 in categories 0, 3, 5, 6 and 8. If we compare their RCA directly, in categories 7 and 8 China is higher than India, while in all other eight categories India is higher than China. This implies a lot of trade opportunity in these categories.

If fully integrated, China and India make one of the largest markets in the world. Put together, China and India have a GDP of US$ 12.4 billion in 2014, accounting for 15.9% of the world's GDP, and a population of 26.3 billion, making up for 36.5% of the world's total population.

(b) Relations of these two countries to the rest of the world is duelling

(i) Market competition with OECD, similar export structure

Although India and China have much potential to cooperate in their bilateral economic relations, they do have competition when faced with the rest of the

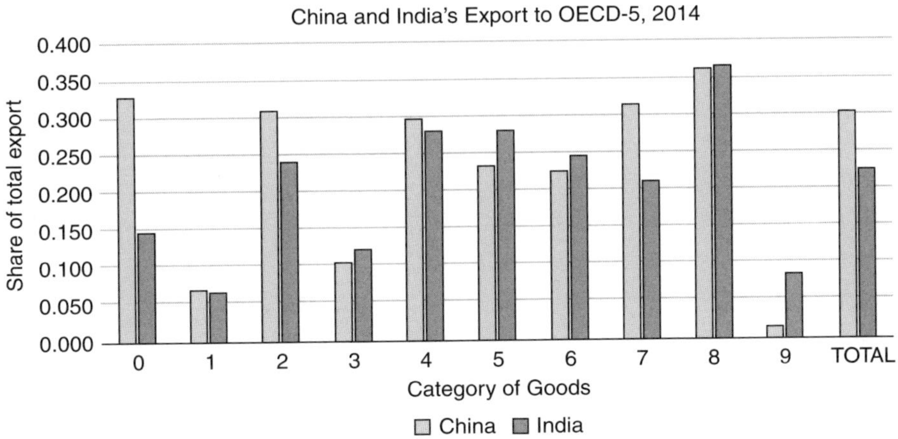

Figure 11. The exports of China and India to five OECD Members, 2014.

Source: UN's Comtrade Database, categories are in SITC, Rev.4.

world. Both are developing countries and their exports to the advanced countries are quite similar. We compute China and India's export to five OECD countries, France, Germany, Japan, UK and USA in 2014. As Figure 11 depicts, in the 10 categories of SITC-4, China and India are very similar in six categories 1, 3, 4, 5, 6 and 8. In total, 30.1% of China's exports went to these OECD-5, while 22.3% of India's exports went to the same five countries in 2014. Therefore, if the market condition changes, China and India will compete for entering these market.

(ii) Relations with developing countries, the competition for resource

Both China and India are in the development stage of industrialisation, therefore they have huge demand on natural resources, such as ironstone, copper ore, oil, natural gas, etc. From Table 9, we can see that in 2010, India's mineral consumption was far smaller than that of China. With India paying more attention on infrastructure construction and industrialisation, India will need to import more minerals, and will compete with China to obtain the resource.

6 The Trade Costs Change between China and India

(a) Definition and Computation of Trade Costs

As in Jacks (2011), here trade costs are defined as all the costs of transaction and transport associated with the exchange of goods across national borders, including obvious barriers such as tariffs and transport costs, but also many other barriers that are more difficult to observe such as the costs of overcoming language barriers and exchange rate risk.

Table 9. Minerals consume of India and China, 2010.

Minerals	India's consume	Increase rate	Rank in the world	Share of the world	China's consume
Coal (100m t)	5.1	6.5	3	7.5	31.8
Oil (100m t)	1.49	3.4	5	3.9	8.43
Natural Gas (100m M3)	519	25	13	2	6466
Raw steel (million t)	66	7.4	4	4.8	537.4
Refined copper (10k t)	55.8	8.1	6	7.8	714
Primary Aluminum (10k t)	130	1.6	5	3.7	1241
Refined Zinc (10k t)	56.68	6.5	3	4.5	530

Source: Xie (2013).

Following the approaches in Jacks (2011), we compute the trade costs between China and India in the period 2009–2014 based on a gravity model method. Such a trade cost measure is consistent with leading theories of international trade and also is micro-founded. As Head and Ries (2001) point out, the trade cost we calculated is an implied cost by the gravity equation, which gauges the difference between observed trade flows and a hypothetical benchmark of frictionless trade.

We only briefly outline the theory for trade cost. Anderson and van Wincoop (2003) derive the following gravity equation:

$$x_{ij} = \frac{y_i y_j}{y^W} \left(\frac{t_{ij}}{\Pi_i P_j} \right)^{1-\sigma}, \tag{1}$$

where y^W is nominal world output and Π_i and P_j are outward and inward multilateral resistance variables. The latter can be interpreted as average trade barriers. The bilateral trade cost factor is $t_{ij} \geq 1$, and $\sigma > 1$ is the elasticity of substitution. The multilateral resistance variables are difficult to proxy empirically, but we can eliminate them using the domestic trade x_{ii}, which is:

$$x_{ii} = \frac{y_i y_i}{y^W} \left(\frac{t_{ii}}{\Pi_i P_i} \right)^{1-\sigma}. \tag{2}$$

Using Equations (1) and (2) and their counterparts x_{ji}, x_{jj}, we can eliminate the multilateral resistance indices and obtain:

$$\frac{x_{ij} x_{ji}}{x_{ii} x_{jj}} = \left(\frac{t_{ij} t_{ji}}{t_{ii} t_{jj}} \right)^{1-\sigma}. \tag{3}$$

From Equation (3), we get the trade cost τ_{ij}, which is defined as:

$$\tau_{ij} \equiv \left(\frac{t_{ij}t_{ji}}{t_{ii}t_{jj}}\right)^{\frac{1}{2}} - 1 = \left(\frac{x_{ii}x_{jj}}{x_{ij}x_{ji}}\right)^{\frac{1}{2(\sigma-1)}} - 1. \tag{4}$$

(b) Trade Costs between China and India

Now we are ready to compute the trade costs between China and India. The bilateral trade data x_{ij} can be acquired from the UN's Comtrade Database, but the domestic trade x_{ii} cannot be found directly. Using the market clearing condition, we can write domestic trade as:

$$x_{ii} = y_i - x_i, \tag{5}$$

where x_i is the total export, which is also available in the Comtrade Database, y_i is the total income, which can be calculated as GDP minus total service value added, these data can be found in World Bank's WDI Database. All the data are in current US$. As to $\sigma - 1$, we follow Eaton and Kortum (2002) and set it equal to 8.3.

We do not discuss more details on the data, and report the trade costs between China and India we calculated in Figure 12.

From Figure 12, we know that the trade costs between China and India dropped to 0.557 in 2010, then recovered steadily, and in 2014 it reached 0.622,

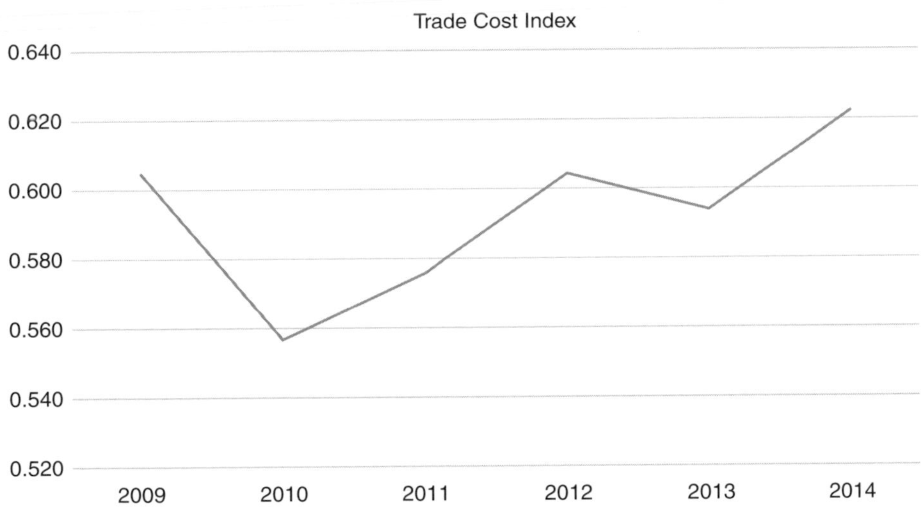

Figure 12. The trade cost between China and India, 2009–2014.

Source: Authors' calculations.

which is higher than 0.604 in 2009. Therefore, the bilateral trade volume still lags behind the potential volume.

7 Concluding Remarks

It seems quite strange why the economic relationship between China and India is not stronger. The two countries share a long geographic border, have similar culture and history experience, and in a similar development stage. Maybe the reason is that both countries paid more attention to the economic relation with western countries before. But this situation is changing since the 2008 global crisis.

China and India each has advantage in some aspects. The manufacturing efficiency of China is higher than that of India, and China's infrastructure is better. On the other hand, India has more comparative advantage in the services and IT sectors. If China and India use more of their potential cooperation, they can push the economic development to a higher level and benefit not only their people, but also the world as a whole.

Acknowledgement

We are grateful to the ORF (Ontario Research Fund) and CIGI (Centre for International Governance Innovation) for financial support.

References

Anderson, J.E. and E. van Wincoop (2003), Gravity with Gravitas: A Solution to the Border Puzzle, *American Economic Review,* 93(1), 170–192.

Eaton, J. and S. Kortum Samuel (2002), Technology, Geography, and Trade, *Econometrica,* 70(4), 1741–1780.

Head, K. and J. Ries (2001), Increasing Returns Versus National Product Differentiation as an Explanation for the Pattern of US–Canada Trade, *American Economic Review,* 91(4), 858–876.

Jacks D.S. (2011), Trade Booms, Trade Busts, and Trade Costs, *Journal of International Economics*, 83, 185–201.

Whalley, J. (2015), China's Rapidly Deepening Economic Relationship with India. In Manmohan Agarwal and J. Whalley (Eds.), *Asia and the World Economy*, Volume 2, *India and China: Comparative Experience and Prospects*. World Scientific.

Xie, F. (2013), The Current Situation and Analysis of India's Mineral Resource, *China Mining Magazine (Zhongguo Kuangye)*, 22(8), 14–17.

Chapter 6

The Trade Performance of Asian Economies During and Following the 2008 Financial Crisis*

Jing Wang

Department of Economics, Western University, Canada
jwang624@uwo.ca

John Whalley

Department of Economics, Western University, Canada
Centre for International Governance Innovation (CIGI), Canada
National Bureau of Economic Research (NBER), USA
jwhalley@uwo.ca

Abstract: This chapter documents and compares the trade performance of the major Asian economies both during and following the 2008 financial crisis. We consider China, India, Thailand, Malaysia, South Korea, Japan, Singapore and Chinese Taiwan. We access separate country data files giving monthly trade performance for both the import and export sides throughout the crisis. We use these to compare the size, speed and acceleration of trade compression with the onset of the crisis, and the reverse effects on recovery. We do this in aggregate and by product and bilateral trading partner. The data reported show considerable diversity of country experience. Among manufacture exporters China has seen a major decline in trade with a slow recovery, whereas Korea experienced smaller initial impact, but a quick rebound. Import impacts are mildest for India and commodity

---

*We are grateful to a seminar group at CIGI for comments, and to Mohan Agarwal, Li Chunding and Shi Xiaojun for discussion.

exporters including Malaysia. On the import side, the falls in world oil prices impact sharply on import values. We also compare trade impacts in the 2008 financial crisis with those in the 1930s, and the Asian financial crisis. In the 1930s, percentage impacts on trade in the first year were similar, but of much longer duration, reducing trade volumes in the US by nearly 80% by 1933, and placing Germany close to autarchy. In the 1998, Asian crisis trade impacts were much smaller since export markets in the OECD were not affected, but negative growth impacts on affected countries were greater.

1 Background and Issues

In September and October 2008, the world experienced the onset of a major financial crisis, triggered in part by a loss of confidence by investors in the value of securitised mortgages in the US during 2007. It also coincided with the reversal of price bubbles in housing, oil, and resource commodities, and resulted in significant stock price declines and exchange rate volatility. These events were followed by a worldwide recession in 2009 with a sharp reduction in world trade and rising unemployment. Although the worldwide crisis seemingly originated in the United States, its effects were felt by all economies around the world. To date, there has been no research which compares the speed, severity and acceleration of both decline in trade and the rebound of Asian economies. This is what we attempt to do here.

We document the trade performance of the Asian economies throughout the crisis. In the preceding two decades, many of these had become major manufacturing exporters. The impacts on auto exports for Japan, consumer electronics exports from China, and manufactured exports from Korea were all major. We use official data for key Asian economies, including China, India, Japan, South Korea (referred to as Korea hereinafter), Malaysia, Chinese Taiwan (referred to as Taiwan hereinafter), Thailand and Singapore, and compare and analyse their trade performance during and beyond the crisis.

Comparison of May 2008 and May 2009 shows that monthly exports of China, India, Japan, Korea, Malaysia, Taiwan and Thailand fell 26.3%, 37.1%, 49.4%, 15.4%, 29.8%, 26.6% and 44.4% respectively. Monthly imports fell more by 43.1%, 37.3%, 42.7%, 24.3%, 30.3%, 40.3% and 56.6% respectively, reflecting in part the oil price decline. Among these countries, Korean trade performed the best, with a smaller drop after the initial onset of the crisis and a quick rebound. Japan's trade was affected most, with a severe and prolonged decline on both the export and import side.

We compare this trade performance both with that of the North American and European economies in the 1930s and with that of the severely impacted Asian economies in the 1997–1998 Asian financial crisis. In the 1930s, initial year trade impacts were similar in percentage terms, but persisted in the North American and

European economies for four years or more. Japan in the 1930s, however, had several years of strong export growth, and China also performed much better than North America and Europe. Trade impacts in Asian were more severe than in either Europe or North America, and were more severe in the recent crisis than in the 1997–1998 Asian financial crisis, but growth impacts on affected countries were more severe in 1997–1998.

2 The Overall Trade Performance of the Asian Economies during the Financial Crisis

We first discuss the overall trade performance of the Asian countries (region) during the financial crisis. We consider China, India, South Korea (Korea for short), Japan, Malaysia, Chinese Taiwan and Thailand for whom monthly data are available for 2008 and 2009, and initial months of 2010. We also consider Singapore, for which there are quarterly data.

Monthly growth rates for exports (compared with the same month in the previous year) are reported for these countries in Table 1. Indian exports grew the fastest and Korean exports grew the second fastest in 2008 pre-crisis. Others showed almost the same performance; Japan was the only country which had export growth rates in single figures in 2008.

For 2009, the picture is different. Korea was still the best performer among these countries (regions), with negative growth in only four months and a smaller decline than other countries. The worst performer was Japan. With sluggish growth pre-crisis, Japan's exports shrank by over 30% for 10 months, and they were almost half of the previous year in the first quarter of 2009. Taiwan also showed a significant decline from November 2008 and had a decline of over 40% in two months. Exports from Malaysia showed the same trend as those of Taiwan, but with a milder decline both on onset and rebound. China's 2009 performance was slightly better than that of India, Malaysia and Taiwan.

The growth rates of imports by the same Asian economies are reported in Table 2. Korean imports fell least among those economies (as for exports). During Pre-crisis, the fastest growth of imports occurred in India and Korea, whereas the lowest growth rates in 2008 were for Malaysia and Japan. Imports by Malaysia and Taiwan started to fall in October 2008, followed by China and Japan one month later, but Korea maintained strong positive export growth for the whole of 2008. Imports of all these economies declined in the first 10 months of 2009, and Korean imports declined the least among these economies. Taiwan's imports dropped the most at the beginning of 2009 and those of Japan fell the most in proportional terms in 2009. Except for Korea, country imports seem to follow a pattern, whereby the faster the growth pre-crisis, the greater the decline during the crisis.

Table 1. Percentage export growth rates of key Asian economies 2008–2010 by month (compared with the same month in the previous year, %).

	Y2008							Y2009						
	CN	IN	JP	KR	MY	CT	TH	CN	IN	JP	KR	MY	CT	TH
Jan	26.6	35.8	7.7	15.6	10.4	11.8	36.1	−17.5	−13.6	−45.7	−7.3	−27.7	−44.1	−26.5
Feb	6.4	44.1	8.7	19.8	14.6	18.3	18.6	−25.7	−21.5	−49.4	20.9	−15.9	−28.6	−11.6
Mar	30.6	34.1	2.2	22.1	5.5	22.7	16.3	−17.1	−25.1	−45.5	18.5	−15.7	−35.8	−23.2
Apr	21.8	63.0	3.9	33.5	20.8	13.9	30.0	−22.6	−35.0	−39.1	9.3	−26.5	−34.3	−26.1
May	28.1	50.0	3.6	40.7	22.9	20.5	24.5	−26.3	−37.1	−40.9	−12.5	−29.8	−31.4	−26.6
Jun	17.3	58.5	−1.8	29.1	18.5	21.2	30.2	−21.2	−32.2	−35.8	5.5	−22.6	−30.4	−26.0
Jul	26.9	52.1	7.9	50.8	25.3	7.9	45.1	−22.9	−30.8	−36.5	−3.2	−22.7	−24.5	−25.7
Aug	21.1	40.5	0.2	30.5	10.6	18.2	15.9	−23.1	−27.2	−36.0	−4.8	−20.0	−24.6	−18.4
Sep	21.4	26.1	1.5	52.2	14.9	−1.6	20.0	−15.0	−13.0	−30.6	−0.3	−24.2	−12.7	−8.5
Oct	19.1	−3.7	−7.9	49.4	−2.7	−8.3	3.0	−13.7		−23.2	−15.4	1.7	−4.6	−3.0
Nov	−2.2	−13.5	−26.8	21.5	−4.8	−23.3	−20.9	−1.2		−6.3	0.0	−3.5	19.3	17.2
Dec	−2.8	−8.6	−35.0	23.6	−14.8	−41.9	−14.6	17.6		12.0	10.7	18.7	46.8	26.1
Y2010							Jan	21.1		40.9	25.0	36.8	75.8	30.9
							Feb	45.7		45.3	7.5	18.4		23.2
							Mar	24.2		43.5				
							Apr	30.4						

Note: CN — China, IN — India, JP — Japan, KR — Korea, MY — Malaysia, TH — Thailand, CT — Chinese Taiwan.

Source: Authors' calculations. China Customs Statistics, Indian DGCIS (Kolkata), Trade Statistics of Japan, Korean Customs Statistics, Official Portal of Ministry of International Trade and Industry Data (Malaysia), Bank of Thailand, Bureau of Foreign Trade of Taiwan.

Table 2. Percentage import growth rates of key Asian economies 2008–2010 by month (compared with same month in the previous year, %).

	Y2008							Y2009						
	CN	IN	JP	KR	MY	CT	TH	CN	IN	JP	KR	MY	CT	TH
Jan	27.5	58.1	9.5	32.6	7.2	14.7	44.2	−43.1	−20.2	−31.8	−3.7	−30.3	−56.6	−35.5
Feb	35.1	51.4	10.7	29.4	11.1	26.0	33.3	−23.8	−31.3	−42.7	2.4	−27.6	−32.1	−40.3
Mar	24.8	37.6	11.4	29.6	2.8	37.5	32.4	−24.9	−29.6	−36.4	−0.7	−29.1	−49.7	−35.1
Apr	26.6	65.0	12.2	36.3	7.9	17.7	43.2	−22.8	−37.3	−35.5	−11.2	−22.5	−41.2	−36.3
May	40.1	39.2	4.8	42.9	9.4	17.5	15.7	−24.8	−33.0	−42.2	−24.3	−27.9	−39.1	−34.7
Jun	31.2	44.6	16.7	47.1	12.4	22.3	34.6	−13.0	−22.1	−41.7	−17.2	−20.7	−33.5	−29.3
Jul	33.6	49.7	18.2	63.5	15.1	11.6	55.9	−14.9	−33.5	−40.6	−20.0	−16.2	−34.1	−32.5
Aug	22.9	64.6	17.1	50.5	4.2	39.3	26.9	−17.1	−36.1	−41.0	−18.1	−18.7	−32.4	−32.8
Sep	20.9	70.9	28.8	71.7	11.5	9.9	39.4	−3.8	−34.3	−36.8	−16.2	−20.4	−21.2	−17.9
Oct	15.4	18.5	7.4	49.3	−5.4	−7.4	21.7	−6.8		−35.5	−20.3	−2.3	−6.7	−17.5
Nov	−18.0	6.3	−14.4	26.6	−8.2	−13.7	2.0	26.3		−16.7	−11.7	2.2	18.0	−2.2
Dec	−21.3	−3.3	−21.5	20.0	−22.5	−44.6	−6.5	55.6		−5.5	1.4	23.5	55.6	28.2
Y2010							Jan	85.8		8.9	9.5	30.8	115.4	44.8
							Feb	44.7		29.5	13.7	28.7		71.2
							Mar	66.4		20.6				
							Apr	50.1						

Note: CN — China, IN — India, JP — Japan, KR — Korea, MY — Malaysia, TH — Thailand, CT — Chinese Taiwan.

Source: Authors' calculations. China Customs Statistics, Indian DGCIS (Kolkata), Trade Statistics of Japan, Korean Customs Statistics, Official Portal of Ministry of International Trade and Industry Data (Malaysia), Bank of Thailand, Bureau of Foreign Trade of Taiwan.

One reason for the decline in imports was falling oil prices in 2009, along with the recession in the real economies. Trade for all economies started to rebound at the end of 2009 and they experienced accelerated recovery. There is a solid rebound shown for 2010 in available data, with Taiwan's imports doubling in January 2010 and China's increasing by over 60% in the first quarter of 2010.

Interestingly, the Korean economy more broadly and Korean financial markets experienced less impact in the current financial crisis than in that of 1997–1998. As Huh and Nam (2010) note, several factors have contributed to this outcome. One was that Korea in 2008 did not have the problem of non-performing assets that needed to deal with through restructuring processes as in the 1997–1998 crisis. Also, policy reactions were more prompt and provided significant resources which stopped the economy's downward spiral during 2008 financial crisis. Also, policy coordination among leading OECD with Asian economies to counter the down turn benefited Korea.

Quarterly growth rates of foreign trade and GDP for Singapore are reported in Table 3. Singapore's trade performance is close to the mean compared with other Asian economies, in both the decline and recovery of growth. Compared with the same period in the previous year pre-crisis, Singapore's real GDP grew by 7.3% (nominal growth rate was 10.6%) in the first quarter of 2008, whereas foreign trade grew by 16.1% (with exports at 11.5% and imports at 21.5%) at the same time. Total trade started to decline in the last quarter of 2008, GDP began to see negative growth and the overall price level shifted to deflation. Overall trade declined by 28% in the first quarter of 2009 and Singapore's real GDP fell by 9.4%. This linkage highlights the pronounced impact of the financial crisis on Singapore as an economy highly dependent on foreign trade.

From the data above, we can also see the collapse of 2009 world trade as reflecting a sharp decline in Asian countries' foreign trade in general. For instance, China's foreign trade halted a trend of export expansion in place since 1999. As a result, China's exports dropped by 26% in May 2009 and imports dropped by 43% in January 2009, compared with the same months in 2008. Also, China's share of

Table 3. Growth rates of Singapore's export, import and GDP during the financial crisis (compared with corresponding period in the previous year, %).

	08Q1	08Q2	08Q3	08Q4	09Q1	09Q2	09Q3	$09Q4_p$	Jan10	Feb10	Mar10
Export	11.5	13.2	11.4	−12.0	−27.8	−25.4	−20.0	4.9	37.0	19.2	29.3
Import	21.5	21.4	22.2	−7.1	−27.6	−28.4	−22.8	−2.7	28.8	16.4	30.8
Real GDP	7.3	2.8	0.1	−4.2	−9.4	−3.1	0.6	4.0			
Nominal GDP	10.6	5.9	2.5	−5.5	−9.1	−5.8	−1.9	3.6			

Source: Growth rates of trade are authors' calculations based on Statistics Singapore data, GDP data are also taken from Statistics Singapore, http://www.singstat.gov.sg/. Accessed on May 18, 2010.

net global export growth in GDP growth dropped from over 10% between 2000 and 2007 to 0.8% in 2008. In the rebound, in March 2010, China's foreign trade was in deficit by US $7.2 billion, the first since 2004. China's trade balance returned to surplus in April 2010, but with only a US$ 1.7 billion surplus, which is less than 10% of the earlier sum.

This overall Asian performance can also be seen relative to the wider global picture of sharp trade compression in the crisis. The volume of world exports and imports fell by 23% and 24% (in current US$) respectively in 2009 according to the WTO (2010)[1] and along with this went substantial variation in trade performance by region and country. On the export side in 2009, oil exporters in Africa saw an export volume fall of 40% and Russian exports dropped by 36% owing in large part to falling prices of oil and other primary commodities. Exports by Asian and North American economies fell less than the global average level with drops of 18% and 21% respectively.

Asian export performance shows China and ASEAN dropped by only 16% and 18% respectively, which accounts for 56.5% of total Asian exports. Exports from Korea even increased by 1% in 2009, whereas those of Japan fell by 28%. These fell more than the world average. On the import side, imports of Africa, Middle East and Asia fell by less than the world average by 16%, 18% and 21% respectively. Imports by Korea and Malaysia dropped by 12% and 17%, which were smaller than world import drops in percentage terms. Imports by Japan and Taiwan fell by 28%, and those of ASEAN and India fell by 23% and 21% in 2009, which contributed significantly to the decline of Asian imports.

The slightly smaller drop of Asian imports than world imports mainly reflects China's imports (which account for about a third of Asian imports) which only fell by 11%. Also, China's Southern trade has grown significantly faster than its Northern trade in the past decade (Wang and Whalley, 2010), and so the smaller compression in trade by Africa, Asia (except Japan) and Latin America partly explains the trade performance of China.

Though Asian trade performance was relatively good for the year 2009, it was affected more severely during the initial impact of the current crisis. Global trade volumes fell by 17.5% between September 2008 and January 2009 in an episode now termed the "Great Trade Collapse" (Gregory *et al.*, 2010, p. 4), and trade volumes of Taiwan and Japan fell by 50% and 46% respectively. Even the trade of Korea and China, good trade performers during the crisis, fell by 29% and 42% respectively during the same period. Trade in India and Malaysia also fell by over 33% during the same period.

[1] WTO press release No. 598, World Trade 2009, Prospects For 2010: Trade to Expand by 9.5% in 2010 after a Dismal 2009, March 26, 2010.

The constant US$ world trade volume reduction of 12% in 2009 is larger than those on the three other occasions (this has happened since 1965 –0.2% in 2001, –2% in 1982, and –7% in 1975). Japan's export fell the most by 24.9% and was over twice the world average level. World GDP declined by 2.3% in 2009. GDP of the Commonwealth of Independent States (CIS), Japan and the EU(27) fell by 7.1%, 5%, and 4.2% respectively, whereas GDP growth in Africa, the Middle East and Asia remained positive at 1.6%, 1.0% and 0.1% respectively, and China grew by 8.5% in 2009.

According to the WTO (2010)[2] the value of world merchandise trade increased by around 25% in the first quarter of 2010 over the same period in 2009, with global exports rising by 27% and imports rising by 24%.

Why trade compression occurred at such a greater rate than GDP growth during the crises, especially in the early stages, and why the rebound also occurred at an equally high rate, is a puzzle that has been noted by others (Baldwin, 2009), but remains largely unexplained. As we note later, in the 1930s, rates of trade compression also exceeded compression rates for GDP, but persisted for much longer.

3 The Bilateral Trade Performance of Asian Economies in the Crisis

Next, we assess the bilateral trade performance of individual Asian countries with four major trading partners, the US, China, the EU and ASEAN. Growth rates of trade between the US and Asian countries are reported in Table 4.

These data indicate that Japan's exports to the US started declining as early as February 2008, and declined the most in the first quarter of 2009, producing less than half the reported exports for the same period in 2008. Asian countries' exports to the US all fell sharply from January 2009 to August 2009, with monthly declines of 23.9% for China, 58.4% for Japan, 28.2% for Korea, and over 30% for other countries. Thailand and China's exports to the US rebounded at the end of 2009, and followed other countries with a significant rebound in 2010. On the import side, the imports by India, Korea, Thailand and Taiwan of US products declined more than their exports to the US, with monthly declines of 46.3%, 44.4%, 41.7% and 65.2% respectively. China's exports to and imports from the US are similar in trend, but imports show a stronger rebound in 2010 than exports, which contributed to China's trade deficit in March 2010. Similar to exports, the most severe decline in imports occurred in the first quarter of 2009.

[2]WTO press release No. 604, First Quarter of 2010 Sees Trade Value Rise by about 25%, June 2, 2010.

Table 4. Growth rates of US trade with key Asian economies during the financial crisis (compared with same month in the previous year, %).

	Exports to US							Imports from US						
	CN	IN	JP	KR	MY	TH	CT	CN	IN	JP	KR	MY	TH	CT
08 May	17.6	9.5	−9.4	−3.1	2.8	6.3	−3.7	29.2	−6.3	−8.2	11.7	−4.3	18.1	−0.6
08 Jun	8.0	16.5	−15.4	9.6	−2.0	5.8	−2.6	15.8	74.3	11.1	2.8	19.5	28.8	7.8
08 Jul	15.2	21.1	−11.4	9.3	6.9	22.8	−6.2	20.1	−46.3	−3.5	19.9	13.6	40.6	−7.2
08 Aug	14.9	31.8	−21.8	1.0	−18.6	8.2	11.6	10.9	0.9	6.2	0.8	30.0	−2.2	10.5
08 Sep	15.4	6.1	−10.9	19.3	−15.2	11.2	4.7	22.2	−16.1	10.5	28.6	8.4	37.0	−3.1
08 Oct	13.1	−5.9	−19.5	5.0	−21.4	−0.7	−11.4	11.9	20.7	−11.1	−1.1	0.8	18.9	−17.6
08 Nov	−6.1	−13.8	−33.8	−14.3	−14.2	−16.3	−14.2	−4.4	−18.6	−17.7	−23.8	−0.4	31.2	−23.4
08 Dec	−4.5	7.4	−36.9	−9.4	−27.0	−19.3	−23.5	7.0	−28.1	−20.5	−21.0	−14.3	−26.7	−50.2
09 Jan	−9.8	−15.9	−52.9	−28.1	−33.1	−27.8	−26.5	−29.9	−17.2	−35.0	−44.4	−18.7	−41.7	−65.2
09 Feb	−23.9	−15.9	−58.4	−18.3	−31.2	−24.9	−24.7	−10.6	−45.5	−36.0	−32.3	−21.1	−35.6	−33.2
09 Mar	−12.6	−31.1	−51.4	−28.2	−28.9	−28.4	−22.1	−12.7	−5.4	−27.1	−39.9	−23.2	−30.4	−56.4
09 Apr	−17.6	−33.2	−46.3	−22.8	−37.7	−28.7	−33.7	−15.7	−21.1	−29.2	−36.8	−21.5	−22.6	−51.7
09 May	−21.2	−25.6	−45.4	−24.0	−37.3	−30.0	−28.0	−17.1	−20.7	−40.1	−32.7	−8.5	−34.7	−38.0
09 Jun	−16.6	−20.7	−38.5	−22.2	−30.5	−22.7	−29.0	−6.5	−11.6	−37.7	−25.8	−23.1	−23.6	−38.2
09 Jul	−14.1	−32.7	−39.5	−20.7	−33.3	−20.8	−28.7	−12.4	−39.1	−34.8	−30.9	−3.6	−27.5	−33.2
09 Aug	−21.8	−30.1	−34.4	−11.4	−21.3	−23.1	−34.4	−3.7	−30.8	−38.3	−26.2	−16.2	−24.0	−38.6
09 Sep	−14.3	−7.9	−33.9	−11.7	−33.9	−13.9	−28.2	−2.9	−38.4	−34.2	−11.6	−25.0	−22.2	−20.5
09 Oct	−9.9		−27.6	−28.1	−2.2	−2.5	−16.5	−0.3		−27.5	−17.6	−11.0	−32.6	0.5
09 Nov	−1.7		−7.9	−0.4	−14.3	4.6	−5.8	16.7		−19.7	9.6	−1.1	−25.5	25.1

(Continued)

Table 4. *(Continued)*

	Exports to US							Imports from US						
	CN	**IN**	**JP**	**KR**	**MY**	**TH**	**CT**	**CN**	**IN**	**JP**	**KR**	**MY**	**TH**	**CT**
09 Dec	15.9		–7.6	–3.8	–13.8	13.3	3.9	41.3		–9.4	15.8	17.5	11.6	51.7
10 Jan	8.3		24.2	16.4	2.9	15.9	13.5	56.6		7.8	54.6	11.2	30.3	130.0
10 Feb	39.2		50.5	24.4	0.9	19.3		19.0		7.3	45.2	24.0	36.0	
10 Mar	19.1		29.5					30.8		2.6				

Note: CN — China, IN — India, JP — Japan, KR — Korea, MY — Malaysia, TH — Thailand, CT — Chinese Taiwan.

Source: Authors' calculations. China Customs Statistics, Indian DGCIS (Kolkata), Trade Statistics of Japan, Korea Customs Statistics, Malaysian Official Portal of Ministry of International Trade and Industry figures, Bank of Thailand, Bureau of Foreign Trade of Taiwan.

The picture is thus of sharper than average declines in US trade with some Asian countries (Japan and Korea), and smaller declines with other countries (China).

The growth rates of other Asian countries' trade with China during the crisis are reported in Table 5. Exports by India, Korea, Thailand and Taiwan to China fell sharply in the last quarter of 2008, and declined more than exports to the US in percentage terms. Japan's exports to China declined less than those to the US during the crisis, which is slightly better than Japan's total export performance. All countries' exports to China rebounded strongly from the end of 2009. These countries' imports from China fell sharply in the first quarter of 2009, lagged a couple of months more than exports to China, and started to rebound from the end of 2009, almost synchronously with exports. The rebound speed for imports is significantly lower than that for exports, which indicates that China's large market for foreign goods contributed to the recovery of neighbouring trade.

Growth rates of trading by China, India, Japan and Thailand with the EU are reported in Table 6. China's and India's trade with the EU grew rapidly on both the export and import side. Also, imports by Thailand of EU products increased faster before the financial crisis. The trade of China, India and Thailand with the EU began to fall from the end of 2008 (imports of Thailand from the EU fell from January 2009) and declined sharply during the first half of 2009. From the end of 2009, trade between China and the EU showed a strong rebound. Similar to trade with the US, Japan's trade with the EU shrank the most among the Asian economies during the financial crisis. Exports by Japan to the EU grew by 10.6% in January 2008; then the growth abated gradually before turning negative from April 2008 onwards. Growth rates of imports by Japan from the EU fluctuated between −10% and 6% during the first nine months, then declined sharply and continuously for 16 months.

The growth rates of trade involving China, India, Japan and Thailand with ASEAN are reported in Table 7. The trade of Japan with ASEAN grew most slowly before the crisis. The proportional decline in exports by India and Japan to ASEAN was approximately the same during the crisis. Exports by India to ASEAN grew at a high rate during the first half of 2008, with a growth rate of 142.5% in June 2008, but started declining sharply from October 2008 onwards. Imports by India from ASEAN grew most rapidly before the crisis and fell the least during the crisis among these countries. The trade of Thailand with other ASEAN countries grew the second most rapidly before the crisis, and dropped less than Japan and India on the export side and less than Japan and China on the import side.

Quarterly growth rates of trade between Singapore and its major partners are reported in Table 8. On the export side, Singapore's exports to China dropped

Table 5. Growth rates of China' trade with key Asian economies during the financial crisis (compared with same month in the previous year, %).

	Exports to China						Imports from China					
	IN	JP	KR	MY	TH	CT	IN	JP	KR	MY	TH	CT
08 May	38.5	12.1	35.3	96.3	13.1	38.1	60.0	−3.9	31.2	−14.8	21.9	23.1
08 Jun	31.2	4.8	33.1	36.3	21.4	49.7	39.9	0.3	33.9	−2.4	31.7	27.4
08 Jul	41.7	16.4	30.1	74.1	37.8	16.4	49.2	5.2	44.1	10.8	50.8	13.7
08 Aug	15.8	8.6	19.3	30.0	1.9	24.2	31.7	−4.6	37.3	−0.8	18.9	35.8
08 Sep	−23.5	1.6	15.0	14.6	6.7	−13.9	45.1	16.1	47.2	4.3	35.8	10.4
08 Oct	−51.8	−1.0	−3.5	−8.6	4.3	−19.7	−2.6	2.8	8.4	1.5	14.2	−2.0
08 Nov	−64.5	−24.5	−33.3	−26.5	−36.5	−42.1	−3.6	−12.0	−14.2	−7.1	−2.1	−9.4
08 Dec	−6.9	−35.5	−35.4	−29.2	−40.1	−57.1	17.0	−12.4	−22.6	−26.4	−10.8	−31.5
09 Jan	−26.7	−45.2	−38.6	−33.7	−40.1	−63.5	−13.6	−16.2	−35.0	−23.5	−26.2	−51.6
09 Feb	−31.1	−39.7	−13.6	7.8	−30.4	−32.6	−15.0	−40.8	−30.8	−29.7	−40.4	−22.0
09 Mar	−40.8	−31.6	−22.4	23.6	−14.2	−44.7	−15.8	−20.6	−29.8	−15.4	−24.6	−33.2
09 Apr	−27.3	−26.0	−19.2	−9.0	−13.4	−34.6	−27.6	−21.7	−39.2	−24.4	−20.5	−39.2
09 May	−41.3	−29.7	−25.6	−28.0	−11.0	−32.4	−32.7	−31.9	−42.1	−0.8	−30.7	−39.2
09 Jun	−21.7	−23.7	−16.1	−10.1	−3.6	−35.8	−9.4	−26.1	−35.6	−6.8	−27.1	−30.8
09 Jul	−29.6	−26.5	−12.9	−16.1	−21.6	−21.5	−22.0	−26.5	−39.0	−14.2	−30.3	−31.4
09 Aug	−5.0	−27.6	−10.3	−9.6	1.2	−18.6	−12.2	−23.3	−37.5	−14.9	−15.8	−31.6
09 Sep	12.8	−13.9	3.4	19.2	4.5	2.1	−20.6	−24.5	−30.9	−12.7	−13.6	−7.8
09 Oct		−14.4	9.5	46.4	2.1	10.5		−26.5	−25.4	−12.8	5.5	−6.1
09 Nov		7.8	54.1	56.2	77.1	56.0		−11.1	−3.9	21.1	20.2	23.0
09 Dec		42.7	93.1	103.9	117.6	96.5		−5.8	20.9	28.8	40.8	42.4
10 Jan		80.0	98.2	136.8	94.3	187.8		−2.3	19.3	19.2	42.5	100.5
10 Feb		47.6	43.1	39.8	75.7			54.5	31.6	32.7	97.8	
10 Mar		47.5						5.5				

Note: IN — India, JP — Japan, KR — Korea, MY — Malaysia, TH — Thailand, CT — Chinese Taiwan.

Source: Authors' calculations. Indian DGCIS (Kolkata), Trade Statistics of Japan, Korean Customs Statistics, Malaysian Official Portal of Ministry of International Trade and Industry, Bank of Thailand, Bureau of Foreign Trade of Taiwan.

Table 6. Growth rates of EU's trade with key Asian economies during the financial crisis (compared with same month in the previous year, %).

	Exports to EU				Imports from EU			
	CN	IN	JP	TH	CN	IN	JP	TH
08 May	35.1	58.4	−1.1	14.2	43.6	14.5	−7.9	26.3
08 Jun	25.3	37.2	−11.2	6.6	31.3	42.2	1.5	6.7
08 Jul	27.6	29.2	4.1	19.2	33.0	16.9	−6.2	43.4
08 Aug	21.9	28.1	−3.5	8.4	18.2	50.0	−7.9	13.0
08 Sep	20.9	19.1	−9.0	13.2	17.0	68.9	5.4	31.6
08 Oct	16.0	0.5	−17.2	3.4	21.7	−9.8	−11.6	2.8
08 Nov	−0.4	−16.4	−30.9	−19.8	−8.7	−9.3	−20.7	6.1
08 Dec	−2.9	13.6	−41.8	−17.5	−6.1	−8.7	−16.1	9.9
09 Jan	−17.5	−4.2	−47.4	−27.7	−21.7	6.1	−23.4	−19.2
09 Feb	−30.2	−8.1	−54.7	−29.3	−4.9	−25.0	−29.7	−8.7
09 Mar	−20.2	−23.0	−56.1	−35.3	−17.4	−17.4	−32.8	−29.9
09 Apr	−27.5	−39.6	−45.3	−34.3	−17.2	−32.7	−31.0	−29.4
09 May	−29.2	−36.7	−45.4	−34.8	−18.4	−37.8	−28.7	−24.7
09 Jun	−23.0	−31.6	−41.3	−27.4	2.1	−25.0	−25.9	−16.0
09 Jul	−26.0	−28.2	−45.8	−24.0	−7.4	−23.3	−30.9	−14.9
09 Aug	−26.6	−26.7	−45.9	−29.1	−6.7	−30.0	−24.1	−11.7
09 Sep	−17.4	−16.8	−38.6	−20.4	7.6	−41.4	−23.0	−11.0
09 Oct	−14.9		−29.0	−11.7	−5.4		−21.8	−9.4
09 Nov	−8.0		−16.0	6.0	22.7		−7.9	0.5
09 Dec	10.2		1.4	16.3	27.6		−6.3	−2.6
10 Jan	17.7		11.2	13.2	46.1		−1.4	8.4
10 Feb	60.1		19.7	28.7	21.5		7.3	20.2
10 Mar	24.6		26.7		56.8		13.4	
10 Apr	28.5				40.8			

Note: CN — China, IN — India, JP — Japan, TH — Thailand.

Source: Authors' calculations. China Customs Statistics, Indian DGCIS (Kolkata), Trade Statistics of Japan, Bank of Thailand.

the least during the crisis and rebounded the most. On the import side, imports from the EU grew the fastest in 2008 and declined the least in 2009 among these partners. Exports to the US and imports from Japan fell the most in 2009.

The overall picture from the above is that of a severe impact of the financial crisis on the trade of Asian countries which affected most trading partners.

Table 7. Growth rates of ASEAN's trade with key Asian economies during the financial crisis (compared with same month in the previous year, %).

	Export to ASEAN				Import from ASEAN			
	CN	IN	JP	TH	CN	IN	JP	TH
08 May	28.4	99.9	11.9	37.5	31.2	60.0	−2.8	0.5
08 Jun	14.6	142.5	6.2	63.2	19.3	39.9	13.2	38.1
08 Jul	30.8	101.2	18.0	70.1	26.9	49.2	7.1	31.9
08 Aug	27.3	30.7	11.0	15.6	8.8	31.7	17.8	9.1
08 Sep	24.2	29.1	5.7	32.4	2.7	45.1	25.9	25.7
08 Oct	21.9	−12.8	3.7	−3.2	0.2	−2.6	10.9	10.2
08 Nov	−2.6	−30.7	−16.0	−28.1	−25.4	−3.6	−9.5	−17.4
08 Dec	−11.8	−28.2	−28.3	−21.3	−31.8	17.0	−14.7	−2.4
09 Jan	−22.0	29.3	−41.4	−35.8	−49.7	−13.6	−29.6	−22.9
09 Feb	−27.7	−35.6	−52.0	−27.6	−26.3	−15.0	−40.9	−35.2
09 Mar	−18.1	−46.8	−43.8	−31.2	−25.5	−15.8	−36.7	−18.0
09 Apr	−20.2	−8.5	−40.8	−30.8	−26.1	−27.6	−34.1	−39.0
09 May	−15.5	−40.6	−40.7	−31.0	−27.1	−32.7	−42.0	−15.5
09 Jun	−14.5	−45.0	−32.6	−36.5	−13.0	−9.4	−38.4	−26.1
09 Jul	−17.4	−26.4	−30.9	−29.2	−12.8	−22.0	−37.1	−21.7
09 Aug	−12.7	−32.0	−30.8	−17.6	−15.6	−12.2	−38.9	−22.2
09 Sep	1.2	−6.4	−24.7	−16.7	1.7	−20.6	−37.8	−10.3
09 Oct	−1.9		−20.4	−2.6	2.6		−37.0	−3.3
09 Nov	20.8		−4.5	22.5	45.1		−20.7	6.0
09 Dec	50.1		17.0	44.3	78.8		−12.6	30.5
10 Jan	52.8		55.9	64.3	118.7		9.9	24.4
10 Feb	53.1		73.4	65.3	51.1		21.1	
10 Mar	36.8		63.5		72.1		24.0	
10 Apr	42.6				61.5			

Note: CN — China, IN — India, JP — Japan, TH — Thailand.

Source: Authors' calculations. China Customs Statistics, Indian DGCIS (Kolkata), Trade Statistics of Japan, Bank of Thailand.

The most severe impact caused by the recession has seemingly been on US imports from Japan and China, but from the end of 2009, the trade of all these Asian economies shows a rebound, and the strongest rebound occurs in trade between ASEAN and China, which suggests the importance of geography in trade recovery.

Table 8. Growth rates of Singapore's trade with major partners during the financial crisis (compared with corresponding quarter in the previous year, %).

	Exports					Imports				
	CN	ID	JP	US	EU	CN	ID	JP	US	EU
08Q1	−1.0	15.8	18.3	−11.5	0.4	0.6	13.7	17.5	8.9	29.0
08Q2	10.5	27.8	17.2	−14.8	11.1	−3.8	13.4	19.3	9.2	17.8
08Q3	10.9	28.0	5.6	−17.7	3.5	11.7	24.3	16.6	14.3	18.2
08Q4	−17.6	−14.3	−6.3	−17.6	−10.6	−11.7	−1.6	−1.0	2.3	−8.6
09Q1	−24.1	−28.0	−32.1	−39.1	−26.1	−29.3	−9.9	−35.8	−19.7	−19.9
09Q2	−21.8	−34.3	−34.9	−27.1	−32.2	−23.7	−31.2	−33.4	−29.5	−14.6
09Q3	−20.1	−28.8	−19.9	−19.5	−27.6	−25.6	−28.2	−26.8	−22.1	−12.4
09Q4	20.7	−3.0	−6.8	−6.2	−5.8	−3.9	7.5	−5.9	−14.7	5.4

Note: CN — China, ID — Indonesia, JP — Japan, US — United States, EU — European Union.

Source: Authors' calculations based on data from Statistics Singapore, http://www.singstat.gov.sg/.

4 Comparing the Trade Performance of Asian Economies by Major Product Group and Type of Trade

We next turn to the trade performance of major export product groups involving Asian countries during and following the crisis as well as look at type of trade (processing/non-processing) and type of enterprise in China's case. Data are presented in Tables 9–15. Performance in terms of total trade varies by country and type of trade, but more by product group than by trade type.

In Table 9, growth rates for China's export of manufactured goods are almost the same as for China's total exports, since manufacture accounts for over 90% of China's total exports. Japan's exports of manufactures increased slowly during the first half of 2008, but experienced a sharp decline with a fall of more than 35% for 10 consecutive months. They showed a rapid rebound in 2010. Korean exports of manufactures grew considerably during the whole of 2008, then experienced a slight recession in the first half of 2009 before resuming growth, interrupted intermittently by months of negative growth. India and Thailand both experienced fast expansion of export of manufactures before October 2008, which then fell sharply as the crisis hit. The rapid growth of India's trade before the crisis and its sharp decline during the crisis suggest an inverted relationship.

For textile, yarns and clothing, exports by India grew faster than for China and Thailand pre-crisis, but fell more sharply during the crisis. Exports by China declined the least. For exports of electronics, Japan and Korea show a different picture. As with other product groups, Japan's exports of electronics declined first

Table 9. Export growth rates of key Asian economies by major product group during and following the crisis (compared with same month in the previous year, %).

	Manufactures					Textile, Yard, Clothing and related					Electronics				
	CN	IN	JP	KR	TH	CN	IN	JP	KR	TH	CN	IN	JP	KR	TH
08 May	27.4	57.5	1.9	34.2	24.8	10.7	14.0	7.0	11.5	4.8	38.1	37.5	2.3	32.5	5.7
08 Jun	15.9	56.4	−3.9	21.7	28.9	−2.2	22.3	−2.7	3.4	−1.6	31.0	65.7	−4.6	21.1	8.5
08 Jul	25.7	46.4	6.1	42.1	42.6	9.4	12.4	3.4	23.9	15.3	34.9	46.6	2.2	21.7	13.5
08 Aug	20.3	40.4	−1.9	25.2	13.6	4.2	1.1	−0.7	5.6	−2.8	26.4	63.9	−4.9	8.6	1.4
08 Sep	20.4	32.4	0.3	46.2	17.9	4.0	−3.1	0.7	29.6	4.0	29.7	51.6	−5.7	30.2	9.9
08 Oct	18.9	5.5	−8.6	46.9	1.8	14.2	−8.4	−7.7	41.7	2.6	19.1	40.4	−10.6	26.1	−5.9
08 Nov	−2.3	−2.7	−27.0	21.5	−20.1	4.2	−23.9	−26.0	19.4	−14.4	22.4	27.6	−29.8	−0.7	−24.2
08 Dec	−3.2	19.2	−35.4	25.9	−12.6	12.3	−4.2	−40.3	34.4	−5.8	17.3	6.6	−39.5	−5.2	−28.8
09 Jan	−17.4	0.4	−45.8	−7.7	−25.1	1.0	−24.5	−44.9	−2.5	−10.9	−4.6	0.2	−47.3	−12.9	−37.7
09 Feb	−25.9	−13.2	−49.7	22.7	−10.0	−33.1	−23.6	−45.1	22.2	−15.0	−9.9	17.2	−49.9	15.8	−33.8
09 Mar	−17.1	−17.0	−45.8	21.4	−22.2	3.5	−19.1	−41.4	21.6	−15.2	−26.9	12.6	−43.9	10.7	−28.5
09 Apr	−22.5	−31.0	−39.3	12.5	−24.8	−11.4	−32.5	−31.6	15.4	−17.4	−24.6	−20.3	−33.9	10.7	−22.8
09 May	−25.9	−35.1	−40.6	−8.5	−25.7	−14.2	−23.5	−37.8	−8.8	−19.8	−21.2	−32.6	−36.2	1.7	−24.8
09 Jun	−20.6	−24.8	−35.5	10.8	−25.1	−9.7	−11.1	−25.8	7.0	−12.9	−23.8	−29.8	−31.6	6.5	−20.4
09 Jul	−22.5	−23.0	−36.1	2.4	−24.0	−12.0	−7.9	−20.5	4.2	−9.4	−23.8	−35.9	−30.8	9.0	−12.7
09 Aug	−23.0	−25.8	−35.3	−1.6	−16.3	−14.6	−6.9	−19.4	−2.6	−18.1	−19.3	−35.7	−30.7	9.1	−12.3
09 Sep	−14.8	−12.8	−30.7	4.2	−6.6	−6.6	−6.7	−13.9	7.3	−13.7	−18.5	−39.7	−27.7	4.3	−8.5
09 Oct			−23.0	−14.5	−2.0			−0.8	−22.0	−8.2	−18.4	−41.9	−21.4	−11.4	4.1
09 Nov			−6.2	0.1	14.9			18.6	−10.4	−3.3	−7.9	−24.0	−5.1	11.8	24.8
09 Dec			11.9	10.3	21.9			49.4	−1.6	9.4			18.9	32.6	34.7
10 Jan			40.7	25.2	27.5			74.4	12.1	5.6			48.7	27.7	51.3
10 Feb			45.7	7.2	21.3			73.8	−4.6	12.5			45.9	5.0	50.9
10 Mar			44.3					69.6					42.9		

Note: CN — China, IN — India, JP — Japan, KR — Korea, TH — Thailand.

Source: Authors' calculations. China Customs Statistics, Indian DGCIS (Kolkata), Trade Statistics of Japan, Korean Customs Statistics, Bank of Thailand.

Table 10. Import growth rates of key Asian economies by major product group during and following the crisis (compared with same month in the previous year, %).

	Oil					Minerals (Exclude Oil)					Base metals				
	CN	IN	JP	KR	TH	CN	IN	JP	KR	TH	CN	IN	JP	KR	TH
08 May	106.0	84.8	46.8	72.5	2.1	85.4	232.0	−22.2	35.8	53.3	17.5	22.4	−4.4	52.2	29.2
08 Jun	92.6	71.8	51.7	90.6	70.3	73.3	241.5	5.6	25.1	96.9	2.8	9.8	5.0	44.6	51.9
08 Jul	88.9	126.3	68.7	113.5	98.9	74.6	55.3	−13.4	58.6	173.4	17.7	30.9	11.2	80.5	82.6
08 Aug	106.4	85.8	62.7	104.3	44.3	70.9	77.3	4.4	31.0	39.7	7.2	11.9	4.2	68.1	36.0
08 Sep	72.3	64.8	62.3	99.7	40.5	67.7	72.4	15.9	77.7	60.4	13.4	46.5	24.2	115.4	72.4
08 Oct	58.4	11.7	23.2	72.0	24.1	41.0	−21.7	3.8	89.3	85.5	13.1	48.3	6.5	61.6	47.9
08 Nov	−15.1	−8.2	−34.8	44.4	−14.3	−11.6	−19.8	−8.8	60.0	21.8	−21.7	8.6	−11.0	39.1	0.1
08 Dec	−31.9	−32.9	−52.2	20.8	3.7	−27.1	1.2	−18.3	37.2	16.9	−19.0	4.7	−18.2	20.2	0.6
09 Jan	−56.4	−46.8	−64.5	6.5	−53.9	−51.0	−41.0	−32.8	−5.9	−37.4	−42.2	−5.7	−29.6	−10.0	−45.8
09 Feb	−54.8	−49.8	−65.0	−1.7	−58.5	−38.9	−45.1	−47.1	−0.3	−65.2	−18.1	−19.4	−52.4	−16.3	−55.9
09 Mar	−54.0	−54.0	−64.7	−11.7	−42.0	−37.9	−53.8	−48.1	−8.8	−27.4	−14.8	−23.8	−49.5	−4.5	−51.7
09 Apr	−45.5	−46.9	−58.1	−25.5	−56.1	−33.3	−82.2	−43.0	40.8	118.3	−1.7	−36.8	−59.6	−29.7	−47.5
09 May	−49.9	−49.5	−62.7	−42.0	−28.8	−38.0	−77.7	−39.5	−6.9	146.8	4.0	−35.9	−64.6	−42.8	−56.9
09 Jun	−45.3	−34.8	−63.4	−38.9	−32.9	−29.5	−70.7	−54.3	1.8	−47.2	27.8	−13.5	−62.6	−35.0	−60.1
09 Jul	−34.5	−42.5	−58.2	−37.6	−45.8	−24.0	−28.2	−37.4	−18.7	−53.4	9.3	−25.7	−59.7	−40.7	−58.1
09 Aug	−44.1	−39.9	−60.8	−33.2	−51.3	−32.4	−48.6	−34.8	−14.0	−40.8	7.8	−10.9	−56.0	−39.8	−48.2
09 Sep	−27.6	−31.5	−50.0	−32.8	0.4	−17.2	−50.7	−46.3	−24.8	−20.6	21.6	−33.7	−54.6	−32.5	−38.2
09 Oct	−18.6		−51.2	−21.7	−21.2			−42.8	−16.2	−38.6			−50.0	−33.1	−24.3
09 Nov	25.5		−8.7	−26.5	4.0			−26.6	−23.2	−1.0			−32.5	−21.6	1.6
09 Dec	90.6		28.9	−2.7	18.2			−6.4	−6.4	19.2			−30.7	−1.7	21.9
10 Jan	116.4		82.7	1.6	55.7			21.6	26.7	53.0			−6.8	4.8	56.6
10 Feb	133.5		71.9	13.8	50.7			36.6	29.0	149.7			39.2	20.2	128.7
10 Mar			68.9					54.9					37.4		

Note: CN — China, IN — India, JP — Japan, KR — Korea, TH — Thailand.

Source: Authors' calculations. China Customs Statistics, Indian DGCIS (Kolkata), Trade Statistics of Japan, Korean Customs Statistics, Bank of Thailand.

Table 11. Growth rates of Singapore's trade by major product group during the financial crisis (over corresponding period in the previous year, %).

	Export					Import					
	Oil	Chemicals	Manufactures	Machinery and equipments	Electrics	Oil	Crude materials*	Chemicals	Manufactures	Iron and steel	Electronic components and parts
08Q1	52.6	–4.8	2.2	3.4	2.7	4.0	29.0	7.7	13.0	20.2	0.9
08Q2	53.4	–6.5	15.8	1.7	2.3	–3.8	12.0	–2.4	16.8	16.5	–2.7
08Q3	77.4	–9.3	4.6	–1.6	–1.0	16.0	20.9	9.3	21.1	73.9	–1.2
08Q4	–10.0	–30.8	–13.5	–11.0	–17.3	18.8	13.8	–16.3	5.1	25.2	–19.5
09Q1	–43.1	–24.4	–22.3	–27.4	–30.1	0.6	7.6	–32.8	–19.3	–29.6	–33.4
09Q2	–46.3	–9.9	–25.8	–20.8	–16.7	0.1	19.9	–15.7	–30.2	–45.5	–21.2
09Q3	–41.5	–2.9	–27.9	–15.3	–12.1	–1.9	2.9	–9.2	–31.8	–51.7	–15.2
09Q4	6.9	31.6	–21.6	–0.1	11.8	–4.2	–2.4	22.5	–19.1	–36.4	1.3

Source: Authors' calculations based on data from Statistics Singapore, http://www.singstat.gov.sg/.

Table 12. Proportion of non-processing and processing trade for China during and after the 2008 financial crisis (%).

	Exports				Imports			
Item	Non-processing trade		Processing trade		Non-processing trade		Processing trade	
Time	Y2008	Y2009	Y2008	Y2009	Y2008	Y2009	Y2008	Y2009
Jan	47.3	50.7	47.3	42.8	50.6	53.4	33.3	30.2
Feb	43.3	39.3	51.5	53.3	49.9	52.6	34.5	31.8
Mar	43.1	44.6	51.3	48.3	51.2	53.7	32.8	31.1
Apr	46.0	45.3	48.0	47.6	51.2	54.2	33.0	31.0
May	47.1	45.3	46.8	47.9	52.5	53.7	32.7	31.8
Jun	47.9	43.7	46.1	49.4	51.3	54.0	32.7	30.2
Jul	48.5	44.7	45.2	48.2	51.7	54.6	32.0	31.3
Aug	48.6	44.2	45.2	48.7	50.7	53.4	32.6	33.0
Sep	46.1	43.6	47.2	49.2	50.0	52.6	33.9	32.8
Oct	44.5	41.5	48.5	51.6	48.0	51.4	36.1	34.5
Nov	44.3	42.1	48.5	51.1	48.6	50.8	35.3	34.3
Dec	48.4	44.0	43.7	48.5	49.7	52.8	33.0	31.8

Note: Processing trade includes processing supplied materials and assembly of supplied parts, imported materials, and exported materials (outward processing). Non-processing trade is total trade apart from processing trade and special trade. Special trade includes materials for aid and donation, compensation trade, consignment trade, petty trade in the border areas, equipments imported for processing trade, export of goods for foreign contracted projects, leasing trade, imported equipment used as investment by foreign funded enterprises, barter transaction, duty-free commodities on payment of foreign currency; inbound and outbound goods in bonded warehouses, merchandise for transit in bonded warehouses, equipment imported in the export processing zones, etc. The total special trade is insignificant.

Source: Authors' calculations based on China Customs Statistics.

and sharply during the crisis, whereas Korean exports only declined slightly in the three months pre- and post-crisis. For Korea and China, this difference reflects the less severe impact of the crisis on the competitiveness of Korean exports.

Table 10 reports Asian countries' imports during the crisis, reporting growth rates of imports by product group. These data reflect the situation of the real, underlying, economies. For oil, imports by these countries all grew rapidly before October 2008, then fell sharply (except for Korea). The global oil price fluctuations influenced all of these countries' trade, the smaller decline in Korean demand for oil reflecting a weaker impact of the crisis on the Korean economy.

For trade in other minerals, India experienced the most rapid growth pre-crisis and the sharpest decline during the crisis. For base metals and related products, Korean imports grew the most rapidly in 2008 and fell sharply in 2009, whereas

Table 13. Growth rates of China's non-processing and processing trade pre- and post-crisis (compared with the same month in the previous year, %).

Item	Exports				Imports			
	Non-processing trade		Processing trade		Non-processing trade		Processing trade	
Time	Y2008	Y2009	Y2008	Y2009	Y2008	Y2009	Y2008	Y2009
Jan	33.1	−11.7	18.3	−25.4	42.0	−39.9	11.7	−48.3
Feb	0.6	−32.6	9.6	−23.1	57.2	−19.5	15.7	−29.7
Mar	48.9	−14.2	16.0	−22.0	42.0	−21.3	11.1	−28.9
Apr	22.3	−23.8	18.0	−23.2	40.2	−18.3	13.6	−27.5
May	29.8	−29.2	23.6	−24.7	66.8	−23.3	17.3	−27.0
Jun	18.2	−28.1	14.5	−15.6	48.4	−8.6	13.4	−19.8
Jul	31.8	−28.9	20.9	−17.7	55.7	−10.0	12.1	−16.9
Aug	31.2	−30.1	10.1	−17.1	40.3	−12.7	2.8	−16.1
Sep	29.5	−19.6	11.0	−11.4	38.8	1.2	3.0	−7.1
Oct	27.1	−19.3	8.5	−8.1	30.6	−0.4	1.8	−11.3
Nov	4.3	−6.0	−11.1	4.3	−13.1	31.9	−25.5	22.8
Dec	6.6	6.9	−15.8	30.2	−17.1	66.0	−29.7	50.9

Note: Processing trade includes processing supplied materials and assembly of supplied parts, imported materials, and exported materials (outward processing). Non-processing trade is total trade, apart from processing trade and special trade. Special trade includes materials for aid and donation, compensation trade, consignment trade, petty trade in the border areas, equipments imported for processing trade, export of goods for foreign contracted projects, leasing trade, imported equipment used as investment by foreign funded enterprises, barter transaction, duty-free commodities on payment of foreign currency; inbound and outbound goods in bonded warehouses, merchandise for transit in bonded warehouses, equipment imported in the export processing zones, etc. The total special trade is insignificant.

Source: Authors' calculations based on China Customs Statistics.

Japan's grew the most slowly pre-crisis and dropped the most post-crisis. China's imports of base metals dropped considerately in the crisis and started to rebound beginning in May 2009, following China's stimulus package. This is almost two quarters (i.e. six months) ahead of the rebound in other countries' imports of base metals.

Quarterly growth rates of Singapore's trade in major product groups are reported in Table 11. On the export side, exports of oil grew fastest pre-crisis and dropped the most in proportion term during the crisis. Exports of chemicals fell first from the beginning of 2008 and showed a strong rebound in the last quarter of 2009. On the import side, imports of iron and steel grew the fastest in 2008, but fell rapidly in 2009. Imports of crude materials (excluding oil) of Singapore saw positive growth in the two years with only a slight drop of 2.4% in the last quarter of 2009.

Table 14. Proportion measured by type of Chinese enterprise during and following the crisis (%).

	Export			Import		
Item	**State-owned**	**Foreign-invested**	**Private**	**State-owned**	**Foreign-invested**	**Private**
08 Mar	17.5	59.1	23.4	31.8	54.1	14.1
08 May	18.6	54.8	26.6	32.5	53.8	13.7
08 Jun	18.3	54.7	26.9	32.5	54.4	13.2
08 Jul	18.9	53.5	27.6	32.3	53.7	14.0
08 Aug	18.5	53.9	27.6	31.9	52.5	15.6
08 Sep	18.1	55.4	26.5	31.3	54.7	14.0
08 Oct	17.0	56.4	26.6	30.2	56.4	13.5
08 Nov	16.6	55.3	28.0	29.2	56.8	13.9
08 Dec	17.6	52.6	29.9	28.0	56.3	15.8
09 Jan	18.4	50.8	30.7	29.2	54.6	16.1
09 Feb	17.5	60.0	22.5	27.9	55.6	16.6
09 Mar	15.7	56.7	27.6	28.9	54.0	17.1
09 Apr	16.5	54.7	28.8	28.8	53.8	17.4
09 May	16.0	55.2	28.9	29.1	53.5	17.4
09 Jun	16.3	55.7	28.0	28.2	54.4	17.4
09 Jul	15.7	55.8	28.6	29.5	53.0	17.4
09 Aug	15.7	55.5	28.8	29.5	53.2	17.3
09 Sep	15.3	56.4	28.3	27.8	54.7	17.5

Source: Authors' calculations based on China Customs Statistics.

To analyse the impact of thc crisis on type of trade, we take China as a more detailed case study and discuss its trade performance in terms of processing and non-processing trade, and also trade by different type of enterprise. The processing trade accounts for a large share of several developing Asian countries including China, India, Vietnam, Malaysia and Indonesia. These countries are all host countries to FDI inflows and the endpoints of manufacturing chains for multinational enterprises. Although foreign-invested companies promote foreign trade for these countries, they also compete with local companies, especially with nationally-owned enterprises in China.

Proportion of China's processing trade and non-processing trade pre- and post-crisis are reported in Table 12 (these sum to a little less than one owing to small amounts of so-called special trade (gifts, for example)). These shares changed relatively little in the crisis. On the export side, shares of processing and non-processing trade were similar pre- and post-crisis, with processing the least at

Table 15. Growth rates of China's trade by type of enterprise during and following the crisis (compared with the same month in the previous year, %).

	Exports			Imports		
Item	**State–owned**	**Foreign–invested**	**Private**	**State–owned**	**Foreign–invested**	**Private**
08 Mar	30.7	21.2	62.6	41.1	15.4	31.8
08 May	21.8	27.9	33.4	61.0	28.4	49.1
08 Jun	12.4	19.6	16.7	49.1	23.4	29.7
08 Jul	23.1	25.0	33.5	47.8	23.5	49.7
08 Aug	21.9	15.7	32.5	39.7	9.2	52.4
08 Sep	29.1	17.2	25.5	41.3	13.0	16.9
08 Oct	15.8	14.3	33.3	31.4	7.7	20.2
08 Nov	−6.2	−8.8	16.2	−14.2	−20.8	−14.6
08 Dec	−4.3	−10.9	17.7	−23.7	−21.9	−12.5
09 Jan	−19.9	−23.2	−4.1	−45.8	−43.4	−35.7
09 Feb	−26.8	−24.7	−27.6	−33.2	−23.0	−3.3
09 Mar	−25.7	−20.5	−2.4	−31.7	−25.0	−9.4
09 Apr	−28.9	−24.5	−14.0	−28.5	−24.9	−1.7
09 May	−36.8	−25.9	−20.0	−32.8	−25.4	−4.8
09 Jun	−30.2	−19.8	−18.1	−24.6	−13.2	14.9
09 Jul	−36.1	−19.5	−20.1	−22.2	−15.9	5.7
09 Aug	−34.9	−20.8	−19.7	−23.4	−15.9	−8.3
09 Sep	−28.1	−13.5	−9.2	−14.6	−3.9	20.5

Source: Authors' calculations based on China Customs Statistics.

43% and non-processing the most at 51% in January 2009. On the import side, non-processing trade was almost half of China's imports with a high of 54% and a low of 48%, whereas processing was over 30% of China's imports, with a high of 36% and a low of 30% during 2008 and 2009. The financial crisis seemingly did not affect China's processing trade pattern greatly.

Table 13 reports growth rates of China's non-processing and processing trade compared with the same month in the previous year. On the export side, China's processing started to fall in November 2008, two months ahead of non-processing trade. Processing trade fell more rapidly than non-processing trade in the first quarter of 2009, and then the situation was reversed. On the import side, non-processing trade grew more quickly than processing trade before November 2008, then processing trade decreased more sharply than non-processing trade for a year. Processing trade then rebounded less strongly than non-processing trade at the end of 2009.

As the majority of FDI inflows into Asian developing countries comes from American and European countries, most processing activities in these countries are completely or partly controlled by developed countries. Goods manufactured by them are mostly shipped back and sold in OECD markets. The trend of China's trade pattern in processing trade is consistent with the general trend in her trade with the US and the EU and reflects the impact of the recession in external markets on China's foreign trade.

We also report changes in China's trade by different types of enterprise during the crisis. Shares of China's trade by type of enterprise are reported in Table 14. Foreign-invested enterprises always account for over half of China's total trade and this did not change markedly during the crisis. Both on the export and import sides, shares of national-owned enterprises decreased slightly and shares of private enterprises increased slightly after the crisis.

Growth rates of China's trade by type of enterprise compared with the same month of the previous year are reported in Table 15. Exports by private enterprises grew the most in 2008 and decreased in 2009, with a two-month lag compared with nationally-owned and foreign-invested enterprises. Imports by nationally-owned enterprises grew the most before November 2008, and declined the fastest after that. Changes in China's processing trade are closely tied to changes in China's trade by type of enterprise.

5 The Trade Compression in Asia During the Financial Crisis, the 1930s and the Asian Financial Crisis

Comparing trade performance with earlier crises is complex and inevitably involves inexact comparisons. For the 1930s, we compare both North American and European trade impacts as well as Asian trade, since in the 1930s Asian trade was insignificant except for Japan (and to a lesser extent China). We use Japan (the worst trade performer among these Asian countries) and China (the average trade performer) for examples of trade in the Great Depression of the 1930s. The annual growth rates of trade are presented in Table 16. China's export and import growth rates declined from 26% and 21% to 17% and 19% between 2007 and 2008, then experienced –16% and –12% negative growth in 2009, respectively. Exports by Japan grew by 11.5% in 2007, then fell slightly in 2008 and sharply by 33% in 2009. Japanese imports reversed a trend of steady growth and declined by 35% in 2009.

The comparison with the 1930s is striking. During the Great Depression, US trade experienced the shortest recession period of all the major economies; three years, far shorter than that of other countries. French trade experienced the longest recession with exports experiencing negative growth each year between 1927 and

Table 16. Comparison of annual growth rates of trade in the 2008 crisis with the 1930s depression (year-on-year, %).

2010's					1930's								
	Exports		Imports			Exports				Imports			
Year	CN	JP	CN	JP	Year	CN	US	GMY	FRC	CN	US	GMY	FRC
2007	25.7	11.5	20.8	8.6	1928	NA	5.4	13.6	−6.5	NA	−2.2	−1.6	0.7
2008	17.2	−3.5	18.5	8.0	1929	NA	2.2	9.0	−2.4	NA	7.5	−4.0	9.0
2009	−16	−33.1	−11.2	−34.8	1930	−11.8	−26.7	−10.5	−12.5	6.4	−30.4	−22.7	−9.8
2010	20.7^{E}	20.5^{E}	18.7^{E}	11.5^{E}	1931	−3.1	−36.9	−18.7	−30.6	16.2	−31.7	−35.3	−19.6
Growth Rate of GDP					1932	−37.8	−33.6	−38.3	−35.3	−23.9	−36.7	−30.6	−29.4
	2007	2008	2009	2010	1933	7.6	4.0	−14.2	−6.3	−11.7	9.6	−9.9	−4.6
CN	13.4	9.0	8.7	9.1^{E}	1934	−12.6	27.3	−14.4	−3.4	−23.4	14.2	5.9	−18.8
JP	2.2	2.0	−0.7	−5.7^{E}	1935	7.7	7.0	1.0	−13.2	−10.8	23.7	−8.3	−9.2

Note: CN — China, JP — Japan, US — United States, GMY — Germany, FRC — France.

Source: Authors' calculations. China's trade between 2007 and 2009 based on China Customs Statistics. China's GDP growth rate is from the Bureau of Statistics of China. Japan GDP growth rates are from the Index of Mundi. Data for China's trade and GDP forecast for 2010 are from, *Analysis and Forecast of China's Economic Situation (Economic Blue Book, Autumn 2010)*. Data for Japan between 2007 and 2009 are based on Trade Statistics of Japan. The forecast for 2010 for Japan is from, *Forecast for the Japanese Economy in Fiscal 2010 and 2011* by Mitsubishi UFJ Research and Consulting. Estimation of Japan trade for 2010 includes trade in service. Data for the US, Germany and France in the Great Depression come from the NBER Macrohistory Database.

1936 and imports falling sharply between 1930 and 1935. On both export and import sides, the trade of the US, Germany, France and China fell sharply during 1930 and 1932. Either because of the magnitude of the drop, or the length of the Depression, the US, Germany, France and China experienced a significantly deeper trade compression in the Great Depression than China and Japan in this financial crisis.

GDP growth rate comparisons for China and Japan pre- and post-financial crisis and in the 1930s are also striking. The average annual GDP growth for China between 2007 and 2009 remained high, whereas Japan's GDP growth rate fell from 2% to –0.7%. During the 1930s, US annual GDP growth rates between 1930 and 1935 were –8.6%, –6.5%, –13.1%, –1.3% and 10.9 respectively (Maddison, 1997), whereas China's GDP growth rates between 1932 and 1936 were 3.68%, –0.72%, –8.64%, 8.30% and 5.87% respectively (Yeh, 1977). Japan's strong growth performance of 3.7% during the Great Depression was higher than China's (average 1.7%) (Maddison, 1997). These data suggest that the impact of the 1930s Depression on real GDP was significantly smaller than that on trade in the Asian countries and trade rebounded more strongly than GDP after the crisis.

We also present quarterly growth rates of Chinese and Japanese trade (compared with the previous quarter). Trade performance during this financial crisis and OECD countries' trade performance during the Great Depression are also reported in Table 17. The trade of Japan and China fell proportionately more in the first quarter of 2009 than for OECD countries in the initial years of the Great Depression, but the trade of Japan and China in the financial crisis shrank less than three quarters before rebounding quickly.

In the 1930s, OECD countries suffered years of decline before recovery; if we compare the proportional decline in individual quarters, the trade of Japan and China fell more in the first quarter of 2009 than OECD countries in the 1930s. Yet, the proportion of decline during the crisis is significantly more than the shrinkage of Chinese and Japanese trade in the 1930s. For the OECD, the fall is smaller. Therefore, the initial impact of the recent financial crisis on the trade of Japan and China is more severe than the impact of the Great Depression, but the duration of the impact is shorter.

We also report data on Asian economies' performance during the Asian financial crisis and make comparisons with trade performance in the crisis. The year-on-year growth rates of exports of Asian economies during the Asian financial crisis are reported in Table 18. Exports by China and Vietnam retained positive growth between 1996 and 2003, whereas others experienced a fall, but at most for two years. The biggest annual proportional trade decline among other Asian economies was 17%, but this is significantly less than exports of Japan, the Philippines and Taiwan in 2009. Thailand and Indonesia, who suffered the severest

Table 17. Quarterly growth rates of trade of China and Japan in the 2008 crisis and OECD economies in the 1930' depression (compared with the previous quarter, %).

	China			Export			Import		
	Exports	**Imports**		**US**	**GMY**	**FRC**	**US**	**GMY**	**FRC**
2008Q1	−10.0	0.5	1929Q1	−9.6	−6.9	−13.3	9.9	−2.4	3.2
2008Q2	17.8	14.6	1929Q2	−15.2	13.6	6.2	3.8	3.2	0.8
2008Q3	13.2	7.4	1929Q3	1.4	0.4	−3.5	−7.8	−3.6	−13.7
2008Q4	−13.1	−26.3	1929Q4	14.5	−0.9	6.9	−3.2	−1.5	8.4
2009Q1	−30.7	−23.7	1930Q1	−19.2	−6.7	−11.0	−14.1	−3.6	−2.5
2009Q2	12.4	31.8	1930Q2	−16.2	−7.7	−6.4	−5.6	−20.1	−8.4
2009Q3	17.7	18.7	1930Q3	−7.4	−1.2	0.9	−21.0	−3.7	−3.4
2009Q4	9.2	2.7	1930Q4	1.6	−1.2	−7.8	−0.9	−7.8	7.4
2010Q1	28.7	64.7	1931Q1	−20.3	−16.6	−17.6	−13.9	−14.7	−11.2
			1931Q2	−14.6	−1.8	−6.7	−5.2	−1.8	−3.5
			1931Q3	−13.3	6.5	−8.5	−5.1	−22.3	−10.7
			1931Q4	10.8	−3.1	−1.6	−7.7	−0.4	−13.1
	Japan		1932Q1	−21.2	−31.8	−24.9	−15.7	−14.7	−16.7
	Exports	**Imports**	1932Q2	−17.0	−13.9	−9.6	−12.2	−8.3	7.1
2008Q1	−5.2	−2.1	1932Q3	−8.8	−3.8	−6.3	−23.0	−7.4	−12.8
2008Q2	−1.0	4.2	1932Q4	21.9	11.2	14.6	14.2	15.4	12.0
2008Q3	5.7	11.2	1933Q1	−22.1	−17.8	−11.3	−10.6	−11.8	1.5
2008Q4	−22.5	−20.2	1933Q2	2.8	−0.2	−3.3	15.6	−6.1	−6.6
2009Q1	−34.4	−31.6	1933Q3	28.4	3.5	2.2	40.0	3.3	−10.8
2009Q2	14.5	−0.8	1933Q4	30.8	2.8	11.0	−7.1	2.8	4.7
2009Q3	12.9	11.9	1934Q1	−7.7	−13.4	−9.7	3.3	6.9	−2.4
2009Q4	8.6	4.4	1934Q2	−3.0	−9.3	−4.7	2.5	0.5	−10.7
2010Q1	2.1	2.6	1934Q3	2.9	1.4	−0.8	−13.4	−8.3	−15.2
			1934Q4	8.9	7.0	11.8	9.1	3.5	8.5

Note: US — United States, GMY — Germany, FRC — France.

Source: Authors' calculations. China's trade between 2007 and 2009 based on China Customs Statistics. China's GDP growth rate is from the Bureau of Statistics of China. Japan GDP growth rates are from the Index of Mundi. Data for China's trade and GDP forecast for 2010 are from, *Analysis and Forecast of China's Economic Situation (Economic Blue Book, Autumn 2010)*. Data for Japan between 2007 and 2009 are based on Trade Statistics of Japan. The forecast for 2010 for Japan is from, *Forecast for the Japanese Economy in Fiscal 2010 and 2011* by Mitsubishi UFJ Research and Consulting. Estimation of Japan trade for 2010 includes trade in service. Data for the US, Germany and France in the Great Depression come from the NBER Macrohistory Database.

Table 18. Export growth rates of key Asian economies before and after the Asian financial crisis (year-on-year, %).

	CN	ID	IN	JP	KR	MY	PH	SG	TH	CT	VN
1996	17.9	5.8	8.0	−6.6	4.1	7.3	17.7	6.7	−1.9	3.7	NA
1997	20.9	12.2	5.8	2.2	6.7	0.7	22.8	0.8	4.1	5.6	26.6
1998	0.5	−10.5	−4.6	−8.6	−4.7	−7.3	16.9	−15.7	−6.9	−9.3	1.9
1999	6.1	1.7	8.2	7.9	9.9	17.0	16.1	6.1	7.6	9.9	23.3
2000	27.9	27.6	17.3	13.8	21.2	17.0	9.1	20.5	19.6	22.8	25.2
2001	6.8	−12.3	3.6	−16.5	−14.0	−10.6	−16.2	−10.8	−7.1	−16.9	4.0
2002	22.4	3.1	14.2	3.1	7.9	6.1	9.9	3.0	4.7	7.1	11.2
2003	34.6	8.4	19.1	13.5	20.7	12.4	2.7	14.9	18.2	11.3	20.6
2009	−16	−15	−4.7*	−33.1	9.8	−15.5	−21.9	−18	−14.2	−20.3	−9.7

Note: CN — China, ID — Indonesia, IN — India, JP — Japan, KR — Korea, MY — Malaysia, PH — Philippines, SG — Singapore, TH — Thailand, CT — Chinese Taiwan, VN — Vietnam.

Source: Authors' calculations. Taiwanese data are based, *on Taiwan Statistics Yearbook 2008*. Others are based on data from World Development Indicators of the World Bank.

recession during the Asian financial crisis, found their exports only declined 6.9% and 4.6% in 1998 respectively, but they dropped about 15% in 2009. Exports of Singapore declined the most among these economies, with a fall of 15.7% in 1998, and exports of Taiwan, Japan and the Philippines fell by over 16% in 2001. Among these economies, only the exports of Korea performed better in 2009 than in the Asian financial crisis. Thus, in general, the impacts of the recent crisis on the exports of the Asian economies are more severe than the impacts of the Asian financial crisis.

The year-on-year growth rates of imports by Asian economies during the Asian financial crisis are reported in Table 19. Except for China, imports kept growing with Vietnam's imports experiencing only a slight decline in 1998. Other countries' imports experienced severe decline during the recent financial crisis. Imports of China, India, Japan, Philippine, Taiwan and Vietnam dropped more in 2009 than in 1998, and imports by Indonesia, Korea, Malaysia and Thailand dropped less in 2009 than in 1998. World oil prices dropped about 40% in 2008, but dropped from US$ 137.1 per barrel in July 2008 to US$ 34.6 per barrel in January 2009, a 75% fall (EIA). Even excluding the impact of the oil price changes, the impact of the financial crisis on Asian imports is still more severe than that of the Asian financial crisis.

Finally, we present data in Table 20 on annual growth rates of key Asian economies before and after the Asian financial crisis and compare them with data

Table 19. Import growth rates of Asian economies before and after the Asian financial crisis (year-on-year, %).

	CN	ID	IN	JP	KR	MY	PH	SG	TH	CT	VN
1996	19.5	8.1	15.4	6.7	12.2	1.8	20.8	6.5	0.8	−1.0	NA
1997	3.7	4.5	4.4	−2.9	−2.2	1.2	14.0	1.2	−13.8	11.7	4.0
1998	0.3	−30.9	−2.0	−18.2	−36.2	−26.5	−18.8	−21.0	−33.7	−8.5	−0.8
1999	15.9	−4.2	1.6	11.4	29.1	13.0	36.2	7.5	17.1	5.7	2.1
2000	35.2	31.9	27.8	22.3	36.2	26.3	7.7	23.0	31.4	26.6	33.2
2001	8.1	−14.1	−2.4	−8.6	−13.4	−10.3	−13.3	−14.2	−2.9	−23.3	3.4
2002	21.3	2.8	6.8	−3.7	7.7	8.1	6.3	2.2	4.5	4.9	22.1
2003	39.8	10.9	24.4	13.6	18.0	5.4	3.1	8.5	17.4	13.0	28.0
2009	−11.2	−25	−8.2*	−34.8	−12.4	−16.6	−24.2	−21	−22.6	−27.5	−14.7

Note: CN — China, ID — Indonesia, IN — India, JP — Japan, KR — Korea, MY — Malaysia, PH — Philippines, SG — Singapore, TH — Thailand, CT — Chinese Taiwan, VN — Vietnam.

Source: Authors' calculations. Data for Taiwan are based on, *Taiwan Statistics Yearbook 2008*. Others are based on from World Development Indicators of the World Bank.

Table 20. Real GDP growth rates of Asian economies pre- and post-financial crises (year-on-year, %).

	CN	ID	IN	JP	KR	MY	PH	SG	TH	CT	VN
1996	10.0	7.8	7.4	2.7	7.0	10.0	5.8	8.2	5.9	6.3	9.3
1997	9.3	4.7	4.5	1.6	4.7	7.3	5.2	8.3	−1.4	6.6	8.2
1998	7.8	−13.1	6.0	−2.0	−6.9	−7.4	−0.6	−1.4	−10.5	4.5	5.8
1999	7.6	0.8	7.1	−0.1	9.5	6.1	3.4	7.2	4.4	5.7	4.8
2000	8.4	4.9	4.0	2.9	8.5	8.9	6.0	10.1	4.8	5.8	6.8
2001	8.3	3.6	5.2	0.2	4.0	0.5	1.8	−2.4	2.2	−2.2	6.9
2002	9.1	4.5	3.8	0.3	7.2	5.4	4.4	4.1	5.3	4.6	7.1
2003	10.0	4.8	8.4	1.4	2.8	5.8	4.9	3.8	7.1	3.5	7.3
2007	13.0	6.3	9.1	2.4	5.1	6.3	7.2	7.8	4.9	5.7	8.5
2008	9.0	6.0	7.3	0.4	2.2	4.5	4.6	1.1	4.8	0.12	6.2
2009^{E}	8.7	4.5	7.2	−0.7	0.2	−1.7	0.9	−2.1	−2.3	−2.5	5.3

Note: CN — China, ID — Indonesia, IN — India, JP — Japan, KR — Korea, MY — Malaysia, PH — Philippines, SG — Singapore, TH — Thailand, CT — Chinese Taiwan, VN — Vietnam.

Source: Taiwanese data are taken from, *Taiwan Statistical Yearbook 2008*. Others are taken from the United Nations Statistics.

for the recent financial crisis. China, India and Vietnam kept growing rapidly during both financial crises. China and Vietnam lost 1.5 points and 2.4 points of GDP growth in 1998, whereas they lost 4.0 and 2.3 points of GDP growth in 2008. Indonesia and Thailand experienced declines of over 10% in GDP in 1998, whereas Indonesia's GDP increased by 4.5% and Thailand declined by 2.3% in 2009. GDP for Korea and the Philippines kept growing between 2007 and 2009, although it declined by 6.9% and 0.6% respectively in 1998. GDP growth rates of Taiwan are positive between 1996 and 2000, but dropped to −2.2 in 2001 then rebounded. GDP growth rates for Taiwan dropped from 5.7% in 2007 to −2.5% in 2009. GDP of Japan and Singapore declined mildly at −2.0% and −1.4% respectively. GDP growth rates of Singapore have fluctuated substantially over the last two decades. They dropped from 8.3% to −1.4% between 1997 and 1998 and from 7.8% to 1.1% between 2007 and 2008.

Thus, in general, the Asian financial crisis affected the Asian economies more severely in terms of GDP growth than the recent financial crisis, but the trade impacts were greater. Green (2010) also analyses Asia's policy response to the 2008 crisis using ASEAN economies as an example, and argues that south-east Asia was slow to mobilise to reduce the impact of the crisis. Fiscal expenditure policy delayed stimulating domestic demand and mitigating the impact on the poor (see also Athukorala and Chongvilaivan, 2010; Basri and Rahardja, 2010).

The impacts of the recent financial crisis on Asian countries' trade thus seem significantly milder, than the impacts of the Great Depression on the trade of OECD countries, but impacts of the Asian financial crisis on the trade of Asian countries were more severe. In terms of GDP growth, the impacts of the financial crisis seem less pronounced than those of the Asian financial crisis on the Asian economies.

6 Conclusion

In this Chapter, we document and compare the trade performance of the major Asian economies both during and following the 2008 financial crisis. We present data for China, India, Thailand, Malaysia, Korea, Japan, Singapore and Taiwan on both the import and export sides on a monthly basis throughout the crisis. We compare their trade performance in aggregate and by product and bilateral trading partner. Except for Korea, which experienced an initial smaller impact but a quick rebound, Asian economies experienced considerable declines in trade in the whole of 2009. In general, imports dropped more proportionally than exports for these economies, which reflects both the consequences of oil price fluctuations and the impacts of the financial crisis on the real economies in the OECD. For Asia, on both the export and import sides, there is a solid rebound in 2010.

We also make comparisons of the impact of the recent financial crisis on Asian trade with both the Great Depression in China and Japan and the Asian financial crisis of 1998. The impact on Asian trade between 2008 and 2009 is milder than for OECD countries during the Great Depression and more severe than for Asian countries during the Asian financial crisis. For GDP growth rates, Asian countries' impacts are greater and declined more in the Asian financial crisis than between 2008 and 2009.

References

Athukorala, P. and A. Chongvilaivan (2010), The Global Financial Crisis and Asian Economies: Impact and Trade Policy Response, *Journal of ASEAN Economic Bulletin*, 27(1), 1–4.

Baldwin, R. (2009), The Great Trade Collapse: What caused it and What Does it Mean?, *VoxEU.org Working Paper*, November 27, 2009, (Online). Available from: http://www.voxeu.org/index.php?q=node/4304 (Accessed April 29, 2010).

Bank of Thailand, International Trade Statistics, (Online). Available from: http://www.bot.or.th/English/Statistics/EconomicAndFinancial/ExternalSector/Pages/StatInternationalTrade.aspx (Accessed April 4, 2010).

Basri, M.C. and S. Rahardja (2010), The Indonesian Economy amidst the Global Crisis: Good Policy and Good Luck, *Journal of ASEAN Economic Bulletin*, 27(1), 77–97.

Bureau of Foreign Trade of Taiwan, Foreign Trade Statistics (Online). Available from: http://cus93.trade.gov.tw/FSCI/ (Accessed March 25, 2010).

China Customs Statistics, China Custom Monthly Report March 2008 — April 2010. (Online). Available from: http://www.haiguan.info (Accessed May 6, 2010).

Chinese Academy of Social Science (2010), *Analysis and Forecast of China's Economic Situation* (Economic Blue Book, Autumn 2010), Chinese Social Science Press Beijing: China.

Green, D.J. (2010), Southeast Asia's Policy Response to the Global Economic Crisis, *Journal of ASEAN Economic Bulletin*, 27(1), 5–26.

Gregory, R., C. Henn, B. McDonald and M. Saito (2010), Trade and the Crisis: Protect or Recover [R], IMF SPN 1007 (Online). Available from: http://www.imf.org/external/pubs/ft/spn/2010/spn1007.pdf (Accessed May 20, 2010).

Huh, C. and K. Nam (2010), A Preview of Tale of Korea's Two Crises: Distinct Aftermath of 1997 and 2008 Crises, *The Journal of the Korean Economy*, 11(1), 1–29.

Index of Mundi, (Online). Available from: http://www.indexmundi.com/japan/gdp_real_growth_rate.html (Accessed May 8, 2010).

Korean Customs Statistics, (Online). Available from: http://www.customs.go.kr/kcshome/site/index.do?layoutSiteId=english (Accessed April 6, 2010).

Maddison, A. (1997), *Review of World Economy in Past Two Hundred Years*[M]. Reform Press, Beijing: China.

Ministry of Commerce & Industry of India: DGCI&S (Directorate General of Commercial Intelligence and Statistics) Database, (Online). Available from: http://www.dgciskol.nic.in/ (Accessed March 29, 2010).

Mitsubishi UFJ Research and Consulting, Forecast for the Japanese Economy in Fiscal 2010 and 2011[R]. (Online). Available from: http://www.murc.jp/english/think_tank/forecast_jp/fc1002.pdf (Accessed April 16, 2010).

National Bureau of Statistics of China, China Statistical Yearbook 1996–2009, (Online). Available from: http://www.stats.gov.cn/tjsj/ndsj/ (Accessed April 25, 2010).

NBER Macrohistory database, (Online). Available from: http://www.nber.org/databases/macrohistory/contents/chapter07.html (Accessed April 10, 2010).

OECD Statistics, (Online). Available from: http://stats.oecd.org/ (Accessed April 14, 2010).

Official Portal of Ministry of International Trade and Industry of Malaysia, International Trade Statistics, (Online). Available from: http://www.miti.gov.my/ (Accessed April 6, 2010).

Statistics Singapore, (Online). Available from: http://www.singstat.gov.sg/statistics (Accessed April 2, 2010).

Taiwan Statistical Yearbook (2008), (Online). Available from: http://eng.dgbas.gov.tw/lp.asp?CtNode=2351&CtUnit=1072&BaseDSD=36&mp=2, (Accessed April 20, 2010).

Trade Statistics of Japan, Ministry of Finance of Japan, (Online). Available from: http://www.customs.go.jp/toukei/info/tsdl_e.htm (Accessed April 2, 2010).

UNCTAD, International Merchandise Trade Database, (Online). Available from: http://comtrade.un.org/ (Accessed May 18, 2010).

United Nations Statistics, (Online). Available from: http://unstats.un.org/unsd/snaama/downloads/Download-GDPgrowth-USD-all.xls (Accessed April 11, 2010).

US Energy Information Administration, (Online). Available from: https://www.eia.gov/petroleum/data.cfm (Accessed May 24, 2010).

Wang, J. and J. Whalley (2010), China's Trade and Investment with the South Pre and Post the Crisis[R]. Paper prepared at World Bank Conference on Trade and the Impacts of the Financial Crisis on Asia, May 10, 2010.

World Development Indicators of the World Bank, (Online). Available from: http://data.worldbank.org/data-catalog (Accessed April 16, 2010).

WTO (2010), Press Releases No. 598, March 26, 2010, World Trade 2009, Prospects For 2010: Trade to Expand by 9.5% in 2010 after a Dismal 2009, WTO reports[N] (Online). Available from: http://www.wto.org/english/news_e/pres10_e/pr598_e.pdf (Accessed April 21, 2010).

WTO (2010), Press Releases No. 604, June 2, 2010, First Quarter of 2010 Sees Trade Value Rise by about 25%[N], (Online). Available from: http://www.wto.org/english/news_e/pres10_e/pr604_e.htm (Accessed June 3, 2010).

Yeh, K.C. (1977), China's National Income, 1931–1936, In Modern Chinese Economic History, The Institute of Economics, Academia Sinica.

Chapter 7

China's Regional and Bilateral Trade Agreements

Chunding Li

Chinese Academy of Social Sciences, China
Department of Economics, Western University, Canada
chundingli@gmail.com

Jing Wang

Department of Economics, Western University, Canada
jwang624@uwo.ca

John Whalley

Department of Economics, Western University, Canada
Centre for International Governance Innovation (CIGI), Canada
National Bureau of Economic Research (NBER), USA
jwhalley@uwo.ca

Abstract: China has been increasingly active on the regional trade agreement front ever since WTO Accession occurred in 2001. These agreements, unlike the US and EU cases, follow no template form of agreement but vary substantially one among the others and are in part an attempt to customise agreements to partner prior agreements. There are presently 12 concluded agreements, 6 under negotiation and 4 others under consideration. Those concluded are in the main with smaller countries Those in prospect are with major trading areas (US, Japan, Korea and India). All are driven in part by China's needs for export access to fuel continuing export lead growth, but other elements enter including using regional agreements to offset unwelcome elements of multilateral arrangements (such as the non-market economy labelling), and attempting to put in place *via* RTA building blocks an Asian trading hub. Outstanding issues not centrally addressed by these agreements include antidumping duties, and investment and competition issues.

1 Introduction

In 2001, China acceded to the WTO driven in large part by the view that integration into the world economy was central to China's development ambitions in helping provide improved access to key export markets. There has since been considerable debate over whether the terms of WTO accession provided much by way of concrete improvement in access commitments by trading partners beyond the technical firming up of MFN by trading partners which some have argued that China already defacto enjoyed. Instead, the claim is often made that the more important impact of WTO accession was in terms of underpinning domestic market oriented reforms and establishing clearer rules of law internationally which proved key in fuelling large increase in foreign direct investment which, in turn, fuelled growth in both GDP and exports.

But China's efforts at international economic diplomacy have not stopped at WTO accession, and since accession, China has been increasingly active in its pursuit of regional and bilateral trade agreements (RTA). Since 2001, China has concluded agreements with 12 different entities (both countries and groups of countries), has 6 other under negotiation and 4 under consideration. While that is a similar picture to elsewhere in Asia (Japan, Korea, for example), the picture in the Chinese case is of initial agreements focusing on local (Hong Kong) or smaller entities (Iceland, for example) that were easier to negotiate, before moving to larger and more consequential agreements (with ASEAN, for instance). Agreements now under consideration emphasise large country arrangements and are more important for China. These include a possible China–US FTA, possible participation in the Trans Pacific Partnership negotiation with 12 other Pacific countries, a bilateral agreement with India, and a trilateral China–Japan–Korea agreement.

China is not alone in pursuing a network of bilateral trade agreements. But China, more than any other larger economy reflects the need to attempt to enhance export access in this way. While export growth which has been falling since the financial crisis and in May 2013 turned negative, given export oriented growth is still the norm, access driven negotiation and bilateralism logically follow. In what following we argue not only that this strategy is now poised to enter a new stage of negotiation with large partners (using TPP, India), but also that China could benefit from a clearer focus on access related problems in such negotiation. Included in the list are antidumping duties, which we discuss in more detail, and where China faces continuing problems.

2 China's Regional and Bilateral Trade Strategy

China clearly sees both RTAs as an increasingly key element of its integration into the global economy, a broader strategy which still underpins her overall growth strategy. The current focus of such agreements is mainly on Asia, and to a further degree the Pacific. The basic idea is to use RTAs to further open up the economy to the outside world and speed up domestic reforms. They are seen as strengthening economic cooperation with other economies, as well as providing a

Table 1. China's RTAs.

1. Existing RTA		**Date concluded**
China–Pakistan	Bilateral-with Developing Countries	November 2006
China–Chile RTA		November 2005
China–Peru FTA		April 2009
China–Costa Rica FTA		April 2010
China–New Zealand FTA	Bilateral-with Developed Countries	April 2008
China–Singapore FTA		October 2008
China–Iceland FTA		April 2013
China–Switzerland FTA		July 2013
China–ASEAN FTA	Multilateral	November 2004
CEPA	Domestic FTAs	March 2003
ECFA		June 2010
China Pilot Free-trade Zone		September 2013
2. RTAs Under Negotiation		**Negotiations Started from**
China–Australia FTA	Bilateral-with Developed Countries	May 2005
China–Norway FTA		September 2008
China–South Korea FTA		May 2010
China–GCC FTA	Multilateral	July 2004
China–Japan–South Korea FTA		August 2013
RCEP		May 2013
3. RTAs Under Consideration		**Joint Feasibility Study Started from**
China–India RTA	Bilateral	2003
China–Columbia FTA		May 2012
China–US FTA		Not Yet
China–TPP FTA	Multilateral	Not Yet

Source: Compiled by authors.

supplement to the WTO based multilateral trading system at a time when given the post Doha Rounds impasse, major progress in the WTO on access seems unlikely.

As Table 1 indicates, China has 12 RTA partners (and with 33 separate economies) with which 11 Agreements have already been signed. These 12 partners are the Association of Southeast Asian Countries (ASEAN), Pakistan, Chile, New Zealand, Singapore, Peru, Hong Kong, Macao, Taiwan, Costa Rica, Iceland and Switzerland. Appendix I to the chapter itemises and gives more details on each of these along with negotiation in progress and in prospect.

Most of the existing RTAs are bilateral and most partners are from Asia and belong to developing countries or country groups. Within the group of existing agreements, the China–ASEAN FTA, CEPA (Hong Kong | Macro) and ECFA (Taiwan) are important RTAs since they involve partners with whom there is large trade. Other RTAs including both developed countries and developing countries are with small countries. China's RTAs under negotiation on consideration mainly involve large partners (US, TPP (12 Trans Pacific Partner countries), RCEP, Japan, Korea and India).

Access for Exports

Since the opening of China to the outside world in 1992, following Deng Xiao Ping's Southern tour, exports have grown rapidly from China. Today around 70% of all goods manufactured in China are exported and manufacturing, while now smaller than services still accounts for nearly 40% of GDP and a similar proportion of employment. Since the early 1990's GDP growth has averaged 10% per year even with the lowered growth rates since the financial crisis of 2008. Continued export growth is thus seen as vital to China in order to continue with high GDP growth, and in recent years export growth which touched 30% a year before the financial crisis has been in the 3–4% range. With a WTO negotiation structure seemingly not yielding much by way of improved access, RTAs seem to offer the most fruitful alternative and hence are being actively embraced by China.

While China's regional trade agreements thus far concluded are mainly with small developing or developed countries, prospective agreements under discussion are with large countries and China's RTA strategy is to move from RTA coverage of perhaps 30% of trade to 70% of trade marking the growing importance of RTAs to China. As such, they clearly reflect the dominant export interest of China in the form of search for access to foreign markets.

Domestic Reform

Another reason China seeks to negotiate RTAs, is to continue to use international disciplines to underpin and support domestic reforms, including enterprise reform,

reform of state owned enterprises, financial sector reform and others reformist directions. The broad idea is that added competition from abroad in the domestic market acts as a spur to improved efficiency of domestic production. In addition, pressures for protectionist and growth slowing policy interventions can be more easily resisted emphasising again the need to compete with foreign producers both at home and abroad. This domestic policy component of trade policy was a key element in Chinese decision making to join the WTO in 2001, and it continues as a key element in underpinning China's RTA strategy.

Dealing with Issues in the Multilateral System

Another Chinese objective in RTA negotiation is to use RTAs as a way of improving on their current treatment multilaterally under the WTO. Two major issues stand out here. One is China's labelling under WTO Accession as a non-market economy. This label, to which China agreed on Accession, has made it both easier to impose antidumping actions against China, and if imposed to do so at (often much) higher duty rates. China has thus used a strategy in her RTA negotiation of bilaterally seeking reclassification as a market economy regionally. This strategy has been successfully followed in China's negotiations with New Zealand. Another is the broad area of antidumping duties. Because China's growth of exports has been so rapid, domestic producers in importing countries seek protection and antidumping duties are often the most effective route for them to pursue. These are special trade restrictions design as to offset alleged unfairness in trade from selling below cost. China is now subject to around 50% of worldwide dumping actions (many from other developing countries)[1] while WTO disciplines under the General Agreement on Tariff and Trade (GATT) do little to help China. China seeks relief, and bilateral arrangements (joint exemptions from dumping and sunset procedures) could help.

Framing New Trade Rules

Since the 2008 financial crisis trade, there has been much discussion of the experience of developing countries with current multinational organisations and rule regimes (World Bank, WTO, IMF). These were framed in the 1940's and were designed to deal with wholly different problems from those today's trading system focuses on. Some argue they do not fit the modern world economy, and global

[1] See the discussions in Bown (2009), "Self-enforcing Trade: Developing Countries and WTO Dispute Settlement", Brookings Institute; Bown (2010), "China's WTO Entry: Antidumping, Safeguards and Dispute Settlement", and Bown (2011) "Taking Stock of Antidumping, Safeguards and Countervailing Duties, 1990–2009".

rules, including in trade, should be reassessed in light of the difficulties in the WTO Doha round. These have reflected developing country frustration with what they often see as a "rich men's club". As such, a further objective China has in participation in RTAs (also including the large country RTAs now being discussed) is to use new RTA structures to help shape the evolution of future global trade rules and arrangements.

3 Characteristics of the RTA Strategy

China's RTA negotiating strategy has been marked by a number of characteristics which can be seen in the documentation in the Appendix. These include the following.

Begin Local/Small

China's strategy has been framed from an initial situation of no regional agreements at the time of WTO accession in 2001. China's strategy was to begin local and small, in part reflecting the ease of negotiation and also the learning experiences involved in sequential negotiation. The first RTA was with Hong Kong and Macro in 2003, and the first developed country RTA was with New Zealand in 2008. With the notable exception of the ASEAN agreement, all of the first 12 China's RTAs have been with relatively small trading entities. In this way, it is easier to achieve precedents in coverage and for later negotiation, as well as pursuing new initiatives. China's RTAs in this initial group also show more variation than is true of US or EU regional agreements. US regional agreements typically offer accelerated tariff elimination bilaterally in return for what is effectively unilateral service liberalisation by the partner. EU agreements emphasise legal structure and competition law and have partners progress through a graduation of agreements before achieving a full FTA. Chinese agreements are in contrast more varied by partners.

Aim to be Inclusive of Key WTO Members

By beginning small and local, China's FTA strategy has implicitly set a goal of aiming to eventually be inclusive of most key WTO members. The list includes the US, the EU, and India, all major trading partners of China. A bilateral agreement with India is the subject of a joint feasibility study, but for now remains blocked by Indian manufacturing interests who fear loss of domestic markets. This strategy has enabled Chinese negotiations to learn about the negotiating process and also gives China the strategic benefits in delaying US/EU negotiation bilaterally until other arrangements are in place. The effective trilateral China/US/EU negotiation which seems likely to happen in the next few years will also help shape the system of trade rules which will guide the world economy in the decades to come, and China through its large country RTAs will have played a major role in this.

BITs as Separate Treaties

A further feature of China's FTAs has been their linkage to bilateral investment treaties (BITs). There are near 3,000 BITs in place today as negotiated bilateral agreements covering dispute settlement over investment related matters, guarantees on repatriation of funds for investors, expropriation limits and other matters. These negotiations typically either predate or follow a full RTA as a separate negotiation and it has been notable in the Chinese case how this separateness has been the norm. Currently for the initial China–Japan–Korea RTA negotiation there is a prior tri initial investment treaty negotiation. BITs negotiations do not typically, however, deal with the rules governing investment flows, including MFN, and so given China's interest now in outward foreign investment a broadening in approach would seem to be in the Chinese interest.

Customise RTAs to Partner

As already noted, the Chinese approach to RTAs has not been to adopt a template, one size fits all, approach to all RTAs. Instead, diversity seems more the norm. This reflects a Chinese negotiating strategy that, by fitting into the preferred broad structure of the partner more can be obtained in the detail of the negotiation. Thus the China–ASEAN agreement devotes considerable coverage to broad commitments of cooperation in development in general. These broad political commitments are in addition to precise and concrete commitments on tariff issues. In the New Zealand agreement in contrast there is less focus on developmental cooperation and more on targeted precise commitments, given New Zealand's developed country status.

4 Some Features of Key Arrangements

Arrangements in Place

Among the already negotiated agreements, the key RTA agreements are with ASEAN and with Hong Kong/Macao. The Hong Kong/Macao agreements are notable in several areas. One is a bilateral agreement to exempt each other from their own antidumping duty arrangements. This is similar to the bilateral exemption in the Australia–New Zealand Closer Economic Relationship RTA. Another is a special arrangement introduced for Hong Kong service companies in their operations in mainland Chinese market. The ASEAN agreement is notable in yielding the largest internal market of 1.7 billion people in one RTA arrangement in the world. At the same time, however, China and ASEAN have more competition in joint country markets (EU) than joint bilateral trade, and hence the focus on economic cooperation mechanisms, in part, for coordinating in third country markets.

Arrangements to Come

The arrangements potentially to come for RTAs with the US, with Japan/Korea, with India and with the TPP countries suggest major potential impact on China's trade and international arrangements generally. The US has, in recent years, repeatedly labelled China as a "currency manipulator" and claimed China keeps an artificially low exchange rate leading to large Chinese trade surpluses. The effective 25% appreciation of the RMB since 2005 has done much to eliminate the large trade surplus, but US concerns remain. US objectives in a bilateral RTA would also involve new rules in trade for state owned enterprises, and heightened enforcement of intellectual property agreements. The Japan/Korea negotiation may be the most straight forward in economic terms, because the joint focuses on economic growth, especially given China's trade deficit with Japan, but political frictions between China and Japan and specially the island dispute threaten to slow the negotiation. India has seen rapid growth in its trade with China (by a factor of 30 since the mid-90s) and so the prospects are for a significant RTA, made complex to negotiate by protectionist pressures on the Indian side. The transpacific partnership situation is one where Chinese participation is neither assumed nor yet sought from the Chinese side.

5 Possible Impacts of RTAs for China

How much will China's RTAs, and especially prospective RTAs, impact on China's growth, trade and overall economic performance. By including all of China's major trading partners in RTAs and with an average current tariff of 10% to be reduced to zero, the medium term impact of the RTA strategy could be substantial as a one off increment to trade growth.

China's problem remains how to keep elevated growth of trade for perhaps two decades while China continues to grow. Under this strategy, the one off contribution of RTAs seems welcome and not inconsequential, but in the long run not the single solution to growth. Much debate currently surrounds growth strategies in China with the prevailing view being, the need to promote domestic consumption growth to replace trade growth as the engine of developments. In this sense of helping with the transition to a new growth strategy, RTAs perhaps take on more significance.

In terms of overall growth impacts, China also faces a situation post the 2008 financial crisis of not being able to continue to rely on infrastructure spending as the latest growth source, to replace trade when growth has slowed. The most rapid component of China's trade growth is with other Southern countries (India, Brazil) and RTAs can have a further positive impact in promoting the most dynamic components of China's trade.

Several researchers have explored various dimensions of China related potential RTAs. For the China–Japan–Korea FTA, Liu *et al.* (2012) have investigated the environmental impacts of China–Japan–Korea FTA on China with CGE methodology, and find that a China–Japan–Korea FTA will lead to a notable environmental impact. Jin *et al.* (2006) evaluate the economic effects of FTA among China, Japan and South Korea on the world economy. Results show that there are strong trade diversion effects.

For the ASEAN+3 FTA, Loke (2013) examines the likely industry effects on China of ASEAN Plus Three (APT), and find that there might be opportunities for agriculture industries fishery to expand. Some manufacturing industries like textiles and clothing are likely to expand even further. However, motor vehicles may face challenges given that Japan and Korea are much more developed in this area.

Siriwardana and Yang (2007) analysed the impact of the proposed Australia–China FTA. Their results suggest that both Australia and China will gain by removing protection on trade bilaterally. The benefits are greater for Australia than for China. Patricio (2011) has also explored Australia–China FTA effects.

For the TPP, Li and Whalley (2013) have explored the TPP effects on China and related other countries, the results reveal that China will be slightly hurt by TPP initiatives in welfare when China is out, but total production and exports will increase. If China takes part in TPP, she will significantly gain and increase other TPP countries' gain as well. Petri *et al.* (2011) has also investigated the potential effects of TPP and other Asia FTAs.

For the China–Pakistan FTA, Shabir and Kazmi (2007) have analysed the economic effects of the Pakistan–China FTA, and reveal that this will enhance interregional trade and export diversification by further deepening cooperation with China.

Other literature include Choi (2013) has analysed the effects of Korea–China FTA, Tan and Li (2009) explore the impact of China–New Zealand FTA.

Appendix: China's RTA Agreements[2]

1 China's Existing RTA Agreements

(1) CEPA (Mainland China with Hong Kong and Macao)

Mainland China and Hong Kong CEPA (Closer Economic Partnership Arrangement) was the first Chinese RTA. It was signed on June 29, 2003 and Macao signed the pact in October 2003.[3]

For Trade in goods, Hong Kong continues to apply zero tariffs to all imported goods of Mainland origin. In the beginning of CEPA enforcement, the Mainland applied zero tariffs to 273 kinds of the import of goods of Hong Kong origin. Since January 1, 2006, all goods of Hong Kong origin importing into the Mainland enjoy tariff free treatment, upon application by local manufacturers and upon the CEPA rules of origin (ROOs) being agreed and met.[4] The two sides undertake that either side will not apply antidumping measures to goods imported and originated from the other side.

For trade in services, mainland China issued various liberalisation measures under CEPA which provides Hong Kong service suppliers with preferential access to the Mainland market. Under CEPA Hong Kong service suppliers receive preferential access to the Mainland market. The preferential treatment takes various forms, including allowing wholly-owned operations, relaxing restrictions on equity shareholding, reducing registered capital requirements, relaxing restrictions over geographical location and business scope, etc.[5] Since 2004, mainland China has issued 41 liberalisation measures covering 18 service areas, and this increased to 338 measures by 2013.[6] Professional bodies of Hong Kong and the regulatory authorities in the Mainland have also signed a number of agreements or arrangements on mutual recognition of professional qualification.[7]

Both sides also agreed to enhance cooperation in various trade and investment facilitation areas to improve the overall business environment. These includes Customs Clearance Facilitation; Commodity Inspection and Quarantine, Food Safety, Quality and Standardisation; Cooperation of Small and Medium-Sized Enterprises (SMEs); Cooperation in Industries; Electronic Business; Trade and

---

[2] The majority of China's RTAs are labelled as FTAs (FTAs). When discussing individual agreements we keep the label used in the legal texts.

[3] http://www.cepa.gov.mo/cepaweb/front/eng/index_en.htm.

[4] http://www.tid.gov.hk/english/cepa/index.html.

[5] http://www.tid.gov.hk/english/cepa/tradeservices/trade_services.html.

[6] http://gaoyan.mofcom.gov.cn/article/speeches/201308/20130800271162.shtml.

[7] http://www.tid.gov.hk/english/cepa/tradeservices/trade_services.html.

Investment Promotion; Transparency in Laws and Regulations; Protection of Intellectual Property; Cooperation on Branding; and Cooperation on Education.[8]

The outward direct investment from mainland to Hong Kong in 2012 was 35.6 billion USD, double than it was in 2007. Hong Kong and mainland China are the largest trading partners for each other, with total trade amounting 341.49 billion USD in 2012, which is three folds larger than as in 2003 (87.44 billion USD). Hong Kong also keeps the position of the largest source and recipient of investment for mainland.

(2) ASEAN–China FTA

The ASEAN–China Free Trade Area (ACFTA) is a free trade area among the 10 Member States of the Association of Southeast Asian Nations (ASEAN) and China. The initial Framework Agreement (FA) was signed on November 4, 2002. The ASEAN–China Free Trade Area is the largest free trade area in terms of population and third largest in terms of nominal GDP.

Under the ASEAN–China Trade in Goods Agreement (ACTIGA), Parties reduced their tariffs for goods listed under the Normal Track 1 (NT1) from 2005–2010 and Normal Track 2 (NT2) from 2010 to 2012. China allowed ASEAN Member States to have a list of products that were granted flexibility until 2012 (NT2) for 150 tariff lines. For the Philippines and Indonesia however, 400 tariff lines were accorded flexibility. The Sensitive Track under the ACFTA consists of a "Sensitive List" (SL) and the "Highly Sensitive List" (HSL). The timeframe for SL requires tariffs to be reduced to 20% in 2012 and shall be subsequently reduced to 0–5% in 2018. For HSL, tariffs will be reduced to 50% in 2015. With these tariff cuts, the average tariff levels under the FTA have declined to 4.5%, compared with the MFN rate of 8.1%. In China's case, the overall simple ad valorem average for 2009 under the ACFTA is 2.5%, compared with the 9.7% MFN rate. The average tariff rate on Chinese goods sold in ASEAN countries decreased from 12.8% to 0.6% on 1 January 2010 pending implementation of the free trade area by the remaining ASEAN members. Meanwhile, the average tariff rate on ASEAN goods sold in China decreased from 9.8% to 0.1%.

Under the ASEAN–China Trade in Services Agreement, services and services suppliers/providers in the region enjoy improved market access and national treatment in sectors/subsectors where commitments have been made. The Agreement provides for liberalisation of substantial coverage of sectors/subsectors especially in more than 60 additional subsectors committed by ASEAN Member Countries which are parties to the GATS/WTO.

[8] http://www.tid.gov.hk/english/cepa/facilitation/summary_invest.html.

The ASEAN–China Investment Agreement is the third of three main agreements concluded under the 2002 ASEAN–China FA on Comprehensive Economic Cooperation. This provides an environment that aims to lead to enhanced investment flows between both sides at a time when ASEAN and China are both key emerging economies with strong economic prospects. China's investment in ASEAN was a cumulative 6.1 billion US $ up to the end of 2008, while ASEAN's investments into China alone totalled 5.6 billion US $ in 2008.[9]

(3) China–Chile FTA (FTA)

The China–Chile FTA was signed in November 2005 and entered into force in October 2006. It includes agreements on goods trade and trade in services. Under the agreement, China and Chile extended zero duty treatment phase by phase to cover 97% of products in a 10 year time frame. The two countries also showed willingness to further strengthen exchange and cooperation in areas such as economy, SMEs, culture, education, science and technology, and environmental protection.

The Supplementary Agreement on Trade in Services under China–Chile FTA was signed on April 13, 2008. An agreement on investment is under negotiation.

(4) China–Pakistan FTA

China and Pakistan started negotiations on a free trade area in April 2005 and reached a FTA in November 2006, which took effect in July 2007. China and Pakistan signed an Agreement on Trade in Service on February 21, 2009, which entered into force since October 10, 2009. The contents of the agreements include an early harvest program, FTAs FTA, trade in services, and supplementary agreements.

(5) China–New Zealand FTA

China–New Zealand FTA is the first comprehensive RTA that China signed, as well as the first RTA that China signed with a developed country. It was signed April 7, 2008 and entered into force since October 1, 2008. The agreements cover areas of trade in goods, trade in services and investment.

Under the agreement, 37% of Chinese exports to New Zealand and 35% of New Zealand exports to China became tariff free by October 2008. All tariffs on Chinese exports to New Zealand will be eliminated by 2016, and 96% of New Zealand exports to China will be tariff free by 2019.[10]

---

[9] http://www.dti.gov.ph/.

[10] https://www.mfat.govt.nz/assets/_securedfiles/FTAs-agreements-in-force/China-FTA/Key-outcomes.pdf.

For trade in service the NZ–China FTA aims to reduce barriers to trade in services. New Zealand and China have also agreed to ensure that their domestic measures affecting trade in services are administered in a reasonable, objective and impartial manner.[11]

On the investment side, both countries have agreed to treat investors and investments of the other country at least as well as they treat their own investors ('national treatment'), and both countries have also agreed to give Most Favoured Nation treatment to investors and investors of the other country, except in respect of fisheries and maritime matters. The FTA contains additional protections for investments, including: International law standards of fair and equitable treatment; Compensation for losses arising from war, armed conflict or similar situations; and protection from the funds of an investor being arbitrarily expropriated or nationalised.[12]

(6) China–Singapore FTA

The China–Singapore FTA (CSFTA) is the first comprehensive bilateral RTA that China signed with another Asian country, covering trade in goods, trade in services, rules of origin, trade remedies, sanitary measures, technical barriers to trade (TBT), customs procedures, economic cooperation and dispute settlement, among others. It was signed on October 23, 2008 and entered into force on January 1, 2009.

The CSFTA provided preferential coverage for about 95% of Singapore's exports to China. More than 85% of Singapore exports to China were at zero-tariff upon the CSFTA's entry into force since January 1, 2009, and an additional 10% became duty-free on January 1, 2010. The agreement consists of general disciplines governing trade in services between Singapore and China, and the committed sectors are subject to market access, national treatment and domestic regulation disciplines.[13]

(7) China–Peru FTA

The China–Peru FTA was signed on April 28, 2009. This is the first comprehensive FTA China has signed with a Latin American country and aims to deepen economic and trade co-operation.

This agreement lead to gradual removal of tariffs on more than 90% of goods ranging from Chinese electronic products and machinery to Peruvian fishmeal and

---

[11] https://www.mfat.govt.nz/assets/_securedfiles/FTAs-agreements-in-force/China-FTA/Key-outcomes.pdf.

[12] https://www.mfat.govt.nz/assets/_securedfiles/FTAs-agreements-in-force/China-FTA/Key-outcomes.pdf.

[13] http://www.iesingapore.gov.sg/~/media/IE%20Singapore/Files/Publications/Brochures%20Free%20Trade%20Agreements/IE_CSFTA%20ACFTA_Mar2012.pdf.

minerals over 16 years. The two nations also pledged to further open their service sectors and offer favourable treatment to investors.

(8) China–Costa Rica FTA

Costa Rica is China's second largest trading partner in Central America while China is the second largest trading partner of Costa Rica. After negotiations for around one year and half, China and the Costa Rica signed the FTAFTA in April 2010.

Provisions in the FTA enabled over 60% of the two countries' products to enter each other's markets duty-free immediately, and allowed tariffs to be removed on another 30% of products gradually over the next 5–15 years. Under the agreement, Costa Rica allowed free service trades in 45 sectors including telecommunications, business services, construction, real estate, distribution, education, environment services, information technology (IT) services and tourism, while China opened seven sectors including IT services, real estate, market research, translation and interpretation, and sports.[14]

(9) Mainland and Taiwan Economic Cooperation Framework Agreement (ECFA)

The Economic Cooperation Framework Agreement (ECFA) is a preferential trade agreement between Mainland China and Taiwan (China) which aims to reduce tariffs and commercial barriers between the two sides. The agreement was signed on June 29, 2010.

Under the agreement, Mainland agreed to cut duties on 539 items from Taiwan valued at $13.8 billion, or about 16% of imports from the island in 2009. Taiwan lowered tariffs on 267 items from Mainland, about 10.5% of the country's shipments to Taiwan in 2009. Tariffs would be cut over two years in three stages to zero. Mainland China will also open markets in 11 service sectors such as banking, securities, insurance, hospitals and accounting, while Taiwan agreed to offer wider access in seven areas, including banking and movies.[15]

(10) China–Iceland FTA

Iceland is the first developed European country to recognise China as a full market economy as well as the first European country to negotiate a FTAFTA with China. The China– Iceland FTA was signed on April 15, 2013. It covers trade in

---

[14] http://www.china-briefing.com/news/2011/08/02/china-costa-rica-fta-comes-into-effect.html.

[15] http://www.bloomberg.com/news/articles/2010-09-11/china-taiwan-economic-agreement-to-take-effect-sept-12-to-boost-trade.

goods and services, rules of origin, trade facilitation, intellectual property rights, competition and investment. With the entry into force of the FTA, tariffs on most goods are removed. On trade in service, Iceland commitments are based on its revised offer under the WTO General Agreement on Trade in Services (GATS) and in recent EFTA FTAs. Commitments are not made in the area of healthcare and education. China's undertaking is in line with their revised offer in the WTO. Certain areas of services will be fully exempted from liberalisation, including public services. The provisions on investment do not go beyond and simply refer to an already existing bilateral agreement between Iceland and China on the promotion and reciprocal protection of investments from 1994.[16]

(11) China–Switzerland FTA

China and Switzerland signed a FTAFTA on July 6, 2013, paving the way for significant reductions in Customs duty rates between both parties that may commence as early as in the middle of 2014. This further solidifies economic relations between the two countries as it came only nine months after Hong Kong entered into a double tax treaty with Switzerland.

Once the FTA goes into effect, as much as 99.7% of Chinese exports to Switzerland will be immediately exempted from tariffs, while 84.2% of Swiss exports to China will eventually receive zero tariffs. The FTA is also expected to facilitate industrial cooperation between both countries and set new rules in areas of environment, labour, intellectual property and government procurement.[17]

(12) China (Shanghai) Pilot Free-trade Zone

The China (Shanghai) Pilot Free-Trade Zone is a free-trade zone launched in Shanghai on September 29, 2013. It is the first free-trade zone launched by the Chinese government. China (Shanghai) Pilot Free-trade Zone is not a FTA arrangement between countries, instead it is a Chinese domestic free trade zone, but we include it here given its potential significance.

According to the Overall Plan for China (Shanghai) Pilot Free Trade Zone "the China (Shanghai) Pilot Free Trade Zone shall expedite the functional transformation of government, expand the opening up of service sectors and promote the reform of the foreign investment administrative system, and develop headquarter economy and new trade forms; shall explore RMB convertibility under capital account items and opening up of financial services; shall explore to improve Customs' supervision efficiency; and shall create a framework to support

[16] http://www.mfa.is/media/fta-kina/China_fact_sheet_enska_15042013_Final.pdf.

[17] See China Daily "China, Switzerland sign FTA", 2013-07-06.

investment and innovation activities to cultivate an internationalised business environment" (State Council, 2013). SFTA introduces a number of changes to the current regulatory framework for foreign investments within the Zone including relaxation of certain foreign investment restrictions within the Zone for 18 service industries spanning six service areas; introduction of a "Negative List" approach towards foreign investment in the Zone; simplification of approval requirements for investments by Zone enterprises outside of China; and facilitation of further financial reform and promotion of new forms of trading within the Zone.

After the successful introduction of China (Shanghai) Pilot Free-trade Zone, some other larger cities in China may also apply for this kind of free trade zone.

2 China's FTAs under Negotiation

(1) China–GCC (Gulf Cooperation Council) FTA

China and the Gulf Cooperation Council (GCC) announced the launch of China–GCC FTA negotiations in July 2004. The two parties have reached agreement on the majority of issues concerning trade in goods. Negotiations on trade in services were also launched. A China–GCC FTA is likely to be concluded in 2014.

(2) China–Australia FTA

China and Australia started negotiations on the establishment of China–Australia Free Trade Area in May 2005. China aims to use this FTA to not only facilitate trade and investment cooperation with Australia, but also for the stable development of the Asian-Pacific region and the liberalisation of global trade. Given only a couple of details to be resolved, there seems a good chance this could be concluded in 2014.[18]

(3) China–Norway FTA

A joint FTA feasibility study on the establishment of China–Norway FTA was initiated in 2007. The first round of negotiations was held on September 18, 2008. Relations between China and Norway maintained a sound momentum from 2008 to 2010. But after October 2010, bilateral relations suffered a serious setback due to the awarding of Nobel Peace Prize. But now, China and Norway are close to the 'final stage' of negotiations for a free-trade agreement.[19]

[18] See China Daily "Australia-China FTA achievable in 12 months", 2013-10-11.

[19] See Teddy Ng, "China-Norway free trade talks nearing agreement", South China Morning Post, 2013-11-14.

(4) China–South Korea FTA

Korea and China launched negotiations on a Korea–China FTA in May 2012. They completed the first-stage negotiations in early September 2013 with a total of seven rounds of talks, agreeing on the modalities or basic guidelines for the Sino-Korea FTA. Second-stage negotiations have moved on to discuss which items that would be liberalised by lowering or removing tariff barriers.

(5) Regional Comprehensive Economic Partnership (RCEP)

The Regional Comprehensive Economic Partnership (RCEP) is a proposed FTAFTA between the 10 ASEAN Member countries and its FTA Partners (Australia, China, India, Japan, Korea and New Zealand). The participants in the RCEP FTA negotiations have a total population of over 3 billion people and a share of around 27% of global trade (based on 2012 WTO figures), covering GDP of around 21 trillion US $ (2012 IMF figures).[20]

RCEP is a significant step in the evolution of trade policy frameworks in East Asia. RCEP's history starts as a study group for an FTA between ASEAN, China, Japan and Korea (known as ASEAN+3), with a parallel study process for an ASEAN+6 FTA, which included the ASEAN+3 partners plus Australia, India and New Zealand.

There were two rounds of RCEP negotiations in May 2013 and September 2013 respectively. Three working groups (on Goods, Services and Investment) were established in the first round. During the second round of negotiation, discussions continued on a services chapter. In goods, among other things sessions were held on Customs Procedures, Rules of Origin, and initial exchanges on tariff negotiations and on non-tariff barriers to market access. A third round negotiation will be held in January 2014 and RCEP is targeted to conclude the negotiations by the end of 2015.

(6) China–Japan–South Korea FTA

The China–Japan–South Korea FTA is a proposed FTA between China, Japan and South Korea. Negotiations on the agreement were started in 2012. Three rounds of talks were held in 2013.

In the first two rounds, the three sides discussed key issues such as ways to lower tariffs and the scope of future negotiations based on terms of reference adopted at the first round of talks. The second round of negotiation also included working-group meetings on goods, service and competition along with expert

[20] https://www.mfat.govt.nz/en/trade/free-trade-agreements/agreements-under-negotiation/rcep/.

dialogue on intellectual property rights and e-commerce. The three Asian countries talked about the trilateral FTA's modality such as how to draft liberalisation for goods at the third round of negotiation. Working group meetings were held to discuss a wide range of topics such as indications of origin, customs, trade remedy, sanitary and phytosanitary (SPS) and TBT along with services, investment, competition, general rules and intellectual property rights. Discussions among experts were on e-commerce, environment, government procurement and food sectors.

3 FTA Agreements under Consideration

(1) China–India Regional Trade Agreement

China and India initiated a Joint Study Group which finalised a report on the feasibility of a China–India Regional Trading Arrangement (RTA) in October 2007. The report supports the position that a China–India RTA would benefit each other. Both sides agreed to explore the possibility of commencing discussions on a RTA.

In the meanwhile, economic relation between China and India have developed in the past decade. As two main emerging countries, China and India have same benefit, and they are near each other in geography (Antkiewicz and Whalley, 2005). These factors suggest that China and India may initiate a regional trade agreement negotiation in the near future.

(2) China–Columbia FTA

China and Columbia signed the Memorandum of Understanding on a Joint Feasibility Study on a Bilateral FTA and officially initiated a joint feasibility study on bilateral free trade area in May 2012.[21]

(3) China–US FTA

There are not yet official statements or discussions on China–US FTA, but at a research level, a China–US FTA has been discussed often. Although there will have a lot of difficulties, as the two biggest countries in the world, it may be possible to initiate a FTA in the future. Trade and investment between the US and China have continued to grow at a substantial rate. As with any relationship between major powers, there is friction and concern on both sides about how the trade relationship is conducted.

---

[21] See the website of Chinese Ministry of Commerce, "Joint Feasibility Study on Free Trade Area Initiated by China and Columbia", 2012-05-10, http://english.mofcom.gov.cn.

(4) China–TPP FTA

TPP is one of important FTA arrangements in the Asia pacific region; and it has received global attention in recent years. As the second largest country in the world, China is not involved in the TPP negotiation. Some researches propose that China should take part in the TPP negotiation (Song and Yuan, 2012).

Recently, there are many debates about whether China should join the TPP negotiations seem quite lively. Not only Chinese media but also some from the US and Europe have expressed interest in this topic and published numerous comments. A Financial Times commentary regarded the US moves around TTP as designed to have an Asia Pacific club that excludes China and doubted such an attempt would be successful. Some media in the US expressed the view that the US never had any idea to exclude China and that the US would welcome China's participation in the negotiation. The Spokesman of the Chinese Commerce Ministry responded positively, claiming that China would positively consider any proposal inviting China to TPP negotiation.[22]

References

Antkiewicz, A and J. Whalley (2005), China's New Regional Trade Agreements, *The World Economy*, 28(10), 1539–1557.

Bown, C.P. (2009), Self-enforcing Trade: Developing Countries and WTO Dispute Settlement, Brookings Institute.

Bown, C.P. (2010), China's WTO Entry: Antidumping, Safeguards, and Dispute Settlement, NBER Chapters, In: China's Growing Role in World Trade, 281–337 National Bureau of Economic Research, Inc.

Bown, C.P. (2011), Taking Stock of Antidumping, Safeguards and Countervailing Duties, 1990–2009, *The World Economy*, 34(12), 1955–1998, December.

CFN. (2013), China FTA Network. http://fta.mofcom.gov.cn/.

China State Council, (2013), Overall Plan for the China (Shanghai) Pilot Free Trade Zone, http://www.china.org.cn/business/2013-10/16/content_30310013.htm.

Choi. N. (2013), Korea–China FTA: Expected Effects and Future Directions. Korea Institute for International Economic Policy, Opinions, May 10.

Jin, H.J., W.W. Koo and B. Sul (2006), The Effects of The Free Trade Agreement Among China, Japan and South Korea, *Journal of Economic Development*, 31(2), 55–72.

Li, C. and J. Whalley (2013), China and The Trans-Pacific Partnership: A Numerical Simulation Assessment of The Effects Involved, *The World Economy*, Forthcoming.

Liu, Z., X. Mao, W. Tang, T. Hu and P. Song (2012), An Assessment of China–Japan–Korea Free Trade Agreement's Economic and Environmental Impact on China, *Frontiers of Environmental Science & Engineering*, 6(6), 849–859.

---

[22] See Ding, Y., "Should China Join the TPP Negotiation", China–US Focus, 2013-07-03.

Loke, W.H. (2013), East-Asia FTA: Effects on China's Selected Industries. The University of Nottingham Ningbo China Working Paper, 6th February.

Patricio, K. (2011), The Welfare Impact of An Australia–China Free Trade Agreement. School of Economics, The University of New South Wales Working Paper, 24 October.

Petri, P.A., M.G. Plummer and F. Zhai (2011), The Trans-Pacific Partnership and Asia-Pacific Integration: A Quantitative Assessment. East–West Center Working Papers No. 119, October 24, 2011.

Shabir, S. and R. Kazmi (2007), Economic Effects of the Recently Signed Pak-China Free Trade Agreement, *The Lahore Journal of Economics*, 173–202.

Siriwardana, M. and J. Yang (2007), Economic Effects of the Proposed Australia-China Free Trade Agreement, Center for Contemporary Asian Studies, Doshisha University Working Paper No. 4, April.

Song, G. and W.J. Yuan (2012), China's Free Trade Agreement Strategies, *The Washington Quarterly Fall*, 35(4), 107–119.

Tan, H. and C. Li (2009), Quantitative Analysis on the Impact of China–New Zealand FTA on Both Sides' Economies.

Chapter 8

The Effect of Regional Trade Agreements on India's Trade

Manmohan Agarwal* and Sunandan Ghosh†

Centre for Development Studies,
Thiruvananthapuram, Kerala, India
**manmohan@cds.ac.in*
†sunandan@cds.edu

Abstract: We analyse the effect of India's regional trade agreements on her trade. We find that both exports to and imports from RTA partner countries have significantly increased in recent years. However, India's trade deficit with these countries has been growing over time mainly because of India's trade with China. We did not find any significant intra-industry trade in India's trade with her RTA partners unlike India's trade with the world. We also found that India's exports to the RTA partners are mainly concentrated in commodities in which India has an RCA with respect to the world.

1 Introduction

There has been a surge in the number of regional trade agreements (RTAs) that have been notified to the World Trade Organization (WTO) over the last two decades.[1] India has started signing RTAs only recently.[2] India's late entry into negotiating RTAs is likely a reflection that India's trade is very well diversified

[1] Out of the 275 RTAs reported in the WTO RTA database, only 17 were formed before 1990 (as on September, 2015).

[2] Apart from GSTP (Bangkok Agreement (BA) of 1975), India started signing RTAs only from 2003 (India–MERCOSUR and India–Afghanistan Preferential Scope Agreements).

geographically and so India benefits more from multilateral trade liberalisation than RTAs (Ghosh, 1999). But increasingly, RTAs are being driven by specific industry interests. A major concern of Indian policy makers is their belief that RTAs have resulted in a burgeoning of the trade deficit. They believe that the trade partners have benefited more from the RTAs than Indian producers. If that is the case, it is reflection on the negotiating ability of Indian officials than the intrinsic merits or otherwise of RTAs. Furthermore, as is well known, the trade or current account deficit is more the reflection of aggregate macro imbalance where investment is greater than savings than of trade policy as such (Johnson, 1958). The role of RTAs is that they redirect the aggregate trade imbalances between countries. But again there is no *a priori* reason that the deficit would increase with countries with which India has signed a RTA. What is more likely is that the overall trade deficit of India has been rising because of macro-imbalance and so the balance has worsened against most of India's trading partners.

In this chapter, we investigate the operation of the different trading arrangements that India has made and their effects on exports, imports and the trade balance. In Section 2, we give some historical information on the various arrangements. We then examine in Section 3 the change in exports, imports and the trade balance over an extended period identifying the break from when the arrangement came into effect. We expect that an arrangement will lead to heightened economic cooperation particularly as many of the agreements are more than trade agreements and cover investment also. So in Section 4 we try to analyse the pattern of India's recent trade and then examine in Section 5 whether the extent of intra-industry trade is greater with countries with which India has arrangements than its overall trade. Section 6 analyses whether the trade generated by RTAs is trade creating or trade diverting. Section 7 concludes the chapter.

2 India's Trading Arrangements

India has entered into a number of trading arrangements. Some are free trade areas (FTAs), some are FTAs and Economic Integration Agreements (EIAs) whereas others are Preferential Scope Agreements (PSAs). Table 1 gives a brief summary of all these agreements.

These agreements have almost all been signed since 2003. While the BA had been negotiated in 1975 by seven developing countries, namely, Bangladesh, India, Cambodia, The Philippines, Republic of Korea, Sri Lanka and Thailand, it had been ratified/implemented by only four countries — India, Bangladesh, Republic of Korea and Sri Lanka. The agreement was energised with the accession of China in 2002. It was renamed as the Asia-Pacific Trade Agreement (APTA) in 2005 and renegotiated in 2006.

Table 1. India's RTA.

RTA name	Present members	Date of entry in to force	Chronology
FTA and EIA			
India–Japan FTA and EIA	India and Japan	August 1, 2011	
India–Malaysia FTA and EIA	India and Malaysia	July 1, 2011	
India–Singapore FTA and EIA	India and Singapore	August 1, 2005	
India–South Korea FTA and EIA	India and South Korea	January 1, 2010	
FTA			
India–ASEAN FTA	Cambodia, Brunei Darussalam, India, Indonesia, Lao PDR, Malaysia, Myanmar, Singapore, Thailand, The Philippines and Vietnam	July 1, 2004	India, Malaysia, Singapore and Thailand (January 1, 2010) Brunei Darussalam, Myanmar and Vietnam (June 1, 2010) Indonesia (October 1, 2010) Lao PDR (January 1, 2011) The Philippines (May 17, 2011) Cambodia (July 15, 2011)
India–Bhutan FTA	India and Bhutan	June 30, 2008	
SAFTA	Bangladesh, Bhutan, India, Maldives, Nepal, Pakistan and Sri Lanka	January 6, 2004	Trade Liberalisation Programme commenced from January 1, 2006
India–Sri Lanka FTA	India and Sri Lanka	June 17, 2002	

(*Continued*)

Table 1. *(Continued)*

RTA name	Present members	Date of entry in to force	Chronology
PSA			
India–Afghanistan PSA	India and Afghanistan	May 13, 2003	
India APTA PSA	Bangladesh, China, India, Lao PDR, South Korea, Sri Lanka	June 17, 1976	BA Signed: 1975 (India, Bangladesh, South Korea, Lao PDR, Sri Lanka) BA came in to force: June 17, 1976 Accession of China: January 1, 2002 APTA renaming: 2005 Amended agreement: September 1, 2006
India–Chile PSA	India and Chile	August 17, 2007	The agreement effectively entered into force in India on September 11, 2007
India–MERCOSUR PSA	India, Argentina, Brazil, Uruguay and Paraguay	June 1, 2009	A Framework Agreement was signed on June 17, 2003 Preferential Trade Agreement was signed on January 25, 2004 Venezuela is not a part of this agreement.
India–Nepal PSA	India and Nepal	October 27, 2009	

Source: Compiled from the RTA Database (WTO).

3 India's Exports, Imports and Trade Balance with RTA Partners

In this section, we try to identify the pattern of export, import and trade balance of India with its RTA partners. For this we used COMTRADE data for the period 1962–2014.[3] India's exports to her RTA partners remained less than $10 billion till 2001, increasing marginally during these years (Figure 1). However, in 2002 there was an unprecedented jump and subsequently India's exports to its RTA partners reached $90 billion in 2013. The average rate of growth of exports to this set of countries is 11.5% for the entire period while it is 18.6% since 2000. A similar story applies to imports from these countries except that the import from these countries reached $140 billion in 2014. India experienced a trade surplus with its RTA partners for only a few years in the early 1990s. Rest of the period it experienced a deficit, though, not at an alarming level. However, India's trade deficit plummeted abruptly to $13 billion in 2005, from $3 billion in 2004, reaching $55 billion in 2014 (Figure 1).

It is evident that India is having a trade deficit with its FTA partners (in aggregate) continuously after 2003 and this deficit is quite significant 2006 onwards. In fact, the series for India's trade balance with all its FTA partners taken together shows an endogenous structural break[4] in the year 2005. This date corresponds to India's signing the initial agreement on trade in goods with the ASEAN in July

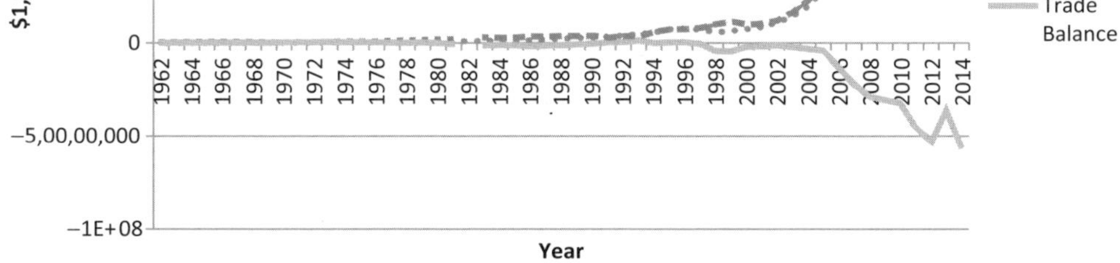

Figure 1. India's exports, imports and trade balance with RTA partners.

[3] However, there is no data on India's imports for the year 1982.

[4] We used the Bai and Perron (1998, 2003) method of estimating endogenous structural breaks in time series.

2004 and India's subsequent trade deficits with Indonesia and Malaysia. Furthermore, India's trade with Japan and South Korea also started registering deficits from the new millennium.

Just as India has been running a trade deficit with its FTA partners, it is running trade deficits with its PSA partners since 1994 (Figure 2). However, India is generating a trade surplus since 2010 with its PSA trade partners less China (PSAswoCh in Figure 2). India's trade balance series with all its PSA partners exhibits two endogenous structural breaks, in 1994 and 2004. In 1994, India registered a significant deficit in trade with both China and Brazil, and 2004 is the beginning of the period from when India started registering a huge trade deficit with China (Figure 3).

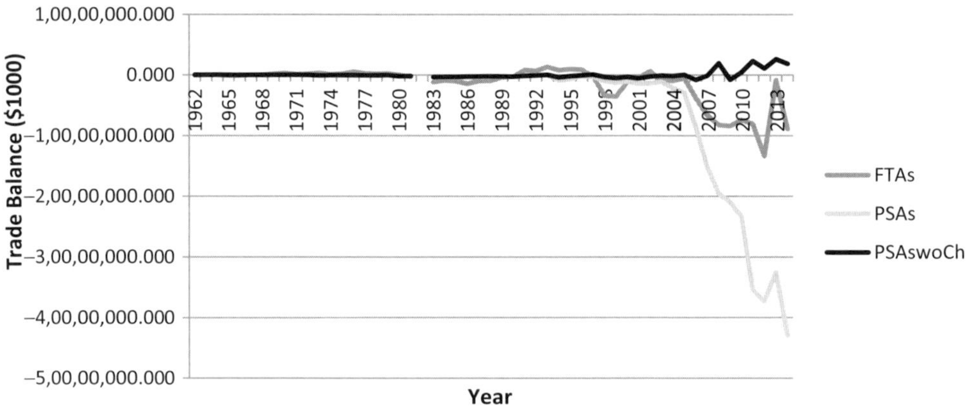

Figure 2. India's trade balance with FTAs and PSAs.

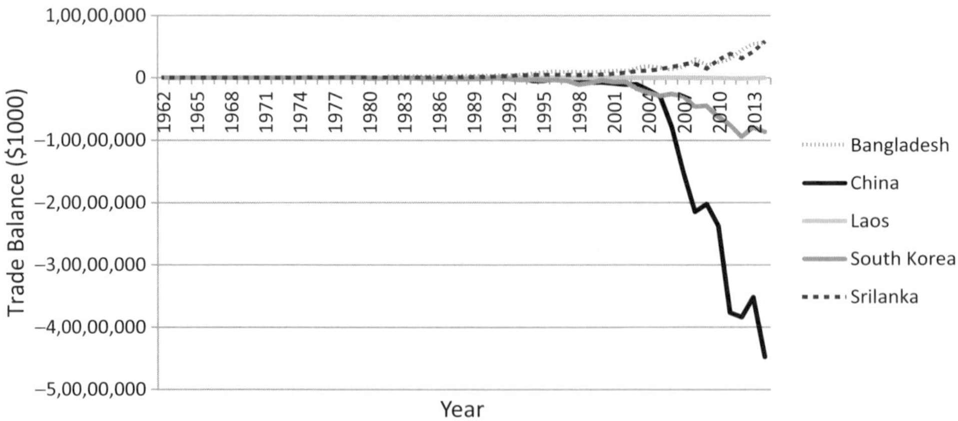

Figure 3. India's trade balance with APTA.

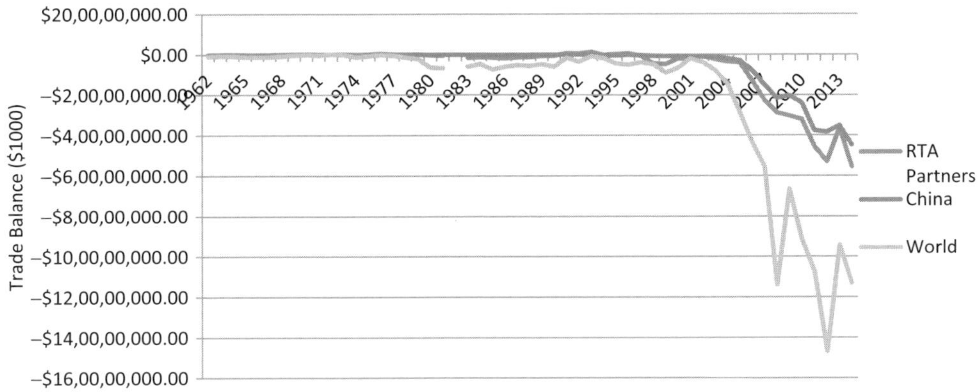

Figure 4. India's trade balances.

To better understand India's trade balance with China, we examine India's trade balances with APTA as India's PSA with China is only through India's PSA with APTA. Interestingly, India's trade balance series with APTA exhibits an endogenous structural break in 2002 — the year of accession of China to the bloc. Though India–South Korea EIA came into force from January 1, 2010, India's trade deficit with South Korea increased continuously from 1998, more rapidly from 2004, in particular.

We analyse further the evolution of India's trade balance with its FTA and PSA partners as India has been running a substantial trade deficit with the world. We find that India's trade deficit with China is 40% of that with the world even though India's trade with China is only 9.6% of its total trade in 2014. Furthermore, the deficit with China is 80% of that with India's RTA partners as a whole so that the deficit with the partners less China is only about 8% of its deficit with the entire world, though its trade with the RTA partners is 30% of its total trade. The trade deficit with China has increased by an annual average of 40% since 2003. Post 2004, India's trade deficit has been continually increasing and a substantial part of this deficit emanates from India's trade deficit with China.

We conclude this section by analysing the export, import and trade shares of the RTA partner countries *vis-à-vis* India's trade with the world. All these shares have increased over time. However, the imports from RTA partners as a share of India's total imports was less than the exports to RTA partners as a share of India's total exports till the early 1980s. Since the late 1980s, there is no unique consistent pattern (Figure 5). The share of exports was usually more in the 1990s, but less around the turn of this century; the share is again smaller in recent years.

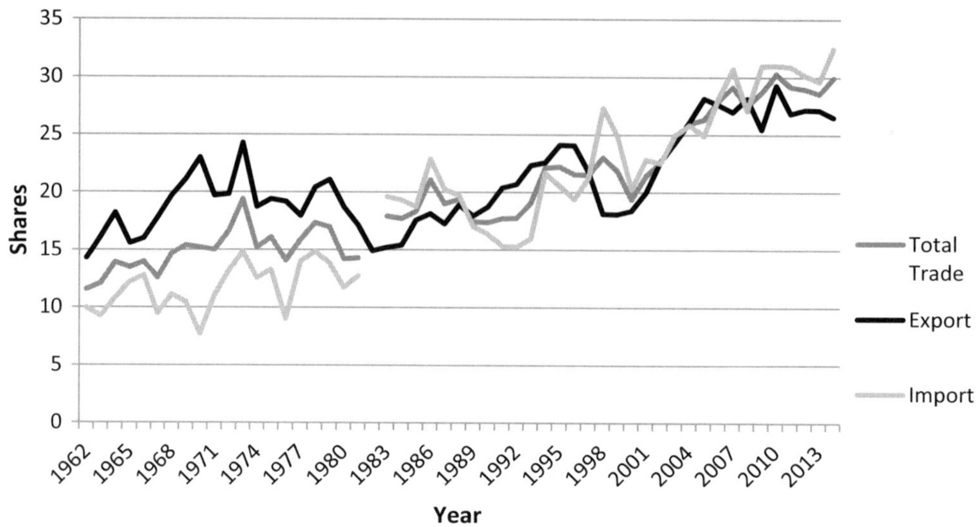

Figure 5. Export, import and trade shares of RTA partners.

4 Pattern of India's Recent Trade

Discussion in the last section clearly indicates two developments regarding India's trade with her RTA partners. First, both exports from and imports to the RTA partner countries have grown exponentially since the new millennium, essentially before the signing of the agreements. This suggests that the agreements may have merely ratified what was happening. Second, the share of trade, either export or import, has grown as well indicating a larger trade with the RTA partners since the late 1990s.

Now, according to the existing theoretical literature on trade, trade patterns can be caused through three major channels. First, the classical Heckscher–Ohlin theorem identifies relative differences in national endowments of factors of production and ensuing comparative advantage being the driver of trade. Second, a different strand of literature (Balassa, 1966; Grubel, 1967; Grubel and Lloyd, 1975; Krugman, 1979; Lancaster, 1980; Brander, 1981; Helpman, 1981; Brander and Krugman, 1983) identifies intra-industry trade as the propellant behind the large volume of trade between developed countries having similar endowments.[5] In fact, empirical evidence of intra-industry trade can be traced back to Verdoorn's (1960) analysis of the impact of economic integration for the case of BENELUX. Third, the literature on global value chain argues that a relatively labour abundant country will specialise in the labour-intensive niche of a hitherto capital-intensive production process (see Krugman (2008) for a lucid exposition). Hence, a labour

[5] See Brulhart (2009) for a detailed historical account of intra-industry trade in the world.

Table 2. Summary of commodities exhibiting intra-industry trade (2013).

GLI ranges	Number of items
Number of items with GLI more than 0.9	17
Number of items with GLI (0.8, 0.9)	20
Number of items with GLI (0.7, 0.8)	23
Number of items with GLI (0.6, 0.7)	25
Number of items with GLI (0.5, 0.6)	14
Number of Items (total)	99
GLI of these 99 items taken together	0.960646

rich country ends up exporting a capital intensive commodity (for example, China exporting i-Pod).

Using COMTRADE data for 2013 we find that there are 99 commodities (at the five digit level of disaggregation, SITC 1) in India's trade basket exhibiting Grubel–Lloyd Index (GLI) values ranging from 0.5 to 0.98. When we consider all these commodities as a group, the combined GLI turns out to be 0.96 (Table 2).

However, not all of these items have a prominent share in India's total trade. We identified 12 commodity groups (at the three digit level of disaggregation, SITC 1) with significant GLI which also have significant export/import shares. Interestingly, these 12 commodity groups made up for one-fourth of India's trade in 2013, exhibiting a high degree of intra-industry trade.

For the rest of the chapter, we will identify these commodities by the product codes rather than by the product name.

5 India's Trade Agreements and Intra-industry Trade

In the last section, we have identified 12 commodities (at the three digit level of disaggregation, SITC 1) which not only exhibited significant intra-industry trade, but such trade constituted one-fourth of India's trade for the year 2013 (Table 3). In this section, we present a time series analysis of extent of India's intra-industry trade with her RTA partner countries *vis-à-vis* the world as a whole. We calculate the GLI for these commodities for both the world and for the partner countries for the time period 1962–2014.

Till about 1986, intra-industry trade was low except for the commodities 667, 711, 722 and 861. However, there is an overall increase in the GLI values for all the commodities after that. Certain commodities like 512, 581, 674, 719 and 931 have exhibited a fall in GLI (in some cases marginal) since the mid-2000s. One interesting point is that the fall in intra-industry trade (as measured by GLI values) has been

Table 3. Intra-industry component of India's trade (2013).

Product code (SITC 1)	Product description	GLI–value	Export share	Import share	Trade share
512	Organic chemicals	0.872578435	3.642978411	3.671938184	3.659246924
581	Plastic materials	0.930970604	2.259418933	2.023985259	2.127161139
599	Chemical materials and products	0.956438704	1.049776359	0.893541055	0.962009233
667	Pearls and precious and semi-precious stones	0.885542916	9.040397017	5.603903775	7.109904196
674	Universals, plates and sheets of iron	0.931958111	1.062722256	0.950098368	0.999454386
711	Power generating machinery, other than electrical	0.820771204	0.758830168	0.850506144	0.810330288
719	Machinery and appliances non-electrical	0.694718517	2.132302806	3.125367437	2.690169214
722	Electric power machinery and switch	0.837875529	1.15108828	1.245485495	1.20411709
734	Aircraft	0.76328268	1.232324348	0.593330804	0.873361777
735	Ships and boats	0.678615891	1.076633273	1.635421691	1.390539617
861	Scientific, medical, optical, meas.	0.528792828	0.543762037	1.180195797	0.901286618
931	Special transactions not classd.	0.607037779	1.500443882	2.685964554	2.166424865
			25.45067777	24.45973856	24.89400535

Table 4. Summary of time-series analyses.

Commodity	IIT (World)	IIT (FTA and PSA Partners)
512	Sharp increase since early 80's	Sharp increase since early 80's
581	Sharp increase since early 80's	Sharp increase since early 80's
599	Sharp increase since early 80's	Sharp increase since early 80's
667	Sharp increase in late 60's followed by a consistent high GLI since mid 70's	Initially very high GLI, followed by a sharp and secular decline from late 60's. Marginal increase since mid-2000s
674	Sharp increase since early 90's	Sharp increase since early 90's followed by a sharp decline since mid 2000s
711	Sharp increase in early 60's followed by a sudden fall in early 80's after which there was gradual increase	Sharp increase in early 60's followed by a sudden fall in early 80's after which there was gradual increase but less than that with World
719	Increasing over time from the beginning, sharp fall after 2012	Almost hovered around 0.4
722	Increased sharply till mid 1970s followed by a drastic fall. Increased gradually since early 80s.	Increased sharply till mid 1970s followed by a drastic fall. Recovered gradually followed by a sharp fall since late 90's.
734	Very inconsistent and predominantly low, except for sudden peaks in early 2000s and early 2010s	Very inconsistent and predominantly low, except for sudden peaks in early 2000s and late 2000s
735	Increasing gradually since early 80s	Increasing (though a little inconsistent) since early 80s
861	Increasing gradually since early 80s (GLI values moderate)	Increasing gradually since early 80s (GLI values low)
931	No consistent pattern (peaks in early 80s and 2000s)	No consistent pattern (peaks in early 80s and 2000s)

more prominent for trade with the RTA partners as compared to trade with the world. In fact, the extent of intra-industry trade for the commodities 667, 711 and 867 has been significantly lower for India's trade with her RTA partners as compared to that with the world. Commodity 722 represents an interesting case where the GLI values have increased for trade with the world while those for trade with RTA partners have decreased since 1998. Table 4 provides a summary of these findings.[6]

Hence, India's trade with her RTA partners does not reveal any significant existence of intra-industry trade although India's trade with the world does.

6 Trade Creation or Diversion: RCA in India's Major Exports to RTA Partners

A major aspect of analysis of RTAs is their welfare implications. Usually, trade between the partner countries can exhibit either trade creation or trade diversion (Viner, 1950). The former occurs when the trade replaces less efficient domestic production and is considered to be welfare improving; the latter occurs when trade between the partners displaces trade with the more efficient rest of the world and is welfare reducing.[7] Usually, trade creation and diversion are identified as the residuals from the expected pattern given by an estimated gravity model.

Table 5. Share of the 22 major export items.

Years	Share of exports of 22 items to RTA partners in India's total export to RTA partners	Share of exports of 22 items to the world in India's total export to the world
2003	60.12304445	59.56074
2004	67.92662773	59.20858
2005	70.8314638	61.85335
2006	74.02335433	63.3172
2007	71.66089033	63.93852
2008	71.48131939	64.81512
2009	69.21449403	61.41817
2010	74.71402929	66.41682
2011	72.91086732	66.49499
2012	70.00876799	62.16763
2013	67.30327025	64.74104

[6] The time series graphs for all these 12 commodities are given in Figures A.1–A.12 in the appendix.

[7] In a multi-commodity world such a simple identification of trade diversion with welfare reduction and trade creation with welfare increase does not hold (Bhagwati *et al.*, 1998). Even Viner's case of trade diversion may not reduce welfare. But most analyses of the welfare effects of RTAs continue to associate trade diversion with welfare reduction and trade creation with welfare creation.

Table 6. India's RCA in the 22 items in the world.

Items	2003	2004	2005	2006	2007	2008	2009	2010	2011	2012	2013	Average RCA values
31	3.06	2.39	2.41	2.08	1.92	1.43	1.30	1.73	1.89	2.06	2.47	2.07
61	3.75	0.62	0.40	2.95	4.15	5.20	0.21	1.95	2.64	3.27	1.64	2.43
81	2.05	3.35	2.50	3.44	3.38	4.03	2.14	2.26	2.28	2.07	2.34	2.71
263	0.88	2.14	3.25	7.77	12.58	10.43	7.26	11.85	7.81	10.26	12.90	7.92
281	6.00	9.21	10.63	7.78	6.60	4.54	4.66	3.10	1.31	0.93	0.53	5.03
332	2.40	2.91	2.97	3.89	4.18	3.85	3.45	3.89	3.55	3.47	3.81	3.49
512	1.44	1.48	1.57	1.79	1.62	1.69	1.38	1.40	1.31	1.58	1.44	1.52
541	1.17	1.09	1.01	1.05	1.12	1.20	0.93	1.02	1.08	1.28	1.32	1.12
581	0.67	0.92	0.76	0.77	0.62	0.53	0.49	0.64	0.91	1.49	0.95	0.79
599	0.84	0.84	1.06	0.92	0.95	1.04	0.83	0.82	0.70	0.84	0.89	0.88
651	6.66	6.70	6.06	6.33	6.50	5.92	4.28	6.35	5.55	6.62	7.22	6.20
653	3.46	3.57	2.93	2.76	2.72	3.18	3.38	3.11	2.62	2.28	2.23	2.93
667	18.28	14.84	14.13	12.69	13.34	12.47	15.38	13.54	13.19	11.24	11.73	13.71
671	1.26	1.14	1.65	1.70	2.45	3.15	2.62	4.06	2.94	3.11	3.50	2.51
672	2.16	1.69	1.67	2.00	1.49	1.42	0.85	0.94	0.86	1.12	1.85	1.46
682	1.49	1.63	1.80	2.38	2.06	1.52	1.14	2.87	1.05	1.09	1.04	1.64
719	0.38	0.42	0.46	0.50	0.49	0.51	0.45	0.44	0.41	0.45	0.46	0.45
722	0.37	0.35	0.43	0.59	0.64	0.78	0.63	0.66	0.48	0.49	0.48	0.54
732	0.23	0.29	0.33	0.33	0.30	0.40	0.46	0.57	0.46	0.57	0.54	0.41
735	0.50	1.22	1.71	1.55	2.42	3.29	4.34	3.78	5.74	3.76	2.87	2.84
841	3.31	3.12	3.16	3.05	2.77	2.66	2.56	2.16	2.12	2.20	2.23	2.67
931	0.46	0.39	0.43	0.36	0.33	0.43	1.10	0.66	1.79	0.31	0.60	0.62

Table 7. India's RCA in the 22 items in RTA partner countries.

Items	2003	2004	2005	2006	2007	2008	2009	2010	2011	2012	2013	Average RCA values	GLI capturing IIT
31	2.58	1.93	1.97	1.81	1.78	1.27	1.33	2.04	2.74	2.56	3.59	2.15	
61	11.22	1.45	0.70	8.32	7.67	9.70	0.31	5.26	4.01	3.75	1.00	4.85	
81	5.93	8.53	6.59	9.51	9.75	10.72	6.34	5.65	6.43	5.12	4.74	7.21	
263	1.21	2.16	3.39	7.84	13.24	11.41	8.96	13.38	9.98	12.67	16.91	9.19	
281	7.72	10.46	11.68	8.81	7.17	4.83	4.84	3.39	1.61	1.15	0.65	5.66	
332	3.37	4.28	3.90	4.76	4.40	3.79	3.40	3.98	4.42	4.14	3.81	4.02	
512	1.64	1.91	1.92	2.24	1.99	1.79	1.54	1.45	1.55	1.93	1.73	1.79	✓
541	2.88	2.47	2.12	2.16	2.14	2.00	1.61	1.34	1.43	1.54	1.56	1.93	
581	1.00	1.35	0.89	1.03	0.70	0.49	0.48	0.54	0.78	0.89	0.91	0.82	✓
599	1.00	0.95	0.99	0.85	1.00	1.16	1.06	1.03	0.91	1.12	1.18	1.02	✓
651	7.39	7.71	6.57	6.95	6.63	6.74	5.35	7.98	6.79	9.74	11.88	7.61	
653	2.05	1.91	1.44	1.19	1.44	2.19	3.98	2.70	1.93	2.17	2.35	2.12	
667	16.19	15.35	22.09	9.95	9.38	7.48	18.86	6.73	5.99	7.33	5.34	11.34	✓
671	2.56	1.83	3.68	3.66	4.19	4.56	4.65	7.44	6.27	6.13	7.30	4.75	
672	3.68	2.17	2.14	2.56	1.49	1.34	1.20	0.52	0.76	1.42	3.07	1.85	
682	1.46	1.88	1.91	2.81	2.36	1.77	1.39	4.86	2.05	2.38	2.25	2.28	
719	0.32	0.32	0.32	0.33	0.31	0.34	0.39	0.32	0.32	0.42	0.45	0.35	✓
722	0.24	0.22	0.19	0.20	0.30	0.37	0.37	0.30	0.35	0.36	0.39	0.30	✓
732	0.83	0.80	0.90	0.85	0.66	0.75	0.71	1.10	0.91	0.97	0.83	0.85	✓
735	0.29	2.58	3.97	5.74	3.86	6.85	10.91	8.55	16.89	10.20	9.05	7.17	✓
841	1.11	1.01	0.81	0.79	0.65	0.72	0.80	0.70	0.85	0.98	0.97	0.85	
931	2.09	2.37	1.08	2.08	1.39	1.65	3.20	1.21	0.29	0.21	0.38	1.45	

In this paper, we follow an alternative approach. RCA calculation from the trade with the rest of the world would identify commodities in which India has a comparative advantage. Then if India exports these commodities to the RTA partners these exports are in line with India's comparative advantage and so the trade is trade creation and welfare enhancing. We have identified 22 items as India's major exports to her RTA partners[8] for this analysis.

These commodities account for almost 70% of India's exports to the RTA partners and only a slightly smaller amount of India's exports to the world (Table 5). We then calculated the RCA for these commodities. India has RCA for most of these commodities in her export to the world. There are five exceptions, mainly in the area of machinery and road motor vehicles (Table 6).

We then examine the RCA of these commodities regarding their export to the RTA partners (Table 7). Again, India has RCA in these commodities, except for the machinery categories, 711, 719 and 722. So our analysis reveals that most of the commodities exported to the RTA partners are commodities in which India has a comparative advantage in the world and so is welfare enhancing.

As far as the export of machinery items is concerned, it has been well documented in the literature that developing countries export these to other developing countries until their productivity in their production increases when they begin exporting these to the developed countries also. India seems to have just started on its journey of establishing comparative advantage in these commodities.[9]

7 Conclusion

In this chapter we try to analyse the impact of India's RTAs on her trade. We find that both exports to and imports from RTA partner countries have significantly increased in recent years. However, India's imports are larger than her exports generating increasing current account deficits over time. However, such an observation is predominantly ruled by India's widening trade deficit with China over the last decade.

Next, we try to analyse the position of India's overall trade in the light of intra-industry trade. We find that as much as 25% of India's trade in 2013 exhibits a high degree of intra-industry trade as measured by the GLI. However, we find no significant intra-industry trade in India's trade with her RTA partners.

We also found that India's exports to the RTA partners are mainly concentrated in commodities in which India has an RCA with respect to the world. Hence, we

[8]The list of these items is given in Table A.1. in the appendix.

[9]This was the original motive behind establishment of regional trading arrangements (Prebisch, 1959). Import substitution had resulted in the establishment of many small plants which could not exploit economies of scale and so were inefficient. So Prebisch recommended establishment of RTAs, whose larger markets would allow exploitation of the economies of scale and so lead to efficient production.

conclude that India's trade with her RTA partners exhibits trade creation and not trade diversion.

However, we have not answered the question as to whether this comparative advantage is being exhibited at the level of final goods (i.e. according to Heckscher–Ohlin) or at the level of intermediate goods which form part of a value chain. At this point, we leave such an exercise for future research.

References

Bai, J. and P. Perron (1998), Estimating and Testing Linear Models with Multiple Structural Changes, *Econometrica*, 66(1), 47–78.

Bai, J. and P. Perron (2003), Computation and Analysis of Multiple Structural Change Models, *Journal of Applied Econometrics*, 18, 1–22.

Balassa, B. (1966), Tariff Reductions and Trade in Manufacturers among the Industrial Countries, *The American Economic Review*, 56(3), 466–473.

Bhagwati, J., A. Panagariya and T.N. Srinivasan (1998), *Lectures on International Trade*, 2nd Edition. Oxford University Press: New Delhi.

Brander, J.A. (1981), Intra-industry Trade in Identical Commodities, *Journal of International Economics*, 11(1), 1–14.

Brander, J.A. and P. R. Krugman (1983), A 'Reciprocal Dumping' Model of International Trade, *Journal of International Economics*, 15(3–4), 313–321.

Brulhart, M. (2009), An Account of Global Intra-industry Trade, 1962–2006, *The World Economy*, 32(3), 401–459.

Ghosh, M. (1999), *The Revival of Regional Trade Arrangements: Implications for Indian Trade Policy*. Unpublished Ph.D. dissertation, Jawaharlal Nehru University, New Delhi.

Grubel, H.G. (1967), Intra-industry Specialization and the Pattern of Trade, *Canadian Journal of Economics and Political Science*, 33(3), 374–388.

Grubel, H.G. and P.J. Lloyd (1975), *Intra-industry Trade*. Wiley: New York.

Helpman, E. (1981), International Trade in the Presence of Product Differentiation, Economies of Scale and Monopolistic Competition: A Chamberlin–Heckscher–Ohlin Approach, *Journal of International Economics*, 11(3), 305–340.

Johnson, H.G. (1958), *International Trade and Economic Growth*. Allen and Unwin: London.

Krugman, P.R. (1979), Increasing Returns, Monopolistic Competition and International Trade, *Journal of International Economics*, 9(4), 469–479.

Krugman, P.R. (2008), Trade and Wages, Reconsidered, *Brookings Papers on Economic Activity*, 1, 103–154.

Lancaster, K. (1980), Intra-industry Trade under Perfect Monopolistic Competition, *Journal of International Economics*, 10(2), 151–175.

Prebisch, R. (1959), Commercial Policies in the Developing Economies, *American Economic Review*, 49(2), 251–273.

Verdoorn, P.J. (1960), The Intra-block Trade of Benelux, in E. A.G. Robinson (Ed.) *Economic Consequences of the Economic Size of Nations*. McMillan: London.

Viner, J. (1950), *The Custom Unions Issue*. Carnegie Endowment for World Peace: New York.

Appendix

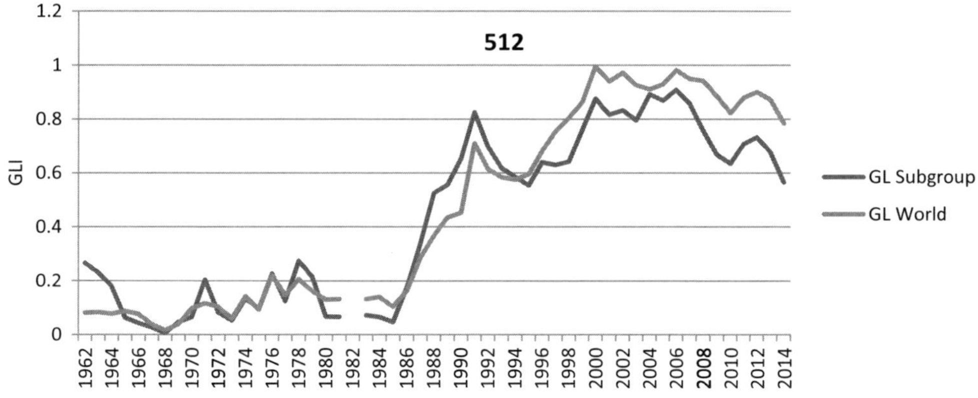

Figure A.1. IIT pattern of commodity 512 (SITC 1).

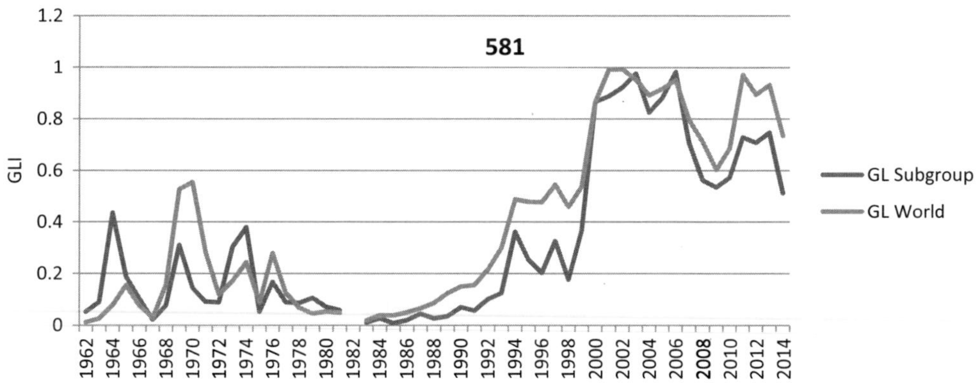

Figure A.2. IIT pattern of commodity 581 (SITC 1).

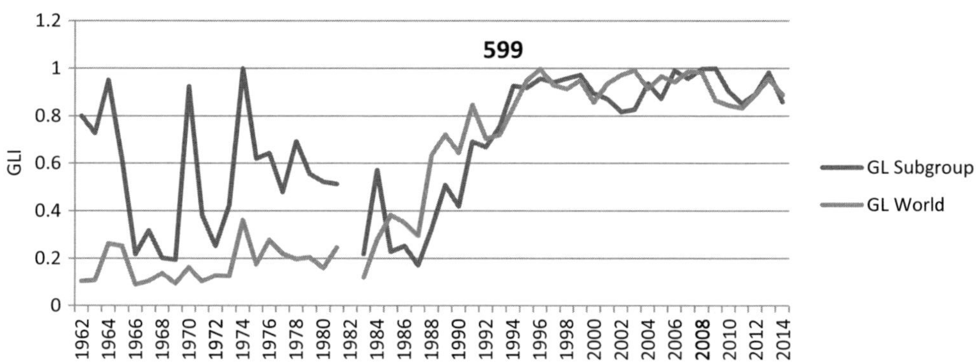

Figure A.3. IIT pattern of commodity 599 (SITC 1).

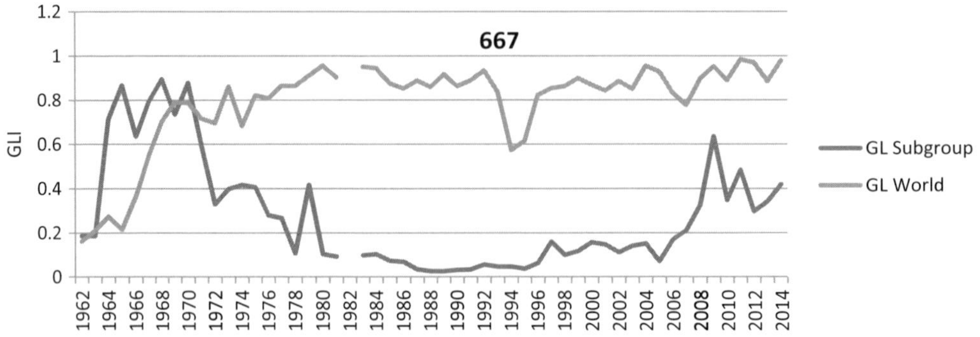

Figure A.4. IIT pattern of commodity 667 (SITC 1).

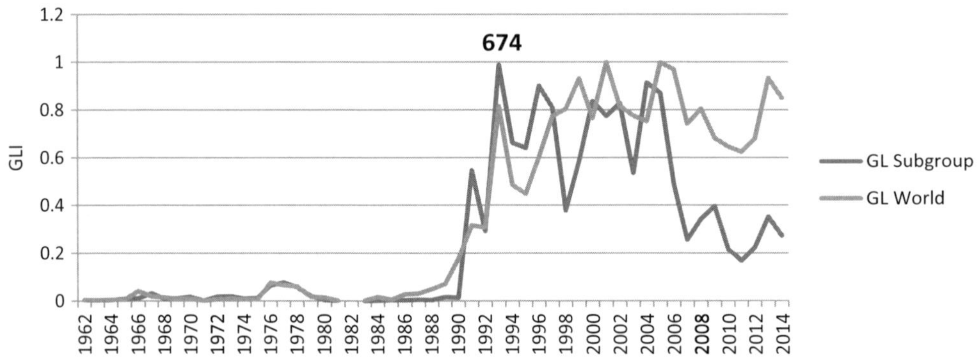

Figure A.5. IIT pattern of commodity 674 (SITC 1).

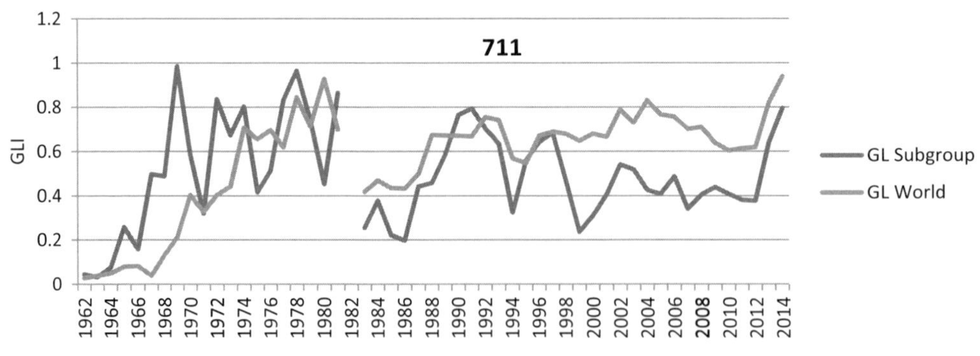

Figure A.6. IIT pattern of commodity 711 (SITC 1).

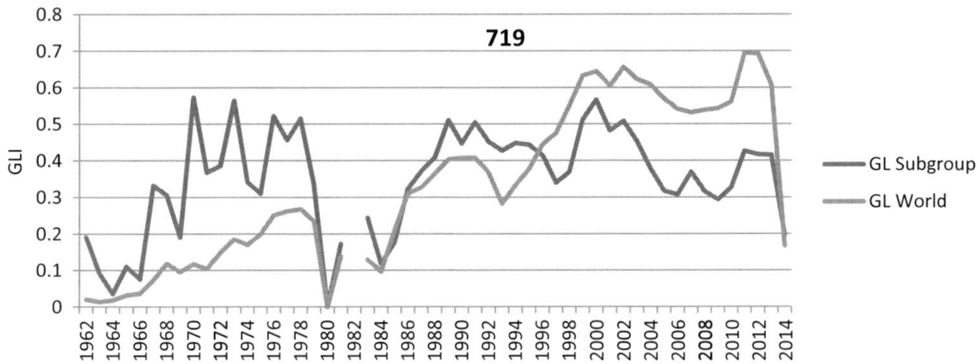

Figure A.7. IIT pattern of commodity 799 (SITC 1).

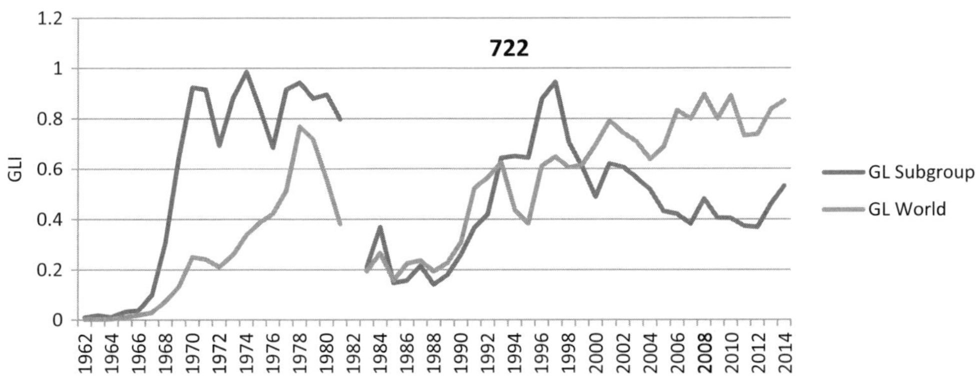

Figure A.8. IIT pattern of commodity 722 (SITC 1).

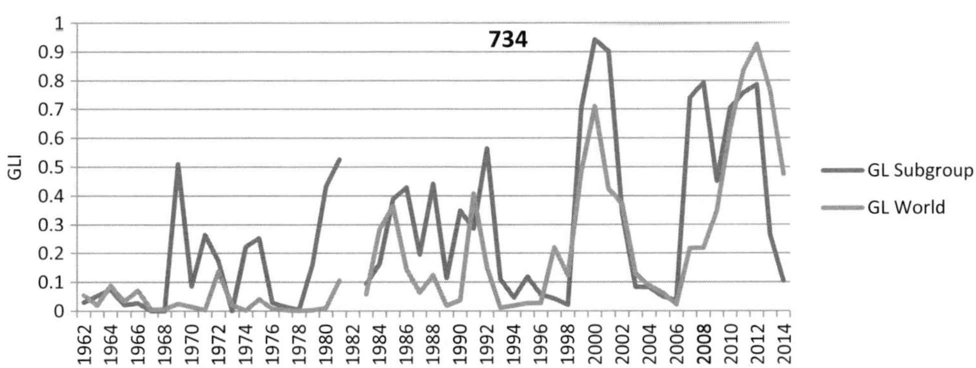

Figure A.9. IIT pattern of commodity 734 (SITC 1).

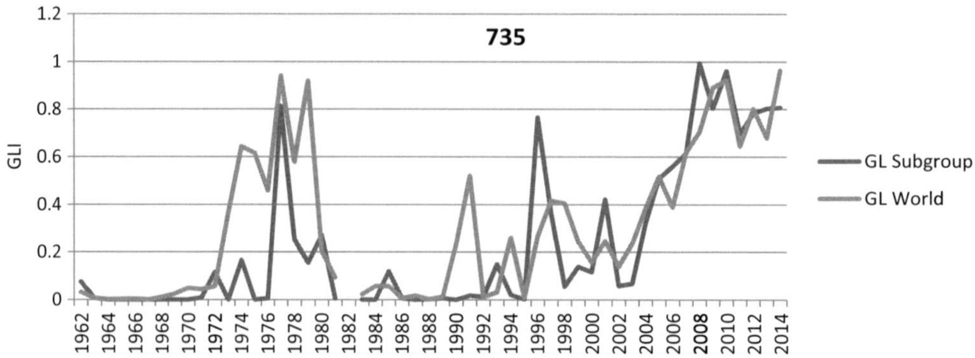

Figure A.10. IIT pattern of commodity 735 (SITC 1).

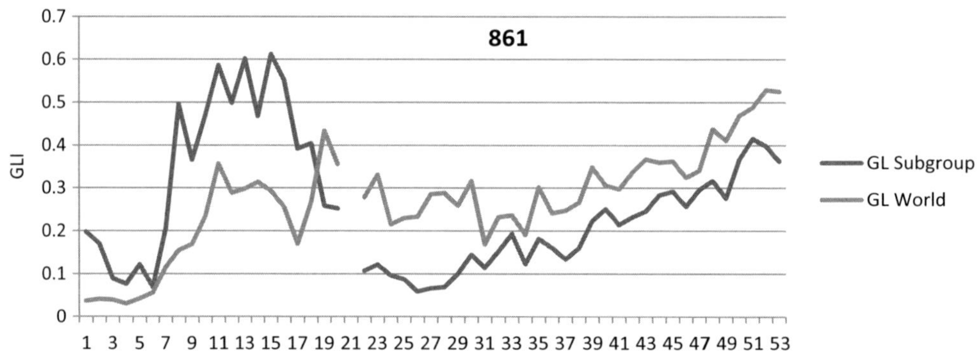

Figure A.11. IIT pattern of commodity 861 (SITC 1).

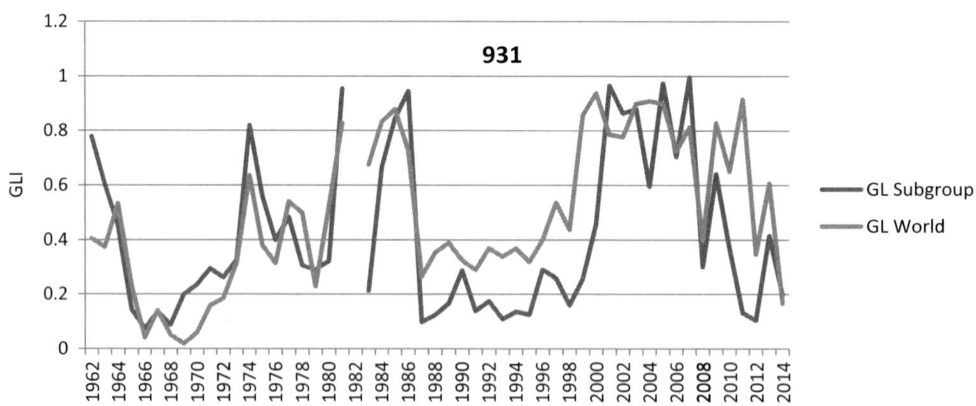

Figure A.12. IIT pattern of commodity 931 (SITC 1).

Table A.1. List of 22 items.

ISIC (1) code	Product description
31	Fish, fresh and simply preserved
61	Sugar and honey
81	Feed. Stuff for animals excl. unmil
263	Cotton
281	Iron ore and concentrates
332	Petroleum products
512	Organic chemicals
541	Medicinal and pharmaceutical products
581	Plastic materials, regenerd. cellul
599	Chemical materials and products, n.
651	Textile yarn and thread
653	Text fabrics woven ex narrow, spec,
667	Pearls and precious and semi-precious stones
671	Pig iron, spiegeleisen, sponge iron
672	Ingots and other primary forms of iron
682	Copper
719	Machinery and appliances non-electrical
722	Electric power machinery and switch
732	Road motor vehicles
735	Ships and boats
841	Clothing except fur clothing
931	Special transactions not classd.acc

Part III

Rural Development

Chapter 9

The Agricultural Tax Abolishment Program and On-farm Labour Time in Rural China*

Haiyuan Wan

Business School, Beijing Normal University, China
Institute for Income Distribution,
Beijing Normal University, China
why842000@163.com

Abstract: This chapter employs difference in differences (DID) method with the microeconomic panel data to study the impact of the Agricultural Tax Abolishment program (ATA) on agricultural labour time in rural China. We find that the policy does exert a significant effect on on-farm working, though a great amount of variables are controlled. In perspective of on-farm working decision, the program promotes 6.19% more of farmers to engage in agriculture industry in 2004. Meanwhile, for the peasants who are already in the agriculture industry, the average net effect of the program is to increase agriculture labour time by 24 hours in 2004. Furthermore, the educated, young male gets more of impacts from the program in the garden product field, while it is not significant any more in the farm and livestock industries. These results are stable and robust in different sub-group datasets, which implies a strong and significant on-farm working effect of the ATA program.

---

*I thank IDRC/CIGI Young Scholar Research Network Program in Canada for funding me this chapter, and great acknowledge should be given to Shi Li from Beijing Normal University who provides constructive suggestions on the draft of this chapter. I would also like to express my gratitude to many people, especially Dr. Hui Xu and Zhilei Tian for their comments on this chapter.

1 Introduction

As Cohen (1959) stated, the dynamic adjustment of tax structure is one of the best indicators to measure the flexibility of an economy. Therefore, the adjustment of tax rate or tax category should be a matter of repeated occurrence in economic operation, and the entry and exit of specific tax categories is also commonly observed in our modern society. Therefore, research on the ways about how to abolish a specific tax category is very important, as analysing the tax exit mechanism provides intuitive knowledge about the future tax design. And distinguishing the tax impacts by different population groups helps us to better understand the priorities for the new added tax category and clarify the main factors that affect the individuals' activity and the overall economy. Moreover, research on the tax exit mechanism enlightens the present similar tax, and it also helps us to rethink our current tax categories and provides much of experiences if establish a new tax category and redesign its structure in the future. However, there is rarely paper devoting to exploring the experience on how to establish a new tax based on the past abolished tax and also few of research analyses the its social and economic impacts in China.

At present, Chinese government plans to levy many new tax categories to improve the tax structure, such as property tax including inheritance tax and gift tax and resource tax. However, many debates are aroused on its potential impacts on production and individual activity, and its heterogeneous impacts across different population groups. So, in this chapter, we will take agriculture tax abolishment for example, to further explore the tax entry and exit mechanism in the past years, and further investigates its heterogeneous impacts on different groups to enlighten the ways on how to design a new tax category in the future.

The agricultural tax in China is a traditional and ancient tax category, which has been lasted for more than 2,600 years. Considering the heavy burden on farmers in rural China, the government begins to launch a program to abolish the agricultural tax and taxes on special agricultural products nationwide ("ATA" program in short) from the beginning of 2001. This large-scale program, which is part of a national agriculture development plans, entailed the objective of raising farmers' income and improving grain production in rural areas. After five years' implementation of the program in China, the agricultural tax is absolutely abolished in China on January 1, 2006. As a result of the ATA program, total agricultural taxation (including agricultural tax, special agriculture products tax and agricultural tax surcharges; see Appendix 1) was reduced from CNY 51.7 billion (about US$ 6.2 billion)[1] in 2003 to CNY 1.62 billion in 2005.

[1] The exchange rate of the Chinese Renminbi Yuan (CNY) against the US $ was 8.28 CNY per USD in 2003 and 2004.

The ATA program provides an excellent social experiment for us to analyse its exit mechanism and process. Although it was abolished five years ago, analysing its continued impacts on socio-economic and individual aspects should still be an interesting topic for us. Meanwhile, some economic literature concluded that the program has achieved the target of income improvement on farmers, as the program abolished the tax and improved farmers' income level in a direct way. However, few papers have been devoted to measuring the program's impacts on farmers' agricultural labour time, though the program impact on-farm labour time input is the core of examining the question of, how this program affect the amount of grain production and finally the farmers' income improvement, a subject of long-time interest to economists in China.

However, the existing literature about the effect of the ATA program on the on-farm working time provides mixed evidence. On one hand, it highlights the attractiveness of the program to households because of the income effect, and finds that it reduces the amount of time spent on on-farm activities as a result of the tax relief on farmers' overall income level. On the other hand, the shadow price of the agricultural products increases because of the substitute effect of the program, so the time spent on on-farm activities increases a lot. Overall, the impact of the ATA program on the on-farm working activities is mixed, and how much is the effect of the program on agricultural labour time, grain production and finally the farmer's income improvement remains unclear, though the national grain production and farmer's income level experienced a rapid and stable increase in the past years.

This chapter tries to fix the gap to explore the tax exit mechanism with an example of ATA program, and distinguish the heterogeneous impacts on individual's time allocation activity. Using the microeconomic data set collected in 2000 and 2004, this chapter evaluates whether and to what extent the ATA program influences the agricultural labour time in China. We focus on the questions: Does the policy exert an impact on agricultural labour time? If yes, to what extent? Do different levitation approaches could also play a role in deciding the heterogeneous impacts on individual's on-farm working time? Does the past agriculture tax provides any experience to help enlighten our tax levitation and similar tax program's exit mechanism in the future?

Compared to the existing literature, we use a recent dataset that covers the full period of the program. The advantage of using the 2000 and 2004 panel data is that it allows us to cover the full implementation period of the program. Meanwhile, our samples also are much larger and more representative than previous. More importantly, we mainly focus on the impact of the program on agricultural labour time, so that we can concentrate on explaining the mechanism that the program affects peasants' time allocation in theoretically and empirically, and then its impact on farmer's grain production and income improvement. The last but not the least, a rigorous econometric approach is employed in this chapter to investigate the net effect of the program on agricultural labour time, which we are not aware of any studies have used this method to evaluate the ATA program in a broad range of developing countries and in China.

The rest of the paper is organised as follows. Section 2 reviews the literature on the program effects on agricultural labour time in China. Section 3 gives an introduction to the ATA program, and develops a mechanism to illustrate how ATA program may affect farmer's time allocation when faced with time and income constraints. Section 4 provides data description. Section 5 gives an overview of the empirical approach and discusses the identification strategy. On this basis, Section 6 reports regression results with the DID method. Section 7 proposes further robustness checks. Section 8 distinguishes the heterogeneous impacts of ATA program on different sub-groups. Section 9 concludes and summarises the results.

2 Literature Review

The ATA implemented in China falls into the category of programs implemented worldwide under a scheme of reducing burdens on farmers. The United States launched such programs in 1996 with the implementation of the Agriculture Subsidy Program ('ASP' in short in here and after), a long-term subsiding program founded by the government. Similarly, Canada implemented an ASP in 1989, while the European Union implemented an ASP program in 1992. Payments for agriculture subsidising programs have also been implemented in a series of developing countries including Gambia, Tanzania, Mexico, Vietnam, and Ecuador, etc.

Generally speaking, these programs have been found to have positive effect on farmers' income (Schiff and Valdes, 1992; Mishra and Goodwin, 1997; Xu *et al.*, 2012). However, regarding the production impacts of ASPs, especially for household activity choice or agricultural labour time for peasants, evidence is rather mixed.

In the developed countries, Higgs (1976) reviewed the history of agriculture tax in European to better understand the effect of ATA program on on-farm working by placing agriculture in a broad theoretical framework and in the context of other economies. It found that the implementation of subsidizing projects have some positive externality, which means that it also improves the agricultural labour time as well. Schneider and McCarl (2005) evaluated both the advantages and disadvantages that ASP brings to the on-farm working in America. They believed that, policies to reduce or abolish the agriculture tax are likely to increase agriculture product price that raise on-farm benefits for farmers. Simultaneously, renewable non-farm working options become more feasible to the low-income agricultural producers because of income subsidy from the ATA program. Considering both of the on-farm and off-farm effects, they finally found that the implementation of this policy activates the labour market and improves agricultural labour time in US Generally, those countries' experience demonstrated that, the not linked agriculture subsidy (e.g., direct income subsidy) do stimulate the labour input for farmers (Woldehanna *et al.*, 2000). On average, the increase of 4500 billion dollar direct income subsidy brought a 7% increase of labour time on corns and 12.8% increase on barley in U.S. (Goodwin and Mishra, 2003). Therefore, Woldehanna *et al.* (2000) concluded that, the agriculture support programs are likely to increase the on-farm time of arable farm households even if controlling the household and farm characteristics.

On the contrary, some of the literature in developed countries found that government subsidy to farmers through agriculture tax abolishment decrease on-farm labour time (Serra *et al.*, 2005). Alig *et al.* (1998) employed a price-endogenous agricultural sector model to analyse the impact of ASP program on farmers' agricultural labour time, and the results showed a negative impact on American's agricultural labour time in the inter-mediate run. Meanwhile, Serra *et al.* (2005) found that the subsidy from the ASP decrease the likelihood of a farmer to work on the farm, as cash subsidies from ASP actually create an important income effect, which makes peasants unlikely to work more on on-farm work. Hertel and Tsigas (1988) also employed a computable general equilibrium model to analyse the effects of eliminating farm tax preferences in 1977. By calculating the benefits and costs of participating in the ATA project, they argued that it is not rational for farmers to allocate more of labour time to the agricultural activities.

As for the ATA program's impact on on-farm working in developing countries, empirical evidence is also mixed. On one hand, there was a large body of literature shows that agriculture subsidy policy has a significant positive impact on agricultural labour time (Ghandi in India, 1966; Valdés in the Dominican Republic, 1996). However, other researches like Orden *et al.* (2007), it analysed the impact of subsidy programs on on-farm working time in India, Vietnam and Indonesia, and the results showed that the policies reduced the agricultural labour time because of the income effect.

In China, researches on the effect of the ATA also exhibit contrasting results. A small number of studies highlighted the positive aspect. For instance, Gu and Ji (2008) pointed out, the acreage and agriculture input in Jiangsu province has increased sharply after the implementation of the ATA program, and the amount of acreage and on-farm working time in Jurong city of Jiangsu province also has grown 2.7% because of the ATA program. With a dataset in three Chinese provinces from the national rural socio-economic survey conducted by the China Ministry of Agriculture (MOA) and a fixed-effect econometric model,

Xu *et al.* (2012) evaluated the effect of agriculture taxation reduction on agriculture factor input and grain production, they found that the ATA itself influences the farmer's time allocation decision, therefore, contributes to increasing of the agricultural labour time. Moreover, they explored the reason that can explain the increase in labour time input beyond the level of direct tax reduction, as the farmers may add their on-farm production input after ATA with the additional tax saving so as to increase their production levels. Yu and Jensen (2010) reviewed past developments in China's agricultural domestic support policy, especially the transition from taxing farmers and agriculture to providing direct subsidies to grain production. With a model-based quantitative analysis, they found that the declared policy goals of increasing grain production and boosting farm income has achieved. Much of the increase in grain production and farm income can be attributed to more labour time reallocation to grain production and extra agricultural employment triggered by the ATA program. Xu *et al.* (2009) evaluated the effect of ATA program based on the data collected from 15 villages of Yangtze River Delta in China. They argued that the ATA policy has a positive impact on agricultural labour time because it changes the benefits and the costs of the farmers. Zhou and Chen (2005) firstly introduced DID methodology to evaluate the effect of ATA on households' income and agricultural labour time and showed that this policy improves the income level and also contributed to increasing agricultural labour time. Furthermore, they also distinguished the program impacts across different groups in the sample.

More researches on agricultural labour time showed that the effect of ATA on agricultural labour time was not obvious and may be negative. For instance, Chen (2004) did a research on the change of farmers' economic situation after attending the ATA program by starting from the attitude of the farmers' behaviour, and it turned out that this policy only has positive effect on the stock of household income but does not have a significant effect on the agricultural labour time itself. Furthermore, some research like Lin and Liu (2007), they found that the direct subsidy program has few of impact on household income as well as agricultural labour time. An explanation provided by Ni (2004), it argued that the ATA policy was not strictly implemented in some regions and had low impact on farmers' employment and labour time allocation decision. Ma and Yang (2005) analysed the factors that affect agricultural labour time by mainly using the data collected in Hebei province, they also estimated the impact of the ATA on households' income and the time spent on agricultural activities, and they did not find any positive evidence of the ATA program on agricultural labour time, especially for the individuals who have larger stock of farmland. As less of farmers are engaging in on-farm working because of the ATA program, Chen (2009) found that China's grain production and food security is facing big challenges in the future, as there was a trend that the households are likely to transfer to high-risk activity (e.g., off-farm employment) because of the income effect from the ATA subsidy. Gale *et al.* (2005) explained that the Chinese government has dual, often conflicting, rural/agricultural policy goals. Policies originally intended to raise rural incomes were given a secondary goal of promoting grain production when Chinese authorities became alarmed by rapid decrease of 2003 grain harvest. And the agriculture subsidies in China did not provide strong incentives to increase grain production as grain typically provides relatively low returns to Chinese farms, so the on-farm working time dropped sharply.

In total, Serra *et al.* (2005) concluded that the effects of ATA program on on-farm labour time are complicated: Eliminating the agriculture tax can have opposing effects on off-farm work decisions, as it has both positive and negative impacts on agricultural labour time and the overall effect in theoretical is ambiguous. Essentially, this makes the issue an empirical question, as the existing paper do not come to a unanimous conclusion. Furthermore, the existing empirical literature in China mostly focuses on the descriptive levels to investigate the impact that agricultural support policy imposes on agricultural labour time based on highly aggregated data rather than data directly relating to farm households. This chapter empirically looks into the impact that ATA program has on agricultural labour time, using research data collected by joint investigation from China Center for Disease Control and Prevention and the University of North Carolina covering both pre and post-ATA periods in 2000 and 2004.

3 The Mechanism of the ATA Policy and its Expected Impact on On-farm Labour Time

3.1 Background of the agricultural tax

3.1.1 *History*

Agriculture tax is a kind of tax levied on all the individuals and units that engage in agriculture production in a country. It usually originates from the rent tax or land tax in western countries. In a feudal society, agriculture is the most important production sector, and it is also the main source of fiscal revenue. However, after entering into the capitalist society, with the development of the industrial and commercial, the role of agriculture is declining all the time. Afterwards, considering the heavy burden on farmers, some countries in the world began to abolish the agricultural tax. Korean cancelled the agriculture tax in 1964, while the Vietnam also abolishes its agricultural tax in 2003. Afterwards, China becomes to be the only country that retains the tax specially levied on the peasants.

For the agriculture tax in China, it was firstly originated from "acres tax" during the Spring and Autumn period (770–221 BC) in the State of Lu, and was completely confirmed in the period of Han Dynasty. And then to the modern China, 'The rule of agriculture tax in PRC. China' was launched on June 3, 1958, which generally includes agriculture tax, special agricultural products tax and agriculture tax surcharge.

In perspective of historical records in China, the ancient agricultural tax has been an important cornerstone of the state's financial system in the past 2600 years. Moreover, according to statistics in NBS (2001), the farmers have paid the state more than 7000 billion kg grain from 1949 to 2000. Considering the heavy burden on farmers, at the beginning of 2001, the State Council began to implement the new agricultural policy to reduce or abolish the agriculture tax. According to statistics, the exemption of agricultural tax could reduce the farmers' burden to more than 500 billion yuan, which directly benefits farmers by more than 800 million yuan by the end of 2005. At the end of 2005, the exemption of agriculture tax was confirmed by the law, so more than 900 million farmers mark the end of the era of paying agriculture tax in the past 2600 years.[2]

3.1.2 *Agriculture tax before the ATA program*

The levitation of agricultural tax in practice is based on the agricultural income, which is calculated according to regular years' output on the land. Moreover, it depends on the land's natural condition and local general operation condition, while it remains the same in the next five years once it is decided.

As for the tax rate, all the categories of agriculture outputs should be transformed into income according to the current price in the market, and then transformed into amount of the local main foods. Overall, the national tax rate on the agriculture output was about 15.5%, while the regional average tax rates at provincial level are different across provinces.[3]

Moreover, according to the Law, some regions could enjoy the preferential if satisfy some specific conditions before 2001, and some of them could even get an exemption of paying the agriculture tax, especially in the developing areas such as areas of regional national autonomy, ethnic minority areas, old revolutionary bases and outlying and poverty-stricken areas, etc. And the specific preference level for

[2] These data are mainly gathered from official documents of the Ministry of Finance, China (http://www.mof.gov.cn)

[3] These data are mainly gathered from official documents of the Ministry of Finance, China (http://www.mof.gov.cn)

each group was decided by the local governments, which again demonstrated that the local governments have much power in deciding the practical operation within the limitation of the law.

3.2 Introduction of the ATA program

At the beginning of 2001, Anhui province starts a pilot of "rural taxes and fees reform", and it gradually expands its pilot scope and spread to all of other provinces in 2003. So, in 2004, the central government decides to exempt the taxes on special agricultural products except tobacco, and promotes its popularisation work on the "exempt of rural taxes and fees".

By the end of 2004, Jilin, Heilongjiang, etc. eight provinces had already completely or partially abolished the agriculture tax. While within Jiangsu and Hubei provinces, some of cities are also terminating the agriculture tax before the first half of the year 2004. Furthermore, the decreased agriculture tax has reached as large as 3% in eleven major grain-producing areas (Hebei, etc.). In total, the agriculture tax only accounted for 1% of the overall tax in 2004. In the first half of 2005, there are more than 22 provinces have evolved into the program of abolishing agriculture tax. And by the end of 2005, all of the 28 provinces in China have engaged in the program. Finally, on December, 2005, the program of abolishing agriculture tax was confirmed by the law, and the agriculture tax was terminated absolutely, totally, and immediately from June 1, 2006.

3.3 The summary of the ATA program

As we know, the ATA program was implemented and promoted in national wide in China, while the tax exemption was also decided in provincial level. Therefore, the individuals in the rural areas did not have option to make a choice whether to attend or not if the program was decided to be implemented in their province. In other words, the ATA program was compulsory and exogenous for the farmers.

Moreover, we have also found progressive characteristics of the ATA program, as the policy was launched and implemented gradually in different provinces (in Table 1). As can be seen from the NBS data set in Table 1, the individuals' first year to participate the ATA program ranges from 2000 to 2006, while almost none of them participate the program in 2000 and 48.23% of them have attended the program in 2004.

Moreover, for the ATA program participation in our dataset during the period of 2000–2004, none of them is evolved in the program before 2000, and all of

Table 1. The first year to participate the ATA program in China.

The first year to participate the ATA program	Percent %	Calculation proportion %
2000	0.38	0.38
2001	1.01	1.39
2002	3.79	5.18
2003	14.52	19.70
2004	28.54	48.23
2005	48.48	96.72
2006	3.28	100.00

Sources: These data is mainly collected from official documents of the Ministry of Agriculture (http://www.moa.gov.cn) in China.

them participate it in 2006. Moreover, some provinces have already participated the ATA program in 2004, while on the contrary, some provinces are not introducing the program in 2004 and before (see in Table 2).[4]

[4] Meanwhile, we also worry about the "seed subsidy policy" and "agricultural machinery purchase subsidy policy" might coincide and confuse the net effect of ATA program, as both of them are implemented around 2004. So, in this chapter, we will take December, 2004 as a split point, as it is an available way to exclude the effects of "seed subsidy policy" and "agricultural machinery purchase subsidy".

As we know, the ATA program begins from January, 2001, so by the end of December, 2004, all the provinces in our treatment group (Heilongjiang, Jiangsu, Hubei, and Shandong) have participated the program, while none of provinces in our control group (Guangxi, Hunan, Guizhou, Liaoning and Henan) have introduced it.

For the "seed subsidy policy", it firstly begins from April, 2004 in Heilongjiang and Jilin provinces, while other provinces introduce the program after 2005. Therefore, in the spilt point of December, 2004, only Heilongjiang in our data have participated the "seed subsidy policy", while all of other provinces have not evolved the policy at all. However, for the treatment group in our data, it includes not only Heilongjiang but also Jiangsu, Hubei, Shandong provinces, so the treatment and control group between "seed subsidy policy" and the ATA program are not the same. Therefore, using December, 2004 as spilt point could separate the effect of "seed subsidy policy" and finally get the net effect of ATA program.

Furthermore, as for the "agricultural machinery purchase subsidy policy", it starts from December, 2004, so none of provinces in our treatment group have participated this policy by the end of December, 2004, the treatment and control group between this policy and the ATA program are completely different. Therefore, the "agricultural machinery purchase subsidy policy" is not able to confuse our net effect of the ATA program.

Table 2. The first year to implement the ATA program.

Before December, 2004[5] (Participating group)		After December, 2004 (Non-participating group[6])	
Regions	**Date**	**Regions**	**Date**
Heilongjiang	March, 2004	Guangxi	July, 2005
Jiangsu province	July, 2004	Hunan	January, 2005
Hubei province	July, 2004	Guizhou	January, 2005
Shandong province	October, 2004	Liaoning	January, 2005
		Henan	January, 2005

Sources: These data are mainly gathered from official documents of the Ministry of Agriculture, China (http://www.moa.gov.cn).

3.4 Channel of ATA program affecting agricultural labour time

As can be seen from the agriculture tax background, it is levied on the basis of agriculture income, which is decided by regular years' output, which again is decided on the land's natural condition and local general operation condition, and it remains unchanged in the next five years once it is decided. So, the tax on farmers is levied according to the quantity and quality of the land.

Generally, the ATA program do not change the marginal cost and benefit for the peasants, so it is regarded as a non-direct subsidy program and cannot affect the agriculture production and factor input activity. However, as a matter of fact, with the consideration of risk factor, the ATA program could probably affect the agriculture factor input activity at least on three aspects. Firstly, the probability for the peasants to get the loan from the bank increases because of the subsidy, and then reduces farmers' budget constraints. Moreover, the direct subsidy from the ATA program could allow the peasants to allocate more financial resources on agriculture production. Most importantly, the extent of risk aversion for the

[5] The reason why we choose December, 2004 as the split point, is that our CHNS2004 investigation is conducted during the September and December in 2004. Therefore, using December, 2004 as a split point could be able to divide the overall CHNS2004 data into two categories: participating group and non-participating group.

[6] As for the observations in the non-participating group, few of them in specific cities/counties are also implementing the ATA program before December, 2004, so we have dropped those individuals to guarantee all the observations are not attending the ATA program in this group. Meanwhile, for the participating group, we also have dropped some individuals to guarantee all the observations in this group are attending the ATA program before December, 2004.

peasants could decrease with the increase of wealth. So, the farmers might transfer from the high-risk grain production to low-risk off-farm employment to capture larger benefits. Therefore, the factor input structure, especially labour time allocation mechanism could be changed because of the ATA program (Young and Westcott, 2000). So, we conclude that the non-direct subsidy program could also be able to affect the farmers' labour time decision in this way.

4 Data and Descriptive Analysis

4.1 Data

This chapter uses the China Health and Nutrition Survey (CHNS) dataset collected by Population Research Center of North Carolina State University and the Nutrition and Food Safety Department of Chinese Center for Disease Control and Prevention. The investigation has been conducted for nine times from 1989 to 2011. In this chapter, we just select the years of 2000 and 2004 to cover both pre and post-ATA periods of the program. Two years data can be organised as a panel data set so as to control as many as possible time-invariant variables. It is a dataset that covered the eastern, central and western areas at the same time in China to investigate the effects of ATA program on time allocation mechanism in China. Most importantly, the large enough sample in nine provinces makes it possible to use the quasi-experiment method as it is only effective when we have larger number of observations. Furthermore, the panel data of 2000 and 2004 can effectively solve the problem of time-invariant and improve the reliability of causal inference.

A stratified random sampling method is used to collect the data, and the survey investigates the information at household and individual level. It requests the enumerators to come to the household and ask them about the related information. Meanwhile, specific questions related to village-level information are also included in questionnaires. In general, the questionnaire inquires much information about family and individuals' basic information, labour time allocation, health and nutritional information, income and expenditure, consumption and agriculture production information. Furthermore, a complete household roster has been used as a reference for subsequent blocks of questions on time allocation at work in and out of the formal market during the previous years.

Moreover, besides randomly selecting major cities in each province, it has also randomly selected four counties in each city according to income clusters and particular weighting factors. Then towns are selected from each county, from which three villages are selected according to clustered income, with each village 20 households.

So as to avoid the imbalanced panel data set, in our classification of individuals by time, we choose to drop individuals in the CHNS2000 survey who are not investigated in 2004 anymore. Similarly, we also drop individuals in the CHNS2004 survey who are not included in the CHNS2000 sample. Meanwhile, we exclude the urban individuals in the sample as our research focus on the on-farm labour time allocation for the farmers. In our classification of the rural households, we extend the peasants' definition to observations in villages, towns and counties as well, so we are also considering the agriculture labour time within generalised rural regions.

In accordance with the accustomed procedure on workers, we also confine our sample to individuals whose age ranges from 15 to 76. Moreover, in order to be qualified to strictly use the DID method, we define the individuals changed the participation status from non-participation before 2004 to participation after 2004 as treatment group, while people who do not participate the program in both of two periods are defined as control group. For the purpose of making our analysis credible, it is compulsory to request the individuals in treatment group not participate the program before 2004 and participate the program after 2004, while in control group individuals do not participate the program all the time.

Finally, as can be seen from Figure 1, we have drawled a sample of about 2,776 households with a total of 5,428 adult individuals in nine provinces, including the provinces of Guangxi, Guizhou, Heilongjiang, Henan, Hubei, Hunan, Jiangsu, Liaoning and Shandong.

According to the split point of December, 2004, we also find that there are 3,059 individuals in the treatment group (who do not participate the program

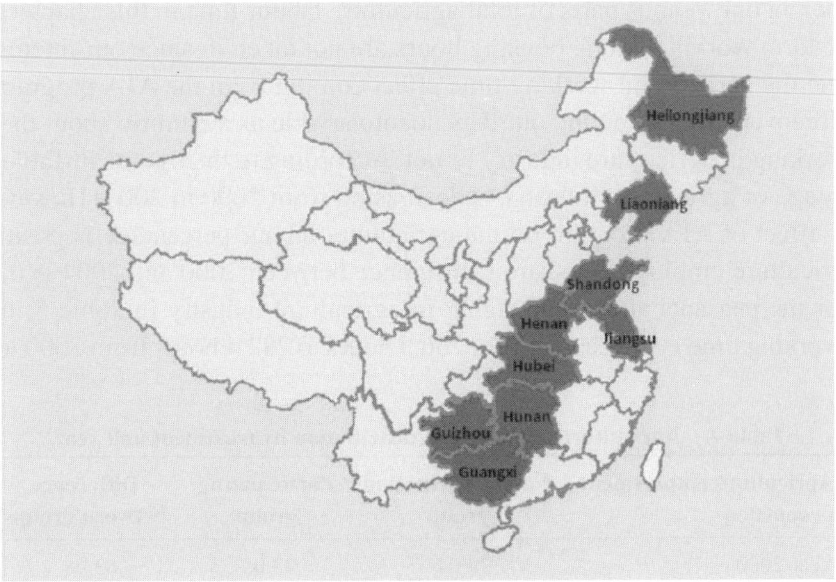

Figure 1. Sample distribution for the CHNS data set.

Note: The darker shaded regions in this map are the provinces in which the survey has been conducted. They are: Guangxi, Guizhou, Heilongjiang, Henan, Hubei, Hunan, Jiangsu, Liaoning, Shandong.

Table 3. Treatment distribution and sample description.

Treatment group	Control group
(Obs = 3059)	(Obs = 2369)
Do not participate the program before January, 2000 and participate it from December, 2004	Do not participate the program all the time from January, 2000 to December, 2004

Source: Authors' estimation from CHNS 2000 and 2004.

before January, 2000 and participate it before December, 2004) and 2,369 individuals in the control group (who do not participate the program all the time) (see in Table 3).

4.2 Descriptive analysis

4.2.1 *Dependent variables (On-farm labour time)*

Agriculture labour time is a central variable in this research. One point we should keep in mind is that our interest in this chapter is to estimate the agricultural working time effect because of the ATA program. Our decomposition of agricultural working time effect in this chapter will be confused if we take off-farm working time, housing time as parts of dependent variable definition. Therefore, we only include the garden labour hours, on-farm working hours, hours in fishing and livestock in one year as parts of total agriculture labour time in this chapter, while the off-farm working hours, housing hours are not taken in since our interest is to evaluate the agricultural working time effect coming from the ATA program.

Moreover, we also define our dependent variable as a dummy about the peasants working in agriculture industry or not. According to the figures in Table 4, the percentage of agriculture industry is decreasing from 2000 to 2004. However, the policy effect of ATA program on the agriculture labour percentage is positive, as the agriculture employment share's difference between 2000 and 2004 is 0.56%.

For the peasants already engaging in agriculture industry in Table 5, the on-farm working time is increasing from 266.3 hours to 282.4 hours from 2000 to 2004

Table 4. Agriculture employment distribution by treatment and year.

Agriculture employment proportion	Non-participating group	Participating group	Difference between groups
Year 2000	29.04	93.03	63.98
Year 2004	23.14	87.68	64.54
Difference between years	−5.91	−5.35	**0.56**

Sources: Authors' estimates from CHNS 2000 and 2004.

Table 5. On-farm labour time by treatment and year during 2000 and 2004.

On-farm labour hours	Non-participating group	Participating group	Difference between groups
Year 2000	205.5	266.3	60.8
Year 2004	150.9	282.4	131.4
Difference between years	–54.6	16.1	**70.7**

Sources: Authors' estimates from CHNS 2000 and 2004.

Table 6. Income improvement by treatment and year during 2000 and 2004.

On-farm income level	Non-participating group	Participating group	Difference between groups
Year 2000	1122.2	5010.1	3888.0
Year 2004	1596.5	6819.3	5222.7
Difference between years	474.3	1809.1	**1334.8**

Sources: Authors' estimates from CHNS 2000 and 2004 (Yuan).

for participating group, while it decreases sharply from 205.5 hours to 150.9 hours for non-participating group during this period. In total, the net effect of ATA program is to increase the agriculture labour time about 70.7 hours from 2000 to 2004.

Overall, from the Tables 4 and 5, we conclude that both of the population engaging in agriculture industry and the amount of on-farm working hours for the peasants already in agriculture industry increases a lot because of the ATA program. Thus, in Table 6, accompanied by the increasing agricultural labour input, the amount of farmers' income raised sharply compared with that of the period before the ATA program, and the farmers' income level raised 1334.8 Yuan triggered by the ATA program.

4.2.2 *Independent variables*

Besides the policy effect from ATA program, time allocation to agriculture activity also depends on a set of various factors that can be summarised as follows: individual and household characteristics variables, opportunity cost, and family assets variables, etc. In general, all the factors that probably affect farmers' time allocation decision should be included as explanatory variables. We expect that the larger the household size, the higher the possibility to move out for off-farm work (Stark and Bloom, 1985). Moreover, younger and more educated people are more likely to engage in off-farm work because of the lower psychological costs and higher revenue streams, so their on-farm working time is less compared to the older and less educated counterpart (Ehrenberg and Smith, 2005). At last, the education, age and related variables are included as independent variables in Table 7.

Table 7. Main factors that possibly affect agricultural labour time.

		Mean		tt test	
	Variables	Non-participating group	Participating group	Mean	Standard errors
Dependent variable	Time (hours)	21.36	255.1	−233.8***	(3.284)
	Time (dummy)	0.117	0.954	−0.838***	(0.00512)
Individual characteristics	Gender (% male)	0.500	0.452	0.0483***	(0.0105)
	Age (years)	46.06	45.83	0.236	(0.248)
	Marry status (married %)	0.830	0.898	−0.0683***	(0.00658)
	Ethnic	0.992	0.994	−0.00207	(0.00159)
	Education (year)	7.034	5.530	1.504***	(0.0792)
	Head (household head% yes)	0.419	0.436	−0.0171	(0.00955)
	Cardre_ind	0.0149	0.00134	0.0135***	(0.00165)
	Health	5.423	4.584	0.838***	(0.0377)
	Household size	3.817	4.063	−0.246***	(0.0287)
	# Children less than 7	0.585	0.681	−0.0961***	(0.0150)
Family characteristics	# Adult	2.731	2.841	−0.109***	(0.0233)
	# Elderly	0.140	0.0996	0.0400***	(0.00842)
	Family wealth	5391.2	4276.9	1114.3***	(84.39)
	Housing condition score	6.043	4.021	2.022***	(0.0397)
	Denc	5.712	5.120	0.591***	(0.0279)
Village/county characteristics	Comm	4.811	4.155	0.656***	(0.0212)
	Econ	5.394	2.373	3.021***	(0.0516)
	Sani	6.179	3.518	2.660***	(0.0489)

Note: Standard errors in parentheses; * $p < 0.05$, ** $p < 0.01$, *** $p < 0.001$
Source: Survey data collected by CHNS.

As can be seen from Table 7, there are indeed some differences between the two groups at 5% level with the two-sample tt test. Take education variable for example, the average education in non-participating group is higher at 1% significant level, which we can conclude that non-participating group peasants get more of education compared to that of participating group. The number of children less than seven within a family also presents an apparently difference, which demonstrates that the participating peasants have much more children less than seven within their families. Moreover, the amount of wealth for participating households is also less than that of the non-participating households at 5% level. Generally speaking, individuals in the participating group are less educated, with more children at school and higher amount of household wealth.

The dependent variable is measured by a continuous variable on the amount of on-farm working days within one year. Table 7 shows that the agriculture labour time pattern is very different between the participating and the non-participating groups. The on-farm working time are significantly higher in the non-participating group compared to that of participating group, because the tt test is apparently different with zero at 1% level.

5 Identification Strategy

Our objective is to test whether there are significant differences in agricultural labour time patterns between the participating and the non-participating group. So as to control for self-selection, we construct a "natural experiment" according to the policy that affects agricultural labour time. The DID method with controlled variables is then used to measure the net effect of the ATA policy on agriculture labour time.

We assume that the participating peasants in 2004 are the treatment group ("1" for short), and the non-participating peasants in 2004 are the control group ("0" for short). The time before the policy implementation is $t = 0$, and the time after is $t = 1$. Our target is to examine the difference before and after the policy for the treatment and the control groups.

The DID estimator is given by:

$$DD = E(Y_1^T - Y_0^T \mid T_1 = 1) - E(Y_1^c - Y_0^c \mid T_1 = 0) = E(G_1 \mid T_1 = 1), \tag{1}$$

where Y_1^T is the outcome of interest (agricultural labour time in our case) for individual i at time t (with $t = 0, 1$). The first term can eliminate separate changes trend for them. And the second term not only can control the time series trend and some other time-varying factors, but also can get the policy's net impacts (Bertrand *et al.*, 2004). We use the 2 × 2 quadrat method and the first order difference method to measure the DID.

Let us define A, B, C and D as the number of agricultural labour time in the following situations: A stands for the non-participating group before the implementation of the policy, B stands for the participating group before the implementation of the policy, C stands for the non-participating group after the implementation of the policy and D stands for the participating group after the implementation of the policy. We use $C–A$ to eliminate the non-participating group's time-varying trend and $D–B$ to eliminate the participating group's time-varying trend. As a result, *(D−B)* — *(C−A)* can eliminate the whole time series trend, and the remaining effect is the net impact of the policy on agricultural labour time.

We can translate this into a basic model:

$$Y = \beta_0 + \beta_1 \times year + \beta_2 \times decision + \beta_3 \times (year\_decision) + \varepsilon \qquad (2)$$

year is a dummy variable (0 before the policy, 1 after the policy); and *decision* is a dummy variable that equals 0 for a ATA non-participating peasant and 1 for a ATA participating peasant. It is straightforward to show that the coefficient β_3 of the interaction term is *(D−B)* – *(C−A)*, that is the net impact of the policy on agricultural labour time in our model.

Another assumption is that during the experiment, all the factors should stay the same or be randomly changed, except program participation changes. As it is very difficult to hold such assumption in social science research, so we control as many variables as possible to fill up this deficiency (Lalonde, 1986). On the basis of the controlled variables, the new DID model can be written as follows:

$$Y = \beta_0 + \beta_1 \times year + \beta_2 \times decision + \beta_3 \times (year\_decision) + X'\gamma + \varepsilon, \qquad (3)$$

X is a vector of control variables, including time invariant or time-varying observable variables, such as gender, ethnicity, family scale, education, age, the number of family labour, and a period dummy. ε is a random error, which reflects the unobservable factors that affect agricultural labour time. Unobservable effects and time-invariant factors could be eliminated by difference. In conclusion,β_1, β_2 and γ in the model are the coefficients to be estimated. Moreover, we also add variables of duration in the program to test whether the duration of participation in the program makes any difference with the "number of months in the program". Thus, heterogeneity of treatment effects can be examined by including interactions between duration and the treatment dummy variable. Moreover, similar variables like the amount of land participated in the program, the dummy variable for individuals within the major grain producing areas are also added into the models.

6 Empirical Estimation with DID Approach

6.1 Estimation results with DID approach

Following the theoretical analysis above, we use the DID method with controlled variables to regress agricultural labour time on ATA policy. Considering the correlation within households, we regress the model using the cluster option to account for clustered errors at the household level. The estimation results are reported in Table 8.

Table 8. Simple DID method with controlled variables analysis.

	(1)	(2)	(3)	(4)
year	−10.44***	−11.39***	−11.39***	−0.0499***
	(3.584)	(3.674)	(3.674)	(0.0110)
treatment	215.3***	214.6***	214.6***	0.804***
	(6.757)	(6.760)	(6.760)	(0.0133)
year_treatment	24.08***	24.93***	24.93***	0.0619***
	(7.554)	(7.592)	(7.592)	(0.0125)
gender	−13.88***	−13.76***	−13.76***	−0.0206***
	(3.321)	(3.322)	(3.322)	(0.00455)
age	−0.0788	−0.0723	−0.0723	0.000713**
	(0.197)	(0.197)	(0.197)	(0.000310)
marriage	−4.685	−4.608	−4.608	0.0273***
	(5.646)	(5.649)	(5.649)	(0.00934)
ethnic	44.40**	41.62**	41.62**	−0.00913
	(19.56)	(19.78)	(19.78)	(0.0450)
eduy	−2.041***	−2.000***	−2.000***	−0.00142*
	(0.581)	(0.584)	(0.584)	(0.000797)
hhsize	2.726	2.731	2.731	−0.00560*
	(2.176)	(2.176)	(2.176)	(0.00306)
child1	−0.964	−0.981	−0.981	0.00116
	(4.330)	(4.334)	(4.334)	(0.00521)
adult1	−2.166	−2.144	−2.144	−0.00394
	(2.763)	(2.763)	(2.763)	(0.00336)
elderly	−12.25**	−12.35**	−12.35**	0.00179
	(5.092)	(5.091)	(5.091)	(0.00786)
wealth	0.000798	0.000797	0.000797	0.00000191**
	(0.000531)	(0.000530)	(0.000530)	(0.000000818)
house	7.048***	7.096***	7.096***	−0.000634
	(2.075)	(2.078)	(2.078)	(0.00243)
denc	−6.711***	−6.722***	−6.722***	−0.00151
	(2.100)	(2.099)	(2.099)	(0.00271)
comm	−6.372**	−6.338**	−6.338**	0.00356
	(2.930)	(2.960)	(2.960)	(0.00399)
econ	−3.106***	−3.107***	−3.107***	−0.00719***
	(0.975)	(0.973)	(0.973)	(0.00156)
sani	−3.364**	−3.362**	−3.362**	−0.00723***
	(1.371)	(1.395)	(1.395)	(0.00184)
province1	−70.07***	−70.09***	−70.09***	0.0121
	(12.26)	(12.06)	(12.06)	(0.0178)

(*Continued*)

Table 8. (*Continued*)

	(1)	(2)	(3)	(4)
province2	−74.68***	−74.62***	−74.62***	−0.124***
	(12.33)	(12.80)	(12.80)	(0.0158)
province3	−67.84***	−68.06***	−68.06***	−0.0498***
	(11.03)	(11.83)	(11.83)	(0.0139)
province4	−73.52***	−73.65***	−73.65***	−0.173***
	(13.84)	(13.59)	(13.59)	(0.0177)
province5	−66.14***	−66.10***	−66.10***	−0.0532***
	(11.03)	(11.19)	(11.19)	(0.0155)
province6	−35.43***	−35.35***	−35.35***	−0.103***
	(12.16)	(12.39)	(12.39)	(0.0148)
province7	−35.13***	−35.36***	−35.36***	0.0679***
	(11.23)	(11.63)	(11.63)	(0.0218)
province8	−50.48***	−50.67***	−50.67***	−0.0255
	(12.27)	(12.52)	(12.52)	(0.0166)
cardre_ind	—	−23.65***	−23.65***	−0.0376
		(8.562)	(8.562)	(0.0273)
health	—	0.0103	0.0103	0.00473**
		(1.609)	(1.609)	(0.00203)
_cons	127.6***	130.1***	130.1***	0.193***
	(27.99)	(28.59)	(28.59)	(0.0558)
R^2	0.349	0.350	0.350	0.762
N	8845	8845	8845	8845

Notes: (1) The marginal effect for a dummy variable is the difference in probability of agriculture labour time relative to the reference group; for continuous variables, the effect is evaluated at the mean. The standard errors are clustered at the household level. (2) Standard errors in parentheses. $^{*}p < 0.10$, $^{**}p < 0.05$, $^{***}p < 0.01$.

Source: Survey data collected by CHNS 2000–2004.

Indeed, in the models (1), (2) and (3) that using OLS regression approach, the coefficients of the interaction term are positive, and all of them pass the 5% level significance test. In perspective of the estimation result, the coefficient is rather robust for the three controlled DID models. Table 8 shows that no matter models and controlled variables we include, the ATA program does exert a significant impact on agriculture labour time. On average, if other conditions remain unchanged, the policy increases the agriculture labour time for 24.08, 24.93 and 24.93 days in 2004 for model 1, model 2 and model 3 respectively. In general, the regression results among the three models are almost the same. Considering the explaining power for the added independent variables, the R2 in model 3 is much higher compared to other two models, and the added variables in model 3 are also have reasonable good explainable power on dependent variable, so we finally choose the model 3 as our final estimation model.

On the basis of model 3, we are also considering the dummy way to measure the dependent variable (whether to participate the on-farm work) to regress the explainable variables in model 4, and the results are the same while on-farm possibility for peasants will increase 6.19% because of the ATA program.

In addition, Table 8 also demonstrates that the on-farm peasants usually are young female, peasants who have those characteristics are more likely to stay in rural areas to engage in on-farm working. In model 4, the female are more likely to engage in on-farm work while the male are migrating out for off-farm work. Likewise, age is identified as positively affecting the probability of peasants engaging in agriculture labour, 10 year older actually increases 0.7% possibility for farmers to engage in agriculture labour activity at 5% level. As for the group of minority and married, their agriculture labour time is also apparently higher compared to the majority and single group even controlled as many as independent variables in different models.

Moreover, education is found to have an apparently effect on decreasing the possibility for peasants engaging in on-farm activity in model 4. Meanwhile, the agriculture labour time for the educated is also apparently less than their counterpart as well, as it pass the significance test at 1% level, which is rather robust in different models. Holding household size and the rest of the variables constant, increasing the number of education by 1% could improve the agriculture labour time by 2.0%. At last, as can be seen from Table 8, the number of elderly within a household is also an important factor to decrease the agriculture labour time in model 3.

6.2 Further effects with DID approach

Considering the positive impact of ATA program on peasants' agriculture labour time, we also reasonably expect that the longer to participate into the program, the larger effect of the program on agricultural labour time. As can be seen from Table 9, one month more to participate into the program for the peasants, 5.48 days more impacts could get from the ATA program.

Meanwhile, as displayed in Table 9, the amount of land is also the reason to explain the heterogonous effects between the households. The households with more of land could get larger impact on agriculture labour time from the ATA program. On average, with all of other variables constant, one more acre of land evolved into the ATA program, 3.27 days more engaged in on-farm working for the peasants.

Table 9. Simple DID — Linear regression estimates.

	(1) Treatment	(2) Duration	(3) Area	(4) Main
year	−11.56***	−12.31**	−46.19***	15.03
	(3.703)	(4.969)	(7.869)	(9.480)
treatment	214.8***	—	—	—
	(6.802)			
year_treatment	25.36***	—	—	—
	(7.645)			
gender	−13.83***	−20.37***	−23.64***	−17.39***
	(3.339)	(3.723)	(4.482)	(3.897)
age	−0.0718	−0.0734	−0.110	−0.378
	(0.199)	(0.232)	(0.275)	(0.247)
marriage	−4.545	2.101	2.101	3.227
	(5.680)	(6.725)	(8.201)	(7.095)
ethnic	41.81**	48.16**	38.00	67.53***
	(19.79)	(20.68)	(35.56)	(20.61)
eduy	−2.004***	−1.768***	−3.095***	−4.262***
	(0.587)	(0.667)	(0.844)	(0.698)
cardre_ind	−23.81***	−43.18***	−149.5***	−59.17***
	(8.579)	(11.48)	(21.54)	(10.50)
health	−0.00571	−0.478	−1.870	0.528
	(1.618)	(1.899)	(2.153)	(1.814)
hhsize	2.673	2.903	1.344	3.188
	(2.184)	(2.578)	(2.888)	(2.696)
child1	−0.966	3.568	3.844	0.496
	(4.357)	(4.972)	(5.504)	(5.247)
adult1	−1.979	−0.890	−2.218	−3.134
	(2.767)	(3.100)	(3.414)	(3.228)
elderly	−12.54**	−14.99***	−12.19*	−15.70**
	(5.103)	(5.762)	(6.986)	(6.276)
wealth	0.000804	0.0000607	-0.000777	0.00125*
	(0.000533)	(0.000578)	(0.000708)	(0.000653)
house	7.150***	4.112*	3.754	−2.380
	(2.087)	(2.361)	(2.770)	(2.130)
denc	−6.719***	−6.969***	−9.861***	−8.004***
	(2.112)	(2.528)	(3.112)	(2.456)
comm	−6.338**	−9.114***	−9.517**	−16.80***
	(2.979)	(3.344)	(3.774)	(3.305)
econ	−3.105***	−8.775***	−10.09***	−12.90***
	(0.977)	(1.183)	(1.335)	(1.223)

(*Continued*)

Table 9. (*Continued*)

	(1)	(2)	(3)	(4)
	Treatment	**Duration**	**Area**	**Main**
sani	−3.391**	−11.38***	−8.760***	−6.559***
	(1.402)	(1.620)	(1.849)	(1.649)
province1	−70.44***	−121.7***	−118.8***	—
	(12.12)	(14.62)	(15.94)	
province2	−74.83***	−249.7***	−156.7***	—
	(12.87)	(14.41)	(18.21)	
province3	−68.47***	−134.5***	−55.36***	—
	(11.90)	(14.59)	(15.32)	
province4	−73.92***	−132.0***	−89.74***	—
	(13.66)	(15.26)	(17.23)	
province5	−66.34***	−132.7***	−138.9***	—
	(11.23)	(13.53)	(14.44)	
province6	−35.53***	−127.0***	−26.53*	—
	(12.46)	(14.26)	(16.11)	
province7	−35.21***	−116.1***	−117.0***	—
	(11.72)	(13.95)	(15.69)	
province8	−50.80***	−98.91***	−89.96***	—
	(12.60)	(15.17)	(16.50)	
duration	—	23.65***	—	—
		(1.398)		
year_duration	—	5.476***	—	—
		(1.716)		
area	—	—	2.441***	—
			(0.631)	
year_area	—	—	3.267***	—
			(0.935)	
main	—	—	—	−25.45***
				(9.554)
year_main	—	—	—	−27.41***
				(10.48)
_cons	129.8***	358.1***	433.3***	360.9***
	(28.67)	(31.64)	(45.17)	(32.44)
R^2	0.348	0.225	0.184	0.151
N	8845	8845	7060	8845

Notes: (1) The marginal effect for a dummy variable is the difference in probability of agriculture labour time relative to the reference group; for continuous variables, the effect is evaluated at the mean. The standard errors are clustered at the household level. (2) Standard errors in parentheses. $*p < 0.10$, $**p < 0.05$, $***p < 0.01$.

Source: Survey data collected by CHNS 2000–2004.

Apart of demographic characteristics for the peasants, the regional factors could also play an important role in deciding the amount of program effects on on-farm working time. As some regions could enjoy the preferential if they satisfy some specific conditions according to the program design, and some of them could even get an exemption of paying the agriculture tax, especially in the developing areas such as areas of regional national autonomy, ethnic minority areas, old revolutionary bases and outlying and poverty-stricken areas, etc. Therefore, the program effects vary across different regions.

Specifically in Table 9, the peasants locating in major grain producing area could get less of 27.41 days impact on on-farm working because of the ATA program. It might come from the ATA program's different subsidy rates on peasants, as the tax burden on agriculture product in the major grain producing area is less compared to its counterpart. Therefore, abolishing of agriculture tax on peasants in major grain producing area gets less of impact from the ATA program.

7 Sensitivity Analysis

Until now, we have implicitly assumed that the ATA Program had the same effect that clearly separated among different agriculture products. However, according to the program design, the tax rate between different agriculture products are not the same, and the regional average tax rates for the specific agriculture product at provincial level are also different across the provinces. Moreover, the agriculture tax's levy approaches also varies widely among different agriculture products. In general, for the grain crops like paddy, wheat, millet, Chinese sorghum, etc., the levitation of agricultural tax is based on the agricultural income, which is decided by regular years' agriculture output on the land. However, for the cash crops like horticultural crops, the tax rate is specially decided by the local governments based on regular year's output and the price of those products in the market, etc.

Therefore, as a sensitivity analysis, we now relax the assumption of the same effect on different agricultural categories and distinguish the ATA program's heterogamous effects on on-farm working time. In this part, in order to do the sensitivity analysis of average treatment effects, we still use the DID as a method to double check the treatment effects of the ATA program on agriculture labour time.

As can be seen from Table 10, average treatment effects varied widely among different agriculture product categories. Specifically, in the garden product field, the ATA program could bring 70.2 hours on-farm working for the peasants. On the contrary, the ATA program negatively affects the peasants' on-farm working for more than 205.1 hours in the fish product field. Moreover, the effect of ATA program on agriculture labour time is not significant any more in the farm and livestock industries.

Table 10. Sensitivity DID — Linear regression estimates.

	(1)	(2)	(3)	(4)
	Garden	**Farm**	**Fish**	**Livestock**
year	−51.82**	63.45	256.7***	−6.075
	(21.35)	(71.57)	(85.84)	(20.73)
treatment	−66.33***	26.13	−15.00	−14.69
	(20.12)	(45.11)	(78.20)	(16.09)
year_treatment	70.22***	−44.53	−205.1**	10.02
	(22.17)	(71.93)	(92.36)	(21.33)
gender	16.92***	7.862	30.36	4.569
	(4.497)	(4.872)	(27.17)	(5.750)
age	−0.566*	−0.583*	0.193	0.716***
	(0.335)	(0.300)	(1.936)	(0.256)
marriage	−8.049	−9.113	−66.58	−15.98*
	(8.256)	(9.619)	(57.58)	(9.007)
ethnic	55.44**	43.91	—	−0.654
	(23.05)	(29.70)		(31.20)
eduy	−1.317	−1.338	−4.461	−1.499*
	(0.951)	(0.974)	(3.253)	(0.795)
cardre_ind	−157.1***	−43.76	—	−95.16***
	(37.35)	(39.69)		(11.67)
health	3.003	−7.656***	4.718	0.481
	(2.304)	(2.337)	(7.205)	(2.299)
hhsize	4.035	6.573**	7.018	1.042
	(2.830)	(2.905)	(12.59)	(2.240)
child1	−4.191	−4.075	−16.33	2.373
	(4.888)	(5.176)	(21.28)	(3.858)
adult1	−2.519	2.864	18.45	2.497
	(2.939)	(3.539)	(12.16)	(2.285)
elderly	−8.795	−15.60	−50.95	−13.02***
	(8.034)	(9.897)	(40.50)	(4.850)
wealth	0.000845	−0.00225**	0.000744	0.00196**
	(0.000944)	(0.000973)	(0.00465)	(0.000794)
house	9.024***	3.723	15.07	5.480**
	(3.229)	(3.629)	(20.35)	(2.572)
denc	−17.52***	−20.22***	11.19	2.194
	(3.965)	(3.954)	(15.92)	(2.568)
comm	4.736	−3.401	−51.23	−9.829***
	(3.789)	(3.768)	(32.18)	(3.100)

(*Continued*)

Table 10. (*Continued*)

	(1)	(2)	(3)	(4)
	Garden	Farm	Fish	Livestock
econ	0.498	−3.782**	20.81	0.455
	(1.867)	(1.768)	(16.45)	(1.689)
sani	−3.134*	−2.639	0.734	0.138
	(1.802)	(2.081)	(13.77)	(1.472)
province1	−29.31**	−76.14***	−398.6**	−0.673
	(14.44)	(15.69)	(163.7)	(12.33)
province2	0.558	−75.17***	110.7	82.79***
	(15.83)	(16.65)	(108.3)	(14.82)
province3	−14.44	−52.40***	12.68	−30.66**
	(13.26)	(15.17)	(75.50)	(14.52)
province4	44.68**	51.14**	197.2*	−6.871
	(17.92)	(24.91)	(102.7)	(11.23)
province5	−48.22***	−34.43**	158.5*	25.30*
	(12.80)	(16.88)	(89.44)	(14.53)
province6	43.68***	−2.471	194.9**	−2.186
	(16.78)	(15.38)	(96.53)	(10.54)
province7	33.82*	−59.79***	146.8	14.68
	(19.27)	(20.97)	(96.77)	(18.09)
province8	15.91	−74.09***	76.68	−10.74
	(13.95)	(17.40)	(73.42)	(11.59)
_cons	164.8***	326.0***	58.62	123.0**
	(44.89)	(69.01)	(164.7)	(51.96)
R^2	0.075	0.079	0.390	0.062
N	3656	3802	121	2775

Note: Standard errors in parentheses; $*p < 0.10$, $**p < 0.05$, $***p < 0.01$.
Source: Survey data collected by CHNS 2000–2004.

8 Program Heterogeneous Effects by Sub-groups

In order to test the heterogeneous effect of the program on various groups of individuals, we further decompose the effect of the program along three dimensions: gender, education and household wealth (see Table 11). As a result, we find notable differences when we stratify by gender, education and wealth.

For the heterogeneous effects by gender, we find that the male group gets more of impact from the ATA program, as the male's on-farm working days are 24.33 more compared to that of the female group.

Apart from gender factor, we have also examined the ATA program's heterogeneous effects on different wealth level. As displayed in model 2 of Table 11, the

Table 11. Impacts of ATA policy on sub-groups.

	(1) Gender	(2) Wealth	(3) Edu1	(4) Edu2
Year	−18.45***	−13.48***	−18.21***	−14.51***
	(4.639)	(4.268)	(3.662)	(3.899)
Treatment	225.0***	204.8***	203.0***	218.6***
	(7.785)	(7.469)	(8.749)	(6.964)
year_treatment	14.90*	38.08***	38.73***	23.23***
	(8.833)	(9.280)	(10.80)	(8.071)
year_treatment_gender	24.33**	—	—	—
	(9.909)			
Gender	−15.10***	−13.53***	−16.50***	−17.31***
	(4.014)	(3.335)	(3.152)	(3.052)
Age	−0.0499	−0.0924	0.0385	0.134
	(0.199)	(0.198)	(0.196)	(0.193)
Marriage	−4.946	−4.333	−4.311	−4.364
	(5.668)	(5.673)	(5.675)	(5.672)
Ethnic	36.10*	40.98**	29.47	27.44
	(19.76)	(19.47)	(19.30)	(19.41)
Eduy	−1.946***	−1.974***	—	—
	(0.589)	(0.587)		
Cardre_ind	−23.07***	−24.23***	−29.10***	−28.56***
	(8.435)	(8.921)	(8.470)	(8.234)
Health	−0.0393	0.0250	−0.0973	−0.0946
	(1.619)	(1.617)	(1.616)	(1.618)
hhsize	2.564	2.642	2.420	2.512
	(2.183)	(2.193)	(2.192)	(2.189)
Child 1	−0.821	−1.061	−0.560	−0.787
	(4.356)	(4.359)	(4.356)	(4.367)
Adult 1	−1.905	−1.995	−1.871	−1.747
	(2.764)	(2.785)	(2.768)	(2.756)
Elderly	−12.40**	-12.11**	−12.30**	−12.30**
	(5.113)	(5.097)	(5.110)	(5.082)
Wealth	0.000742	0.000178	0.000588	0.000623
	(0.000535)	(0.000605)	(0.000530)	(0.000533)
House	7.118***	7.048***	6.668***	6.717***
	(2.088)	(2.087)	(2.075)	(2.074)
Denc	−6.726***	−6.822***	−6.815***	−6.737***
	(2.114)	(2.117)	(2.117)	(2.110)

(*Continued*)

Table 11. (*Continued*)

	(1) Gender	(2) Wealth	(3) Edu1	(4) Edu2
Comm	−6.317**	−6.222**	−6.366**	−6.395**
	(2.980)	(2.965)	(2.989)	(2.977)
Econ	−3.098***	−3.149***	−3.185***	−3.278***
	(0.978)	(0.980)	(0.976)	(0.974)
Sani	−3.382**	−3.482**	−3.300**	−3.367**
	(1.402)	(1.402)	(1.404)	(1.401)
Province 1	−70.79***	−72.71***	−70.97***	−71.97***
	(12.12)	(12.19)	(12.12)	(12.17)
Province 2	−74.88***	−75.57***	−76.91***	−77.37***
	(12.87)	(12.79)	(12.84)	(12.84)
Province 3	−68.88***	−70.13***	−68.10***	−68.37***
	(11.90)	(11.92)	(11.93)	(11.94)
Province 4	−73.86***	−76.02***	−74.44***	−75.15***
	(13.66)	(13.76)	(13.69)	(13.69)
Province 5	−66.57***	−67.81***	−67.89***	−68.47***
	(11.23)	(11.28)	(11.24)	(11.21)
Province 6	−35.46***	−36.36***	−36.78***	−36.42***
	(12.46)	(12.44)	(12.45)	(12.45)
Province 7	−35.30***	−37.18***	−37.09***	−37.34***
	(11.72)	(11.78)	(11.65)	(11.67)
Province 8	−51.21***	−52.28***	−52.33***	−53.09***
	(12.59)	(12.60)	(12.61)	(12.64)
year_gender	14.04***	—	—	—
	(4.399)			
treatment_gender	−22.75***	—	—	—
	(7.224)			
year_treatment_ incomed	—	−48.92***	—	—
		(17.03)		
year_incomed	—	5.935	—	—
		(6.084)		
treatment_incomed	—	38.22***	—	—
		(12.74)		
year_treatment_ belowprim	—	—	−20.83	—
			(13.18)	

(*Continued*)

Table 11. (*Continued*)

	(1) Gender	(2) Wealth	(3) Edu1	(4) Edu2
year_belowprim	—	—	7.298 (4.730)	—
treatment_belowprim	—	—	19.62** (9.162)	—
year_treatment_ abovemid	—	—	—	46.48** (23.45)
year_abovemid	—	—	—	−3.795 (4.443)
treatment_abovemid	—	—	—	−52.34*** (15.29)
R^2	0.349	0.349	0.347	0.348
N	8845	8845	8845	8845

Note: Standard errors in parentheses; $*p < 0.10$, $**p < 0.05$, $***p < 0.01$.
Source: Survey data collected by CHNS.

wealthy peasants could get 48.92 days less of impact from ATA program compared that of the poor peasants. It might come from the less budget constraint on the wealthy farmers as they can easily migrate to non-farm regions to engage in off-farm employment before the program.

Finally, the heterogeneous effects from the ATA program on different education groups are also considered. The better educated group is found to receive a significantly larger effect from the program on average. As can be seen from Table 11, the coefficient of the ATA program's effect are significantly different with zero in columns 3 and 4, which further demonstrate the larger effect of ATA program on on-farm working time for the educated. In column 4 of Table 11, the group with college and above could get more of 46.48 hours impact coming from the ATA program compared to the group with an education level of primary school.

9 Conclusion

The past decades have witnessed a stable agricultural tax burden on farmers in rural China. As a result, lots of problems emerge in the rural area because of the high agriculture tax burden, especially the increasing urban–rural income inequality and social segmentation, the unharmonious relationship between carders and peasants, and the decreasing grain production in rural China, etc. Therefore, improving rural households' income level and grain production has become a prime task from the beginning of 2000s and tax cutting projects are part of the agenda. The background of the implementation of such policies can be traced back to 2001 in Anhui province when they launched a pilot project to gradually reduce the agriculture tax on farmers.

The ATA program implemented from 2002 aimed at reducing burden on farmers or protecting agriculture activity by abolishing the agriculture tax burden and subsidising on the farmers. From January, 2006, the ATA has been national wide conducted by the central government with the same criterion in provincial level, which makes it exogenous and compulsory for the individuals to participate the program. Therefore, it can be treated as a "natural experiment" for ordinary peasants.

To assess the net effect of policy on agricultural labour time, we use a DID method with controlled variables. We find that the ATA Program does exert significantly positive effects on agricultural labour time, which is different from some existing researches (such as Gale *et al.*, 2005; Chen, 2009). In perspective of peasant' possibility to engage in agriculture industry, the peasants have a higher of 6.19% possibility to engage in agriculture industry because of the ATA program. In other words, the program promotes more of people to engage in agricultural labour activities. Furthermore, in the perspective of peasant' on-farm working time for the peasants that already in the agriculture industry, the average net effect of the program is to increase agriculture labour time by 24 hours for the participating group in 2004.

Moreover, we find a larger impact of the program for the group of less educated young female in the garden product field, while it is not significant any more in the farm and livestock industries. And the impact coefficients are positive for all the models, which is stable and robust in the different models. Most importantly, those impacted groups are the disadvantaged in rural China, this might seem rather interesting as agriculture taxation abolishment has been seen as distortionary in our case, and its immovability on land makes agriculture taxation an attractive tax base in the face of growing tax competition for government (Heady, 2002). In particular, the increasing agriculture labour time leads to higher grain production and more agriculture income for the disadvantaged because of the ATA program, we also provides a reasonable explanation for the increasing grain production and farmer' income in recent years.

Furthermore, taxation on land may be particularly attractive in developing countries, because land ownership is often strongly concentrated amongst the rich, especially in western rural China. In addition, tax on land is a tax that is difficult to avoid, and so should be attractive to developing countries with limited administrative capabilities.

Therefore, it is acceptable if the government could provide more of similar programs to improve the grain safety and raise the farmers' income, especially for the disadvantaged to shrink the income inequality within rural areas and then the income inequality between urban and rural areas.

Appendix 1. Agricultural Tax Reform in China: 2003–2005

	2003	**2004**	**2005**
Agriculture tax	39,220	20,403	1,272
Special agricultural products tax	2,828	0	0
Agriculture tax surcharge	9,660	4,894	351
Total	51,709	25,297	1,622

Note: Numbers in the table are in million CNY.
Source: These data are collected from the official website of Ministry of Agriculture, China (http://www.agri.gov.cn).

Appendix 2. Definition of Variables

	Variable definition
Dependent variable	
Time (hours)	The amount of hours engaging in on-farm activity
Timed (dummy)	To engage in on-farm work or not (yes = 1)
Program variables	
Treatment	Dummy variable: program participation = 1.
Year	Dummy variable: after the policy = 1.
Year ´Treatment	Interaction term of "Treatment" and "Year".
Duration in Program	Number of months participating in the program
Program area	Number of land for the households to participate the program
Program region (Main)	Major grain producing areas or not (yes=1)
Year × Duration	Interaction term of "Duration" and "Year"
Year × Program area	Interaction term of "Program area" and "Year"
Year × Main	Interaction term of "Program region" and "Year"

(*Continued*)

(Continued)

	Variable definition
Individual level variables	
Gender	Dummy variable: male = 1
Age	Individuals' age
Marry status	Dummy variable: being married = 1
Ethnic	Dummy variable: Majority = 1
Education year	The amount of received education (years)
Household level variables	
Household size	Number of permanent members in the household
# Children	Number of children less than 7 within a family.
# Adult	Number of adult (the age ranges from 15 to 66)
# Elderly	Number of elderly members
Family wealth	Total amount of family wealth per capita
Other variables	
Province	Dummy variables (yes = 1)

References

Alig, R.J., D.M. Adams and B.A. Mc Carl (1998), Impacts of Incorporating Land Exchanges between Forestry and Agriculture in Sector Models, *Journal of Agricultural and Applied Economics,* 30(2), 389–401.

Bertrand, M., D. Esther and S. Mullainathan (2004), How Much Should We Trust Differences-in-Differences Estimates? *Quarterly Journal of Economics*, 119(1), 249–275.

Chen, X. (2009), Review of China's Agricultural and Rural Development: Policy Changes and Current Issues, *China Agricultural Economic Review*, 1(2), 121–135.

Chen, X. (2004), Issues Concerning the Increasing of Grain Output and Farmers' Incomes, *Xuexi Shibao*, In Chinese, Translated by Foreign Broadcast Information Service, June 30, 2004.

Cohen, L. (1959), An Empirical Measurement of the Built-in Flexibility of the Individual Income Tax, *American Economic Review*, 49(2), 532–541.

Ehrenberg R. G., R. S. Smith (2005), *Modern Labor Economics*. Addison Wesley: USA.

Gale F., B. Lohmar and F. Tuan (2005), China's New Farm Subsidies, USDA/ERS, Url: http://Ers.Usda.Gov/Publications/WRS0501(Last Date Accessed: 13 February 2008).

Ghandi, U. P. (1966), *Tax Burden on Indian Agriculture*. 1966 , pp. 240.

Goodwin, B. K. and A.K. Mishra (2003), *Acreage Effects of Decoupled Programs at the Extensive Margin.* Paper Prepared for Presentation at the American Agricultural Economics Association Annual Meeting, Montreal Canada, July, 2003.

Gu, H. and J. Yueqing (2008), The Impact of Agricultural Tax Abolishment Program on Factor Input for Farmers — Based on the Data In Jurong, Jiangsu Province, *Journal of Agrotechnical Economics,* 37–42. (In Chinese)

Hertel Thomas and W., E. Tsigas (1988), Tax Policy and U.S. Agriculture: A General Equilibrium Analysis, *American Journal of Agricultural Economics*,70(2), 289–302.

Higgs, E. S. (1976), The History of European Agriculture, *Philosophical Transactions of Royal Society*. B, 275, 159–173.

Lalonde Robert, J. (1986), Evaluating the Econometric Evaluations of Training Programs with Experimental Data, *American Economic Review*, 76(4), 604–620.

Lin, J. Y. and M. Liu (2007), Rural Informal Taxation in China: Historical Evolution and an Analytic Framework, *China & World Economy*, 1, 1–18.

Ma Y. and Y. Yun (2005), The Direct Subsidies to Grain Producers: The Policy's Impacts on Farmers' Willingness to Grow Grain Crops, Their Income and Inputs-A Case Study in Hebei Province, *Journal of Agrotechnical Economics*, 2005(2), 7–13.

Mishra, A. K. and B.K. Goodwin (1977), Farm Income Variability and the Supply of Off-farm Labor, *American Journal of Agricultural Economics*, 79, 880–887.

NBS (National Bureau of Statistics), China Statistical Yearbook, *China Statistical Publishing House*, Beijing, various years (2000–2012).

Ni,H. (2004), Five Major Issues Needing Resolution in the Abolition of the Three Agricultural Taxes, *China Economic Daily*, Online Edition in Chinese, Translated by Foreign Broadcast Information Service, June 24, 2004.

Orden, D., F. Cheng, H. Nguyen, U. Grote, M. Thomas, K. Mullen and D. Sun (2007), *Agricultural Producer Support Estimates for Developing Countries: Measurement Issues and Evidence from India, Indonesia, China, and Vietnam* — IFPRI Research Report 152 Washington, DC.: International Food Policy Research Institute.

Schiff, M. and A. Valdes (1992), *The Plundering of Agriculture in Developing Countries*, The World Bank Washington, DC.

Schneider Uwe A. and A. Mccarl Bruce (2005), Implications of a Carbon-Based Energy Tax for U.S. Agriculture, *Agricultural and Resource Economics Review,* 34(2), 265–279.

Serra, T., K. Goodwin Barry and M. Featherstone Allen (2005), Agricultural Policy Reform and Off-Farm Labour Decisions, *Journal of Agricultural Economics*, 56 (2), 271–285.

Stark, O. and D. Bloom (1985), The New Economics of Labor Migration, *American Economic Review*, 75(2), 173–178.

Valdés, A. (1996). Surveillance of Agricultural Price and Trade Policy in Latin America during Major Policy Reforms. *World Bank Discussion Paper* 349. Washington, DC.

Woldehanna, T., A. Oude-Lansink and J. Peerlings (2000), Off-Farm Work Decisions on Dutch Cash Crop Farms and the 1992 and Agenda 2000 CAP Reforms, *Agricultural Economics*, 22, 163–171.

Xu, C., W. H. Holly and S. Qinghua, (2012), Farmers' Income and Production Responses to Rural Taxation Reform in Three Regions in China, *Journal of Agricultural Economics*, 63(2), 291–309.

Xu, C., Q. Shi and H. Wang (2009), The Impact of Rural Taxation Reform on Farmer Households' Income: Evidences from 15 Villages of Yangtze River Delta in China, *Chinese Rural Economics*, 290, 22–33. (In Chinese)

Young, C.E. and P. Westcott (2000), How Decoupled is U.S. Agricultural Support for Major Crops? *American Journal of Agricultural Economics*, 82, 762–767.

Yu, W. and H.G. Jensen (2010), China's Agricultural Policy Transition: Impacts of Recent Reforms and Future Scenarios, *Journal of Agricultural Economics*, 61, 343–368.

Zhou, L. A. and Y. Chen (2005), The Policy Effect of Tax-For-Fees Reforms in Rural China: A Difference-In-Differences Estimation, *Economic Research Journal*, 8, 44–53. (In Chinese)

Chapter 10

Rural Land Transfer and Registration in China: Perspectives from Stakeholders

Jun Li* and Pei Guo†
College of Economics and Management,
China Agricultural University, Beijing, China
**sirlijun@cau.edu.cn*
†guopei@cau.edu.cn

Abstract: The purpose of this chapter is to contribute to land transfers and land registration which are presently the central issues in rural China, and which get increasing concern in academia. The chapter uses the dataset from interviewing "farmer households" with questionnaires and the "focus group" approaches, besides interviewing a bunch of individuals, this approach incorporated government officials at different levels as well as the associated stakeholder organisations. The results indicate a comprehensive figure of the opinions and attitudes of those involved. 'Focus group' approach provided rural land contracts, rural land transfers, land disputes, limitations of current contract certification system. The household interviews provided respondents views on general land issues, land registration and rural land transfers. The value of this chapter indicates that the perspectives from stakeholders capture the characteristics of the land transfers and land registration in order to put forward feasible policy implications.

1 Introduction

Since the adoption of the Household Responsibility System (HRS) in the late 1970s, China's agriculture has enjoyed a significant growth and the living standards of farmers have increasingly grown higher as well. In 2002, a specific law governing rural land contracts granted farmers' inheritance rights to their land and the ability to transfer out and transfer in land, and the rural land contract has a term of 30 years. Rural welfare is at the top of the Chinese government's priority list today, while rural land is at the heart of most rural issues and disputes. The most prominent issue is that with its ever worsening rural–urban income disparity, farmers' incomes have been lagging far behind their urban counterparts. Numerous studies indicate that land has a substantial direct and indirect bearing on issues of income disparity in China's rural areas (Lin, 1992; Dong, 1996; Li *et al.*,1998; Yao, 2000; Deininger and Jin, 2002).

Under the HRS, practically all rural households are able to contract and farm land from their rural collectives. The central government also provided further protection for farmers' rural land use and contracting rights through the 1998 *Land Management Law* and the 2007 *Property Rights Law*. Yet, farmers' land use and contracting rights established by law is far from fully implemented.

Based on independent research, not many farmers actually possess any written documentation — a Rural Land Use and Contracting Certificate or a Rural Land Use and Contracting Contract — that confirms their legal rights to land. For the already issued Certificates or Contracts, a vast majority of them do not comply with the law and lack legal validity. Further, the insecurity of farmers' land rights is demonstrated by frequent illegal land expropriations, administrative readjustments, or re-contracting to outside developers against farmers' wishes. (Carter and Yang, 1999) Finally, the level of land transactions has been relatively low due to the insecurity of rights, the lack of institutional safeguards, and high transaction costs.

Secure, long-term, and marketable land rights is one of the fundamental prerequisites for the assurance of a basic rural livelihood, sustainable investments in land by farmers, the orderly development of a rural land transfer market and the continuing growth of rural income. Land registration is an important means of implementing and confirming the land rights.

One of the classical land registrations, named "Fish-Scale Register" (*yulin tuce*), which was field cadasters for the purpose of taxation and recorded information about owner, boundary, area of the land parcel. The institution emerged during the Southern Song period (1127–1279) in Yangtze river basin and extended across the nation from Ming Dynasty (1368–1644) to the middle of 20th century (Zhao, 2010).

However, the current registration system of rural land rights has been grossly ineffective for two reasons. Firstly, the ownership rights and contracting rights of rural land registered by two Ministries are incomplete, inconsistent, or even contradictory. Secondly, there are no clear laws on how land rights should be registered. The utility of the current registration system is minimal and serious reform is required.

Chinese Central Government chooses one area to be addressed by its first policy document each and every year — so-called "No. 1 Document" — to indicate its top priority. In the past nine consecutive years, the topics are all about agricultural and rural development with different focuses. In each No.1 Document, the rural land transfer and registration are mentioned and some measures are put forward to be implemented.

Correspondingly, the Chinese Ministry of Agriculture implemented agricultural land registration pilot projects in eight provinces in 2009. However, agricultural land registration is still new and a challenge to China's vast rural areas with regard to the design of a rural land registration system, the data to be registered, and the support and expectations of stakeholders. In preparation for the larger-scale pilot projects, it was necessary to gather further up-to-date information on the development of rural land markets and the attitudes of various stakeholders towards land registration, as a vital input into the understanding of how rural land registration systems will be used, and as a potential and timely input into the design of large-scale piloting exercises.

In anticipation of this, a rural land registration pilot project was undertaken in two villages of Feidong County of Anhui Province, during the period July 2005 to January 2009 by the Chinese government, with assistance from FAO, the World Bank and the Canadian International Development Agency (CIDA). The objective was to establish a functioning rural land registration system for 89 farmer households and 810 land parcels involved. The experiences and lessons learned have been invaluable and used in formulating recommendations for further larger-scale pilot projects which will in turn eventually lead to a national roll-out strategy.[1]

This chapter is to examine the stakeholders' perspectives on rural land transfer and land registration in China in order to put forward feasible policy implications. Part 1 introduces the background of this research, while Part 2 provides the methodology and data. Parts 3 and 4 attempt to indicate the preliminary findings from focus group discussions as well as farmer households surveys, and further discussions and policy implications are drawn in Part 5.

2 Methodology and Data

As land markets fluctuate according to a range of factors, some of which are outside the immediate locality, it is important to contextualise data generated by surveys. Therefore, this study has undertaken a review of selected existing written literatures on land markets and land registration in China, in order to provide a broader context in which to view the results of the survey analysis.

---

[1] *A Preliminary National Strategy on Land Registration in China* January 15, 2009 — FAO, WB & CIDA.

A questionnaire on key issues relating to land market development, perceptions and expectations relating to land registration was prepared for interviewing individual farmer households. Separate lists of questions were prepared as a basis for structured discussions with focus groups, which included government officials and other stakeholders.

The objective of the interviews and group discussions was to determine:

(1) the type of transactions that are likely to needed to be recorded in a future title registration system;
(2) the volume of each of these types of transaction, both systematic and sporadic;
(3) the likely cost of performing transactions and related land surveys;
(4) the willingness of farmers to pay for registration and surveys;
(5) farmers' attitudes towards precision of boundary measurements, and therefore the cost of land surveys;
(6) farmers' attitudes toward individual or communal property rights;
(7) capacity to carry out land surveys, both systematic and sporadic;
(8) legal support in rural areas to assist with land transactions; and
(9) the opinions of other stakeholders such as government officials, financial institutions, law firms and other agencies towards establishing a land registration system.

Anhui and Shandong provinces were selected to conduct the surveys. Anhui Province represents the southern and inland provinces, while Shandong Province represents the northern and coastal provinces. Both are representative of rural development models in China, particularly reflecting the trend and direction of China's rural land reform. These two provinces are also the provinces adopted by the Ministry of Agriculture in 2009 for the agricultural land registration pilot projects. Government officials, agencies and farmers in these two provinces have exposure to, and experience of, land registration issues and thus were expected to be useful sources of information about the practical issues involved in the implementation of an agricultural land registration system.

Two counties and villages in each province were selected on the advice of the Provincial and County level Agriculture Commissions using criteria relating to levels of market activity — Qingyang and Feidong counties in Anhui province and Tengzhou and Feicheng counties in Shandong Province. Field visits were undertaken in December 2009, January 2010 and August 2012, respectively.

Approximately, 30 farmer households were selected by random sampling from each of the eight villages identified from the two selected provinces. A total of 250 interviews were held, which resulted in 244 valid questionnaires (representing 97.6% of the interviews). Eight focus group meetings were held in the two provinces, which comprised a total of 35 government officials from different administrative levels and 20 representatives from other agencies.

3 Findings from Focus Group Discussions

The rural land registration process in China is a complicated procedure, involving the farmer household contractors, different levels of government and various other agencies. In order to obtain a comprehensive figure of the opinions and attitudes of those involved, the survey was extended from the farmer households to incorporate these different groups. Rather than interviewing a series of individuals, a 'focus group' approach was adopted incorporating government officials at different administrative levels as well as the associated stakeholder organisations.

In addition to sharing experiences on land certification and registration, these group discussions provided a wide range of information regarding social development, agricultural production, household income, land use, agricultural land transfers and land management in the cities and counties involved. Data collected on the general economic situation and social development include the local geographical environment, population structure, level of education, employment and levels of economic and social development. The agricultural production data mainly concern local agricultural production levels and individual farm household production. The land management data provided is based on the published land policy of the local government, which includes the recognition of the right to transfer contracted land use rights and the handling of legal disputes on rural land.

3.1 Land transfer

3.1.1 *Rural land contracts*

During the period of 1995–2005, most of China's regions adopted the second round of 30-year agricultural land contracting. Agricultural land was allocated based on household population, with women having equal rights as men. Currently, the average per capita of cultivated land in Anhui Province is 1.4 mu[2] and in Shandong Province 1.2 mu.

Under Chinese law, contracted agricultural land cannot be readjusted during the contract period, even if the number of household or village member changes. However, the population has changed significantly within the last 10 years resulting in uneven land holding patterns in some areas. Besides population changes, land acquisitions and other reasons (such as marriages of offspring thus creating new

[2] 1 mu is equal to 0.1647 acres (1 acre is equal to 6 mu).

households) have resulted in an increase in the number of rural landless. Anhui agricultural officials estimate that landless farmers account for as much as 10% of the total number of individual farmers. The number of landless rural households, however, is much less, estimated at a mere 0.1% of the total rural households, as usually at least one person in the household is likely to possess a parcel of contracted land.

This marked imbalance between farmers and land, has prompted some local officials to support rural land readjustment prior to land registration. For example, one village leader in Feicheng suggested that agricultural land should be reallocated more evenly, based on the number of the village population, prior to land registration. A number of landless peasants wanted the land to be readjusted during the registration.

3.1.2 *Rural land transfer*

The proportion of agricultural land transfers in China has increased gradually with economic development and with increases in rural migration. According to a sample survey in Anhui Province in 2008, the agricultural land turnover ratio[3] was 12.4% based on area. The agricultural land transfer area in Shandong province amounted to 5.49 million mu in 2008, which accounts for 6.1% of the total contracted area, and involves about 1.51 million farmers, or about 7.8% of the total.

The consensus indicated that government officials generally support and encourage agricultural land transfer. For example, Tengzhou City has set up agricultural land transfer trading centres at both county and township levels. Favourable local land policies aimed at increasing productivity through economies of scale and mechanisation also encourage land transfer. On the other hand, some agricultural officials stated that they are concerned that rural land transfers may lead to land disputes and may result in a decline in grain output.

The discussants generally agreed that rural land registration is conducive to the development of land markets, and the number of rural land transfers will increase in the next 5–10 years, but the scale of the increase would be limited. One provincial agricultural official in Shandong stated that as rural land transfers were related to the level of economic development and the amount of labour migration, higher transfer ratios are not necessarily a good thing. One official in Qingyang County stated, that farmers' willingness to transfer out their land may be impeded to some extent by the current system of agricultural subsidies.

[3] Turnover ratios are often given based on area. From a land registration view point, the number of land parcels transferred may be of greater significance than the amount of land transferred. Further, this is not an annual ratio but a cumulative one.

3.1.3 *Land disputes*

Land is one source of disputes in rural areas. In Shandong Province, around 70% of Farmers' petitions are related to land. A lawyer in Feicheng classified land disputes into three categories: the first kind, land transfer disputes were raised from farmers who want to take back land they had previously transferred, particularly where returning migrant labourers want to re-establish their farming income; the second concern disputes over the amount of compensation received for expropriated land; and the third category of disputes is related to land readjustments (or lack of them, where increases in local populations occur without a corresponding reallocation of contracted land).

There also exists a further type of land dispute associated with land tax reform. Before the tax reforms of 2006, many farmers did not want to keep their contracted land, as the rural land tax represented a relatively heavy burden. Village collectives often took back contracted land that was offered to them and in many cases rented it out to large grain producing farmers or enterprises. These subsequent agreements were often on the basis of long-term contracts, at rental levels that were only equal to, or even lower than, the agricultural taxes and fees charged on the original farmer households. Following the implementation of new tax exemption and subsidy policies, disputes have arisen when many farmers wanted to take back their original land, because long-term leases had already been signed, their requests been rejected.

3.1.4 *Limitations of current contract certification system*

Currently, land contracts and land certificates are designed by each province or county. The law requires the Village Collective to issue land contracts to each farmer household and to submit an application to register the Collective's ownership with the county government. The law also requires that the county government issues land user rights certificates to farmers, and maintains a register of such rights.

During the discussions, it was found that some local cadres felt that the existing contracts worked well. However, there were also many local cadres who recognised that the current contract certification system contains many defects and that the establishment of an improved rural land registration system is needed. One of the main problems identified is that there are two certification-issuing agencies involved in the current system. According to the Land Departments in both provinces, Anhui and Shandong have more or less completed the registration of agricultural land ownership (as at the end of 2009) with most ownership certificates having been issued to the village collectives. These activities are conducted by the Land Departments of each province. However, the certificate of rural land contract (or use) rights is issued by the Agricultural Department. This separate certification by two different departments creates a lot of problems and most discussants thought that there should be a single department responsible for issuing the two certificates.

Another concern is associated with the accuracy of the recorded land area. A large number of land parcels in the initial certification were 'measured' only by rough estimate and there are likely to be significant differences between the actual land area and that recorded in the certificate. The discussants generally agreed that registration should be based on accurate measurement of the land area. Based on the evidence from the pilot project in Anhui recorded land allocations can be as much as, 30% lower than the actual land area.

3.2 Land registration

3.2.1 *Requirements for land registration*

The majority of cadres interviewed thought that an improved system of rural land registration would have important practical implications and therefore they largely supported undertaking this work. The village leaders of Huolong and Hucun indicated that registration would help to further stabilise farmers' contract rights and secure higher compensation where land expropriations take place. An improved land registration system would also promote the land transfer market since a more comprehensive register would contain rich information about the original contractor and also accurate land areas. One county leader in Feidong County pointed out that land registration would help the capitalisation of the land assets and augment the investment and rural consumption, which in turn would promote domestic demand and economic growth.

One provincial official in the Agricultural Department of Shandong Province said that land registration is important where there is inheritance or inter-generational transfer of property rights, which is of greater significance since introduction of the Chinese government's policy of 'perpetual rural land contract rights'. A lawyer from Feicheng County agreed that land registration will help to protect farmers' property rights since China's new Property Law treats rural land contract rights as property rights. It was also noted that there was no need to register agricultural land if reallocation of land happens frequently.[4]

[4]The reallocation/readjustment of rural land in China was mainly adopted by the village administration without paying any compensation to the land-decreased farmer households. Therefore, farmer households are unlikely to generate much demand for accurate land registration if they feel that their rights are insecure.

Some cadres considered that more accurate measurement of land parcels would lead to a greater number of disputes, which would be a difficult problem for the authorities. A small number of cadres also stated that once farmers had registration certificates, this might lead to difficulties in public land acquisitions which might delay the construction of public facilities.

3.2.2 *Registration costs*

Some cadres expressed their concerns regarding land registration, in particular, that it would not be affordable to local authorities. Land registration is considered to be relatively expensive. For example, in the Hucun Village of Tengzhou County, the cost of registration is around RMB 215 yuan per household, even though they use relatively simple mapping techniques to register the larger land parcels. Costs will be much higher when dealing with parcels in difficult terrain such as mountains or hilly areas. One of the main concerns expressed was who would share these costs and how would they be apportioned?

The majority of cadres felt that registration costs should not be borne by the farmers, mainly because they could not afford any additional financial burden, as agricultural income is still relatively low. Farmers should only bear the cost of the registration certificate fee (currently less than RMB 10 yuan). They also felt that farmers may not be able to clearly identify the benefits of registration and therefore might not be willing to pay the full cost. Another reason given was that land ownership still belonged to the Village Collective and farmers only possess contract/use rights, and therefore, farmers should not bear the registration costs.

One agribusiness manager in Feicheng City said that enterprises would be prepared to bear the costs involved in registration of land transfers (that is, subsequent registrations) together with a portion of the initial registration costs — but not the full cost of the initial registration. One official in Hefei City pointed out that this would only provide a small portion of the total cost of initial registration (as the number of enterprises involved in land transfers is relatively small) and therefore, this would not resolve the problem. The majority of interviewed cadres held that the initial registration of rural land was a kind of government action and the cost should therefore be borne by government, but not local government, which could not afford such a huge expenditure, concluding that central government should bear the cost.[5]

[5] Yet a central government official has stated that the provincial government should take the responsibility for financing rural land registration, in keeping with current fiscal policy. Government's position on this still needs to be confirmed. Meanwhile, both provincial and local levels of government have indicated a lack of budgetary resources to deal with this.

3.2.3 *Mortgaging of rural land*

The *Guarantee Law* in 1995 provides that user rights to land (in certain circumstances) but it specifically prohibits the mortgaging of arable land rights. The *Property Law* in 2007, classifying contracted rural land rights as 'usufruct' rights, which theoretically could be used as collateral for bank loans, remains silent on the issue. This has created a degree of legal ambiguity with regard to interpreting the latest government thinking. In any event, the registration of rural land will make the registration of rural land rights technically possible.

The discussants claimed that a considerable proportion of farmers support the position that rural land should be mortgageable and rural enterprises are particularly enthusiastic for this. Two managers of agricultural enterprises in Qingyang and Feidong counties, and one large-scale grain producer, agreed that they were looking forward to having access to land mortgages. Most of the agricultural sector cadres were also inclined to support the introduction of rural mortgages. Two provincial officials in Anhui and Shandong agreed that rural land mortgages would allow small farmers to get micro-credit from banks. One village leader in the pilot village of Tengzhou City stated that there would be little risk involved in the mortgaging of rural land, but that loans should be used for agricultural production purposes, the reason being that, compared with non-farming activities, farming would be more secure and less risky.

Banking institutions have different views about the mortgaging of agricultural land. One banker in Feicheng indicated that rural credit cooperatives may welcome rural land mortgages, but they will nevertheless carefully assess the total household income and ability to make their repayments, rather than assessing the value of the land as collateral. Another banker in Feicheng stated that registration certificates would make it easier for farmers to get loans but that the amounts involved are likely to be very small. Similarly, one banker in Qingyang County argued that agricultural land as loan collateral is not ideal for several reasons. Firstly, the lack of developed secondary land markets would make it difficult for banks to liquidate the collateral in the event of defaults. Secondly, there is a lack of rural land valuation agencies and therefore no fair valuation standards that could be applied in assessing the amount of loans. It was also noted that starting from 2008, Anhui Province has successfully introduced the mortgaging of forest warrants, following the forest tenure reforms, but in only a very small number of cases.

4. Findings from the Farmer Household Surveys

The household interviews provided a wealth of information on the circumstances and views of individual farming families in the two provinces. The results of the 244 completed questionnaires have been summarised under the headings,

(1) Respondents Views on General Land Issues, (2) Respondents Views on Land Registration and (3) Respondents Views on Rural Land Transfers, as follows.

4.1 Rural land transfers

4.1.1 *Land fragmentation*

China is a country with large mountains and hilly areas, and as a result arable land tends to be widely scattered and fragmented. The implementation of HRS started in early 1980's brought about the first and second rounds of farmland contracting, which highlighted the degree of fragmentation. The average size of individual arable land parcels in China is 1.38 mu. However, this varies considerably from region to region and within the sample it can be seen that the average parcel size in Anhui is 0.97 mu and in Shandong 1.57 mu. This difference is probably explained by topographical variations, Anhui being hilly, while Shandong comprises flat farmlands. It is also interesting to note that the average size of transferred land parcels is are much smaller, being 0.74 mu and 1.12 mu in Anhui and Shandong respectively. In addition, the average number of parcels held by households in Anhui province is 7.5 compared with Shandong province which is 4.9.

4.1.2 *Number of land transfers*

The data from this survey illustrate that the land-transfer rate appears to be relatively high, both in Anhui and Shandong provinces, whether considering the number of transfers or the area of land transferred. There were 95 land parcels transferred out of a total of 580 in the sample, which represents 16.38% by number or 11.59% by area of land transferred. Of these, the proportion by number is 18.90% and 12.71% for Anhui and Shandong respectively, and by area 11.59% and 9.03% respectively. Thus, from the viewpoint of both the number of transferred land parcels and the area of land transferred, the land transfer ratio in Anhui is significantly higher than in Shandong.

Table 1. Land transfer data.

Land parcel data	Anhui	Shandong	Total/Average
Number of Land Parcels	344	236	580
Number of Land Transfers	65	30	95
Land Transfer Ratio by number	18.90%	12.71%	16.38%
Area of Land Parcels (mu)	333.89	370.35	704.24
Area of Land Transferred (mu)	48.2	33.45	81.65
Land Transfer Ratio by Area	14.44%	9.03%	11.59%

4.1.3 *Reasons for high level of land transfers*

According to the survey, 64.79% of land parcel transfers are due to labour shortages; 23.94% are due to farmers' unwillingness to cultivate (due to age, low benefit level, etc.); while 5.63% are due to having no time to cultivate and the remaining 5.63% transferred their lands for other reasons.

Thus, it is clear that the main reason for transferring land is the lack of labour force to continue working the land caused by the migration of rural labour to cities. This was more apparent in Anhui province, where it was found that 68.29% of interviewees cited this as the reason for land transfer compared with 60% in Shandong.

4.1.4 *Types of land transaction*

According to the survey, the most popular types of land transactions are leasing and sub-contracting. Taking Anhui and Shandong provinces together, it was reported that, 52.11% of cultivated land was transferred by sub-lease, and 28.17% by sub-contract, together accounting for 80.28% of the transactions. Other forms of transfers, not recognised in the regulations, such as entrusting the land to village committees or transferring in other ways, accounted for 20%.

In Anhui and Shandong, land transfers by leasing account for 58.53% and 43.33% respectively; while 24.39% and 33.33% were transferred by sub-contracting. The difference between sub-lease and sub-contract is, whether the transferee is the member of village collective. With the development of rural land markets, more and more transferees are from outside of the village. As a result, the number of sub-contract transactions is dropping and sub-lease transactions is going up and

Table 2. Land transactions by type.

Pattern	Anhui	Shandong	Total	%
Sub-contracting	10	10	20	28.2
Leasing	24	13	37	52.1
Transferring	0	0	0	0.0
Swapping	0	0	0	0.0
Others:				
Share Holding	0	0	0	0.0
Entrust to Village Committee	1	1	2	2.8
Uncertain	6	6	12	16.9
Total	41	30	71	100.0

becoming the main form of land transfer. Swapping rarely occurs, because a swap usually requires that both parties have similar size land and that the respective land parcels would be contiguous after the swap. Entrusting to the village committee is becoming less and less common as village committees tend to transfer the land to others on behalf of village collective.

4.1.5 *Rural land transferees*

In rural China, land is often transferred to relatives, local villagers, non-local farmers, enterprises, land cooperatives, and others. In accordance with relevant land policies, village collectives do not act as transfer-in parties for rural land. From the survey of Anhui and Shandong provinces, it can be seen that the bulk of transfers were to farmers' relatives and neighbours (local villagers) which accounted for 81.70% of the transfers. Only 14.08% of the transfers were to non-local farmers and a mere 4.22% were to enterprises. There were no transfers to Land Co-operatives and few cases of entrusting to Village Committees.

This point was more pronounced in Anhui province where it was found that 48.78% of the land transactions were to local villagers, 34.15% were to relatives, with only 12.20% and 4.88% of the land being transferred to non-local farming households and enterprises. In Shandong, 43.33% of the land transfer was to relatives and friends, 36.67% was to the local villagers, and only 16.67% and 3.33% respectively was to non-local farmers and enterprises.

4.1.6 *Forms of contracts*

As noted above, in Anhui and Shandong provinces the vast majority of land transfers took place between relatives and neighbours/acquaintances in the same village, which would explain why most land transfers were made by oral agreement. Only farmers who transferred their lands to non-local farming households and enterprises signed formal contracts. It was reported that among all 41 transferred land parcels in Anhui, only three were subject to contracts, accounting for 7.32% of total number of land parcels. In Shandong, 30 transferred land parcels were investigated, and only one parcel (3.33%) had a formal contract.

4.1.7 *Length of term of sub-lease or sub-contract*

As most of the land transactions occurred mainly among relatives, friends or local villagers (94.37% of the transfers, and 91.18% by land area) and did not have formal contracts, most land transfers had no clearly defined term. A total of 55 land parcels out of the 71 transferred were subject to being reclaimed by the

Table 3. Length of lease terms.

	Anhui		Shandong		Total	
Land Transfer term	**Parcel**	**Area**	**Parcel**	**Area**	**Parcel**	**Area**
Subject to Reclaim	28	29.8	27	30.05	55	59.85
1 Year	3	4.4	2	1.4	5	5.8
2 Years	1	1.3	0	0	1	1.3
3 Years	3	2.7	0	0	3	2.7
5 Years	3	5.2	1	2	4	7.2
15 Years	3	4.8	0	0	3	4.8
Total	41	48.2	30	33.45	71	81.65

'owner' upon his return. Of the remaining 16, 4 had written contracts, 2 with terms fixed at one year and 2 with terms fixed at five years. The remaining 12 transfers were oral agreements with length of terms agreed at between one and five years (though in three cases in Anhui terms of 15 years were agreed).

Based on the analysis, 4.4 mu and 1.4 mu of transferred land had terms of 1 year, in Anhui and Shandong, respectively, and 5.2 mu and 2.0 mu of transferred land had terms fixed at five years.

4.1.8 *Land transfer prices*

It is interesting to look at variations in transfer prices over time, in order to establish price patterns and trends. It is difficult to extrapolate with certainty where the land market is, or has been, relatively unsophisticated, where parties may be uninformed or have a close relationship, and where sample size is relatively small, however, it would appear that there is a general trend towards increasing rental levels over time.

With regard to rental variations or increases within the term of a sub-contract or lease, most agreements are based on fixed rents for the term of the transfer and few have provided for rental variations or 'floating' rents, where the rent is agreed, for example, annually. The data showed only eight parcels, or 11.27% of the transfers, adopting a floating rent. Of the 41 transferred parcels in Anhui, six parcels (9.2 mu) were subject to a floating rent, while only two (1.42 mu) of the 30 transferred arable land parcels in Shandong had provided for variations in rental levels. This suggests that either the transferors are not fully aware of the local market conditions and possible trends in increasing rental values or, that the rental income generated from the transfers is relatively low compared with non-farming income and not a major concern for the transferor (Figure 1).

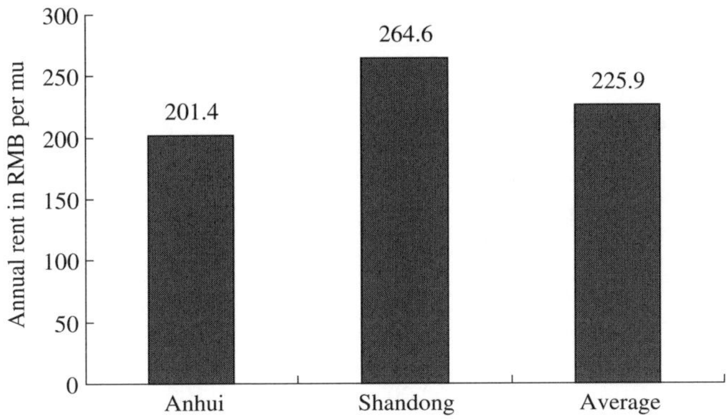

Figure 1. Average rentals per mu per annum.

4.1.9 *Comparison of income before and after land transfers*

According to the survey results, the income before land transfers was much higher than the rent received under the transfer agreements. In Anhui and Shandong, the average income per mu before land transfers was RMB 476.87 yuan. This seems to suggest that farmers are not prepared to invest time and labour in the land as, compared with the income from migrant work, many farmers are willing to lease out their land at relatively low charges, many even at no charge at all.

Before land transfers, the annual income of 20 parcels ranged between RMB 0 and 200 yuan per mu, accounting for 23.20%; 18 parcels were in the range RMB 200–300 yuan per mu, accounting for 25.54%, six ranged from RMB 300–500 yuan per mu, accounting for 5.06%, four had an income of RMB 540 yuan per mu, accounting for 3.45%, six of them were RMB 720 yuan per mu, accounting for 8.64%, nine of them were RMB 800 yuan per mu, accounting for 13.65% and two of them were RMB 900 yuan per mu, accounting for 9.87%.

4.1.10 *Trends in land transfers*

Notwithstanding the relatively small sample size and the data incomplete for the earlier years, there appears to be an increasing number of transactions taking place since the new millennium, peaking at 12–16 transactions per year out of a survey group of 244 households, which represents 4.9–6.6%. There are however, marked fluctuations, in particular 2009 which saw only three transactions within the survey group. And in the same year, this tailing-off in the number of transactions is likely to be the result of the global financial crisis, which resulted in huge numbers of migrant workers losing their jobs and returning to their rural homes to resume farming activities (Figures 2 and 3).

Table 4. Average income (RMB per mu) before land transfer.

	Anhui		Shandong		Total	
Level of revenue	**Area**	**%**	**Area**	**%**	**Area**	**%**
(0–200)	12.8	26.56	6.0	17.94	18.8	23.03
(200–500)	15.8	32.78	9.0	26.91	24.8	30.37
(500–800)	9.6	19.92	13.85	41.41	23.45	28.72
(800+)	4.0	08.30	4.0	11.96	8.0	9.80
Unclear	6.0	12.45	0.6	1.79	6.6	8.03
Total	48.2	100.00	33.45	100.00	81.65	100.00

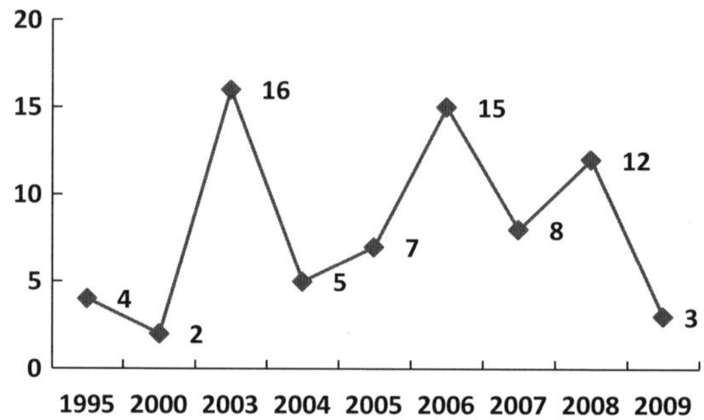

Figure 2. Transfers of cultivated land (By number of land parcels).

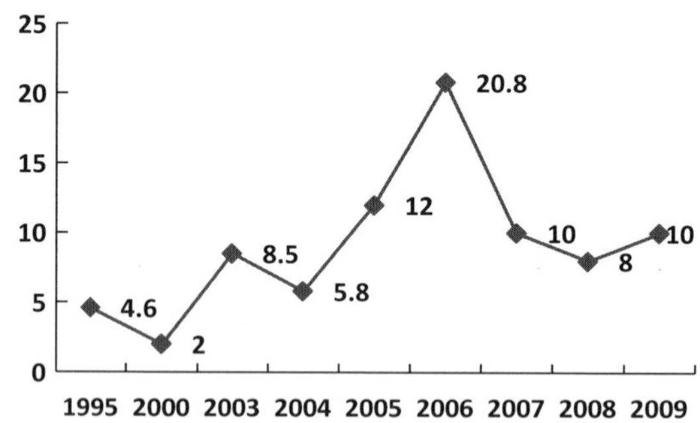

Figure 3. Transfers of cultivated land (By area — mu).

4.2 Land registration

4.2.1 *Current documentation and registration system*

Currently, land contracts and land certificates are designed by each province or county, or even at the township level, resulting in a wide variety of deviations from the law that reduce or nullify the legal force of such documents. Previous surveys have found that large numbers of households have no contracts or certificates, or if they have, they are missing essential elements (such as adequate land descriptions, accurate acreage or boundary demarcation).

The survey in Anhui Province found that only 5.3% of the respondents had not been issued with land contract certificates. However, of those that did, many were lost (13.6%) or damaged, indicating that farmers often did not attach much importance to them. Significantly, only 55.26% of the certificates issued contained clear registration details, meaning that nearly half of the contract certificates in the sample were defective. Thus, the current land registration system in Anhui Province could not be considered to provide adequate protection for all. In Shandong Province, land contract certificates have basically been issued to all farmer households with clear registration details.

4.2.2 *Expectations from rural land registration*

In many areas of China, insufficient legal regulation and ineffective rural land right protection has often resulted land disputes and in farmers' land being taken illegally and converted into non-farming use. It was therefore not surprising to find that the majority of interviewed farmers hoped that the legal effect of land contracting could be effectively reinforced. More accurate and detailed land registration would increase the effectiveness of the Rural Land Contract Law, which in turn would help to resolve land disputes.

As indicated in Figure 4 below, 60.00% and 54.84% of the interviewees in the two provinces thought that land registration should be legally binding, while 38.18% and 41.94% of the respondents would like to see more precise land

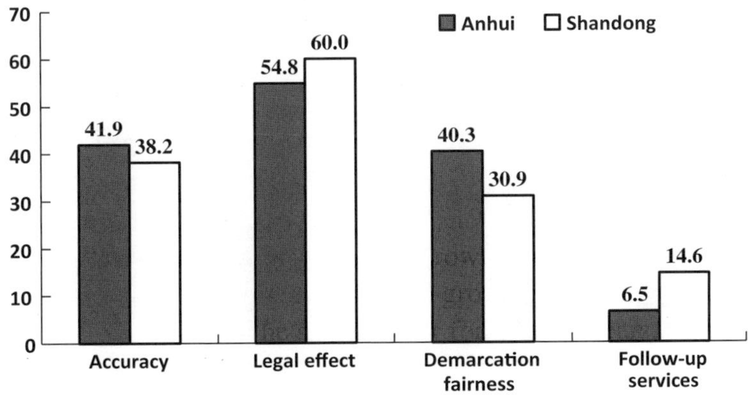

Figure 4. Expectations from rural land registration (%).

surveys. 30.91% and 40.32% of the respondents considered that accurate demarcation of land parcels would be fair and would not cause new disputes, while 14.55% and 6.45% thought that follow-up services should be in place to enable registration of subsequent transfers. This suggests that at present farmer households are on the whole not aware of the benefits of subsequent transfer registration.

4.2.3 *Contract details to be registered*

The interviewees on the whole were of the opinion that the land registration certificate should amongst other things include the contractor's name, the dimensions of the plot and its area, the quality or grade of the land, the duration of the contract, the responsibilities and rights of the contractor and the defaulting penalties.

In Shandong and Anhui, 51.06% and 50.00% respectively considered the location and dimensions should be registered, and 59.57% and 55.36% considered that the land area should be included. 36.17% and 32.14% believed that the land contract period should be registered; 42.55% and 26.79% wanted the quality and grade of the land to be included; 74.47% and 48.21% thought that the rights and responsibilities of contractors should be registered; and 27.66% and 16.07% thought that the records of subsequent land transfers should also be registered (Figure 5).

4.2.4 *Responsible authority for issuing land registration certificates*

While the Rural Land Contracting Law in 2002 (RLCL) requires that the county government issue land rights certificates to farmers, in reality, the certificate-issuing agencies (usually part of the Agricultural Department) may be a different

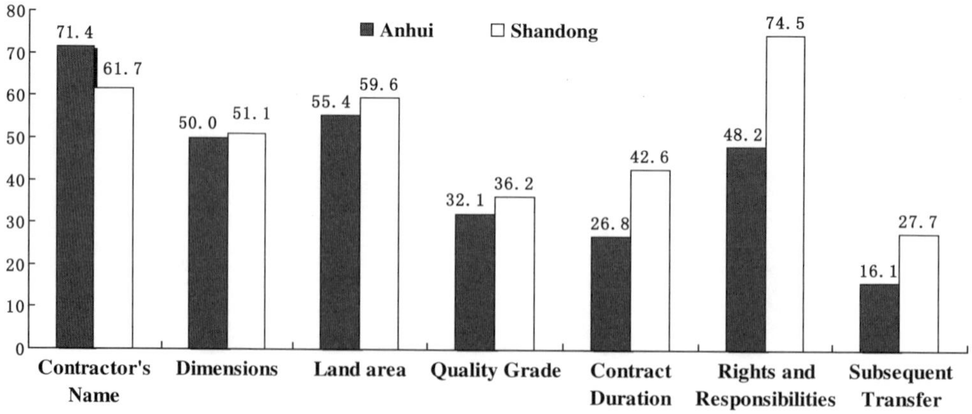

Figure 5. Views on the contract details to be registered (%).

level of government. In China, the administrative level of the land registration office is related to the degree of authority of the registration, as well as the level of operating costs. Usually, the higher the administrative level, the more serious the certification is taken, and the higher the fees that would be charged.

On this point, the majority of interviewees in Feidong County of Anhui Province thought that the certificate should be issued by either township or county level government, as this would make issuing certificates easier and would facilitate dispute resolution. For instance, 67.9% of respondents thought that land registration should be carried out by township government and 22.3% thought the county level government should be responsible. Only 8.9% thought that municipal government was the appropriate level, while 0.9% of did not care which level of governments was responsible.

4.2.5 *Funding rural land registration*

The costs associated with land registration increases with the level of detail recorded, but in any event, are considered to be relatively high. The results of the recent FAO rural land registration pilot project in Huolong Village, Shitang Town in Anhui Province, indicated a total cost averaging about RMB 80 yuan per parcel. Meanwhile, the pilot project conducted by Ministry of Agriculture in Tengzhou City, Shandong Province, indicated the cost at RMB 215 yuan per rural household. However, it is likely that larger-scale roll-out programs would achieve significant savings over these figures.

Perhaps because land contract certification is perceived as playing a significant role in protecting farmer's land use rights and stabilising agricultural production, the majority of the respondents stated that a more accurate and detailed registration and certification system is required. When asked if, in the event of mass or systematic registration, they would be willing to pay a land registration fee, more than half said they would.

In Anhui and Shandong, approximately 70% (68.85% and 70.37% respectively) of the respondents said they needed more accurately measured and detailed land registration certificates, with 57.26% saying they were willing to pay a fee. However, 41.88% said they could only afford RMB 10 yuan or less, while 15.38% said they could pay between RMB 10–50 yuan.

5. International Experiences for China

Experiences of the land administration projects carried out by the World Bank has shown that the stable and long-term rural land rights transfer is one of the imperative conditions to guarantee the basic livelihood of the rural areas, to promote sustainable investment in the land by the producers, and to achieve the sound development of rural land transfer market so as to sustain the growth of farmers' income.

Countries can be divided into three groups regarding to their rural land right systems. The first group includes those countries in which the distribution of rural land rights is still going on and has not yet been completed. The original allocation of rural land rights has been implemented and ended up in the countries in the second group in which, the rural land management system are already in place and effective, or the system has taken shape but needs to further roll out to cover the regions and sectors nationwide. The third group embraces the countries where the basic rural land rights system and management mechanism are in full-fledge and going quite well.

In the above sense, China can be classified into the second group, so the rural land related system needs to be further improved. From the World Bank practices, some elements should be considered by the Chinese policy makers to ensure the scale-up of the rural land registration system.

Firstly, the establishment of a single agency responsible for land registration and cadastral management is the most effective mode, but it requires the strong political will of the government to achieve. Taking Romania as an example, the urban and rural land management system was separately administrated by different government agency historically, but Romania eventually established an independent agency to take charge of land registration and cadastral management with strong political will and government support, and the rural land registration system was speeded up to take shape.

Secondly, the sustainability of the rural land system must be taken into account at the both design and implement phrases. Land registration is not a one-time action, and a continued action can provide updated information and services in a very long-term. Therefore, it is vital to encourage farmers to continuously use the system voluntarily and the land registration department could really provide the convenient and reliable services to the public for a long time. Some countries had failed when they attempted to carry out land registration system mainly due to a not-well-designed rural land system.

Thirdly, the public awareness and community participation are the solid foundations to guarantee the sound development of land registration system. In Vietnam, the information dissemination and farmer mobilisation were well done and farmers were much clear that the purpose of land registration is to further ensure their own legal and long-term rights of the contracting land. Moreover, the women, disabled, illiterate, poor households, migrant workers and the like vulnerable people were also acknowledgeable to the rural land registration system establishment. All the above public awareness activities have achieved satisfying effect.

Fourth, controlling the cost of land registration played important role for a successful rural land registration practice. According to the World Bank's studies in the 1990s, the registration cost of each land parcel averaged between USD 20 and USD 50 in many developing countries, and the break-down was: land survey accounted for 22%, land mapping 24%, arbitration and adjudication 18%, paper work 23% and institution-building 13%. The possible avenues to significantly reduce the land registration cost is to simplify the registration procedure for reducing the staff labour time, to increase the farmers' participation to help determine the land boundary, to produce the necessary documents of ownership and reduce the recording errors and disputes. In addition, selection of suitable land registration technology will also make big difference in the total registration costs, so the IT systems need to be revised and updated from time to time.

Fifth, the government should enact legislation for the land registration and certification based on the pilot practices. In Ukraine, for example, the pilot rural land registration practices of restructuring the small farm land rights makes the public and government decision-makers recognise the positive significance of the land registration and certification. Eventually, the government enacted new land registration legislation and issued new land rights certificates accordingly. Based on the new registration reform, farmers have to update the stored land information to ensure the subsequent land transfer or trading.

Last but not least, charging a reasonable fee for land registration and related transactions is another factor to ensure a successful land registration system. Land registration can be an income-generating activity for land registration authority. The World Bank project experienced that, although the initial registration of land was usually government-funded in many countries, the current trend is to ensure the land registration services financial sustainable, that simply means the revenue can surpass its cost. Therefore, the government needs to develop a reasonable fee for land registration and related information inquiries. In addition, the registration fee could also help the land registration agencies provide customers with quality service according to the public demands, and to simplify improve the transparency of procedures and reduce the possibility of wrongdoing of land registration agency.

6 Further Discussions and Policy Implications

6.1 Further discussions

Based on the subsequent interview in Anhui Province in 2012, more questions which lie in the issues of land registration have no clear answers.

The land values and the urgency of registration: One official in Feidong County proposed that registration should be carried out as soon as possible while land values are low in order to reduce the potential disputes, otherwise the number of disputes could be enormous. But, according to the classical theories of property rights, the increasing values of resources, such as land, enlarge the demand of clear definition of rights bundle, namely, the higher the values of land becomes, the clearer the definition is, and *vice versa*. Actually, the lands in urban fringe with higher market value need land registration or certificates more urgently. Therefore, the responsible authority confronts the trade-off between fewer disputes and less urgency or demand of land registration. One official suggested that registration should start first in the richer regions and then gradually expand to less developed regions because they would tend to have a higher demand for registration and could afford the costs.

Certainly, China's historical experience could give one path on how to deal with that question. "Fish-Scale Register" (*yulin tuce*) in Ming Dynasty was firstly employed in some areas of Zhejiang Province and Jiangsu Province, where were the richest areas in that period of time.

Secondly, the government or the responsible authority need pay more attention to the coordination between land registration and other agricultural projects, especially in the mainstream of land registration over the country pushed by the Chinese Ministry of Agriculture. The Ministry of Land and Resources launched the "1,000 Village Model and 10,000 Village Land Consolidation Project" in 2009.[6] Some provinces are carrying out the land consolidation which will undoubtedly erase the geographical boundaries. It was not strange that some government officials, such as the county leader from Feidong County, suggested that land registration should be carried out only after land consolidation had taken place.

6.2 Policy implications

Agricultural land registration in China is very imperative and this initiative should be actively and steadily pushed forward. China's current agricultural land ownership registration is implemented by the Ministry of Land and Resources while agricultural land contacting rights registration is implemented by Ministry of Agriculture. A government authority involving these two ministries and coordinating different government sectors to carry out the agricultural land registration is badly needed. To designate one of them or set up a new government authority to carry out the land registration should be placed on the top of agenda. Corresponding organisations should also be set up at the county or township levels to implement the initial and mutation registration.

---

[6]These initiatives aim to facilitate the implementation of policies on land reclamation and development, and link changes in urban and rural construction land and collective construction land transfers, by promoting economies of scale, farmland protection, speedier rural land transfers and helping farmers to generate greater incomes.

China should conduct more pilots to roll out the rural land registration and it could be at township level or even up to county level. The criteria for location selection could be: (1) frequency of land transferring; (2) urban fringe; (3) contract possession percentage; (4) pro-active county/township government; (5) good contracts records management and (6) transportation access. The agricultural land registration should be gradually implemented and methods selection should be adapted to local conditions. The land registration then could be gradually expanded to the economically underdeveloped areas with accumulated experiences. Appropriate mapping method should be selected according to the local economic conditions, terrain and other factors. More accurate measurement methods, such as full-field measurement, can be utilised in the economically developed areas while in economically underdeveloped areas the photogrammetry and other lower-cost measurement method can be employed.

The survey participants expressed demands for the additional functionalities of rural land registration, such as agricultural land transfer, agricultural land mortgage loans, agricultural land use monitoring. These will in turn attract farmers and local governments to participate positively in the agricultural land registration. Therefore, the further pilot should aim to maximum it in order to generate popular support.

References

Carter, M. and Y Yang (1999), Market versus Administrative Reallocation of Agricultural Land in a Period of Rapid Industralization. *World Bank Policy Research Working Paper 2203.*

Deininger, K. and S.Q. Jin (2002), Land rental markets as an alternative to government reallocation? *World Bank Policy Research Working Paper 2930*, November 2002.

Dong, X.Y. (1996), Two-tier Land Tenure System and Sustained Economic Growth in Post-1978 Rural China, *World Development* 24(5), 915–928.

Li, G., S. Rozelle and L. Brandt (1998), Tenure, Land Rights, and Farmer Investment Incentives in China, *Agricultural Economics* 19, 63–71.

Lin, J.Y. (1992). Rural Reform and Agricultural Growth in China, *American Economic Review* 82, 34–51.

Liu, W. and D. Yang (1990), China's land use policy under change, *Land Use Policy* 7, 198–201.

Yao, Y. (2000), The Development of the Land Lease Market in Rural China, *Land Economics*, May 2000. http://econpapers.repec.org/article/uwplandec/v_3a76_3ay_3a2000_3ai_3a2_3ap_3a252-266.htm.

Zhang, X.Q. (1997), Urban Land Reform in China, *Land Use Policy* 14(3), 187–199.

Zhao, G. (2010), *Study on Fish-Scale Register*, Huang Shan Publishing: China.

Chapter 11

Public Works Programme in India: An Evaluation of the Rural Employment Guarantee Programme in West Bengal

Upasak Das* and Indrajeet Kumar†

Centre for Development Studies,
Thiruvananthapuram, Kerala, India
**upasakdas@cds.ac.in*
† indrajeetkumat17@gmail.com

Abstract: Public works programmes have been increasingly adopted by developing economies as a strategy to tackle unemployment and poverty. In India, the Mahatma Gandhi National Rural Employment Guarantee Act was passed which guarantees unskilled employment to all rural households. This chapter reviews the performance of the implementation of the programme in the state of West Bengal and compares it with the rest of the country. It evaluates the programme in terms of number of person-days generated and its inclusiveness in reaching out to the poorest and deprived households. Findings suggest that apart from the tribals, the programme has been able to reach the vulnerable and deprived population more than that in other parts of the country. However, in terms of getting the full entitlement of work, performance has not been exactly inclusive. The results show that it is necessary for the state to improve on intensive margin, that is, to provide more work to the participants and also improve woman and tribal participation.

1 Introduction

Public works programmes have been increasingly adopted by low and middle income economies as a strategy to tackle unemployment and poverty. In the lines of economic theories propounded by Keynes, they are designed to create purchasing power in the hands of the poorest, which can propel demand in the economy. They are also viewed as income stabilising interventions especially in countries with high unemployment and underemployment rates and in places where macroeconomic shocks and natural disasters can affect livelihoods. For example, the Government of Argentina enacted a workfare programme, *Programa Jefes* in the year 2001 to target unemployed household heads. Bangladesh also runs the Food for Work programme for the landless and marginal farmers during the slack season (Devereux and Solomon, 2006).

In India too, public employment programmes have been extensively used as policy instruments to alleviate rural distress. Going back to the 4th century BC, Kautilya, the Indian political economist emphasised public relief works particularly during famines. Employment programmes later became important interventions for famine prevention in India (Dev, 1996). Post-independence, there have been numerous centrally sponsored programmes which focused on public works in exchange for wages. Some of these include the National Rural Employment Programme (NREP) during 1980–1989, the Jawahar Rozgar Yojana (JRY) during 1989–1999 and the Sampoorna Grameen Rozgar Yojana (SGRY) from 2001. The Maharashtra Employment Guarantee Scheme (MEGS) is a programme sponsored by the state government which was brought into force from January 26, 1979.

Back in 2005, with a view to provide employment to rural households and reduce abject poverty, The National Rural Employment Guarantee Act (NREGA)[1] was passed unanimously by the Indian Parliament. Initially, it was implemented in 200 rural districts of India on February 2, 2006 and has been extended to the whole country at present. Under this Act any adult living in rural areas willing to do unskilled manual labour at the statutory minimum wage is entitled to be employed for at least 100 days every year on public works within 15 days of his application. If employment is not provided, an unemployment allowance has to be paid as laid down by the Act.

Using Government of India data and other field level studies, this chapter reviews the performance of the implementation of Mahatma Gandhi National Rural Employment Guarantee Act (MGNREGA) in the state of West Bengal in India and compares it with the rest of the country. It evaluates the programme in terms of number of person-days generated and its inclusiveness in reaching out to the poorest and deprived households. The chapter finds that apart from the Scheduled Tribe (ST) households, the programme has been able to reach the vulnerable and deprived population more than that in other parts of the country.

[1] NREGA was renamed Mahatma Gandhi National Rural Employment Guarantee Act (MGNREGA) on October 2, 2009.

However, these households have not been able to get their full quota of 100 days of employment. This shows that while the performance of the programme in West Bengal has been inclusive in terms of an extensive margin, it has not been as good in terms of an intensive margin.

The structure of the chapter is as follows. Section 2 elaborately presents the situation before the implementation of MGNREGA and then its features. The next section discusses why West Bengal is an interesting state to analyse the performance of the programme. Section 4 gives an overview of the data used in our analysis. Section 5 presents the results and the next section reviews the findings based on literature and field surveys. The chapter then concludes with the inferences drawn from our study and examines the way forward.

2 Implementation of MGNREGA and Its Features

Despite India's very high rate of growth of Gross Domestic Product (GDP) over the past two decades that has made India one of the fastest growing economies, abject widespread poverty has raised questions about the inclusiveness of this growth process, especially in rural areas. Recent estimates by the Planning Commission show that around 25.7% of the rural population lived below the poverty line in 2010–2011 (Government of India, 2014).[2] This amounts to about 216.5 million rural people. Notably, concentration of poverty and distress is higher in dryland farming areas along with hilly and tribal areas of the country as the report finds states like Jharkhand, Chhattisgarh, Odisha as well as Manipur, Mizoram and Arunachal Pradesh having rural poverty of more than 35%. Along with widespread poverty, substantial socioeconomic inequalities in various economic and non-economic outcomes have been observed as well (Jayadev *et al.*, 2007; Singh *et al.*, 2013). In terms of rural unemployment, the situation is no better. Mukhopadhyay and Rajaraman (2007) find overall rise in rural unemployment from 1999–2000 to 2004–2005, especially among the tribal population. Interestingly, they also show that the decline in rural unemployment among highly educated males is significantly higher than the illiterate ones.

It is in this context that MGNREGA acquired great importance. After the Indian National Congress (INC) won the general election in 2004, the alliance government led by the INC with outside support from the Left Front parties, prepared the National Common Minimum Programme (NCMP), which included

[2] There has been huge criticism regarding the poverty line that was used to estimate the poverty rates. A monthly per-capita consumption expenditure (MPCE) of Rs. 816 is used for rural areas, while for the urban areas, it is Rs. 1,000.

the provision for an Employment Guarantee Act.[3] After this, on August 23, 2005, the NREGA was passed unanimously.[4] The draft that was passed in parliament defined it as "An Act to provide for the enhancement of livelihood security of the households in rural areas of the country by providing at least one hundred days of guaranteed wage employment in every financial year to every household whose adult members volunteer to do unskilled manual work and for matters connected therewith or incidental thereto."[5] Hence, the provisions of the Act ensure 100 days of work to every rural household at a mandated minimum wage rate. It has been also stipulated that the work has to be provided within 15 days of applying, failing which an unemployment allowance has to be paid to the household. Initially it was implemented in 200 rural districts of the country (with effect from February 2, 2006). In 2007–2008, it was extended to an additional 130 rural districts. Since 2008, the programme has covered all the rural parts of the country. In 2009, the name was changed from NREGA to MGNREGA.

According to the salient features of the Act, all adult members of the rural household, willing to work under the programme have to register at the Gram Panchayat (GP).[6] Once the place of residence and age of the individuals (only adult individuals are allowed to work under MGNREGA) is verified, a job card for every household is issued, which is mandatory for work to be provided. After the receipt of the job card, a written application has to be made to the GP or block office stating the time and duration of work. The work has to be provided within 15 days of this application, failing which an unemployment allowance has to be paid by the state. It should be noted that all members above the age of 18 years are eligible to work from a household. State wise wages are notified by the Government of India and have to be paid through banks/post offices on a weekly basis. Notably, wages for men and women have been kept equal.

The work that is provided should also follow stipulated guidelines. It has to be provided within a 5 kilometres radius of the village. If it is more than 5 kilometres, 10% extra wage has to be paid to meet the transportation and other costs. Priority also has to be given to women as the Act mandates at least one-third representation of women among the beneficiaries. The nature and choice of works are decided in open assemblies of the Gram Sabha (GS) and ratified by the GP.[7] To ensure that the workers are benefitted directly, use of contractors or machinery is prohibited under the Act. The Act also mandates that the wage expenditure to

[3] The alliance is known as the UPA.

[4] For more information on how the Act was passed, please refer MacAuslan (2008).

[5] This is retrieved from http://nrega.nic.in/rajaswa.pdf (Accessed on October 17, 2015).

[6] A GP is the primary unit of the three tier structure of the local self-government in rural India. It may consist of one or more than one village.

[7] A GS is the body of all individuals entered as electors in the electoral roll of the GP.

material expenditure ratio should be 60:40. The worksites should have basic facilities like crèche, drinking water and shade. In terms of cost sharing, the Government of India bears 100% of the wage cost of manual labour and 75% of the material expenditure.

3 The Case of West Bengal

Evaluation of MGNREGA in West Bengal is especially important for two reasons. Firstly, the Left Front government ruled in the state for 34 years from 1977 to 2011 with the Communist Party of India (Marxist) (CPIM) and other allied parties like the Revolutionary Socialist Party (RSP) and the Forward Block. This set of parties was part of the government at the centre as part of the UPA with the INC and other political outfits after the 2004 general elections.[8] The left back then was instrumental in getting the MGNREA adopted (MacAuslan, 2008). In this context, it is, therefore, interesting to study the implementation of the programme in the state in comparison to other parts of the country that were ruled mostly by non-Left political parties.

Second, the state of West Bengal is among the poorer in the country. The state ranks fourth poorest with about 19 million poor in 2011–2012 in terms of the absolute number of poor across India, according to the latest estimates by the Rangarajan Expert Group (Government of India, 2014) and thereby pointing to the need for such a social welfare programme. Furthermore, in 2006 the state ranked 22 out of the 35 states of India in terms of the Human Development Index (HDI), (Government of India, 2009). Since MGNREGA is formulated and designed to target the ultra-poor and deprived rural population through self-targeting,[9] evaluating its implementation in West Bengal is a worthwhile exercise.

4 Data

The data used in the paper is drawn from the MGNREGA website, managed by the Ministry of Rural Development, Government of India (http://nrega.nic.in/netnrega/home.aspx). A data portal maintained by the ministry and Evidence for Policy Design, Harvard University containing time-series information on various indicators of MGNREGA implementation has been used for the study (Public Data Portal). The portal contains state-wise information on job-cards, allocation of work, employment days generated for different groups of population and expenditure details. The time frame is 2011–2012 to 2014–2015.

---

[8] These parties supported the government from the outside and were instrumental in providing it a majority that it otherwise lacked.

[9] It is self-targeting as the person has to apply for a job card and for a job.

5 Findings

5.1 Performance of MGNREGS in West Bengal

This section highlights three aspects of the programme (MGNREGA) — inclusiveness, guarantee of 100 days employment and works expenditure at the national level and also at the state level with a greater emphasis on West Bengal for the time period 2011–2012 to 2014–2015. The reason for taking this short time period is that the Public Data Portal for MGNREGA provides extensive information for the stated time period only and not for the time before. Each of the three aspects, as stated above, attempt to evaluate the performance of the programme in West Bengal *vis-à-vis* the other neighbouring states like Bihar, Jharkhand, Odisha and Assam.

Inclusiveness is the first and foremost indicator of success or failure of the programme in terms of guaranteeing employment to the most marginalised sections of the rural society- Scheduled Castes (SC), STs, women, the poor and the disabled. This can be evaluated through inquiring into person-days worked, number of individuals participating and number of households working from these sections of the society. Moreover, if this guarantee is not fulfilled to a certain threshold to make the change visible and sustainable in the long run, the objective of the programme is achieved only partially (see Ravallion 1991, for gains generated by an antipoverty programme). To examine inclusiveness the fulfilment of the guarantee of 100 days' work for these marginalised groups has been analysed. In this regard, number of SC/ST families/households completing 100 days out of total participating families will further guarantee inclusiveness to bring a sustainable source of income generation for deprived people. So, to know exactly how many of the people are really able to get sustaining income from the programme, it is important to study the proportion of SC/ST households that have completed 100 days of work out of the total SC/ST families participating.

Finally, to know both participating and non-participating benefits originating from the programme, it is important to know the proportion of labour or material expenditure allocated under the programme. This is because labour payments are individual payments, while material expenditure gets transformed into infrastructural creation for the rural economy in the form of roads, canals and other works. It has the property of public goods and generates positive externalities to non-participants too at large. These participatory and non-participatory benefits can be gauged in terms of labour to capital expenditure ratio for states and India. The more the labour expenditure, the better off the participants will be in terms of more days of work with less rationing. But, a combination of labour and material is required to assimilate labour at potential level. For measuring these concerns, the chapter digs deeper into the debate of sustainable and long term benefits generated by the scheme. The labour to material ratio is used to know whether the scheme generates more participatory (individual payment-wages), or non-participatory (positive externalities- out of infrastructural development) benefits in states. The following are the three aspects discussed in detail.

Inclusiveness

Person-days worked by the SC under the programme out of the total SC population in rural India gives per capita person-days worked by SC. We also compare the person-days worked by SC, as compared to those worked by the non-SC population. Table 1 presents the figures for all the states. From the table, it is quite evident that per capita person-days work performed by SCs is volatile and

Table 1. Per capita person-days by SC population.

State	2011–2012	2012–2013	2013–2014	2014–2015
Andhra Pradesh	3.27	7.05	1.96	3.27
Assam	0.70	1.03	1.54	0.70
Bihar	0.64	1.69	2.54	0.64
Chhattisgarh	2.39	4.31	1.95	2.39
Gujarat	0.55	1.06	1.40	0.55
Haryana	0.72	1.76	2.12	0.72
Himachal Pradesh	3.21	4.65	1.56	3.21
Jammu and Kashmir	0.76	2.82	3.56	0.76
Jharkhand	1.95	2.30	0.91	1.95
Karnataka	0.92	1.39	1.66	0.92
Kerala	5.66	7.30	1.42	5.66
Madhya Pradesh	2.26	3.19	1.13	2.26
Maharashtra	0.83	1.04	0.83	0.83
Odisha	1.36	1.55	1.38	1.36
Punjab	0.76	0.79	2.09	0.76
Rajasthan	3.48	4.55	1.10	3.48
Tamil Nadu	8.18	13.51	1.41	8.18
Uttar Pradesh	1.27	1.34	1.36	1.27
Uttarakhand	1.79	2.28	1.16	1.79
West Bengal	3.23	3.84	1.39	3.23
India	2.26	3.34	1.45	2.26

Source: Public data portal available from MGNREGA website.

meagre over the years across the states. Around 2–3 person days of work is the norm for all India for the years studied. The year 2013–2014 has observed a decline in participation of SC across all the states. Das and Maiorano (2015) argue that the recent decline in demand and participation of rural households in MGNREGA is due to the crunch in fund allocation, which mainly decreased around 2013–2014. Nevertheless, West Bengal is performing better as the figures are better than the all India average for all the years, except 2013–2014, which is the worst year for all states and at the all-India level too. That is to say, per capita availability of person-days work for SC is more inclusive for WB as compared to the all India average. In addition West Bengal's performance is better than that of the neighbouring states, e.g., Bihar, Jharkhand, Odisha and Assam. It should be noted that analysis based on per capita person-days for the population who participated in MGNREGA would have made more sense. However, due to paucity of data on total population working under the programme for different social groups, we have to resort to per capita person-days for total population.

In terms of ST participation, the same person-days work criterion is used for measuring inclusiveness. Here, West Bengal lags behind the participation rate for all India. For all the years under the study availability of per capita person days' work for STs in the state is below the all India average (Table 2). Nevertheless, West Bengal's performance for inclusiveness of STs in per-capita person-days work is better than in the neighbouring states of Jharkhand (with ST population share of 26%) and Assam (a share of 12.4% ST population), which has higher proportion of ST population as compared to WB. Immediate concern arises from the fact that in both the all India average and across the states, person-day employment generation for STs is declining over the years (2011–2012 to 2014–2015). This problem is quite visible in major tribal populated states like Jharkhand, Madhya Pradesh and Assam.[10]

To infer more on inclusiveness, we compare the indicators based on participation in MGNREGA and the person-days worked for SC and ST with that of the non-SC/ST population for the states. For this purpose, we take the ratio of ST (or SC) population that worked in the programme to that of the non-SC/ST population and the ratio of person-days worked by ST (or SC) to that of the non-C/ST population. Tables 3 and 4 presents the results for ST and SC respectively. The findings are similar to what we found through Tables 1 and 2. For the ST population, inclusiveness in West Bengal is questionable as we find both these indicators to be

[10]There has not been a major structural change in the employment scenario in these states especially for the tribes. We also did not find any major decline for SCs. So we think there is no major reason to think that this decline is because of a shift to other employment opportunities.

Table 2. Per capita person-days worked done by ST.

State	2011–2012	2012–2013	2013–2014	2014–2015
Andhra Pradesh	10.31	9.65	8.42	3.53
Assam	2.19	1.78	1.32	0.87
Bihar	0.96	1.44	1.43	0.44
Chhattisgarh	6.30	6.35	7.21	2.46
Gujarat	1.58	1.35	1.18	0.90
Himachal Pradesh	4.41	4.78	5.56	4.20
Jammu and Kashmir	2.39	3.99	3.82	1.72
Jharkhand	3.06	2.91	2.06	2.05
Karnataka	1.69	1.62	1.66	1.04
Kerala	3.55	5.08	5.87	5.18
Madhya Pradesh	3.43	2.80	2.82	2.36
Maharashtra	1.69	1.63	1.13	1.27
Odisha	1.93	2.29	3.23	2.47
Rajasthan	6.02	6.14	5.53	5.12
Tamil Nadu	5.83	8.15	7.26	4.53
Uttar Pradesh	3.21	1.40	1.75	1.05
Uttarakhand	2.15	1.82	1.63	1.53
West Bengal	3.20	4.14	4.56	2.96
India	5.56	5.35	4.86	3.17

Source: Public data portal available from MGNREGA website.

low for the state in comparison to the all-India figure. Apart from Bihar, it is lower than in the neighbouring states of Assam, Odisha and Jharkhand as well for all the four years. However, the picture seems different for the SC population in West Bengal as we find these indicators showing higher figures compared to all-India and all the neighbouring states also. In fact, the figures for West Bengal is higher than most of the states barring Punjab and Haryana for a few years. This reiterates the fact that the benefits have been inclusive of the SC population in West Bengal, however not as much for the ST population.

The issue of inclusiveness has further been challenged in some recent literature. The analysts claim that, as far as women participation in MGNREGA is concerned, the implementation of the scheme is not women friendly in the context of wages and rationing in certain states (Das, 2015a; Narayanan and Das, 2014; Liu and Barrett, 2013). In terms of women participation rate through per capita person-days worked by women, West Bengal's performance is below the all-India average, except for the year 2011–2012 (Table 4). However, the

Table 3. Comparison of ST with the non-SC/ST population.

	Total ST working/Total Non-SC/ST working				Total ST person-days/Total Non-SC/ST person-days			
State	**2011–2012**	**2012–2013**	**2013–2014**	**2014–2015**	**2011–2012**	**2012–2013**	**2013–2014**	**2014–2015**
Andhra Pradesh	0.225	0.210	0.205	0.155	0.335	0.252	0.237	0.182
Assam	0.270	0.277	0.237	0.242	0.317	0.284	0.210	0.192
Bihar	0.026	0.029	0.030	0.023	0.024	0.028	0.031	0.023
Chhattisgarh	0.647	0.659	0.691	0.597	0.719	0.732	0.789	0.560
Gujarat	0.845	0.852	0.894	0.900	0.782	0.729	0.801	0.748
Haryana	0.001	0.000	0.000	0.000	0.001	0.000	0.000	0.000
Himachal Pradesh	0.099	0.099	0.107	0.114	0.095	0.106	0.115	0.128
Jammu and Kashmir	0.214	0.198	0.198	0.268	0.209	0.195	0.204	0.267
Jharkhand	0.869	0.897	0.830	0.792	0.828	0.862	0.741	0.699
Karnataka	0.109	0.115	0.099	0.100	0.109	0.121	0.104	0.108
Kerala	0.028	0.029	0.033	0.039	0.030	0.032	0.037	0.048
Madhya Pradesh	0.570	0.576	0.670	0.599	0.569	0.543	0.654	0.520
Maharashtra	0.245	0.252	0.288	0.262	0.272	0.227	0.279	0.262
Odisha	0.822	0.759	0.809	0.844	0.861	0.843	0.953	0.974
Punjab	0.002	0.001	0.001	0.001	0.001	0.001	0.001	0.001
Rajasthan	0.363	0.399	0.420	0.430	0.425	0.432	0.485	0.490
Tamil Nadu	0.020	0.021	0.021	0.017	0.018	0.020	0.019	0.016
Uttar Pradesh	0.018	0.016	0.016	0.014	0.019	0.016	0.016	0.013
Uttarakhand	0.039	0.035	0.033	0.038	0.036	0.032	0.033	0.035
West Bengal	0.161	0.161	0.158	0.152	0.185	0.173	0.170	0.143
India	0.305	0.318	0.324	0.345	0.400	0.361	0.345	0.312

Source: Public data portal available from MGNREGA website.

Table 4. Comparison of SC with the non-SC/ST population.

	Total SC working/Total Non-SC/ST working				Total SC person-days/Total Non-SC/ST person-days			
State	2011–2012	2012–2013	2013–2014	2014–2015	2011–2012	2012–2013	2013–2014	2014–2015
Andhra Pradesh	0.442	0.406	0.397	0.388	0.491	0.382	0.373	0.349
Assam	0.081	0.084	0.083	0.084	0.078	0.082	0.085	0.077
Bihar	0.348	0.402	0.411	0.378	0.342	0.389	0.424	0.398
Chhattisgarh	0.187	0.180	0.183	0.184	0.185	0.173	0.177	0.189
Gujarat	0.152	0.155	0.145	0.129	0.151	0.162	0.149	0.130
Haryana	1.109	1.107	0.923	0.863	1.000	1.029	0.941	0.779
Himachal Pradesh	0.457	0.442	0.440	0.428	0.464	0.441	0.443	0.419
Jammu and Kashmir	0.100	0.086	0.085	0.073	0.087	0.074	0.077	0.063
Jharkhand	0.265	0.259	0.256	0.255	0.269	0.273	0.257	0.266
Karnataka	0.216	0.227	0.213	0.209	0.208	0.228	0.209	0.208
Kerala	0.169	0.167	0.179	0.202	0.191	0.194	0.210	0.222
Madhya Pradesh	0.380	0.356	0.347	0.310	0.395	0.359	0.344	0.288
Maharashtra	0.103	0.126	0.138	0.140	0.108	0.120	0.141	0.142
Odisha	0.398	0.387	0.374	0.362	0.394	0.394	0.382	0.371
Punjab	4.015	4.078	3.433	3.767	3.430	3.653	3.335	3.295
Rajasthan	0.294	0.341	0.354	0.358	0.295	0.351	0.368	0.366
Tamil Nadu	0.398	0.443	0.422	0.413	0.419	0.466	0.430	0.414
Uttar Pradesh	0.507	0.525	0.552	0.553	0.497	0.519	0.549	0.532
Uttarakhand	0.230	0.222	0.224	0.216	0.234	0.223	0.237	0.229
West Bengal	0.558	0.544	0.540	0.542	0.600	0.566	0.589	0.550
India	0.370	0.375	0.382	0.373	0.372	0.369	0.381	0.365

Source: Public data portal available from MGNREGA website.

performance is better than in the neighbouring states of Bihar, Jharkhand and Assam. The states of Andhra Pradesh, Chhattisgarh, Kerala, Rajasthan and Tamil Nadu lead in this category.

Participation of poor households in MGNREGA can be measured by the indicator- number of households that participated in the programme which have also either gone through a land reform or are beneficiary of the Indira Awas Yojana (IAY), which provides housing to the rural poor, out of the total number of poor HHs in rural India.[11] This is because being a beneficiary of land reform or IAY a household must qualify to be a BPL household. In this criterion of inclusiveness of the poor, proportion of household participation in the programme is higher for West Bengal as compared with the all-India average (Table 6). For all India, this proportion of participation is around 4%, except for the year 2014–2015, for which it is about 2%; in contrast the WB figure is around 8–9% over the years of the study. And this is also better than all the neighbouring poor states — Bihar, Jharkhand, Assam and Odisha (Table 5).

The disabled are the most marginalised group of society because of their inability to participate in the rural job market for employment and livelihood creation. For measuring inclusiveness of this group, proportion of the disabled population out of total disabled people in the respective states and India is analysed.[12] In MGNREGA, their participation is quite visibly monitored and guaranteed as this is the only direct employment opportunity for these groups of people who are not able to translocate themselves. In this indicator of inclusiveness, West Bengal is doing better than the all India average and that in the neighbouring states (Table 7). For West Bengal participation of disabled people is around 5–7% over the years in comparison to the all-India average of 2–3% only. As far as neighbouring states are concerned, their participation rate is less than 1%.

Our findings show that by and large, guarantee of employment in WB has been inclusive. The fact that performance in terms of participation of SC and the poor population has been better than in the rest of the country taken together and the neighbouring states shows that allocation of work under the programme has been inclusive. However, in terms of participation of the ST population and women, the performance of West Bengal has been poorer though in comparison to the neighbouring states, it is better.

---

[11] To convert number of poor people taken from Rangarajan Committee Report (2014) across all the states taken, in number of households, we find the rural household size by dividing the rural population with number of households in rural parts. Thereafter, this obtained household size is used to convert the number of people Below Poverty Line (BPL) into number of households.

[12] Number of Disabled individuals is taken from the employment–unemployment schedule of the 68th round of the National Sample Survey (NSS), which is of age group 18 and above.

Table 5. Per capita person-days worked by women.

State	2011–2012	2012–2013	2013–2014	2014–2015
Andhra Pradesh	6.04	6.79	6.25	3.24
Assam	0.67	0.62	0.56	0.45
Bihar	0.44	0.65	0.68	0.30
Chhattisgarh	5.68	5.71	6.43	2.83
Gujarat	0.86	0.72	0.60	0.46
Haryana	0.52	0.66	0.64	0.33
Himachal Pradesh	5.23	5.19	5.76	3.79
Jammu and Kashmir	0.90	1.68	1.81	0.70
Jharkhand	1.56	1.51	1.13	1.18
Karnataka	1.74	1.54	1.81	1.10
Kerala	6.49	8.60	8.92	5.99
Madhya Pradesh	2.85	2.34	2.06	1.99
Maharashtra	1.18	1.29	0.75	0.89
Odisha	1.01	1.13	1.37	1.04
Punjab	0.34	0.37	0.86	0.45
Rajasthan	5.91	6.11	5.01	4.63
Tamil Nadu	12.05	16.31	16.64	12.33
Uttar Pradesh	0.62	0.37	0.52	0.44
Uttarakhand	2.53	2.56	2.11	2.12
West Bengal	1.60	2.24	2.70	2.31
India	2.68	2.98	2.92	2.12

Source: Public data portal available from MGNREGA website.

Guarantee of 100 Days Work

Per capita person-days availability of work does not give a clear picture of long term inclusiveness, but rather only participation in the scheme. Since just participation in MGNREGA is not sufficient to ensure sustainable income and livelihood creation, unless it is utilised for its full potential of 100 days employment. Sustainability requires that people graduate from the programme. This may only be possible if the income generated by participation is sufficient to enable households to begin the process of asset accumulation. Generation of such a surplus would be easier if the full quota of 100 days employment is created. In that too, conversion of 100 days limit among the deprived social groups and within the groups of its own is essential. In this respect total SC/ST households who worked over the 100 days limit out of the total SC/ST households in rural India (Tables 7

Table 6. Proportion of land reform or IAY beneficiary out of the total poor participating in MGNREGA.

State	2011–2012	2012–2013	2013–2014	2014–2015
Andhra Pradesh	0.81	0.92	0.91	0.43
Assam	0.01	0.01	0.01	0.01
Bihar	0.00	0.00	0.00	0.00
Chhattisgarh	0.00	0.00	0.00	0.00
Gujarat	0.01	0.01	0.01	0.01
Haryana	0.00	0.00	0.00	0.00
Himachal Pradesh	0.07	0.06	0.06	0.05
Jammu and Kashmir	0.03	0.03	0.04	0.02
Jharkhand	0.00	0.00	0.00	0.00
Karnataka	0.01	0.01	0.02	0.01
Kerala	0.04	0.04	0.05	0.07
Madhya Pradesh	0.00	0.00	0.01	0.01
Maharashtra	0.01	0.01	0.01	0.01
Odisha	0.01	0.01	0.01	0.01
Punjab	0.00	0.00	0.01	0.00
Rajasthan	0.00	0.00	0.00	0.00
Tamil Nadu	0.03	0.03	0.03	0.03
Uttar Pradesh	0.00	0.00	0.00	0.00
Uttarakhand	0.01	0.01	0.01	0.02
West Bengal	0.10	0.07	0.08	0.08
India	0.04	0.05	0.05	0.03

Source: Public data portal available from MGNREGA website.

and 9) would give within conversion rate of 100 days limit. While, proportion of the total SC/ST households, who worked for over 100 days (Tables 8 and 10) will ensure social groups conversion rate of 100 days limit. In the first scenario for SCs, WB performance is below the all-India average (Table 7). In this respect, even the neighbouring states of Bihar, Odisha and Jharkhand are performing better than West Bengal. For India this conversion rate varies from 6–11% and for the same reference, West Bengal accounts 2–6% of the total households that participated in the programme. In terms of conversion rate for ST households, the performance of West Bengal is below the all India average and also the ratio in the neighbouring states, except for the state of Assam (Table 9). As the per capita person-days for ST households have been declining, the proportion getting more

Table 7. Proportion of disabled individuals participating in MGNREGA.

State	2011–2012	2012–2013	2013–2014	2014–2015
Andhra Pradesh	0.103	0.150	0.164	0.084
Assam	0.006	0.006	0.006	0.004
Bihar	0.006	0.007	0.006	0.003
Chhattisgarh	0.171	0.143	0.134	0.083
Gujarat	0.067	0.041	0.029	0.020
Haryana	0.002	0.002	0.002	0.001
Himachal Pradesh	0.028	0.023	0.022	0.017
Jammu & Kashmir	0.025	0.047	0.048	0.013
Jharkhand	0.035	0.029	0.022	0.025
Karnataka	0.006	0.006	0.007	0.005
Kerala	0.002	0.002	0.002	0.002
Madhya Pradesh	0.019	0.019	0.057	0.068
Maharashtra	0.021	0.015	0.012	0.012
Odisha	0.006	0.008	0.007	0.006
Punjab	0.000	0.000	0.001	0.001
Rajasthan	0.006	0.006	0.006	0.007
Tamil Nadu	0.034	0.061	0.065	0.053
Uttar Pradesh	0.016	0.010	0.010	0.008
Uttaranchal	0.005	0.005	0.006	0.008
West Bengal	0.065	0.070	0.073	0.053
India	0.031	0.035	0.038	0.027

Source: Public data portal available from MGNREGA website.

than 100 days of work has been falling (6–12% in 2011–2012). This again is a cause of concern for inclusiveness of ST households.

In terms of the share of SC households working for more than 100 days out of those households participated in the programme, West Bengal scenario is better than the all India average (Table 10). Among the neighbouring states, the performance for West Bengal is found to be better than all, but Assam. This implies that as far as sustainable inclusiveness of SC is concerned in the programme, West Bengal has fared well. On the other hand, the performance in Bihar, Jharkhand and Odisha has not been overwhelming. In comparison to the national average WB is lagging behind in the participation of STs. The findings from ST populated states like Assam, Chhattisgarh and Odisha show better performance both as compared to West Bengal and the all India average (Table 11).

Table 8. Proportion of SC households working for 100 days out of the total SC households participating in MGNREGA.

State	2011–2012	2012–2013	2013–2014	2014–2015
Andhra Pradesh	0.00	0.15	0.11	0.19
Assam	0.01	0.01	0.02	0.02
Bihar	0.09	0.08	0.06	0.14
Chhattisgarh	0.06	0.07	0.11	0.16
Gujarat	0.06	0.11	0.06	0.08
Haryana	0.05	0.06	0.04	0.07
Himachal Pradesh	0.10	0.08	0.10	0.13
Jammu and Kashmir	0.07	0.09	0.09	0.22
Jharkhand	0.04	0.07	0.07	0.07
Karnataka	0.03	0.08	0.08	0.11
Kerala	0.10	0.26	0.30	0.30
Madhya Pradesh	0.09	0.06	0.06	0.07
Maharashtra	0.14	0.14	0.11	0.11
Odisha	0.03	0.05	0.09	0.10
Punjab	0.01	0.02	0.03	0.04
Rajasthan	0.07	0.11	0.12	0.12
Tamil Nadu	0.11	0.21	0.15	0.17
Uttar Pradesh	0.04	0.01	0.03	0.04
Uttarakhand	0.05	0.05	0.08	0.07
West Bengal	0.02	0.05	0.05	0.06
India	0.06	0.10	0.09	0.11

Source: Public data portal available from MGNREGA website.

Work and Expenditure

On the issue of labour to material expenditure, which is an indicator of labour wage payments *vis-à-vis* material used for infrastructural creation in rural India, labour expenditure has been increasing over the years both for all-India and for West Bengal. In all the years, labour expenditure has been about twice that of material expenditure (Table 12). Direct benefits are more targeted than the indirect benefits. Better performing states like Andhra Pradesh and Kerala have a higher labour expenditure as compared with material expenditure, which can be counted as one of the reasons of success for the programme in these states. As compared to neighbouring states, West Bengal share for labour expenditure is higher than in Bihar, Odisha, Jharkhand and Assam.

Table 9. Proportion of SC households out of all those whose who have worked for over 100 days.

State	2011–2012	2012–2013	2013–2014	2014–2015
Andhra Pradesh	0.00	0.21	0.21	0.21
Assam	0.05	0.08	0.09	0.06
Bihar	0.23	0.26	0.31	0.29
Chhattisgarh	0.09	0.08	0.08	0.13
Gujarat	0.10	0.11	0.09	0.08
Haryana	0.48	0.50	0.47	0.35
Himachal Pradesh	0.31	0.28	0.29	0.25
Jammu and Kashmir	0.06	0.06	0.06	0.05
Jharkhand	0.13	0.14	0.13	0.16
Karnataka	0.15	0.17	0.16	0.16
Kerala	0.16	0.16	0.17	0.18
Madhya Pradesh	0.22	0.20	0.18	0.16
Maharashtra	0.08	0.09	0.10	0.10
Odisha	0.18	0.18	0.16	0.16
Punjab	0.71	0.79	0.78	0.64
Rajasthan	0.16	0.21	0.20	0.21
Tamil Nadu	0.31	0.33	0.30	0.29
Uttar Pradesh	0.33	0.35	0.36	0.34
Uttarakhand	0.20	0.19	0.21	0.25
West Bengal	0.35	0.34	0.36	0.31
India	0.14	0.21	0.21	0.21

Source: Public data portal available from MGNREGA website.

6 Qualitative Insights and Review

Our findings above are similar to those in the literature. We find that MGNREGA has been inclusive in terms of allocation of benefits to the deprived groups such as SC households and the poor. Existing literature also points out to similar findings. Liu and Barrett (2013) find the probability of households seeking but not getting work in 2009–2010 for all-India to be not as pro-poor as West Bengal. Das (2015b) using nationally representative data found West Bengal to be performing better in terms of allocation of work to the poor and disadvantaged households. This observation is found to be valid not only for 2009–2010 but also for 2011–2012.

However, there are other problems we find that cannot be overlooked. One among them is women participation in the programme, where West Bengal has

Table 10. Proportion of ST households working for 100 days out of the total ST households participating in MGNREGA.

State	2011–2012	2012–2013	2013–2014	2014–2015
Andhra Pradesh	0.00	0.24	0.17	0.17
Assam	0.02	0.01	0.01	0.01
Bihar	0.06	0.08	0.06	0.03
Chhattisgarh	0.10	0.12	0.17	0.02
Gujarat	0.04	0.06	0.04	0.02
Haryana	0.02	0.00	0.00	0.09
Himachal Pradesh	0.07	0.09	0.10	0.06
Jammu and Kashmir	0.07	0.11	0.09	0.02
Jharkhand	0.04	0.06	0.05	0.06
Karnataka	0.02	0.08	0.09	0.04
Kerala	0.08	0.20	0.22	0.11
Madhya Pradesh	0.08	0.05	0.06	0.05
Maharashtra	0.15	0.12	0.10	0.14
Odisha	0.04	0.06	0.11	0.07
Punjab	0.04	0.00	0.11	0.01
Rajasthan	0.10	0.11	0.15	0.08
Tamil Nadu	0.08	0.17	0.12	0.05
Uttar Pradesh	0.06	0.02	0.04	0.02
Uttarakhand	0.05	0.04	0.06	0.01
West Bengal	0.03	0.05	0.05	0.03
India	0.12	0.11	0.09	0.06

Source: Public data portal available from MGNREGA website.

lagged behind substantially. Of note is the fact that the key features of MGNREGA provide considerable incentives for women to participate in the programme. First, the scheme mandates that at least one-third of the participants should be women. Second, it provides equal wages for men and women. In addition to these aspects, there are provisions for childcare facilities at the worksites that can reduce the barriers to women's participation (Khera and Nayak, 2009). All these provisions of the programme collectively can incentivise women to come forward and work, which might lead to higher bargaining power and empowerment in the household. Yet, Narayanan and Das (2014) find that the demand rate of women seeking work under MGNREGA is lower in West Bengal, than in most of the states. They also find that administrative rationing for females is much higher in the state compared to that for males, in the sense

Table 11. Proportion of ST households out of all those whose who have worked for over 100 days.

State	2011–2012	2012–2013	2013–2014	2014–2015
Andhra Pradesh	0.00	0.18	0.18	0.14
Assam	0.39	0.14	0.09	0.11
Bihar	0.01	0.02	0.02	0.01
Chhattisgarh	0.45	0.45	0.46	0.30
Gujarat	0.37	0.31	0.36	0.32
Haryana	0.00	0.00	0.00	0.00
Himachal Pradesh	0.05	0.08	0.07	0.09
Jammu and Kashmir	0.13	0.15	0.14	0.14
Jharkhand	0.39	0.38	0.32	0.32
Karnataka	0.07	0.08	0.08	0.08
Kerala	0.02	0.02	0.02	0.05
Madhya Pradesh	0.29	0.28	0.33	0.26
Maharashtra	0.20	0.16	0.19	0.19
Odisha	0.44	0.42	0.46	0.46
Punjab	0.00	0.00	0.00	0.00
Rajasthan	0.30	0.24	0.29	0.24
Tamil Nadu	0.01	0.01	0.01	0.01
Uttar Pradesh	0.02	0.01	0.01	0.01
Uttarakhand	0.03	0.02	0.02	0.02
West Bengal	0.13	0.11	0.10	0.07
India	0.25	0.20	0.19	0.20

Source: Public data portal available from MGNREGA website.

that the proportion of females demanding work but not getting it is more than that for males.

The literature also points out the issue of low employment days generated under MGNREGA. Dey and Bedi (2010) reported a low number of employment days in Birbhum district and found that work is not more likely to be generated during the agricultural slack season. Mukherjee (2010) and Das (2009) found similar issues in the Sunderban delta and Jalpaiguri district of West Bengal respectively. One reason responsible for this is low awareness of the provisions of the programme as pointed by Das *et al.* (2012) in northern parts of the state. Citing the cause for poor implementation of MGNREGA, Dreze and Oldiges (2007, p. 3) mentioned, "The government of West Bengal, for its part, had an ambivalent attitude towards NREGA from the beginning."

Table 12. Labour expenditure/material expenditure.

State	2011–2012	2012–2013	2013–2014	2014–2015
Andhra Pradesh	3.363	6.552	3.785	6.204
Assam	1.895	1.888	2.127	2.075
Bihar	1.268	1.806	1.218	1.429
Chhattisgarh	3.209	2.863	3.143	2.960
Gujarat	1.530	1.803	2.341	1.741
Haryana	3.217	3.101	3.447	5.452
Himachal Pradesh	2.044	2.265	2.373	2.874
Jammu and Kashmir	1.843	1.285	1.262	0.645
Jharkhand	2.029	1.628	1.983	2.267
Karnataka	1.855	1.795	2.341	1.496
Kerala	29.891	30.781	29.794	41.974
Madhya Pradesh	1.612	1.564	2.067	1.899
Maharashtra	2.769	2.307	1.599	1.161
Odisha	1.142	1.350	2.307	1.598
Punjab	1.921	2.525	3.396	3.866
Rajasthan	2.045	2.241	2.701	1.668
Uttar Pradesh	2.105	2.554	2.494	2.200
Uttarakhand	1.911	2.211	2.150	2.133
West Bengal	2.436	2.779	2.814	3.259
India	2.746	3.133	3.315	3.556

Source: Public data portal available from MGNREGA website.

A string of field surveys conducted by one of the authors presents insights, which closely match with the inferences drawn from our empirical findings and literature. One major survey was conducted back in 2012 in the Cooch Behar district of West Bengal covering 556 households from four villages.[13] One observation from the survey was the low number of employment days that most of the households got under the programme. The average person-days generated for three out of the four villages varied between 7 and 12 days. Excerpts from two interviews, one in the Devanganj Gram Panchayat of the Haldibari block and the other in the Falimari GP of the Cooch Behar-I block are as follows:

We have been asking for more work from the authorities every year. However we have to remain satisfied with only a week's work every year. It is better to dismantle the programme rather than giving work for so few days.

[13] For details of the survey, please refer Das (2015b).

(Raju Mandal (name changed for anonymity), agricultural labourer, Devanganj GP)

> *I cannot go to Delhi or Mumbai to work as I have my wife and two small daughters in my home. We have been suffering from agricultural loss for the last few years. In this condition, we can only depend on the 100-days work programme (MGNREGA). Yet we end up getting only 20 days of work.*

(Suleman Miya (name changed for anonymity), farmer working on 1.2 acres of land, Falimari GP).

Despite these problems, a few positives need to be acknowledged. A paper based on this survey finds that poorer and disadvantaged households such as those belonging to scheduled groups (SC/ST), those whose main occupation is agricultural labour and those with an illiterate household head have a higher probability of receiving work after demanding (Das, 2015b). A survey in the Phasidewa block of the Darjeeling district of West Bengal in March, 2011 indicates similar findings. In fact, a supervisor appointed by the Panchayat head responsible for implementing MGNREGA at the ground level says the following:

> *"I have one objective in my mind: to provide work to as many poor households as I can. So if you go for a survey, you will find many with only 20 to 25 days of work. Hence you may not find households working for 100 days. But you would not find any really poor households who have not got work even if for few days."*

(Shyamal Basak (name changed for anonymity), supervisor for MGNREGA, Ghoshpukur GP).

7 Conclusion

These findings should be an inspiration to authorities and give an impetus to them and the Government to improve on women and ST participation and intensive margin. One possible way is public mobilisation through effective civil societies. For example, the areas where the non-governmental organisation, PRADAN (Professional Assistance for Development Action) has been in operation have seen better performance.[14] As an instance, in Saltora block of the Bankura district, where the organisation has been operating since 2008–2009, the average person-days in 2013–2014 is found to be about 57 days with more than 43% of the workers being women. Further, about 16% of the households get the full

[14] For more on PRADAN, please refer to http://www.pradan.net/index.php (Accessed on August 30, 2014).

quota of at least 100 days in 2013–2014 (Government of India, c.2014b). The Paschim Banga Khet Majoor Samiti, led by social activists can also play a part in ensuring effective implementation. During the field survey conducted in the Falimari Gram Panchayat of the Cooch Behar-I block of the Cooch Behar district, it was found that the Satmile Satish Club, a community based organisation that works for the small farmers, scheduled groups and women organised several awareness campaigns. This has helped villagers to get their entitlements under the programme.[15]

One of the main objectives of casting the programme in the right based framework is to create accountability. For example, it is often found that an individual despite repeated demand does not receive work or does not get the legal entitlement of 100 days; yet no one is held accountable for such shortcomings. As Dreze and Sen (2013, p. 205) point out, "The future of NREGA depends a great on activation of these accountable provisions and on the creation of effective mechanisms for grievance redressal. Failing that, NREGA is likely to be gradually reduced to a lame top-down scheme, instead of a demand-driven, rights-based programme as it has been envisaged." Hence, it is imperative for the newly formed central government led by the Bharatiya Janata Party (BJP) and the existing state Government (All India Trinamool Congress) to ensure effective implementation of the programme and create an opportunity for higher welfare for the most deprived and vulnerable sections of the country.

References

Das, U. (2009), Survey shows discrepancy in NREGS, *The Kolkata Age, The Asian Age*, September 25. (This is a newspaper article).

Das, U. (2015a), Rationing and Accuracy of Targeting in India: The Case of the Rural Employment Guarantee Act, *Oxford Development Studies*, 43(3), 361–378.

Das, U. (2015b), Evaluation of the 100-days work programme in West Bengal. Ph.D. Thesis, Indira Gandhi Institute of Development Research, Mumbai, India.

Das, U., A. Singh and N. Mahanto (2012), Awareness about Mahatma Gandhi National Rural Employment Guarantee Act: Some evidence from the northern parts of West Bengal, India, *Economics Bulletin*, 32(1), 528–537.

Das, U. and D. Maiorano (2015), Is the MNREGA fund crunch making the programme clientelistic? *Ideas for India*, September 2. (Available at: http://www.ideasforindia.in/article.aspx?article_id=1497).

Dev, S.M. (1996), Experience of India's (Maharashtra) Employment Guarantee Scheme: Lessons for Development Policy, *Development Policy Review*, 14(3), 227–254.

[15] For more information on the organisation, please see http://www.satmilesatishclub.org/ (Accessed on April 24, 2014).

Devereux, S. and C. Solomon (2006), Employment creation programmes: The international experience, Discussion paper 24, Economic and Labour Market Analysis Department, Geneva: International Labour Office.

Dey, S. and A.S. Bedi (2010), The National Rural Employment Guarantee Scheme in Birbhum, *Economic and Political Weekly*, 45(41), 19–25.

Dreze, J. and C. Oldiges (2007), How is NREGA Doing. Accessed from http://knowledge.nrega.net/651/1/How_is_NREGA_Doing.doc (Accessed on March 30th, 2014).

Dreze, J and A. Sen (2013), *An Uncertain Glory: India and its Contradictions*. Princeton University Press: USA.

Government of India (2009). HDI and GDI estimates for India and the states/UTs: results and analysis. New Delhi: Ministry of Women and Child Development (Available at: http://icds-wcd.nic.in/publication/GDIGEReport/Part2.pdf).

Government of India (2014), Press note on poverty estimates, 2011–2012. New Delhi: Planning Commission. (Available at: http://planningcommission.nic.in/news/pre_pov 2307.pdf).

Jayadev, A., S. Motiram and V. Vakulabharanam (2007), Patterns of Wealth Disparities in India during the Liberalisation Era, *Economic and Political Weekly*, 42(38), 3853–3863.

Khera, R. and N. Nayak (2009), Women workers and perceptions of National Rural Employment Guarantee Act, *Economic and Political Weekly*, 64(43), 49–57.

Liu, Y. and C.B. Barrett (2013), Heterogeneous Pro-poor Targeting in India's Mahatma Gandhi National Rural Employment Guarantee Scheme, *Economic and Political Weekly*, 48(10), 46–53.

MacAuslan, I. (2008), India's National Rural Employment Guarantee Act: A Case Study for How Change Happens. From Poverty to Power.'Oxford: Oxfam International.

Mukherjee, S. (2010), The Year After, The Telegraph, Kolkata, March 25. Accessed from http://www.telegraphindia.com/1100325/jsp/opinion/story_12138868.jsp (Accessed on June 10th, 2011).

Mukhopadhyay, A. and I. Rajaraman (2007), Rural unemployment 1999–2005: Who gained, who lost?. *Economic and Political Weekly*, 42(30), 3116–3120.

Narayanan, S. and U. Das (2014), Women Participation and Rationing in the Employment Guarantee Scheme, *Economic and Political Weekly*, 49, 46–53.

Ravallion, M. (1991), Reaching the Rural Poor Through Public Employment: Arguments, Evidence and Lessons From South Asia, *World Bank Research Observer*, 6(2), 153–175.

Singh, A., U. Das and T. Agarwal (2013), How Inclusive has Regular Employment been in India? A dynamic view, *European Journal of Development Research*, 25(3), 486–494.

Part IV

Sector Issues Manufacturing, Technology

Chapter 12

Growth of the Manufacturing Sector Future Constraints[1]

Manmohan Agarwal* and Aritri Chakravarty†
Centre for Development Studies
Thiruvananthapuram, Kerala, India
**manmohan@cds.ac.in*
†aritri.chakravarty@gmail.com

Abstract: Despite the unprecedented growth of GDP in developing countries during 2001–2007, the manufacturing sector lagged so that the share of manufacturing in GDP fell in many regions and counties. We find that the share of value added in gross value of output fell and the use of imported inputs increased in Brazil, China, India and Russia. Also, the share of manufacturing output exported has increased in Brazil, China and India but decreased in Russia. There has been considerable transformation of the manufacturing sector during this period only in India. Manufactures of these countries do not compete in the world market as their export baskets are very different. The only exception is that the export baskets of China and India are very similar and have become more similar over the period.

We then decompose the sources of growth for the manufacturing sector and the sub-sectors. The chapter goes on to argue that improved performance requires better sources of long-term finance and here the New Development Bank (NDB) could have a role.

1 Introduction

This chapter examines the likely impact of the NDB on economic performance of developing countries. This is done by analysing in Section 1 the economic

[1] We wish to thank Susmita Mitra for help with accessing the WIOD data base.

performance of developing countries in recent years and what that reveals about possible weaknesses in their economic performance. A major shortcoming in their economic performance has been the performance of the manufacturing sector. The performance and structural characteristics of the manufacturing sector are analysed in detail in Section 2. This detailed discussion of the manufacturing sector stems from the importance that developing countries have placed on its development as that is supposed to draw surplus labour from agriculture and other low productivity areas and thus lead to more productive employment and higher incomes.[2] The chapter then examines in Section 3 the growth in employment and productivity in the four countries. In Section 4, we discuss the issues involved in providing long-term finance for manufactures concentrating on the situation in India. The declining role of aid provides an opportunity for the NDB set up by the BRICS. However, apart from the finance it would provide, we argue that the NDB can affect the current international aid architecture by demonstrating the irrelevance of conditionalities and so forcing reform on the current international aid institutions. We end with concluding remarks in Section 6.

2 Economic Performance of Developing Countries

The period 2001–2007 before the onset of the financial crisis was a golden period for growth in developing countries. Developing countries as a group were catching up with the high income countries because of the marked acceleration in their rate of growth in this period despite a significant slowdown in growth in high income countries. This is in contrast to the previous "golden age" of capitalism (Marglin and Schor, 1990) when developing countries had grown rapidly but the developed countries had grown even faster (Agarwal, 2008).

This rapid growth in developing countries in the face of the slowdown in developed countries raised hopes that the growth process in developing countries had developed its own momentum.[3] However, the subsequent slowdown in growth in most groups of developing countries shows their continuing vulnerability to the state of the world economy. Obviously, the current institutions of international

---

[2] For a discussion of these aspects in development policies see Rosenstein-Rodan (1943), Nurkse (1953).

[3] The growth in South–South trade and in FDI flows among developing countries provided a basis for this hope (Agarwal, 2015).

Table 1. Growth of per capita GDP (annual average %).

	1991–2000	2001–2007	2008–2010	2011–2013
High Income	2	1.9	–0.7	1.2
Middle Income	2.4	5	4.2	4
Upper Middle Income	3	5.3	4.5	4.5
Lower Middle Income	1.4	4.7	4.1	3.5
Low Income	–0.2	3	3.5	3.5
Least Developed	0.3	4.3	3.2	2
Brazil	1	2.2	3.2	1.2
China	8.8	10.1	9.2	7.7
India	3.7	5.9	6.1	4.1
Russia	–3.5	7.2	0.6	2.7
South Africa	–0.4	2.8	0.4	1.3

Source: World Bank, World Development Indicators.

governance are not able to insulate developing countries from the vagaries of the world economy. This vulnerability could be reduced by greater wide ranging South–South Cooperation (SSC) (Agarwal and Whalley, 2015) as this would make them less dependent on the developed countries for trade, foreign direct investment and technology.

Brazil, Russia, India, China, South Africa (BRICS) countries also had seen an acceleration of growth rates in the period 2001–2007, though growth rates continued to be modest in Brazil and South Africa (Table 1). Growth rates have declined across the BRICS countries after the financial crisis falling to particularly low levels in Brazil, Russia and South Africa.

An important positive feature of recent developments in developing countries is the maintenance of high rates of investment despite the growth slowdown; and these investments have been financed largely by high rates of domestic savings (Table 2). The share of gross capital formation (GCF) in GDP has increased in all the developing regions despite the economic slowdown and in all the BRICS countries except Russia. Also gross domestic savings (GDS) as a share of GDP has usually continued to increase. However, the savings investment gap has tended to worsen. Though the gap has remained manageable, partly because of accumulated foreign exchange reserves, and growth reducing measures have not had to be implemented, this is a worrisome factor for the future. In the past, large current account deficits have called for corrective measures that have reduced the rate of

Table 2. GCF and GDS (% of GDP).

		1965–1973	1974–1982	1983–1990	1991–2000	2001–2007	2008–2013
EAP	(i)	26.7	32.7	34.4	36.4	36.7	42.7
	(ii)	32.9	33.9	38.2	41.4	46.5	
LAC	(i)	21.1	24.2	20.2	19.6	19.6	21.2
	(ii)	20.4	23.1	23.6	18.6	20.3	20.1
SA	(i)	15.3	18.9	22.1	23	28.9	33
	(ii)	13.6	16	18.9	21.4	26.2	27
SSA	(i)	24.6	25.5	18.1	16.7	17.6	20.6
	(ii)	22.5	23.2	20.4	16.8	17.1	18.8
Low Income	(i)	12.4	15.1	16.9	18.2	21.3	25.1
	(ii)	8.2	6.7	8.7	9.8	10.8	11.7
Low Middle Income	(i)	15.8	22	22.8	22.7	25.5	29.1

Note: Row (i) is GCF as percent of GDP and row (ii) is GDS as percent of GDP.
Source: World Bank, World Development Indicators.

growth.[4] Historically this gap has been large in low income countries and has worsened as the investment share in GDP increased without a concomitant increase in the share of domestic savings.

3 The Performance of the Manufacturing Sector

3.1 Manufacturing in the developing world and in the BRICS

3.1.1 *Share of manufacturing in GDP*

While the overall macroeconomic growth situation may not generate undue anxiety, the sector composition of growth is worrying. The performance of the manufacturing sector has been poor. The share of manufacturing in GDP had stagnated in the low income countries in the years from 1974 to 2000, though the share had increased in the middle income countries.

[4] The Contingent Reserve Arrangement that was also agreed upon cold provide an additional source of balance of payment financing. But it does not provide for a new model for the operation of the international monetary system and so is not a solution for the ills of the current international monetary system (Agarwal, 2015).

Table 3. Share of manufacturing (% of GDP).

	1965–1973	1974–1982	1983–1990	1991–2000	2001–2007	2008–2013
EAP	27.5	33.4	31.1	30.9	31.2	30.6
LAC	24.3	25.5	25.9	19.5	17.9	16
SA	13.4	15.6	15.8	15.7	15.4	16.2
SSA	16.7	15.6	13.9	12.5	11.1	
Low Income		11.3	11.3	11.3	12.5	12.5
Lower Middle Income	13.6	15.3	16.5	17.6	17.5	17.1
Brazil	28.3	31.5	32.3	20.3	17.7	15
China	31.8	38.5	34.7	32.9	32.4	32.2
India	13.7	16	16	15.7	15.3	16.4
Russia					17.4	15.4[4]
South Africa	22.2	22.2	22.8	20.6	19.1	14.2

Source: World Bank, World Development Indicators.

In this century, the share had increased in the low income countries before the financial crisis, but has stagnated since then. In the middle income countries, the share has tended to decline since the 1990s.[6]

The share of manufacturing in GDP which had been rising in earlier years in developing countries has been declining in recent years (Table 3). The exact timing of the reversal from an increasing share to decreasing share varies between the regions. In EAP and SSA it started decreasing after the period 1974–1982 whereas in LAC the decline has been particularly sharp since the 1983–1990 period. There is a further difference in the performance of the sector in more recent years. Its share has declined continuously in LAC and SSA whereas in EAP it is almost constant and in SA there is an overall increase though with fluctuations.

The BRICS countries exhibit a pattern similar to that of their regions (Table 3). The share of manufacturing in GDP was rising in Brazil and South Africa till the period 1983–1990 and has fallen precipitously since then. In Brazil, it is now less than half and in South Africa slightly more than half. The share in Russia also has

[5]A longer series of data is available for share of industry, which includes manufacturing, in GDP. The share drops from 49.3% in 1989–1990 to 40.6% in 1991–2000 to 35.6% in 2001–2007 and is 35.8% in 2008–2013.

[6]The share of the upper middle income countries declined from 23.9% in the period 1991–2000 to 23.1% in 2008–2013.

been declining over the more limited period for which data is available. In China, it increased till the 1974–1982 period and since then has declined though it has been relatively constant since the 1991–2000 period. In India, the share has fluctuated with periods when it has increased and periods when it has decreased. However, overall the share has increased since the financial crisis.

3.1.2 *Labour productivity and the manufacturing sector*

The performance of the manufacturing sector is of vital importance as it is a source of employment, and rising productivity and thereby of wages and living standards.[7] We examine the evolution of productivity growth in the non-agricultural economy.[8] We find a distinct difference in the behaviour of per worker value added in non-agriculture in Asia from that in LAC and SSA.

The changes in labour productivity show a common pattern among the regions. The pace of productivity increase speeds up in the 1990s compared to the 1980s except in SSA, then further accelerates in the period 2001–2007. It then slows in the period after the crisis (Table 4). As far as the three countries, Brazil, China and India are concerned, per worker value added in the non-agriculture sector continuously falls in Brazil, whereas it increases in the other two. So the declining share of manufactures in GDP in Brazil is not accompanied by a leaner more efficient sector.[9] We further discuss below growth of productivity in Brazil, Russia, India and China (BRIC).

Table 4. Annual growth in per worker value added in non-agriculture.

	1983–1990	1991–2000	2001–2007	2008–2013
EAP	5	6	7.6	5.8
LAC	–1	–0.9	0.8	0.5
SA	2.3	3.1	5	3.5
SSA	–1.6	–2.1	1.3	–0.9
Brazil	–4.4	–6.1	–4.7	–4.2
China	4.9	5.1	4.9	2
India	1.6	1.9	4.1	1.1

Source: Lele *et al.* (2011).

[7] A major source of productivity and wage growth during development is because of shift of labour from low productivity activities to higher productivity activities. This is the classic path of development of dual economies (Lewis, 1954)

[8] Employment data is not available for manufacturing but is available for the total economy and for agriculture. So we can get employment in the non-agriculture economy. .

[9] The analysis suggests that the sectors with higher labour productivity are shrinking. Why this is happening is not very east to determine from the data.

3.2 The manufacturing sector in Brazil, China, India and Russia[10]

3.2.1 *The behaviour of the manufacturing sector*

The percentage of value added in the gross value of output has declined in four of the BRICS countries, BRIC, during the period 1995–2011 (Table 5).[11]

However, the share of value added increased between 2005 and 2011 in Brazil, though overall it decreased in the period 1995–2011. China and Brazil used the least amount of intermediate goods whereas India and Russia used the most. Furthermore, Russia which had a low value added to gross value ratio in 1995 saw the ratio fall further in this period.

When we examine the use of imported and domestic inputs we find that the percentage of imported inputs to value of output declined during 1995–2011 only in the case of Russia (Table 6).

Table 5. Value added % of value of gross output.

	1995	2000	2005	2011	Decline between 1995 and 2011
Brazil	33.2	31	29.4	32.2	3.3
China	34.9	37.4	32.4	31	11.3
India	23.3	23.4	23.6	23	2.5
Russia	27.1	27.5	24	22.3	17.9

Table 6. Use of inputs (% of gross output).

	Imported Inputs				Domestic Inputs			
	1995	2000	2005	2011	1995	2000	2005	2011
Brazil	5.6	7.9	7.3	8.5	55.2	54.9	56.9	52.4
China	7.7	8.2	10.4	9	64.7	63.8	65	68.2
India	7.6	11.4	13.4	12.7	64.7	60.2	58.6	59.9
Russia	8.5	11.8	9.2	8.4	53.4	47.7	54	56

[10] All the tables in this section have been calculated by the author from the data available in the WIOD data set. The data set can be accessed at http://www.wiod.org/new_site/home.htm. For use of the data set consult Dietzenbacher *et al.* (2015).

[11] South Africa is excluded from this analysis as the WIOD data base that we use does not provide data on South Africa.

The largest increase was in India which uses more imported inputs than the other countries.[12] The changes in the use of domestic inputs are in the opposite direction to that for imported inputs. It increases, when the use of imported inputs decreases and *vice-versa*. The only exception is China where the use of both domestic and imported inputs has increased.

3.2.2 *The structure of the manufacturing sector*

We next examine how the structure of the manufacturing sector has changed between 1995 and 2011. We calculated the share of the different sectors in total value added for the manufacturing sector for the years 1995, 2000, 2005 and 2011.[13] We next calculated the correlation between the structures for the different years.

The very high and significant correlation coefficients[14] suggest that there is little change in the structure of the manufacturing sector in these countries over a decade and a half (Table 7) which includes a period of very rapid growth and another period of adjustment to the financial crisis and a slowdown of the world economy.

We next compare the structure of the manufacturing sector in the four countries.[15]

The correlation between the sector distribution of the manufacturing sector in Brazil in 1995 with that in China in 1995 is 0.65 and it decreases to 0.44 when we calculate the correlation between the sector distribution in the two countries

Table 7. Correlations of the structure of manufactures in 1995 with other years.

	2000	2005	2011
Brazil	0.97	0.95	0.96
China	0.94	0.85	0.84
India	0.93	0.87	0.87
Russia	0.95	0.83	0.75

[12] Indian industry is believed not to be an important participant in global value chains.

[13] There are 14 different sectors (i) food and beverages, (ii) textiles, (iii) leather, (iv) wood, (v) pulp, (vi) coke, petroleum, etc. (vii) chemical, (viii) rubber, (ix) other non-metallic minerals, (x) basic metals, (xi) machinery, (xii) electrical machinery, (xiii) transport equipment, (xiv) manufacturing n.e.c.

[14] For 12 degrees of freedom the 1% significant value for the correlation coefficient is 0.661 and the 5% significance level is 0.532.

[15] Here we report only the correlations between the structures for 1995 and 2005 and for 1995 and 2011.

Table 8. Correlations between the structures in manufacturing in the countries.

	China		India		Russia	
	1995	**2011**	**1995**	**2011**	**1995**	**2011**
Brazil	0.65	0.44	0.71	0.7	0.85	0.72
China	0.77	0.58	0.7	0.32		
India	0.71	0.79				

in 2011 (Table 8). The only two correlations that are not significant at the 5% level are between Brazil and China in 2011 and between China and Russia in 2011.[16] The correlation coefficient between the structure of manufacturing in China and India also declined between 1995 and 2011 though it remained significant at the 5% level. This suggests that the structure of manufacturing in China is becoming different from that in the other three countries. Overall, there is a marginal decline in the correlation coefficients over time. This suggests that the sector composition of the manufacturing sector may be becoming less similar among these countries, though at a very slow pace.

3.2.3 *Exports of manufactures*

We next analyse the behaviour of exports of manufactures.

The share of the manufacturing sector that has been exported has increased for all the countries except Russia, where it has steadily declined from its peak in 1999 (Figure 1). The peak export share for China was in 2005 and for Brazil in 2004. For India, the share has increased over the period 1995–2011 period though with some fluctuations. Among the four countries, India is exporting the highest

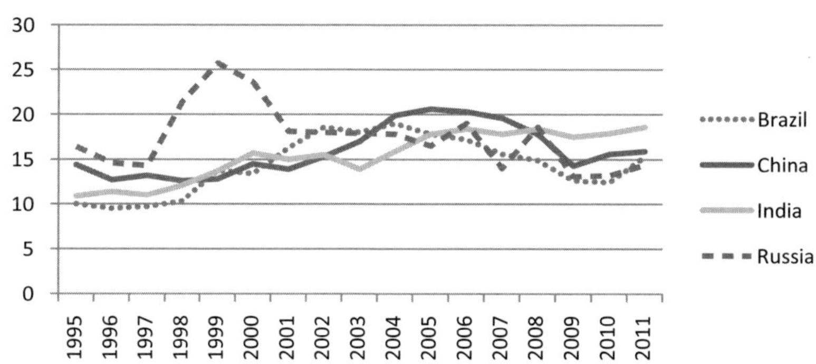

Figure 1. Share of manufactures exported, 1995–2011.

[16]The correlation coefficients for the shares of the different sectors for other years are also very high.

Table 9. Correlations between export shares for the years 1995–2011.

	China	India	Russia
Brazil	0.72	0.6	0.13
China	0.67	–0.17	
India	–0.18		

share of its manufacturing output in 2011. Brazil which exported the lowest share of its output in 1995 had become the country exporting the largest share of its output in 2002. However, by the end of the period in 2011 it was again the country that was exporting the smallest share of its manufacturing output.

We next try to assess whether the overall pattern of change in the export shares over the period 1995–2011 are similar by calculating the correlation between the shares of manufactures exported by the four countries over the years 1995–2011.[17]

The correlations between the shares of manufactures exported in the years 1995–2011 are very high among Brazil, China and India despite the differences between the behaviour of the manufacturing sector among these countries (Table 9). This similarity suggests that the export performance of the manufacturing sector was governed more by common international factors than individual country policies. The pattern of behaviour of shares of manufactures exported by Russia is very different from that of the other countries.

3.2.4 *Concentration of gross output and exports of manufactures*

We examine the structure of the gross output of the different sub-sectors of the manufacturing sector and also of exports by the different sub-sectors of manufacturing. We calculated the Herfindahl index of concentration both for the gross output of the sectors and also of their exports.

The major conclusions are (Table 10)

(a) Levels of concentration are quite low for gross output.[18] But for exports the index for China would suggest moderate concentration and for Russia high concentration.

[17] We take the share of output exported by say Brazil and China for the years between 1995 and 2011 and calculate the correlation between them.

[18] There is no test of significance for the value of the Herfindahl Index. Generally in the analysis of market concentration of firms a value between 0.15 and 0.25 is taken to indicate moderate concentration and a value greater than 0.25 is taken to imply high concentration.

Table 10. Herfindahl concentration index.

	Gross Output		Exports	
	1995	**2011**	**1995**	**2011**
Brazil	0.1	0.11	0.13	0.15
China	0.1	0.11	0.17	0.21
India	0.1	0.14	0.1	0.13
Russia	0.12	0.14	0.25	0.24

(b) There is a weak tendency for concentration levels to rise during the 1995–2011 period. This is most pronounced for China where the concentration index for exports reached 0.24 in 2006 before declining a bit.

(c) The concentration index is in most cases greater for exports than for output.

(d) The different country's output concentration ratios are very similar.[19]

(e) As far as export concentrations are concerned, only Russia's export concentration ratio is significantly different from that of the others. Russia's export concentration in 1995 is significantly different from that of Brazil at the 5% significance level and from that of India at the 1% level. But these differences had narrowed by 2011 as the concentration ratios of Brazil and India had increased. In 2011, Russia's export concentration was only different from that of India at the 5% level of significance.

3.2.5 *Structure of exports*

We next examine changes in the structure of manufacturing exports. We examine two aspects of this. First, how does each sector's contribution to the total exports of manufactures varies over time, namely, how is the export basket of manufactures varying over time. Second, we examine the variation over time in the share of the output of each sector that is exported.

The share of the different sectors in the total exports of manufactures has not changed significantly over the years in Brazil, China and Russia (Table11). The correlation coefficients for the sector contributions for different years are all at least 0.73 which is significant at the 1% level for 12 degrees of freedom. The conclusion is that the export basket has not changed very much. We had seen earlier that the structure of the manufacturing sector has remained relatively constant in these countries. The constancy of the export shares suggests that the export

[19] The variance can be calculated from the index. Then the F-test can be used to see whether the ratio of the variances is significantly different.

Table 11. Correlation between the sector composition of exports.

Correlation coefficients for sector shares of exports between

Brazil	**2000**	**2005**	**2011**
1995	0.86	0.91	0.93
2000	0.97	0.86	
2005	0.94		
China	**2000**	**2005**	**2011**
1995	0.94	0.82	0.78
2000	0.96	0.94	
2005	1		
India	**2000**	**2005**	**2011**
1995	0.96	0.69	0.32
2000	0.77	0.46	
2005	0.88		
Russia	**2000**	**2005**	**2011**
1995	0.98	0.94	0.73
2000	0.95	0.76	
2005	0.91		

markets have not been a force for changes in the structure of the manufacturing sector.

The only exception is India. The correlation coefficient for the export structure in 1995 and 2011 is 0.32 and for the export structure between 2000 and 2011 is 0.46, both of which are not significant at the usual levels of significance. This suggests that there has been a significant shift in the sector composition of India's exports of manufactures.

We next look at how the share of output of each sector that is exported varies over time. The only country for which there seems a significant change in the share of output that the different sectors export is India (Table 12). The correlation between the shares of output of the different sectors that are exported in 1995 and 2011 is only 0.32, which is not significant.[20] So the share of the output of a sector that is exported in 2011 is not similar to the share of that sector's output that was

[20] For 12 degrees of freedom the 1% significant value for the correlation coefficient is 0.661 and the 5% significance level is 0.532.

Table 12. Correlations of the structure of manufactures and of the use of imported inputs.

	Structure of Manufacturing		Share of Imported Inputs	
	1995–2000	**1995–2011**	**1995–2000**	**1995–2011**
Brazil	0.84	0.92	0.9	0.84
China	0.93	0.84	0.87	0.66
India	0.89	0.32	0.91	0.35
Russia	0.91	0.79	0.14	0.05

Table 13. Correlation between the export compositions by country pairs and over time.

	1995	**2011**
Brazil–China	–0.04	–0.31
Brazil–India	0.04	–0.32
Brazil–Russia	0.42	0.2
China–India	0.61	0.95
China–Russia	–0.42	–0.43
India–Russia	–0.43	–0.28

exported in 1995. The structure of the share of output of different sectors exported seems to have changed after 2005.

We then compared the export basket of the four countries, are they similar or different and how has the composition changed over time.

The exports baskets of the different countries are very different, so they are not competing with each other (Table 13). The differences in the export baskets have grown over time.

Only China and India have similar export baskets and this similarity has grown over time. Chinese and Indian manufactures compete but not manufactures of other countries. We then examined the use of imported inputs. We calculated the value of imported inputs in gross value of output for the different sectors. The structure of use by the different sectors is very similar for Brazil and China as the correlation coefficient is larger than the boundary for the 1% level of significance. Again for India we find a sharp change after 2005 as the correlation between the shares of imported inputs sector wise between 1995 and 2005 is 0.95 but drops to merely 0.35 for the sector wise use of imported inputs between 1995 and 2011. The change for Russia occurs even earlier as the correlation between the shares exported by the different sectors in 2000 is not significantly correlated with that in 1995.

One of the significant findings of the literature on global value chains is that very often successful exporting requires the use of appropriate inputs. It is concluded that the share of imported inputs in the value of the output can be significant and that this has been rising.

When we analyse the different sectors of manufacturing we do not find any significant correlation between the share of imported inputs in gross value of output and the share of the output that is exported (Table 14). The only exception is India. There is a significant positive relation between the use of imported inputs and export success at the sector level in 2005 and 2011.

We next examine whether the exports of these countries are concentrated in the labour intensive sectors. We calculated share of labour income in value added for each of the 14 sectors. We then correlated the export share with this labour share.

We found that for none of the countries was the relation strong and also even if it was significant at a point in time it was not consistent across time (Table 15). Only for Brazil in 2005 and for India in 2000 was the correlation coefficient significant at the 5% level of significance. We also calculated the share of labour that was highly skilled labour, that was of medium skilled labour and unskilled labour. We

Table 14. Correlation between export share and share of imported inputs.

	1995	2000	2005	2011
Brazil	–0.4	–0.11	–0.05	–0.26
China	0.4	0.03	0.05	–0.23
India	–0.24	–0.2	0.61*	0.76**
Russia	–0.34	–0.16	–0.28	–0.42

Note: * significant at 5% and ** significant at 1% for 12 degrees of freedom.

Table 15. Correlation between Export share and share of labour in value added.

	1995	2000	2005	2011
Brazil	0.36	0.31	0.54*	0.36
China	–0.03	0.01	–0.14	–0.24
India	0.46	0.55*	0.46	–0.22
Russia	–0.28	–0.03	–0.1	–0.02

calculated the correlation between the share of output exported and the shares of these different forms of labour. Again, we found no significant correlation.

In brief, the structure of the manufacturing sector and that of manufacturing exports shows remarkable stability despite very contrasting performances of the sector in the individual countries. In Brazil and Russia, there seems to have been destruction as share of manufacturing in GDP has fallen but this has not been creative as there seems to have been little construction.

The only country where there has been a structural shift has been India. Considerably more of the output of the sector is being exported and this success seems to be tied to the use of imported inputs whose use has increased considerably. In India, there is a strong correlation at the sector level between export success and use of imported inputs. The substantial change in the manufacturing sector during 1995–2011 is most probably the result in change in policies that started in 1991. Tariffs have been substantially reduced. Import controls had to be eliminated after India lost a dispute at the World Trade Organisation (WTO). Entry of private capital, particularly, foreign private capital has been progressively liberalised. The new policies have resulted in a different structure of manufacturing.

4 Growth in Employment and Productivity

We now examine the growth of employment and productivity in the manufacturing sector for the four countries.

Manufacturing employment fell in Russia while it increased in the other three countries (Table 16).

Per hour productivity increased in all the countries. But per worker productivity declined in Brazil whereas it increased in the other three countries. This was because the hours worked per worker increased in China, India and Russia. Brazil was the only country where the hours worked per worker declined.

Table 16. Annual % growth of employment and productivity in manufacturing, 1995–2009.

		Productivity	
	Employment	Per-Worker	Per-Labour Hour
Brazil	1.8	–0.5	0.1
China	3.6	11.8	11.1
India	1.8	4.6	3.6
Russia	–3.3	5.4	4.9

Table 17. Decomposition of growth of value added.

	Solow Residual	Contribution of Capital	Contribution of Labour
Brazil	–3%	5%	1%
China	4%	3%	4%
India	1%	5%	1%
Russia	3%	1%	1%

We now decompose the growth of manufacturing value added into the Solow residual, the contribution of capital and the contribution of labour.

Brazil is the only country with a negative contribution from productivity growth. It also has a much larger contribution from capital growth than from labour growth. The contribution of capital has been large. As we saw above the spectral composition has not changed. So the capital labour ratio has been rising, perhaps in an attempt to increase productivity. Productivity must have gone up in some segments as exports of manufactures increased rapidly in the early part of the period 1995–2011. But this stalled in the second half of the period. This phenomenon needs further analysis. Productivity growth in India, though positive, is small. In India, capital increase contributed much more to growth than the employment increase did. In contrast, both China and Russia had much larger contributions from growth of productivity. The difference is that the contributions from increase in capital and in employment contributed much less to growth in Russia than they did in China. China had the largest Solow residual and the largest contribution from labour. The contribution from labour was greater in China than the contribution from capital despite the very high rates of investment in China.

5 Availability of Long-term Finance

Availability of long-term finance is very important for the growth of the manufacturing sector. In the UK, the initial country to undergo industrialisation, personal and family savings and retained profits were sufficient to finance the small scale plants that prevailed at that time. But later in the 19th century, plants had become larger and additional sources of finance were required. In the absence of a share market in Germany banks stepped in to provide this finance whereas British banks supplied only working capital (Gerschenkron, 1962). To protect their investments banks were represented on the management of the companies. Later, as in the case of Russia the state stepped in to provide the finance (Gerschenkron, 1962). In the case of Japan, the state set up the first factories and when they were running successfully sold them cheaply to private entrepreneurs (Allen, 1946). Innovative methods have been adopted to finance industrialisation.

When developing countries attempted to industrialise their economies after the Second World War a major challenge they faced was to provide finance for investment in manufacturing. Stock markets then were almost non-existent in developing countries. Even now they have only limited capacity to mobilise resources for investment. A report on the Brazilian stock market noted that even in Brazil the stock market played a very limited, almost no role as there were hardly any initial public offerings by Brazilian companies. Companies were delisting and preferring to raise money in New York and trading volume was declining.[21]

Governments established domestic finance companies (DFCs) to provide finance mainly for manufacturing companies. These DFCs raised money through deposits from the public and through loans from the government and bilateral and multilateral aid giving institutions. DFCs particularly in Latin America have not been successful as they have been reluctant to lend long-term because of the uncertainty created by high rates of inflation, balance of payments deficits and macro instability.[22] The only successful DFC in Latin America is BNDES in Brazil. But even BNDES provides only limited finance for manufacturing and raises its money mainly from the government. For instance, 75% of its lending in 2012 was to the oil and gas, mining and power industries (Coutinho, 2010). Also, "about 60 per cent of BNDES lending goes to large conglomerates rather than small and medium-sized enterprises (SMEs), with ready access to western capital markets, and do not need public money, critics say" (Financial Times, 2015). Liberalisation and competing in international markets leads to more uncertainty and so banks are reluctant to lend to industries.

India had developed a complex system consisting of the share market, development finance banks, other government institutions such as life insurance companies and mutual funds to provide finance for the manufacturing sector. India's capital market was relatively underdeveloped at independence in 1947. As merchant bankers and underwriting firms were almost non-existent and commercial banks did not provide long-term industrial finance, no institutions existed to meet

[21] This is from a case prepared by Aaron Mihaly under the supervision of Professors Roger Leeds and Francis Fukuyama of Johns Hopkins School of Advanced International Studies for class discussion. For further discussion of the operations of BMDES see Lazzarini *et al.* (2011).

[22] "Over the decades, particularly during Brazil's period of runaway inflation in the 1970s and 1980s, long-term finance was not available from the market, so BNDES stepped into the breach." FT online edition for January 11, 2015.

the demand for long-term capital. In this situation, the government established. The Industrial Finance Corporation of India (IFCI) on July 1, 1948. IFCI was the first DFC that could provide loans to corporate borrowers at concessional rates because of its access to low-cost funds through the central bank's statutory liquidity ratio. Later in 1954, the Industrial Development Bank (IDBI) was established by an Act of Parliament to provide credit and other financial facilities to the fledgling Indian industry. Then in 1955, The Industrial Credit and Investment Corporation of India Limited (ICICI) was incorporated at the initiative of the World Bank, the Government of India and representatives of Indian industry, to provide medium and long-term project financing to Indian businesses.

In 1974, the Indian Government passed the Foreign Exchange regulating Act (FERA) under which a company with more than 40% foreign shareholding faced restrictions on its operation and its expansion. Many transnationals issued shares to Indians and these were priced very conservatively by the Controller of Capital Issues so that Indians who got allocations made large capital gains apart from owning shares which paid large dividends. The late 70s and 80s were a period of high inflation partly because of periodic increases in the price of oil. Inflation made fixed deposits in banks unattractive and so Indians increasingly invested in shares. The pattern of allocation of financial savings completely changed in the 80s. As a consequence of this shift in investor preferences big companies could raise large sums of money from the share market. Somewhat smaller enterprises had access to the DFCs and to the Life Insurance Corporation of India for long term funds. Almost 20% of financial savings were invested in shares either directly or indirectly through the Unit Trust of India (UTI) a government mutual fund (Table 18).

Subsequent to the liberalisation started in 1991, a number of scams hit the stock market hurting the small investor who did not have access to privileged information nor could protect himself. Later at the turn of the century the asset value of the UTI fell and the burden of this was disproportionately borne by the small investor as larger investors were able to cash their units in a timely manner so as to earn the usual high returns As a result of this, the small holders had to take larger losses than if the loss of value had been more evenly distributed. As a consequence investments in shares and in the UTI have lost favour and bank deposits have become more attractive (Table 18). This has had unfortunate consequences for the banks. Infrastructure needed large investments and the government persuaded the public sector banks to lend large sums for infrastructure. Construction of infrastructure is a time consuming activity and returns can be long delayed and so the banks have been saddled with a large proportion of non-performing assets. As banks try to rectify their balance sheets, they are reluctant to lend to enterprises with an uncertain international financial outlook.

Table 18. Allocation of household financial savings.

		Currency	Bank Dep	NB Dep	Life Insurance	Provident Fund	Govt.	Shares	UTI	Trade Debt
5th Plan	1974–1977	9.9	50.4	2.5	8.5	20.2	5.9	1.3	0.3	0.9
	1978–1979	14	47.1	3.6	7.4	17	3.8	2.3	0.6	4.2
6th Plan	1980–1984	12.3	41.9	4.9	7.3	17	10.5	3.4	1.3	1.6
7th Plan	1985–1989	12.1	37.7	4.2	7.9	18.1	12.3	4.3	3.5	–0.1
	1990–1991	11.3	28.8	2.8	9.9	18.6	10	9.3	9.9	–0.7
8th Plan	1992–1996	10.7	34.4	11.1	9.4	17.4	7.3	7.6	3	–0.8
9th Plan	1997–2001	8.6	38.7	1.8	12.8	19.8	14.8	4.1	0.1	–0.8
10th Plan	2002–2006	9.1	45.8	0.8	14.8	11.4	14.2	4.3	–0.6	0.2
11th Plan	2007–2011	11.4	50.8	1.3	22	11	0.4	2.6	–0.1	0.7
12th Plan	2012–2013	9.6	56.2	1.5	17.1	8.9	0.3	3.2	0	0.4

Source: Reserve Bank of India, Handbook of Statistics in the Indian Economy, 2014.

Meanwhile, the DFCs that had been established in India were converted into banks so that they also dried up as a source of long term capital. However, a positive development has been the establishment of a number of private venture capital funds. It is unclear as yet whether they can entirely fill the gap left by the withdrawal of small savers from investing in stocks and the changeover of the DFCs.

Bilateral and multilateral aid agencies had provided loans to DFCs to lend to manufacturing. But, now not only is the importance of aid declining but only a very small proportion of bilateral aid is given for productive purposes to the agricultural and manufacturing sectors or to infrastructure development (Agarwal forthcoming, 2016).

The future of aid is even bleaker. The World Bank will reach its lending limit if its capital is not increased and the developed countries do not seem to be keen to do so in the current fiscal situation. Essentially, Brazil, India and China have reached their individual country borrowing limits. The future of IDA is also uncertain as many major borrowers from IDA will graduate in the next decade (Todd and Leo, 2011).[23]

With the uncertain aid outlook the NDB and also the Asian Infrastructure Development Bank (AIIB,) could provide new important sources of funds for developing countries.[24] Both these new initiatives would provide funding for

[23] For a more detailed discussion of the aid situation see Agarwal (2016).

[24] Whereas the NDB has been set up by the BRIC,S the AIIB is a Chinese initiative that has garnered considerable support. 57 founding members had joined by April 15, 2015.

infrastructure only. However, as noted above the need is also for long-term finance for manufacturing and so an important lacuna in the current aid architecture persists.

6 Concluding Remarks

The GDP of developing countries had grown at unprecedented rates in the period 2001–2007. Growth has slowed after the 2008 crisis but continues to be high. However, growth of the manufacturing sector has lagged so that the share of manufacturing in GDP has fallen in many regions and counties. A detailed analysis of the manufacturing sector in BRIC shows that over the period 1995–2011 the share of value added in gross value of output has fallen and the use of imported inputs has increased. Also, the share of manufacturing output exported has increased in Brazil, China and India and decreased in Russia. But only India shows an almost continuous increase in the share because in the case of Brazil and China the peak was reached around 2004–2005. Furthermore, the structure of the manufacturing sector shows considerable stability over the period 1995–2011. The only country where there has been considerable transformation of the manufacturing sector has been India. The share of the output exported has increased considerably, the sector composition of output and of exports has shifted over the years and the use of imported inputs has increased. Another feature of the manufacturing sector is that the export basket of the different countries is very different so that they are not competing in world markets .The only exception is that the export baskets of China and India are very similar and have become more similar over the period.

Manufacturing employment has increased in China, India and Brazil, but fallen in Russia. The working hours have expanded in China, India and Russia so that the increase in employment is less than the increase in hours worked. But the working week has decreased in Brazil. The contribution from productivity growth to growth of value added is low for Brazil, actually negative, and India. In both Brazil and India, increases in capital contributed more to growth of value than did labour growth. In contrast, both China and Russia had much larger contributions from growth of productivity. The difference is that the contributions from increase in capital and in employment contributed much less to growth in Russia than they did in China. China had the largest Solow residual and the largest contribution from labour. The contribution from labour was greater in China than the contribution from capital despite the very high rates of investment in China.

The chapter goes on to argue that one of the reasons for the lackluster performance of the manufacturing sector has been the shortage of long-term finance. Availability of long-term finance has been a problem in Brazil for a considerable period. India had developed a complex system to provide long-term finance in the 1970s and 1980s. But that has collapsed after 1991. Long-term finance for manufacturing is also not readily available from multilateral and bilateral aid agencies. The establishment of the NDB by the BRICS countries and the Chinese initiative to set up the AIIB does not solve the problem of the lack of finance for investment in the manufacturing sector.

References

Agarwal, M. (2015), Reconfiguring International Financial Institutions: The BRICS Initiative, *Discussion Paper No. 196*, Research and Information Systems for Developing Countries, New Delhi.

Agarwal, M. (2013), South–South Economic Cooperation: Emerging Trends and Future Challenges, Background Research Paper Submitted to the High Level Panel on the Post-2015 Development Agenda, May 2013, UN, New York.

Agarwal, M. (2008), Changing Economic Power in the World Economy Research and Information Systems, *Discussion Paper No. 143*, Research and Information Systems for Developing Countries, New Delhi.

Agarwal, M. and W. John (2015), South–South Economic Cooperation, STECO and the Financial Crisis, in Manmohan Agarwal and John Whalley (Eds.) *India and China: Comparative Experience and Prospects*.

Allen, G. C. (1946), *A Short Economic History of Modern Japan*, London: Allen & Unwin.

Coutinho, L. (2010), Challenges for Industrial Policy, Innovation and Competitiveness in Brazil, Woodrow Wilson International Center for Scholars Brazil U.S. Business Council U.S. Chamber of Commerce, July 2010. Accessed from https://www.wilsoncenter.org/sites/default/files/BNDES%20in%20Woodrow%20Wilson%20BR-US%20BCouncil%2015%20July%202010.pdf

Dietzenbacher, M. P., E. Los, B. Stehrer and G. J. de Vries (2015), An Illustrated User Guide to the World Input–Output Database: the Case of Global Automotive Production, *Review of International Economics*.

Financial Times (2015), online edition for January 11, 2015 8:46 pm BNDES: Lender of first resort for Brazil's tycoons, Accessed from http://www.ft.com/intl/cms/s/0/c510368e-968e-11e4-922f-00144feabdc0.html.

Gerschenkron, A. (1962), *Economic Backwardness in Historical Perspective*, Praeger, New York.

Lazzarini, Sergio G., A. Musacchio, R. Bandeira-de-Mello and R. Marcon (2011), What Do Development Banks Do? Evidence from Brazil, 2002–2009, Working paper No 12–047, Harvard Business School, Cambridge Mass. Accessed from http://www.hbs.edu/faculty/Publication%20Files/12-047.pdf

Lele, U., M. Agarwal, P. Timmer and S. Goswami (2011), Patterns of Agriculture and Structural Transformation in 109 developed and Developing Countries with Special Focus on Brazil, China, India and Indonesia, presented at Conference on Policy

Options and Investment priorities for Accelerating Agricultural Productivity Growth, Organized by Indira Gandhi Institute for Development Research, 9–11 Nov 2011, New Delhi.

Lewis W.A. (1954), Economic Development with Unlimited Supplies of Labour, *Manchester School of Economic and Social Studies*, 22, 1–31.

Marglin, Stephen A. and J. Schor (1990), (Eds.) *The Golden Age of Capitalism: Reinterpreting the Postwar Experience*, Clarendon Press, Oxford.

Moss, T. and B. Leo (2011), IDA at 65: "Heading Toward Retirement or a. Fragile Lease on Life?" *CGD Working Paper 246*. Washington, D.C.: Center for Global Development, Washington DC.

Nurkse, R. (1953), *Problems of Capital Formation in Underdeveloped Countries*, Basil Blackwell, Oxford.

Rosenstein-Rodan, P. (1943), Problems of Industrialisation of Eastern and South Eastern Europe, *Economic Journal*, 53, 202–211.

Chapter 13

BRICS and MDGs

Manmohan Agarwal

Reserve Bank of India Chair Professor,
Centre for Development Studies,
Thiruvananthapuram, Kerala, India
manmohan@cds.ac.in

Abstract: This chapter looks at the progress made towards achieving the Millennium Development Goals (MDGs). The analysis is conducted at the aggregate regional level and also at the individual country level for the BRICS in order to see how their performance compares to other countries in the region. The chapter tries to examine the impact of the acceptance of the MDGs by the countries. The chapter then goes on to analyse how social progress relates to economic growth.

1 Introduction

In this chapter, we analyse the progress that the BRICS countries have made in achieving the MDGs. Their performance is important as they are significant countries whose performance can carry lessons for developing countries as a whole and for countries in their regions in particular. In addition three of them, Brazil, India and South Africa have formed IBSA that provides funds to other developing countries and they have cooperated to implement a number of projects in developing countries particularly in the area of health. The BRICS countries have also established the New Development Bank to provide funds mainly for infrastructure projects but also for projects that improve sustainability of development.

The MDG declaration was accepted at the UN in 2000. It was the culmination of a long process; many different factors contributed to the acceptance of the

MDGs. The debt crisis of the 1980s had shifted attention from development to macro stability though the goal of macro stability was claimed to be to establish the conditions for growth. However, the structural adjustment programmes espoused by the International Monetary Fund (IMF) and the World Bank did not result in growth, as per capita incomes grew by only 0.7% a year between 1982 and 2000 in LAC, while they declined by 0.8% a year in SSA.[1] Meanwhile other concerns about these programmes were raised as the social condition of people began to worsen and there were calls for a change in policies (Jolly *et al.*, 1987). During this phase of pre-occupation with macro stability, aid ministers and bureaucrats had lost influence. This was also true at the international level, particularly the UN which earlier had been a leader on development issues. They were keen to regain the initiative. Furthermore, The UN had been holding conferences on many social issues and each conference issued a set of recommendations. These different factors resulted in the enunciation of a set of development goals by the Development Assistance Committee of the OECD.[2] After further negotiations at the UN, a final set of goals was accepted and called the MDGs.[3]

In Section 1, we analyse briefly the performance of different developing country regions. Then in Section 2, we analyse the effect of growth on the social indicators, namely the effectiveness of growth in achieving the MDGs. In Section 3, we discuss the performance of the BRICS countries. We contrast the behaviour of the BRICS with that of their regions in order to see, whether the performance of these countries is much better than the regional average so that they may have useful lessons to provide to their neighbours. In Section 4, we analyse the performance of the BRICS in the context of how other developing countries were faring. In Section 5 we analyse the health expenditures in the regions and in the BRICS to see whether these expenditures can explain the differential progress. We end in Section 6 with some concluding observations.

1.1 Progress in reducing poverty and malnourishment in different regions

Substantial progress has been made over the past two decades in reducing poverty. This effort to reach the target of reducing poverty by half had already been met by 2010 led by phenomenal progress in EAP where poverty was reduced by over

[1] For an analysis of IMF programmes see Mosley *et al.* (1991).

[2] For a more detailed discussion of these issues see Agarwal (2013), Bradford (2002) and Hulme and Fukuda-Parr (2009).

[3] For a full list of the objectives and the indicators to measure the success in reaching the objectives see the United Nations' Secretary-General's Road Map towards the Implementation of the MDGs, http://www.un.org/documents/ga/docs/56/a56326.pdf.

Table 1. Regional poverty (% of population).

	1990	2000	2005	2010	Annual rate of decline 1990–2000	2000–2005	2005–2010	1990–2010
EAP*	57	36	17	10	4.5	13.9	10.1	9.3
LAC	12	11	7	5	0.9	8.6	6.5	4.3
MNA	6	5	3	2	1.8	9.2	7.8	5.3
SA	54	48	39	29	1.8	2.8	5.8	3.1
SSA	57	59	53	48	–0.4	2.1	2.0	0.8

Note: The regions are a defined by the World Bank.
Source: World Bank (2003, 2008, 2012). UN (2015) The MDGs Report, World Bank and IMF (2013) Global Monitoring Report 2013 Rural–Urban Dynamics and the Millennium Development Goals.
*This region as used by the World Bank covers East Asia, and South East Asia.

80%, supported by decreases of about 60% in LAC and MNA (Table 1).[4] While SA had not yet reached the goal of reducing poverty by 50% it was only 2% away from it and was likely to achieve it. The only region which will be far from achieving the target would be SSA.

All the regions and particularly EAP, LAC and MNA saw a considerable acceleration in the decline of the poverty rate after the acceptance of the MDGs by the UN in 2000. This indicates the likely importance of the international community specifying development goals as it seems to energise governments and other actors. The inadequate progress in SSA was the result of slower growth in the region, particularly in the 1990s as per capita income declined because of poor agricultural performance caused perhaps by declining terms of trade which also affected their export performance and worsened their external accounts (United Nations, 2010).

We now examine the decrease in rates of malnourishment in the different regions. Here also, the goal was to reduce malnourishment by 50%.

LAC and EAP regions experienced rapid decreases in malnutrition and had reached the goal (Table 2). As a consequence, malnutrition levels in these two regions are negligible. MNA also has a low level of malnutrition and despite the decline being at a slower pace than in the other two regions had reached the goal by 2013. These three regions which have all met the target have malnourishment rates almost comparable to those in the developed countries. Unfortunately,

[4] One caveat must be kept in mind. Data on social indicators is collected at irregular intervals and is often not very reliable which makes statistical analysis difficult. For instance, the 2011 World Development Indicators says that 31.4% of the people were poor in South Africa in 2000, whereas the 2003 volume gives the 2000 number as less than 2%.

Table 2. Regional prevalence of malnourishment.

	Rate of malnourishment					Annual rate of decline				
	1990	2000	2005	2010	2013	1990–2000	2000–2005	2005–2010	2010–2013	1990–2013
EAP	20	11	8	6	5	5.8	6.2	5.6	5.9	5.8
LAC	8	5	3	2	—	4.6	9.7	7.8	—	6.7*
MNA	12	9	8	7	6	2.8	2.3	2.6	5.0	3.0
SA	52	43	39	35	32	1.9	1.9	2.1	2.9	2.1
SSA	39	25	24	22	21	1.5	0.8	1.7	0.5	1.4

Source: World Bank (2003, 2008, 2012), UN (2015) The MDGs Report, World Bank and IMF (2013), Global Monitoring Report, 2013 Rural–Urban Dynamics and the MDGs.

malnourishment declined at the slowest pace in the two regions where levels of malnutrition were the highest. Furthermore, SA had a very low rate of decrease of malnutrition despite the economies in the region growing rapidly. But once again, there is acceleration in the rate of improvement after the announcement of the MDGs suggesting the usefulness of the MDG declaration.

1.2 Mortality rates

The goals for mortality rates are to reduce infant and child mortality by two thirds and maternal mortality by three fourths.

Infant mortality for the world decreased between 1990 and 2015 by 49%, from 90 deaths per 1,000 live births in 1990 to 46 in 2013.[5] As far as developing country regions are concerned, EAP, LAC and MNA had the greatest declines between 1990 and 2015 even though they had low rates in the base year, 1990 (Tables 3 and 4). The infant mortality rate is under 5 for the developed countries, so that developing country regions still have some way to go before they catch up with the developed countries.

In 2013, the under-five mortality rate in low-income countries was 76 deaths per 1,000 live births — more than 12 times the average rate of 6 in high-income countries.[6]

While EAP and LAC have achieved maternal mortality rates comparable to those in the developed countries, where they average 16, their rates of infant and child mortality are still considerably higher than in the developed countries.

[5] See http://www.un.org/millenniumgoals/childhealth.shtml.

[6] See Levels & Trends in Child Mortality Report, 2014. Estimates Developed by the UN Inter-agency Group of WHO, UNICEF, WB, UN, 2014.

Table 3. Infant mortality rates by regions.

	Mortality rates					Annual rates of decline				
	1990	2000	2005	2010	2013	1990–2000	2000–2005	2005–2010	2010–2013	1990–2013
EAP	45	33	25	19	16	2.8	5.4	5.3	5.6	4.3
LAC	44	27	21	18	16	5.0	4.9	3.0	3.9	4.4
MNA	52	36	29	23	21	3.6	5.6	3.2	3.0	3.9
SA	92	69	58	50	45	2.9	3.4	2.9	3.5	3.1
SSA	107	95	80	67	61	1.2	3.4	3.5	3.1	2.4

Source: Levels & Trends in Child Mortality Report, 2014. Estimates Developed by the UN Inter-agency Group of WHO, UNICEF, WB, UN, 2014.

Table 4. Child mortality rates by regions.

	Mortality rates					Annual rates of decline				
	1990	2000	2005	2010	2013	1990–2000	2000–2005	2005–2010	2010–2013	1990–2013
EAP	59	42	30	23	20	3.9	6.5	5.2	4.6	4.1
LAC	55	33	25	23	18	5.0	5.4	1.7	7.8	4.7
MNA	67	43	36	28	26	3.9	4.4	4.9	2.4	4.0
SA	129	94	77	64	57	3.1	3.9	3.6	3.8	3.5
SSA	179	156	129	103	92	1.4	3.7	4.4	3.7	2.9

Source: http://www.un.org/millenniumgoals/childhealth.shtml.

Table 5. Maternal mortality rates by regions.

	Mortality rates					Annual rates of Decline				
	1990	2000	2005	2010	2013	1990–2000	2000–2005	2005–2010	2010–2013	1990–2013
EAP	170	130	110	82	75	2.6	3.3	5.7	2.9	3.5
LAC	150	110	97	90	87	3.5	2.8	1.5	1.1	2.3
MNA	160	110	97	83	78	3.7	2.5	3.1	2.0	3.1
SA	550	370	280	220	190	3.9	5.4	4.7	4.8	4.5
SSA	990	830	680	560	510	1.7	3.9	3.8	3.1	2.8

Source: Trends in maternal mortality: 1990–2013. Estimates by WHO, UNICEF, UNFPA. The World Bank and the United Nations Population Division.

Again, the two regions with the highest infant and child mortality rates, SA and SSA, saw smaller decreases in mortality rates.

However, the pattern is different for declines in maternal mortality (Table 5). The greatest decline was in SA. But SSA again lagged behind the other regions.

Again, the rate of improvement increased after the 2000 acceptance of the MDGs. The only exceptions were LAC where the improvement in all the three indictors of mortality slowed after 2000 and MNA where the improvement in maternal mortality declined after 2000. Significantly, the decline in maternal mortality was considerably greater in SA than the decline in infant and child mortality in contrast to the other regions. Overall, as women have gained access to family planning and skilled birth attendance with backup emergency obstetric care, the global maternal mortality ratio has fallen from 380 maternal deaths per 100,000 live births in 1990 to 210 deaths per 100,000 live births in 2013, a 45% decline.[7] This has resulted in many countries halving their maternal death rates. At a country level, India (19% or 56,000) and Nigeria (14% or 40,000) accounted for roughly one third of the maternal deaths in 2010. Furthermore, Afghanistan, Bangladesh, Democratic Republic of the Congo, Ethiopia, Indonesia, Pakistan, Sudan and the United Republic of Tanzania each accounted for 3–5% of maternal deaths. Together these 10 countries accounted for about 60% of all maternal deaths.[8] Greater attention needs to be given to maternal care in these countries if the world is to see further substantial reduction in maternal mortality. This may not be easy because generally, it is held to be more difficult to reduce maternal mortality than infant and child mortality as maternal deaths can take place due to a number of reasons and general improvement in the health delivery system is required, rather than a few specific interventions.

2 Responsiveness of Social Indicators to Income Growth

We calculated the change in the social indicator relative to the rate of growth of per capita income for the different regions, namely the elasticities of reduction. The calculation of the elasticities reveals a number of interesting facets of the nature of the growth process in the different regions.

1. The elasticities are usually less than 1 in Asia, particularly East Asia, whereas they are greater than one in LAC and SSA and usually substantially greater than 1 (Table 6).
2. The elasticities for reduction of poverty are usually greater for the entire period 1990–2010, than for 1990–2000, implying that the elasticities are greater for the period after the MDGs had been accepted than the period before. The acceptance of the MDGs meant faster social progress not only because faster growth was achieved, but also greater responsiveness of social indicators to growth in per capita income. This could be because the nature of

[7] See http://www.unfpa.org/maternal-health.

[8] For a detailed analysis see the report prepared jointly by the WHO, UNICEF, UNFPA and the World Bank. Available at http://www.un.org/millennium/declaration/ares552e.htm.

Table 6. Elasticity of reduction with respect to growth in per capita income.

	Poverty rate		Malnourishment	
	1990–2000	1990–2010	1990–2000	1990–2013
EAP	0.7	1.1	0.9	0.8
LAC	0.8	2.9	4.1	4.3
SA	0.6	0.7	0.6	0.5
SSA*	0.5	1.0	–2.0	1.7

Note: Per capita income declined in SSA during the years 1990–2000. In the case of poverty, the poverty ratio increased as per capita income declined. But in the case of malnourishment, its extent declined despite falling per capita income.
Source: Author's calculations based on the above data and on growth of per capita, income from World Bank (2003, 2008, 2012).

Table 7. Elasticity of reduction of mortality rates with respect to growth of per capita income.

	Infant mortality		Child mortality		Maternal mortality	
	1990–2000	1990–2013	1990–2000	1990–2013	1990–2000	1990–2013
EAP	0.4	0.6	0.5	0.6	0.4	0.5
LAC	4.4	2.8	4.4	3.1	2.7	5.1
SA	0.9	0.7	1.0	0.8	1.2	1.1
SSA	–1.6	2.9	–1.8	3.4	–2.4	3.4

Source: Author's calculations based on the above data and data on growth of per capita income from World Bank (2003, 2008, 2012).

the growth process had changed or that it was now accompanied by more or better special social programmes.

3. This greater responsiveness is, however, not true for reduction in malnourishment. Here except for LAC the elasticities are smaller in the second period (Table 6).
4. That growth in incomes is not necessary for social improvement is borne out by most social indicators improving in SSA during the period 1990–2000 despite declining per capita income.

The picture for reductions in mortality rates is more varied than that for reduction in poverty and malnourishment. It must again be noted that the elasticity for SSA for the period 1990–2000 is of the opposite sign than all the other elasticities as mortality rates declined despite falling per capita incomes. Also, elasticities in Asia both East and South are lower than in the other two regions (Table 7). But there is no uniformity in the behaviour of the elasticities in the two periods.

Whereas, the elasticities are higher in the second period for EAP, they are lower in LAC and SA.

3 Progress Towards the MDGs in the BRICS Countries

All the BRICS countries had already achieved the MDG goal of halving the poverty ratio before the target date (Table 8). Brazil had reduced the poverty rate by about 86%, India by just over 50% and South Africa by almost 60% between 2000 and 2004.[9] These rates were faster than those achieved by countries in their regions. China, despite reduction of its poverty rate by almost 70% found its progress lagging behind that of other countries in its region. Furthermore, China is the only BRICS country where the elasticity of reduction of the poverty rate with respect to growth of per capita income is lower than its regional elasticity. The other three countries are more effective in turning economic growth into poverty reduction.

Table 8. Poverty ratios.

	Poverty ratios				
	1990	**2000**	**2012**	**Elasticity**	
Brazil	25.6	14.4	3.5	3.3 (1990–2000)	5.1 (1990–2012)
China	57.0	28.4 (2002)	17.5 (2011)	0.6 (1990–2002)	0.6 (1990–2011)
India	52.0	45.0	24.0 (2010)	0.3 (1990–2000)	0.6 (2000–2010)
Russia	—	1.1	o*	—	—
S. Africa	—	17.0	7.4 (2004)	—	10.8 (2000–2004)

Note: *The actual poverty rate for 2008 was 0.04 and so we take it as basically zero.

Source: Brazil, Objectivos de Desenvolvimento do Milenio, Realtorio Nacional de Acompanhamento, Presidencio da Repub;ica March 2010 and May 2014. Accessed from http://www.undp.org/content/dam/undp/library/MDG/english/MDG%20Country%20Reports/Brazil/140523_relatorioodm.pdf;

China report on China's Implementation of the Millennium development Goals (2000–2015), Ministry of Foreign Affairs and The UN system in China, Beijing. Accessed from http://www.undp.org/content/dam/china/docs/Publications/UNDP-CH-SSC-MDG2015_English.pdf;

India Central Statistical Organization, Ministry of Statistics and Programme Implementation, Government of India www.mospi.nic.in. Accessed from http://www.undp.org/content/dam/undp/library/MDG/english/MDG%20Country%20Reports/India/MDG_India_2011.pdf;

Russia National Human Development Report in the Russian Federation 2010: Looking into the Future, UNDP Russia, Moscow, 2010. Accessed from http://www.undp.org/content/dam/undp/library/MDG/english/MDG%20Country%20Reports/Russian%20Federation/2010_ENG.pdf;

South Africa Millennium Development Goals, Country Report, 2013. Accessed from http://www.undp.org/content/dam/undp/library/MDG/english/MDG%20Country%20Reports/South%20Africa/MDG_October-2013.pdf.

[9] The data from different annual World Development Reports of the World Bank gives different numbers so it is difficult to be very confident about the individual country numbers.

Table 9. Malnourishment rate.

	Malnourishment rate			
	1990	**2000**	**2013**	**Elasticity**
Brazil	7.1 (89)	1.8 (2006)	—	7.8
China	23.9	16.1	10.6 (2012–2014)	0.4 (1990–2000) 0.4 (1990–2013)
India	52.0	43.0 (98–99)	—	0.8
Russia	—	5.7	—	—
S. Africa	13.2 (93)	—	8.3 (2008)	1.6

Source: Brazil, Objectivos de Desenvolvimento do Milenio, Relatorio Nacional de Acompanhamento, Presidencio da Repub;ica March 2010 and May 2014, Accessed from http://www.undp.org/content/dam/undp/library/MDG/english/MDG%20Country%20Reports/Brazil/140523_relatorioodm.pdf.

China report on China's Implementation of the Millennium development Goals (2000–2015), Ministry of Foreign Affairs and The UN system in China, Beijing. Accessed from http://www.undp.org/content/dam/china/docs/Publications/UNDP-CH-SSC-MDG2015_English.pdf;

India Central Statistical Organization, Ministry of Statistics and Programme Implementation, Government of India www.mospi.nic.in. Accessed from http://www.undp.org/content/dam/undp/library/MDG/english/MDG%20Country%20Reports/India/MDG_India_2011.pdf;

Russia National Human Development Report in the Russian Federation 2010: Looking into the Future, UNDP Russia, Moscow, 2010. Accessed from http://www.undp.org/content/dam/undp/library/MDG/english/MDG%20Country%20Reports/Russian%20Federation/2010_ENG.pdf.

South Africa Millennium Development Goals, Country Report, 2013. Accessed from http://www.undp.org/content/dam/undp/library/MDG/english/MDG%20Country%20Reports/South%20Africa/MDG_October-2013.pdf.

As far as malnourishment is concerned, only Brazil has reduced the rate of malnourishment faster than its neighbours (Table 9). The other three BRICS countries are lagging behind their neighbours. But only China has a lower elasticity of reduction of malnourishment with respect to growth of per capita than its neighbours whereas the other three have a higher elasticity.

We now discuss mortality rates. Brazil and China had achieved the targets for reducing infant and child mortality rates by 2013 (Table 10, Trends in maternal mortality: 1990–2013, Estimates by WHO, UNICEF, UNFPA, The World Bank and the United Nations Population Division).

India and Russia had reduced these mortality rates by about 60% rather than the required two-thirds. An acceleration in the rate of improvement may see them achieve the targets, or come close. But South Africa will not achieve the targets as the decline in infant and child mortality till 2013 was only 30%.

However, only China and India are likely to achieve the goal of reducing the maternal mortality rate by three quarters having already by 2013 reduced the rate by 33–34% at an annual rate of 4.6–4.7% (Table 11). The other three will not reach the goal.

Table 10. Mortality rates

	Infant mortality rate			Child mortality rate			Maternal mortality rate		
	1990	2000	2013	1990	2000	2013	1990	2000	2013
Brazil	51	32	12	62	33	14	120	85	69
China	42	30	11	54	37	13	97	63	32
India	88	69	41	126	91	53	560	370	190
Russia	22	17	9	26	23	10	74	57	24
S. Africa	47	62	33	61	74	44	150	150	140

Source: Levels & Trends in Child Mortality Report, 2014. Estimates Developed by the UN Inter-agency Group of WHO, UNICEF, WB, UN, 2014.
http://www.un.org/millenniumgoals/childhealth.shtml.

Table 11. Annual rate of change of mortality rate.

	Infant mortality rate		Child mortality rate		Maternal mortality rate	
	1990–2000	1990–2013	1990–2000	1990–2013	1990–2000	2000–2013
Brazil	4.6	6.1	6.1	6.5	3.4	2.4
China	3.3	5.7	5.1	6.3	4.2	4.7
India	2.4	3.3	3.2	3.8	4.1	4.6
Russia	2.5	3.8	1.2	4.1	2.6	4.8
S. Africa	–2.8	1.5	–2.0	1.4	0	0.3

Table 12. Elasticities of reduction of mortality rates.

	Infant mortality rate		Child mortality rate		Maternal mortality rate	
	1990–2000	1990–2013	1990–2000	1990–2013	1990–2000	2000–2013
Brazil	4.6	3.7	6.1	3.9	3.4	1.4
China	0.4	0.6	0.6	0.7	0.5	0.5
India	0.6	0.7	0.9	0.8	1.1	1.0
Russia	–0.7	3.4	–0.3	3.7	–0.7	4.3
S. Africa	6.9	1.7	4.9	1.6	0.0	0.3

The rate of decrease of mortality accelerated in the second period for all the countries, except Brazil for maternal mortality. Again when we look at the elasticities of the rate of reduction we find that the elasticities fell for all three kinds of mortality in Brazil and for child and infant mortality in South Africa (Table 12).

For China and India, the elasticities were constant whereas for Russia they showed a considerable increase. The effectiveness of growth in reducing mortality rates seems to have stagnated in the second period.

4 Progress in BRICS in the Context of Developing Countries

We have seen above how the performance of the BRICs compares to that of other countries in their regions. We now relate their performance to other large developing countries. We chose 31 large developing countries for whom data on the MDGs was available; 11 were from SSA, 7 from LAC, 5 from EAP and 4 each from MNA and SA. We took 11 indicators which were to be used to measure the first five goals of the NDGs. These goals represent the main features that go into the calculation of the UNDP's human development index. We used principal component analysis to aggregate these indicators to form an index (Nagar and Basu, 2002). We derived the index for 1990, 2000 and 2009 and ranked the countries by the index (Table 13).[10] The countries from LAC region are clustered round the top of the rankings and the countries from SSA and SA are generally at the bottom of the rankings. For 2009, all the countries from SSA are clustered at the bottom, except India and Pakistan which also have low ranks.

The correlation between the ranks for the different years is very high, over 0.8 which is more than four times the standard deviation, indicating that there is not very much change in the ranks of the countries. A few countries greatly improved their ranks, e.g., Bangladesh (7 ranks), China (6), Pakistan (5), Senegal (5), Tunisia (5). At the same time the ranks of some countries deteriorated considerable, e.g., Colombia (8), South Africa (6), Zambia (6), Cameroon (5), Tanzania (5), Nigeria (4), Thailand (4). Among the BRICS, China improved its rank from 13 in 1990 to 7 in 2009. India improved its rank by a mere two positions from 24 to 22. Brazil maintained its rank. However, South Africa saw its rank fall from 14 to 20.

Even though the countries in SSA were lagging behind countries in the other regions, it doesn't seem that South Africa can provide lessons on how to improve the social condition of the people. We next tried to relate economic performance and social achievement. We calculated the rate of growth of per capita GDP for these countries in three periods, 1980–1990, 1990–2000 and 2000–2009. We ranked the countries according to the rate of growth. We then calculated the rank correlation between the ranks according to the growth rates for the different periods and the ranks according to the social index for various years.

[10] For an earlier analysis see Agarwal and Samanta (2006).

Table 13. Ranks according to the MDGs.

	1990	2000	2009
Argentina	1	2	1
Chile	2	1	3
Uruguay	3	3	2
Colombia	4	10	12
Malaysia	5	5	4
Thailand	6	8	10
Mexico	7	5	6
Sri Lanka	8	9	8
Brazil	9	7	9
Tunisia	10	6	5
Iran	11	11	11
Philippines	12	14	14
China	13	13	7
South Africa	14	17	20
Egypt	15	12	13
Bolivia	16	15	16
Morocco	17	16	17
Indonesia	18	18	15
Kenya	19	19	21
Ghana	20	20	19
Tanzania	21	28	26
Cameroon	22	22	27
Zambia	23	26	29
India	24	23	22
Bangladesh	25	21	18
Nigeria	26	29	30
Uganda	27	27	25
Pakistan	28	24	23
Senegal	29	25	24
Burundi	30	30	28
Mali	31	31	31

Source: Agarwal and Samanta (2015).

Table 14. Correlation between growth and social index.

	Index		
Rate of growth	**1990**	**2000**	**2009**
1980–1990	0.2	0.31	0.54*
1990–2000	0.44**	0.52**	0.69*
2000–2009	–0.1	–0.11	0.02

Note: *Significant at 1%; **Significant at 5%.
Source: Author's Calculations.

We find that a higher growth in per capita GDP is usually associated with a better social index in a later year (Table 14). But a better index in a year does not always translate itself into higher growth in the subsequent period. The only exception is the index value for 1990 which is correlated to growth in all three decades, 1980–1990, 1990–2000 and 2000–2009. But the size of the correlation coefficient is higher for later periods.

5 Health Expenditures

We now analyse whether variations in regional health expenditures can explain differences in mortality outcomes. Asian countries, both EAP and SA, spend much less on health than countries in the other regions (Table 15). Furthermore, health expenditures as percentage of GDP, have been rising in all the regions, except SA.

In addition, public expenditures on health are much lower in SA than the other regions, and have been stagnant whereas they have been increasing in the other regions.

We now examine health expenditures in BRICS. Total expenditures on health as a percent of GDP are much higher in Brazil and South Africa than in the other countries (Table 16).

Furthermore, India is the only country where they are lower as a percent of GDP in 2010, than the average percentage during 1990–1995. Also, India has the lowest percentage of public health expenditures as a share of GDP. The contrast is particularly striking when we compare the two rapidly growing economies, China and India. China spent $13.47 billion in 1990 on health of which, $7.45 billion was in the public sector. While India spent almost an equal amount on health, $12.75 billion, it spent only about a third in the public sector, $2.22 billion. By 2000, China spent $63.5 billion on health of which $22.77 billion was by the government. India,

Table 15. Health expenditures (% of GDP).

	1990–1997		2003		2005		2008		2010	
	Total	Public	Total	Public	Total	Public	Total	Public	Total	Public
EAP	3.6	1.8	5.0	1.9	4.3	1.8	4.2	2.0	4.7	2.5
LAC	6.3	2.6	6.8	3.3	7.1	3.3	7.2	3.6	7.8	3.9
MNA	4.7	2.3	5.6	2.7	5.8	3.0	5.0	3.6	4.7	2.4
SA	5.0	0.8	4.4	1.1	4.5	0.9	4.0	1.3	3.8	1.1
SSA	2.7	1.7	6.1	2.4	6.1	2.6	6.1	2.6	6.5	2.9

Source: World Bank, World Development Indicators, 2003, 2008, 2012.

Table 16. Health expenditures in BRICS (% of GDP).

	1990–1995		1997–2000		2010	
	Total public sector		Total public sector		Total public sector	
Brazil	7.4	2.7	8.3	3.4	9.0	4.2
China	4.8	2.1	5.3	1.9	5.1	2.7
India	5.6	0.7	4.9	0.9	4.1	1.2
Russia	4.8	4.1	5.3	3.8	5.1	3.1
S. Africa	7.9	3.6	8.8	3.7	8.9	3.9

Source: World Bank, World Development Indicators, 2003, 2008, 2012.

on the other spent only $22.55 billion on health with about $4 billion spent by the government. By 2010, the gap had further widened China spent $302.24 billion of which 162 was by the government whereas India spent $70.81 billion of which, $20.68 billion was by the government. In 1990, India had spent more on health than China though less than a third of China's expenditure by the public sector. By 2010, China was spending more than four times as much as India in total and the public sector in China spent more than eight times what the public sector did in India.

6 Concluding Remarks

An analysis of the overall achievement in the different regions finds that the countries from LAC region are clustered round the top of the rankings and the countries from SSA and SA are generally at the bottom of the rankings. For 2009, all the countries from SSA are clustered at the bottom, except India and Pakistan which also have low ranks. Among the BRICS, China improved its rank from 13 in 1990 to 7 in 2009. India improved its rank by a mere two positions from 24 to 22. Brazil maintained its rank. However, South Africa saw its rank fall from 14 to 20.

We also find that a higher growth in per capita GDP is usually associated with a better social index in a later year. But a better index in a year does not always translate into higher growth in the subsequent period.

When we look at the regional performance in the different areas we find considerable variation. But by and large EAP and LAC are likely to achieve most of the goals and SA and SSA unlikely to do so. This factor is reflected also in the performance of the BRICS, with India and South Africa unlikely to meet most of the goals.

The target of reducing poverty by half had already been met by 2010 led by phenomenal progress in EAP where poverty was reduced by over 80% supported by decreases of about 60% in LAC and MNA. SA is also likely to achieve it. The only region which will be far from achieving the target would be SSA.

LAC, EAP and MNA regions had all reached the goal of reducing malnutrition by half by 2013. These three have malnourishment rates almost comparable to those in the developed countries. Unfortunately, malnourishment declined at the slowest pace in the two regions where levels of malnutrition were the highest.

There has overall been less progress in achieving the goals of reducing infant, child and maternal mortality. Again, the two regions with the highest infant and child mortality rates, SA and SSA, saw smaller decreases in mortality rates. However, the greatest decline in reducing maternal mortality was in SA. But SSA again lagged behind the other regions.

All the regions and particularly EAP, LAC and MNA saw a considerable acceleration in the decline of the poverty rate after the acceptance of the MDGs by the UN in 2000. This indicates the likely importance of the international community specifying development goals as it seems to energise governments and other actors. The inadequate progress in SSA was the result of slower growth in the region, particularly in the 1990s, as per capita income declined because of poor agricultural performance caused perhaps, by declining terms of trade which also affected their export performance and worsened their external accounts.

We then relate the improvements in social indicators to the increase in per capita income. We find that the elasticities are usually less than 1 in Asia, particularly East Asia, whereas they are substantially greater than one in LAC and SSA. Furthermore, the elasticities are often greater for the period after the MDGs had been accepted than the period before. The faster social progress after the acceptance of the MDGs was not only because faster growth was achieved, but also greater responsiveness of social indicators to growth in per capita income. This could be because the nature of the growth process had changed or that it was now accompanied by more or better special social programmes. But growth in incomes is not necessary for social improvement, at least in the short run, as most social indicators improved in SSA during the period 1990–2000 despite declining per capita income.

All the BRICS countries had already achieved the MDG goal of halving the poverty ratio before the target date. These rates, except for China, were faster than those achieved by countries in their regions. Furthermore, China is the only BRICS country where the elasticity of reduction of the poverty rate with respect to growth of per capita income is lower than its regional elasticity.

As far as malnourishment is concerned, only Brazil has reduced the rate of malnourishment faster than its neighbours. The other three BRICS countries are lagging behind their neighbours. But only China has a lower elasticity of reduction of malnourishment with respect to growth of per capita than its neighbours whereas the other three have a higher elasticity.

As far as mortality rates are concerned, Brazil and China had achieved the targets for reducing infant and child mortality rates by 2013. India and Russia had reduced these mortality rates by about 60% rather than the required two thirds. An acceleration in the rate of improvement may see them achieve the targets, or come close. But South Africa will not achieve the targets as the decline in infant and child mortality till 2013, was only 30%.

However, only China and India are likely to achieve the goal of reducing the maternal mortality rate by three quarters having already by 2013 reduced the rate by almost 70%, at an annual rate of 4.6–4.7%. The other three will not reach the goal. In general, the slower progress in Asia in the area of health is that Asian countries, both EAP and SA, spend much less on health than countries in the other regions. Furthermore, health expenditures as percentage of GDP have been rising in all the regions except SA. In addition, public expenditures on health are much lower in SA than the other regions, and have been stagnant whereas they have been increasing in the other regions. Government provision of social services is important for achieving social goals.

Furthermore, India is the only country where they are lower as a percent of GDP in 2010 than the average percentage during 1990–1995. Also, India has the lowest percentage of public health expenditures as a share of GDP.

References

Agarwal, M. and S. Samanta (2006), Structural Adjustment, Governance, Economic Growth and Social Progress, *Journal of International Trade and conomic Development*, 15(3), 387–401.

Agarwal, M. (2013), *Reshaping international institution for achieving MDGs*, in Hany Besada and Shannon Kidornay (Eds.), Multilateral Development Cooperation in a Changing Global Order, Palgrave Macmillan.

Agarwal, M. and S. Samanta (2015), Financial Crisis of 2008 and Shifting Economic Power: Is there Convergence in Manmohan Agarwal and John Whalley (Eds.) *India and China: Comparative Experience and Prospects.*

Bradford, C. (2002), *Towards 2015: From consensus formation to implementation of the MDGs — The historical background. 1990–2002*, Mimeo, Brookings Institution Washington DC.

David, H. and S. Fukuda-Parr (2009), International Norm Dynamics and 'the End of Poverty': Understanding the Millennium Development Goals (MDGs), *Brooks World Poverty Institute Working Paper Series 9609*, BWPI, The University of Manchester.

Jolly, R., A. Cornea, and F. Stewart (1987), *Adjustment with a Human Face* Protects Vulnerable Growth, Oxford University Press, Oxford. UK.

Moseley, P., J. Hartigan, and J. Toye (1991), *Aid and Power: The World Bank amd Policy Based Lending*, Volume 1, London: Routledge.

Nagar, A.L. and S.R. Basu (2002), Weighting socio economic indicators of human development: A latent variable approach, in *Handbook of Applied Econometrics and Statistical Inference (Eds.* A. Ullah, A. T.K. Wan, and A. Chaturvedi), Marcel Dekker, New York.

United Nations (2010), Trade and Development Report 2010, UNCTAD, Geneva.

Chapter 14

Measuring Changes in the Bilateral Technology Gaps between China, India and the US 1979–2008[1]

Keting Shen

Department of Economics,
Zhejiang Gongshang University, China
ktshen1998@gmail.com

Jing Wang

Department of Economics,
Western University, Canada
jwang624@uwo.ca

John Whalley

Department of Economics,
Western University, Canada
jwhalley@uwo.ca

Abstract: Popular literature suggests a rapid narrowing of the technology gap between China and the US based on large percentage increases in Chinese patent applications, and equally large increases in college registrants and completed PhDs (especially in sciences) in China in recent years. Little literature attempts to measure the technology gap directly

[1] We are grateful to the Ontario Research Fund (ORF) for financial support and to seminar participants at UWO for comments.

using estimates of country aggregate technologies. This gap is usually thought to be smaller than differences in GDP per capita since the latter reflects both differing factor endowments and technology parameters. This chapter assesses changes in China's technology gaps both with the US and India between 1979 and 2008, comparing the technology level of these economies using a Constant Elasticity of Substitution (CES) production framework in which the technology gap is reflected in the change of technology parameters. Our measure is related to but differs from the Malmquist index. We determine the parameter values for country technology by using calibration procedures. Our calculations suggest that the technology gap between China and the US is significantly larger than that between India and the US for the period before 2008. The pairwise gaps between the US and China, and the US and India remain large while narrowing at a slower rate than GDP per worker. Although China has a higher growth rate of total factor productivity than India over the period, the bilateral technology gap between China and India is still in India's favour. India had higher income per worker than China in the 1970's, and China's much more rapid physical and human capital accumulation has allowed China to move ahead, but a bilateral technology gap remains.

1 Introduction

In this chapter, we report calculations of the technology gaps between China and the US as well as China and India between 1979 and 2008 using a CES production framework. A technology gap is defined as the difference in output using foreign technology and domestic (or foreign) factors relative to output using domestic technology and domestic (or foreign) factors. Our measure is related to but differs from the Malmquist productivity index discussed by Caves *et al.* (1982a, 1982b). An advantage of using the technology gap measure instead of the Malmquist productivity index is that our concept is flexible to the structure of the aggregate production function, and can be conveniently generalised to include technological improvements embodied in the production function besides the multiplicative productivity factor (for example, technological improvements due to a change in the substitution elasticity or factor-augmenting technological change in a CES production function, or increasing returns to scale).

Our results suggest that although China has a higher growth rate of total factor productivity than India over the period, the bilateral technology gap between China and India is still in India's favour. India had higher income per worker than China in the 1970's, and China's much more rapid physical and human capital accumulation has allowed China to move ahead, but a bilateral technology gap remains. Also, we find that the technology gap between China and the US is significantly larger than that between India and the US for the period before 2008. The pairwise gaps between China and the US, and India and the US remain large while narrowing at a slower rate than GDP per worker.

The chapter is organised as follows. We provide a brief background related to our analysis in Section 2, and discuss the technology gap concept and the methodology we apply in Section 3. We describe the data sets we use in Section 4, and present our empirical results in Section 5. As a comparison, and also for robustness purposes, we report technology gap calculations for the widely used Cobb–Douglas case in Section 6. We offer concluding remarks in Section 7.

2 Background

A major development in the world economy over the last quarter of the 20th century has been strong economic growth and poverty reduction in both China and India. The Penn World Tables show that the real GDP (or real GDP per worker) in 2008 was almost 14.6 (or 9.4) and 5.3 (or 2.9) times that in 1979 for China and India respectively, while the same number for the US was 2.3 (or 1.6). Figure 1 reports indices of real GDP per worker for these three countries between 1979 and 2008 (year of 1979 = 100). All of these data are in constant 2005 purchasing power parity dollars.

China and India's large economic size combined with rapid growth has meant that their economic rise has had large impacts on the global economy, although their absolute income levels are still quite low (the real GDP per worker of China and India in 2008 were about 12.9 and 9.2% of that of the US, respectively). Recent literature analyses China and India's growing presence in the world economy (see Wang *et al.* (2011) for related discussion), and also conducts comparative growth accounting studies for these two countries (see Herd and Dougherty, 2007; Bosworth and Collins, 2008.

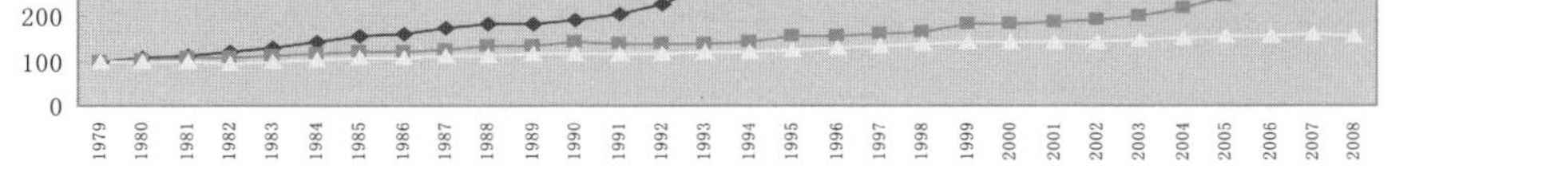

Figure 1. Indices of Real GDP/Worker for China, India and the US 1979–2008.

Note: Year of 1979 = 100.

Source: Authors' calculations using Extended Penn World Tables v.4.0, Marquetti and Foley (2011).

It is widely recognised that technology or efficiency is at least as important as physical and human capital accumulation in explaining income differences across different countries (Hall and Jones, 1999; Caselli, 2005). Since the Cobb–Douglas specification is the most widely used for the aggregate production function, differences in technology or efficiency across countries can be simplified as Total Factor Productivity (TFP) differences, or in other words, can be summarised by the multiplicative factor *A*. Howitt (2000) and Klenow and Rodríguez-Clare (2005) show how large TFP differences can emerge in a world with slow technology diffusion from advanced countries to other countries, while Hsieh and Klenow (2009) estimate the effects of resource misallocation on China and India's manufacturing TFP and find that if capital and labour are hypothetically reallocated to equalise marginal products to the extent observed in the US, the TFP could be boosted by 30–50% in China and by 40–60% in India.

But as Caselli (2005) emphasises, the Cobb–Douglas specification is key to the literature explaining income differences across countries, and a generalisation of the TFP assumption from Cobb–Douglas to CES specification can lead to major changes in results. Notably, there has been increasing recent empirical evidence that rejects the (unitary-elasticity) Cobb–Douglas specification in favour of CES (generally below unity substitution elasticity) aggregate production functions (see Chirinko *et al.*, 1999; Duffy and Papageorgiou, 2000; Chirinko, 2008; Klump *et al.*, 2007, 2011.

It is also noteworthy that China's real GDP per worker did not surpass that of India until the year 1998–2000 (as shown in Figure 2). We can conjecture naturally that the more rapid accumulation of physical capital in China (as shown in Figure 3) may suggest a lower technology level for China compared to that of India at least before the middle of the 1990s.

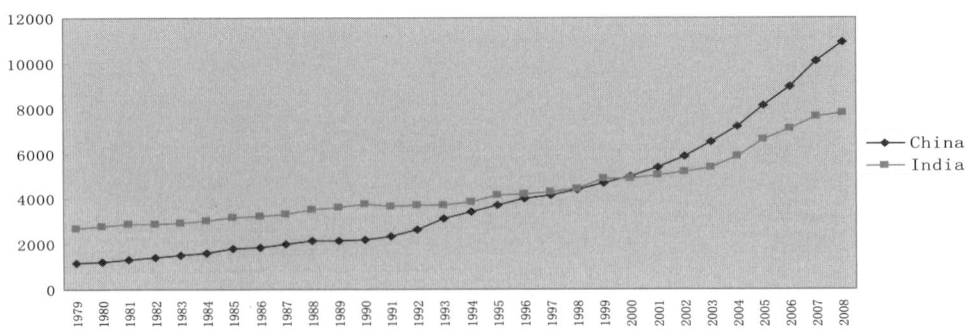

Figure 2. Real GDP per worker for China and India 1979–2008.

Note: In Chain indexed constant 2005 purchasing power parity dollars.

Source: Data from Extended Penn World Tables v.4.0, Marquetti and Foley (2011).

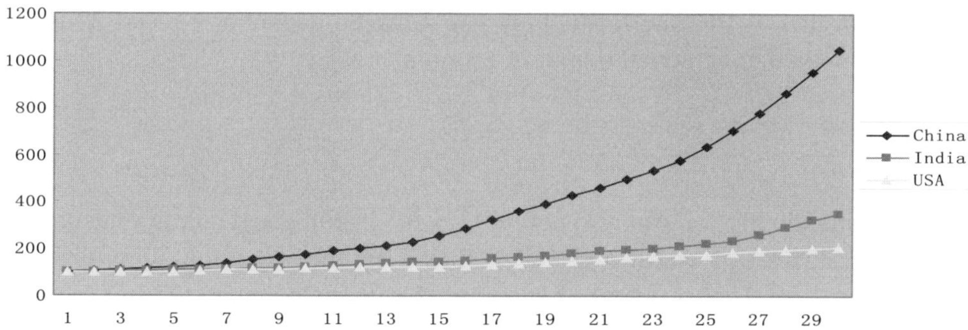

Figure 3. Indices of capital labour ratio for China, India and the US 1979–2008.

Note: Year of 1979 = 100.

Source: Authors' calculations using Extended Penn World Tables v.4.0, Marquetti and Foley (2011).

3 Methodology

In this section, we set out the methodology we use to measure the pairwise technology gaps between China, India and the US over time. We measure the technology gap between two economies 1 and 2 in terms of the ratio between actual output in economy 1 using economy 1's technology and inputs, and hypothetical output using economy 2's technology with economy 1's inputs. The roles of economies 1 and 2 in such a comparison can be reversed to yield an alternative pairwise measure. We assume that each of the two economies produce a single final good *Y* with two factors, capital and labour. However, the two economies can have different technologies in production, i.e. they may have different parameters in (or even have different structures of) production function. They can also have different factor endowments.

Specifically, we can write the production function as follows:

$$Y_i = F_i(K_i, L_i) \quad i = 1, 2. \tag{1}$$

Here, $i = 1, 2$ refers to the two different economies, and F_i represents different technologies for production.

We denote $\hat{Y}_1$ as the actual output of economy 1, i.e. $\hat{Y}_1$ is realised with endowments K_1 and L_1 using its own technology of production F_1. $\hat{Y}_2$ is defined as the hypothetical output of economy 1 that it could produce with endowments K_1 and L_1 using the technology of economy 2, F_2. Thus, we have:

$$\hat{Y}_1 = F_1\left(K_1, L_1\right), \tag{2}$$

$$\hat{Y}_2 = F_2\left(K_1, L_1\right). \tag{3}$$

We can then define the technology gap between economies 1 and 2, as the ratio of hypothetical to actual output in economy 1:

$$G_{12} = \frac{\hat{Y}_2}{\hat{Y}_1}. \tag{4}$$

Correspondingly, we can also define $\overline{\overline{Y}}_1$ as the hypothetical output of economy 2 that it produces with endowments K_2 and L_2 using the technology in production F_1, while $\overline{\overline{Y}}_2$ is the actual output of economy 2 with endowments K_2 and L_2 using its own technology, F_2. Thus we have:

$$\overline{\overline{Y}}_1 = F_1(K_2, L_2), \tag{5}$$

$$\overline{\overline{Y}}_2 = F_2(K_2, L_2). \tag{6}$$

And we can define the reverse technology gap as:

$$G_{21} = \frac{\overline{\overline{Y}}_2}{\overline{\overline{Y}}_1}. \tag{7}$$

If we use a CES production function with Hicks-neutral technological change

$$Y_{it} = \gamma_i e^{\lambda_i \cdot t}\left(\delta_i K_{it}{}^{\rho_i} + (1-\delta_i) L_{it}{}^{\rho_i}\right)^{\frac{1}{\rho_i}}. \tag{8}$$

Here $i = 1, 2$ refers to the two different economies, t is a time variable, γ_i is an efficiency parameter, λ_i is the rate of disembodied (or Hicks-neutral) technological change, δ_i is the distribution parameter, and ρ_i is the substitution parameter. Then from Equations (2), (3) and (5), (6), we have:

$$\hat{Y}_{1t} = \gamma_1 e^{\lambda_1 \cdot t}\left(\delta_1 K_{1t}{}^{\rho_1} + (1-\delta_1) L_{1t}{}^{\rho_1}\right)^{\frac{1}{\rho_i}}, \tag{9}$$

$$\hat{Y}_{2t} = \gamma_2 e^{\lambda_2 \cdot t}\left(\delta_2 K_{1t}{}^{\rho_2} + (1-\delta_2) L_{1t}{}^{\rho_2}\right)^{\frac{1}{\rho_2}}, \tag{10}$$

$$\overline{\overline{Y}}_{1t} = \gamma_1 e^{\lambda_1 \cdot t}\left(\delta_1 K_{2t}{}^{\rho_1} + (1-\delta_1) L_{2t}{}^{\rho_1}\right)^{\frac{1}{\rho_1}}, \tag{11}$$

$$\overline{\overline{Y}}_{2t} = \gamma_2 e^{\lambda_2 \cdot t}\left(\delta_2 K_{2t}{}^{\rho_2} + (1-\delta_2) L_{2t}{}^{\rho_2}\right)^{\frac{1}{\rho_1}}. \tag{12}$$

We can thus calculate the technology gaps G_{12} and G_{21} as in Equations (4) and (7).

Similarly, for the CES production function with factor-augmenting technological change

$$Y_{it} = \left(\delta_i \left(\gamma_{Ki} e^{\lambda_{Ki} \cdot t} K_{it} \right)^{\rho_i} + (1 - \delta_i) \left(\gamma_{Li} e^{\lambda_{Li} \cdot t} L_{it} \right)^{\rho_i} \right)^{\frac{1}{\rho_i}}. \tag{13}$$

and the Cobb–Douglas production function

$$Y_{it} = \gamma_i e^{\lambda_i \cdot t} K_{it}^{\ \alpha} L_{it}^{\ 1-\alpha}. \tag{14}$$

We can also calculate the technology gaps G_{12} and G_{21} using Equations (2)–(7).

Our definition of technology gaps is related to but differs from the Malmquist productivity index, a widely used productivity measure developed by Caves, Christensen and Diewert (CCD) (1982a, 1982b). An advantage of using the technology gap measures G_{12} and G_{21} set out above rather than a Malmquist productivity index is that our concept is flexible in the structure of the aggregate production function, and can be conveniently generalised to include technological improvements embodied in other parts of the production function besides the multiplicative productivity factor $A_{it} = \gamma_i e^{\lambda_i \cdot t}$ (for example, improvements due to a change in the elasticity of substitution or factor-augmenting technological change in a CES production function, or increasing returns to scale). It is also worthy of note that if the aggregate production functions of the two economies (as Equations (9)–(10) or (11)–(12)) have the same values for parameters δ_i and ρ_i, and only differ from each other on the multiplicative productivity factor $A_{it} = \gamma_i e^{\lambda_i \cdot t}$, then both the technology gaps G_{12_t} and G_{21_t} can be simplified to A_{2_t} / A_{1_t}. As Bjurek (1996) mentions, to establish a relationship between the productivity indices and the corresponding Malmquist indices, CCD made the assumption that the underlying technologies were translog with equal second-order parameters. Although CCD (1982b) showed that their superlative index numbers could also be used to make multilateral output, input and productivity comparisons, if we allow for different assumptions on the production technologies, the productivity index might not be expressed easily in terms of a quantity index.

For a CES production function with Hicks-neutral technological change as in Equation (8), or a CES function with factor-augmenting technological change as in Equation (13), the key issues in calculating the technology gap measures G_{12} and G_{21} are how to parameterise the corresponding production functions by the observed data of the two economies, and specifically, for the production function equation (8) how to parameterise the two Equations (9) and (12). Parameterisation of the production function and calculation of the technology gap measures G_{12} and G_{21} can be made using a variety of techniques. Earlier literature uses the Kmenta approximation (Kmenta, 1967) or estimates a restricted translog function with traditional econometric methods. Klump *et al.* (2007) estimate a supply-side system for the US economy using a normalised CES function with factor-augmenting technological change. Henningsen and Henningsen (2011) offer an R-package to estimate the CES function directly using different nonlinear optimisation algorithms. Luoma and Luoto (2010) estimate a normalised CES production function with factor-augmenting technological change of the Finnish economy directly with Bayesian approach.

However, estimation of restricted translog functions or utilisation of the Kmenta approximation has been proved unsuitable when the underlying CES function differs from the Cobb–Douglas form (Thursby and Lovell, 1978; Henningsen and Henningsen, 2011). Results based on using nonlinear optimisation techniques in many cases seem not to be stable; while the estimation of the supply-side system presented by Klump *et al.* (2007) encounters problems of data availability. As a result, the calibration approach is now the more commonly used method in recent literature (Caselli, 2005). Since we also compare results from different forms of production function (a Cobb–Douglas function and a CES function with Hicks-neutral or factor-augmenting technological change) or different values of the elasticity of substitution, considering the number of experiments we report on in this chapter, we adopt the calibration approach.

We specify as our benchmark a CES production function with Hicks–neutral technological change that also incorporates human capital. As in Caselli (2005), we use a Hall and Jones' (1999) formulation for human capital

$$Y_{it} = \gamma_i e^{\lambda_i \cdot t} \left(\delta_i K_{it}^{\rho_i} + (1-\delta_i)(h_{it} L_{it})^{\rho_i} \right)^{\frac{1}{\rho_i}}, \tag{15}$$

where K_{it} is the aggregate capital stock of economy i at time t, L_{it} is the corresponding number of workers, h_{it} is their average human capital, and $h_{it}L_{it}$ can be interpreted as the "quality adjusted" workforce.

In per-worker terms, the production function (15) can be rewritten as

$$y_{it} = \gamma_i e^{\lambda_i \cdot t} \left(\delta_i k_{it}^{\rho_i} + (1-\delta_i) h_{it}^{\rho_i} \right)^{\frac{1}{\rho_i}}, \tag{16}$$

where y_{it} is the output per worker of economy i at time t, and $k_{it} = K_{it}/L_{it}$ is the corresponding capital–labour ratio.

Accordingly, the technology gaps at time t, G_{12_t} and G_{21_t}, can also be rewritten as

$$G_{12_t} = \frac{\hat{y}_{2_t}}{\hat{y}_{1_t}}, \tag{17}$$

$$G_{21_t} = \frac{\overline{\overline{y}}_{2_t}}{\overline{\overline{y}}_{1_t}}. \tag{18}$$

Here $\hat{y}_{1_t}$ and $\hat{y}_{2_t}$ are actual and hypothetical output per worker of economy 1 at time t, respectively; while $\overline{\overline{y}}_{1_t}$ and $\overline{\overline{y}}_{2_t}$ are hypothetical and actual output per worker of economy 2 at time t, respectively (corresponding to Equations (4) and (7)).

In order to calculate the technology gaps of interest here using a CES production function with Hicks-neutral technological change as in Equation (16), we need the data sets for y_{it}, k_{it} and h_{it}, and the value of the efficiency parameter γ_i, the rate of technological change λ_i, the distribution parameter δ_i, and the substitution parameter ρ_i.

4 Data Sets for China, India and the US

The data sets used in this chapter combine variables from two different sources. The first is Version 4.0 of the Extended Penn World Tables (EPWT version 4.0, Marquetti and Foley, 2011). We extract from the EPWT Version 4.0 data set for the countries we study data on labour productivity (output per worker y_{it}, expressed in real GDP per worker in chain indexed 2005 purchasing power parity dollars), and capital-labour ratio (physical capital per worker k_{it}, expressed in 2005 purchasing power parity dollars). The EPWT Version 4.0 data set includes time series for China from 1965 to 2008, time series for India from 1963 to 2008, and those for the US from 1963 to 2009. We extract data from these sources for the period 1979 to 2008.

To construct data on human capital, we use Barro and Lee (2011) estimates of the average years of schooling in the population over 15 years old (Barro and Lee v.1.2). Data on the average years of schooling of China, India and the US used here are available online (at http:/www.barrolee.com/, Last Updated: 2011.09.04). Barro and Lee's (2011) data set has both the average years of schooling in the population over 15 and 25 years old. However, as Caselli (2005) suggests, the average years of schooling in the population over 25 years old may be more appropriate for rich countries with a large share of college graduates, but it may be less appropriate for developing countries.

Following Caselli (2005), we turn these data into a measure of human capital using the formula of Hall and Jones (1999):

$$h = e^{\varphi(s)}, \tag{19}$$

where S is the average years of schooling, and $\varphi(s)$ is a piecewise linear function with slope 0.134 for $s \leq 4$, 0.101 for $4 < s \leq 8$, and 0.068 for $s > 8$. The Hall and Jones's (1999) measure involving the parameter values 0.134, 0.101, and 0.068 is used here to accommodate the log-linearity in the wage-schooling relationship at the country level consistent with the convexity of returns to education across countries. Specifically, the function $\varphi(s)$ can be written as:

$$\varphi(s) = \begin{cases} 0.134 \cdot s & \text{for } s \leq 4, \\ 0.134 \cdot 4 + 0.101 \cdot s & \text{for } 4 < s \leq 8, \\ 0.134 \cdot 4 + 0.101 \cdot 4 + 0.068 \cdot s & \text{for } s > 8. \end{cases} \tag{20}$$

Barro and Lee's (2011) data set of average years of schooling s is available for every five year period between 1950 and 2010. Since s changes slowly over time, we treat s as invariant before new data is available, i.e. we apply the 1980 data of s to the period 1980–1984, the 1985 data to the period 1985–1989 and so forth.

As is common in calibration exercises, besides data on y_{it}, k_{it} and h_{it}, we also need to determine the values of key technology parameters (the substitution parameter ρ_i, the distribution parameter δ_i, the efficiency parameter γ_i, and the rate of technological change λ_i).

Recent empirical evidence suggests that the US and other developed economies should be better represented by a CES aggregate production function with an elasticity of substitution below unity, rather than the unitary-elasticity Cobb–Douglas specification (Chirinko, 2008; Klump *et al.*, 2007, 2011). While according to Duffy and Papageorgiou's (2000) estimates, elasticity of substitution with human capital adjusted labour could be lower than estimates without human capital. As a result, we set as a benchmark the elasticity of substitution between capital and labour $\sigma_i = 0.8$, which gives a substitution parameter $\rho_i = -0.25$ (also giving $\rho_i = \sigma_i - 1/\sigma_i$).

The distribution parameter δ_i in a CES aggregate production function (in per-worker terms as in Equation (16)) can be written as a function of the capital–labour ratio k_{it}, the average human capital index h_{it}, the substitution parameter ρ_i, and the capital share θ_i. As in Caselli (2005), we assume that factor markets are competitive, and for the aggregate CES function in Equations (15) or (16) we have

$$\delta_i = \frac{\theta_i k_{it}^{-\rho_i}}{\theta_i k_{it}^{-\rho_i} + (1-\theta_i) h_{it}^{-\rho_i}}. \tag{21}$$

Since the distribution parameter δ_i is a function of the two time series k_{it} (capital–labour ratio) and h_{it} (the average human capital), in the calibration procedure we can firstly calculate a series of δ_{it}, and then take δ_i as the geometric mean of the series δ_{it}. Before calculating the country distribution parameters δ_i, we also need the value of the capital share θ_i. For our benchmark situation, as elsewhere in the literature (Caselli, 2005; Hsieh and Klenow, 2009), we use US data on the capital share for all the three country parameters θ_i. The long-run average value is around 1/3, and we adopt this setting. Due to problems of data quality and availability, we have not adopted the actual capital shares for China and India. We will vary these parameters later in robustness analyses.

Given the values of the substitution parameters ρ_i and the distribution parameters δ_i, we can then estimate the efficiency parameters γ_i and the rates of technological change λ_i. Following Caselli (2005), we define $y_{it}^{kh} = \left(\delta_i k_{it}^{\rho_i} + (1-\delta_i) h_{it}^{\rho_i}\right)^{\frac{1}{\rho_i}}$, and rewrite Equation (16) as

$$y_{it} = \gamma_i e^{\lambda_i \cdot t} \cdot y_{it}^{kh}, \tag{22}$$

or

$$\gamma_i e^{\lambda_i \cdot t} = \frac{y_{it}}{y_{it}^{kh}}. \tag{23}$$

It is noteworthy, however, that the values of the series y_{it}^{kh} and the distribution parameters δ_i, and consequently the estimates of parameters γ_i and λ_i are sensitive to the measurement (or unit) of time series k_{it} (capital–labour ratio), h_{it} (the average human capital) and y_{it} (output per worker). For consistency and reliability, we normalise all the time series of y_{it}, k_{it} and h_{it} by the corresponding US data in 1979.[1] We also choose different years or different countries as reference points. Both different reference points for the normalised CES function and different measurements (or units) of time series for un-normalised CES function will change the estimates of the parameters γ_i and λ_i. Results are, however, comparatively more consistent with a normalised CES production function.

[1]The normalized CES production function was introduced by La Grandville (1989) and advanced by Klump and de La Grandville (2000), Klump and Preissler (2000) and Klump and Saam (2008), see Klump *et al*. (2011) for a recent survey of the related literature.

Following Klump and Saam (2008), for a reference point with y_0 as output per capita at k_0 and h_0, we assume

$$\delta_i = \frac{\theta_0 k_0^{-\rho_i}}{\theta_0 k_0^{-\rho_i} + (1-\theta_0) h_0^{-\rho_i}}, \tag{24}$$

$$\gamma = y_0 \left(\theta_0 k_0^{-\rho_i} + (1-\theta_0) h_0^{-\rho_i}\right)^{\frac{1}{\rho_i}}, \tag{25}$$

where θ_0 is the capital share at the reference point, and γ is a efficiency parameter. With Equations (24) and (25), we can then express Equation (16) as

$$\frac{y_{it}}{y_0} = \gamma_i^* e^{\lambda_i \cdot t} \left(\theta_0 \left(\frac{k_{it}}{k_0}\right)^{\rho_i} + (1-\theta_0)\left(\frac{h_{it}}{h_0}\right)^{\rho_i}\right)^{\frac{1}{\rho_i}}. \tag{26}$$

Here $\gamma_i^* = \gamma_i / \gamma$. By defining $y_{it}^{kh*} = \left(\theta_0 (k_{it}/k_0)^{\rho_i} + (1-\theta_0)(h_{it}/h_0)^{\rho_i}\right)^{\frac{1}{\rho_i}}$, Equations (22) and (23) now become

$$\frac{y_{it}}{y_0} = \gamma_i^* e^{\lambda_i \cdot t} \cdot y_{it}^{kh*}, \tag{27}$$

$$\gamma_i^* e^{\lambda_i \cdot t} = \frac{\frac{y_{it}}{y_0}}{y_{it}^{kh*}}. \tag{28}$$

The series y_{it}/y_0, k_{it}/k_0 and h_{it}/y_0 used in Equations (26)–(28) are data normalised with the reference point (US data in 1979 in the benchmark situation). The key to the normalisation procedures used here is to normalise all the data y_{it}, k_{it} and h_{it} of the three countries using a common reference point. Otherwise, all the efficiency parameters γ_i^* of these countries will become 1, and the differences in efficiency or technology level will disappear.

5 Empirical Results

Figure 4 presents the indices of technology or efficiency level $A_{it} = \gamma_i^* e^{\lambda_i \cdot t}$ between 1979 and 2008 for China, India and the US calculated using Equation (28), and also the estimated parameters γ_i^* and λ_i derived from a standard curve fitting procedure. The technology level index for the US in 1979 is 1, as all the time series

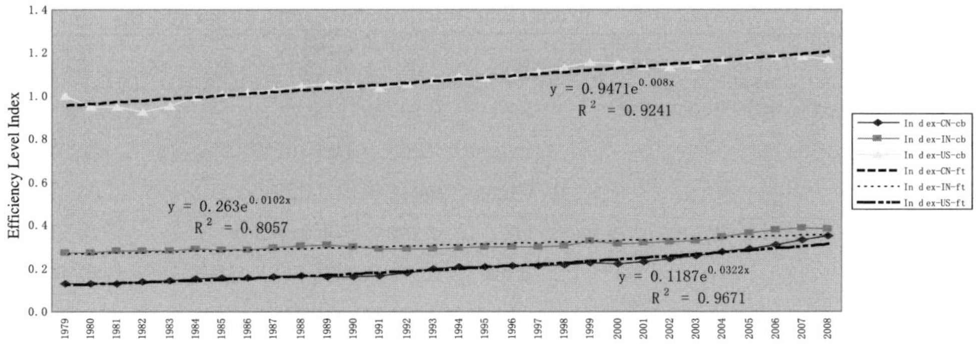

Figure 4. Technology levels with CES function for China, India and the US 1979–2008.

Notes: Index of "CN", "IN" and "US" denote China, India and the US; and Index of "cb" and "ft" denote calibrated and fitted data, respectively.
Source: Authors' calculations.

of y_{it}, k_{it} and h_{it} are normalised by the corresponding US data in 1979. We can see from Figure 4 that the rate of technological change in China is much higher than India (as emphasised in literature on TFP growth rates), while the latter is still higher than that of the US However, while both the efficiency or technology levels of China and India are much lower than that of the US, at least before the year 2008, the technology level of India is higher than that of China. Although factor accumulation rates in China exceed those of India, and economic growth rates in China also exceed those of India, the technology gap is in favour of India before 2008 since the initial gap is in India's favour and closing more slowly than relative GDP growth rates.

Using the data presented in Figure 4, we can also parameterise Equation (26) for China, India and the US, respectively. Results are shown in Table 1. Since different reference points or reference countries may have substantial impacts on the estimates, for comparative purposes, we also give results using time series normalised by China and India's data in 1979. As shown in Table 1, estimated growth rates of technological change λ_i in China and India are close to the results of Herd and Dougherty (2007) and Bosworth and Collins (2008). The estimated efficiency parameters γ_i^* of the US are about 3.6, 4.5 or 4.9 times of India, and 8.0, 11.1 or 12.3 times of China, and those of India are about 2.2, 2.4 or 2.5 times of China, when we use time series normalised by the US, India or China's data in 1979 respectively. It is also noteworthy that by comparing estimates with different reference points, the results show that rates of technological change λ_i seem lower with a decrease in the efficiency parameters γ_i^*. Nevertheless, trends are similar as shown in Figure 4.

Table 1. Parameters of CES production functions for China, India and the US

Parameter		γ_i^*	λ_i	θ_0	σ_i	ρ_i
Normalised with 1979 data of US	US	0.9471	0.008			
	India	0.263	0.0102	1/3	0.8	–0.25
	China	0.1187	0.0322			
Normalised with 1979 data of India	US	4.2904	0.0103			
	India	0.9461	0.0134	1/3	0.8	–0.25
	China	0.3882	0.0406			
Normalised with 1979 data of China	US	10.984	0.011			
	India	2.2537	0.0145	1/3	0.8	–0.25
	China	0.8965	0.0433			

Source: Authors' calculations.

The technology gaps of China and India both with the US and with each other calculated using Equations (17) and (18) are shown in Figure 5 ($\hat{y}_{it}$ and $\overline{\overline{y}}_{it}$ are calculated from Equation (26); the reference point is US data in 1979). These calculations suggest that if China and India's input factors were hypothetically used with US technology, the hypothetical output would be much larger; and if China's input factors were hypothetically used with India's technology, the hypothetical output would also be higher. Conversely, if US inputs were hypothetically used with China or India's technology, the hypothetical output would be much lower; and if India's input factors were hypothetically used with China's technology, the hypothetical output would also be lower. Note that since we assume the aggregate production functions of all the three economies (as Equation (26)) have the same values for parameters δ_i and ρ_i, and only differ from each other on the multiplicative productivity factor $A_{it} = \gamma_i e^{\lambda_i \cdot t}$, as mentioned earlier in Section 3, both the technology gaps G_{12_t} and G_{21_t} are simplified to A_{2_t}/A_{1_t}.

Figure 5 also indicates that between 1979 and 2008, the technology gaps of China and India relative to the US decrease from about 7.79 and 3.59 to 3.86 and 3.37, respectively. These results confirm that the technology gap between China and the US is larger than that between India and the US, while both the gaps of China and India narrow at a slower rate than GDP per worker (also consistent to the pattern shown in Figure 4). The technology gap of China between 1979 and 2008 relative to India decreases from 2.17 to 1.15. Since all the measures of the technology gap of China relative to India over the period are greater than 1, the technology gap is in favour of India before 2008 since the initial gap is in India's favour. These trends of the pairwise measures of technology gaps between China,

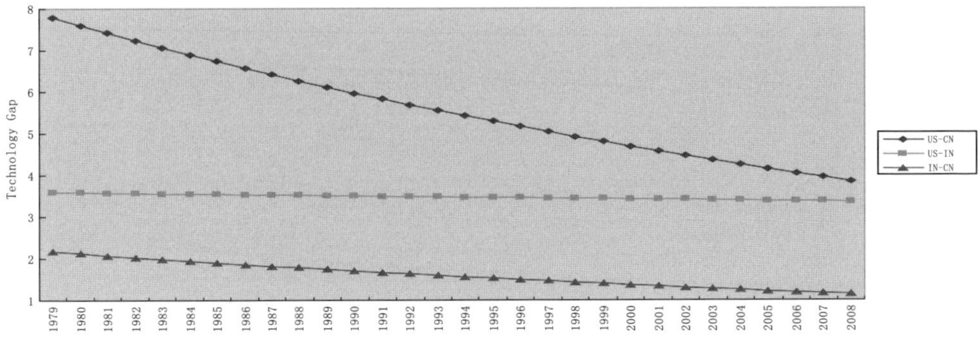

Figure 5. Pairwise technology gaps with CES function between China, India and the US

Notes: Technology gaps denote "US–CN" and "US–IN" are China and India's hypothetical output/worker with US technology divided by their estimated output/worker with own technology, and technology gap "IN–CN" is China's hypothetical output/worker with India's technology divided by its estimated output/worker with own technology.

Source: Authors' calculations.

India and the US as shown in Figure 5 are consistent with different estimated values for parameters of γ_i^* and λ_i shown in Table 1, i.e. different reference points or reference countries do not change the trends described here.

These findings are noteworthy, since recent literature emphasises the much higher growth rate of total factor productivity in China than in India, and misses China's comparatively lower technology level compared to India.

6 Robustness Checks

For comparative purposes, we also present results calculated using an aggregate Cobb–Douglas production function

$$\frac{y_{it}}{y_0} = \gamma_i^* e^{\lambda_i \cdot t} \left(\frac{k_{it}}{k_0} \right)^{\alpha_i} \left(\frac{h_{it}}{h_0} \right)^{1-\alpha_i} . \tag{29}$$

We use US data on the capital share for α_i again, i.e. we again use its long-run average value $\alpha_i = 1/3$ (capital share α_i is θ_0 in Table 1, Section 5). Thus the only difference between the Cobb–Douglas production function used here and Equation (26) used in Section 5 is the elasticity of substitution σ_i (or equivalently the substitution parameter ρ_i).

Figure 6 presents the indices of technology level $A_{it} = \gamma_i^* e^{\lambda_i \cdot t}$ for China, India and the US between 1979 and 2008 calculated using Equation (29), and also the estimated parameters γ_i^* and λ_i derived from a standard curve fitting procedure, with US data of 1979 as the reference point (the efficiency level index of the US

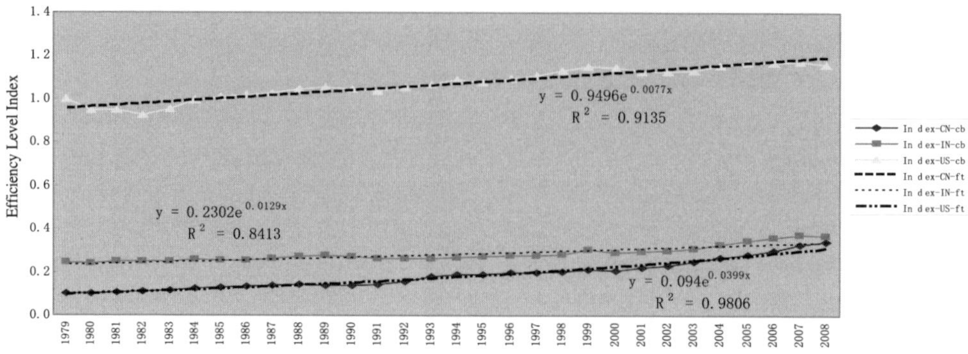

Figure 6. Technology levels for China, India and the US Using C-D function 1979–2008.

Notes: Indices of "CN", "IN" and "US" denote China, India and the US; and Indices of "cb" and "ft" denote calibrated and fitted data, respectively.

Source: Authors' calculations.

in 1979 is 1). Comparing Figures 4 and 6, we can see that these two figures give similar trends: the growth rate of technological change in China is higher than India, and the latter is still higher than that of the U.S; while both the technology levels (measured by the efficiency level indices in the figures) of China and India are much lower than that of the US, the technology level of India is higher than that of China. Our previous conclusion that the technology gap is in favour of India before 2008 since the initial gap is in India's favour still holds. The major difference between Figures 4 and 6 is that with a Cobb–Douglas production function, efficiency level indices are slightly lower, and the rates of technological change are slightly higher for China and India than that for the CES case in Section 5; while for the US, the contrary is true.

For comparative purposes, we also present results with different reference points (China, India and US data in 1979) in Table 2. As shown in Table 2, the estimated growth rates of technological change λ_i in China and India are still close to the results of Herd and Dougherty (2007) and Bosworth and Collins (2008). The estimated values of efficiency parameters γ_i^* of the US are about 4.1 times of India and 10.1 times of China, and those of India are about 2.4 times of China. Data in Table 2 also confirm that when the aggregate production function is Cobb–Douglas, different reference points (for y_{it}/y_0, k_{it}/k_0 and h_{it}/h_0) or different measures (or units) of the times series (such as y_{it}, k_{it} and h_{it}) only change the levels of the efficiency parameters γ_i^*, while having no effects on both the ratios of γ_i^* and the values of λ_i.

The technology gaps of China and India both with the US and with each other calculated with a Cobb–Douglas aggregate production function are shown in

Table 2. Parameters of C-D production functions for China, India and the US

	Parameter	γ_i^*	λ_i	θ_0	σ_i
Normalised with 1979 data of US	US	0.9496	0.0077		
	India	0.2302	0.0129	1/3	1
	China	0.094	0.0399		
Normalised with 1979 data of India	US	3.9203	0.0077		
	India	0.9503	0.0129	1/3	1
	China	0.3879	0.0399		
Normalised with 1979 data of China	US	9.2667	0.0077		
	India	2.2462	0.0129	1/3	1
	China	0.9168	0.0399		

Source: Authors' calculations.

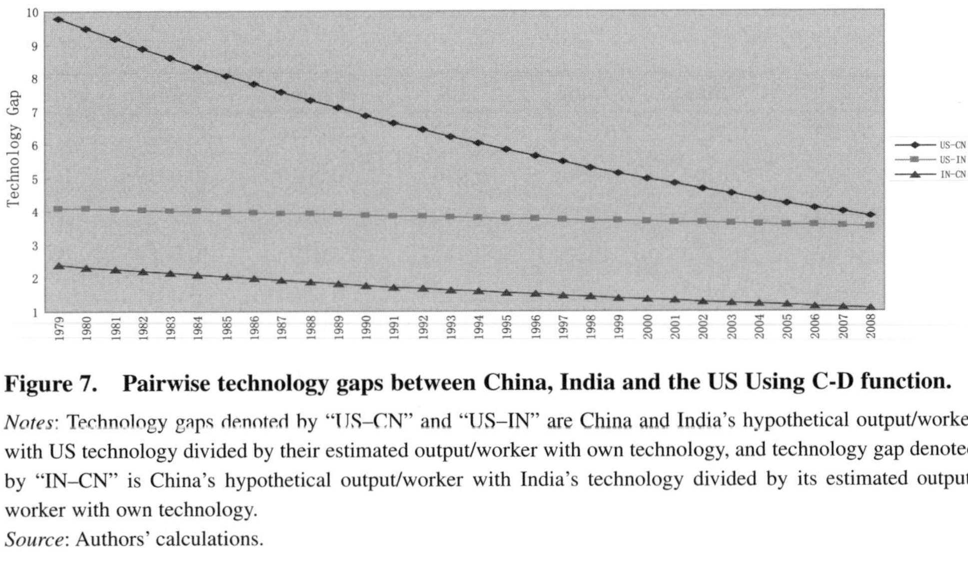

Figure 7. Pairwise technology gaps between China, India and the US Using C-D function.

Notes: Technology gaps denoted by "US–CN" and "US–IN" are China and India's hypothetical output/worker with US technology divided by their estimated output/worker with own technology, and technology gap denoted by "IN–CN" is China's hypothetical output/worker with India's technology divided by its estimated output/worker with own technology.

Source: Authors' calculations.

Figure 7 ($\hat{y}_{it}$ and $\overline{\overline{y}}_{it}$ in Equations (17) and (18) are calculated from Equation (29); the reference point is US data in 1979). Since we assume the Cobb–Douglas aggregate production functions of all the three economies have the same values of capital share α_i, and only differ from each other in the multiplicative productivity factor $A_{it} = \gamma_i e^{\lambda_i \cdot t}$, both the technology gaps G_{12_t} and G_{21_t} are simplified to A_{2_t}/A_{1_t}. We can see from Figure 7 that between 1979 and 2008, the technology gaps of China and India relative to the US decrease from about 9.78 and 4.10, to 3.84 and 3.53, respectively. While the technology gap of China relative to India during the period decreases from 2.38 to 1.09. Although the measures of the pairwise technology gaps in Figure 7 change slightly compare to Figure 5, and the initial gaps in the Cobb–Douglas scenario become larger, our previous conclusion still holds.

For robustness, we now consider relaxing further the assumptions on the elasticity of substitution σ_i and the capital share θ_0. We investigate the variation of the estimated efficiency parameters γ_i^* and technological change rate λ_i hence the variation of the technology gaps, by increasing the elasticity of substitution σ_i with a step of 0.1 from 0.3 to 1.2. Due to problems of data quality or availability in China and India, we previously set the capital share θ_0 (or α_i) of all the three countries at the US long-run average value 1/3. Based on recent Chinese literature (see Zhang and Zhang (2010)), we set the capital share θ_0 for China in an interval from 1/3 to

Table 3. Sensitivity analysis of calibrated technology parameters γ_i^* and λ_i to elasticities of substitution and capital share.

	γ_i^*			λ_i		
Parameter	**China**	**India**	**US**	**China**	**India**	**US**
$\sigma_i = 0.3; \theta_0 = 1/3$	0.4174	0.6146	0.9301	–0.0044	–0.0045	0.0104
$\sigma_i = 0.4; \theta_0 = 1/3$	0.316	0.4901	0.936	0.0019	–0.0017	0.0096
$\sigma_i = 0.5; \theta_0 = 1/3$	0.2338	0.3957	0.9401	0.0104	0.002	0.009
$\sigma_i = 0.6; \theta_0 = 1/3$	0.1773	0.3321	0.9431	0.019	0.0054	0.0086
$\sigma_i = 0.7; \theta_0 = 1/3$	0.1414	0.2906	0.9453	0.0264	0.0081	0.0083
$\sigma_i = 0.8; \theta_0 = 1/3$	0.1187	0.263	0.9471	0.0322	0.0102	0.008
$\sigma_i = 0.9; \theta_0 = 1/3$	0.1039	0.2439	0.9485	0.0366	0.0117	0.0078
$\sigma_i = 1.0; \theta_0 = 1/3$	0.094	0.2302	0.9496	0.0399	0.0129	0.0077
$\sigma_i = 1.1; \theta_0 = 1/3$	0.0869	0.22	0.9506	0.0425	0.0138	0.0075
$\sigma_i = 1.2; \theta_0 = 1/3$	0.0817	0.2122	0.9514	0.0445	0.0146	0.0074
$\sigma_i = 0.8; \theta'_0 = 1/3$	0.1187	0.263	0.9471	0.0322	0.0102	0.008
$\sigma_i = 0.8; \theta'_0 = 0.4$	0.1464	0.3064	0.9471	0.0271	0.0082	0.008
$\sigma_i = 0.8; \theta'_0 = 0.5$	0.1971	0.3814	0.9471	0.02	0.0054	0.008
$\sigma_i = 0.8; \theta'_0 = 0.6$	0.2604	0.4697	0.9471	0.0136	0.0028	0.008
$\sigma_i = 1.0; \theta'_0 = 1/3$	0.094	0.2302	0.9496	0.0399	0.0129	0.0077
$\sigma_i = 1.0; \theta'_0 = 0.4$	0.1146	0.2662	0.9496	0.0352	0.011	0.0077
$\sigma_i = 1.0; \theta'_0 = 0.5$	0.1544	0.3311	0.9496	0.0281	0.0082	0.0077
$\sigma_i = 1.0; \theta'_0 = 0.6$	0.2079	0.4119	0.9496	0.0209	0.0054	0.0077

Notes: Changes in θ'_0 only applies to China and India, θ_0 for the US does not change.
Source: Authors' calculations.

Table 4. Sensitivity analysis on technology gaps G_{12t} and G_{12t} for China relative to India.

	G_{12t}		G_{12t}	
Parameter	**1979**	**2008**	**1979**	**2008**
$\sigma_i = 0.3; \theta_0 = 1/3$	1.472	1.468	1.472	1.468
$\sigma_i = 0.4; \theta_0 = 1/3$	1.545	1.392	1.545	1.392
$\sigma_i = 0.5; \theta_0 = 1/3$	1.678	1.315	1.678	1.315
$\sigma_i = 0.6; \theta_0 = 1/3$	1.848	1.246	1.848	1.246
$\sigma_i = 0.7; \theta_0 = 1/3$	2.018	1.187	2.018	1.187
$\sigma_i = 0.8; \theta_0 = 1/3$	2.167	1.145	2.167	1.145
$\sigma_i = 0.9; \theta_0 = 1/3$	2.290	1.112	2.290	1.112
$\sigma_i = 1.0; \theta_0 = 1/3$	2.384	1.089	2.384	1.089
$\sigma_i = 1.1; \theta_0 = 1/3$	2.460	1.070	2.460	1.070
$\sigma_i = 1.2; \theta_0 = 1/3$	2.521	1.059	2.521	1.059
$\sigma_i = 0.8; \theta_0^i = 1/3; \theta_0^C = 0.4$	2.140	1.139	2.033	1.167
$\sigma_i = 0.8; \theta_0^i = 1/3; \theta_0^C = 0.5$	2.101	1.129	1.861	1.199
$\sigma_i = 0.8; \theta_0^i = 1/3; \theta_0^C = 0.6$	2.064	1.114	1.719	1.225
$\sigma_i = 0.8; \theta_0^i = 3/5; \theta_0^C = 1/3$	1.874	1.341	2.250	1.220
$\sigma_i = 0.8; \theta_0^i = 3/5; \theta_0^C = 0.4$	1.850	1.333	2.111	1.243
$\sigma_i = 0.8; \theta_0^i = 3/5; \theta_0^C = 0.5$	1.816	1.321	1.933	1.277
$\sigma_i = 0.8; \theta_0^i = 3/5; \theta_0^C = 0.6$	1.784	1.305	1.784	1.305
$\sigma_i = 1.0; \theta_0^i = 1/3; \theta_0^C = 0.4$	2.347	1.076	2.195	1.099
$\sigma_i = 1.0; \theta_0^i = 1/3; \theta_0^C = 0.5$	2.290	1.056	2.004	1.104
$\sigma_i = 1.0; \theta_0^i = 1/3; \theta_0^C = 0.6$	2.237	1.040	1.872	1.163
$\sigma_i = 1.0; \theta_0^i = 3/5; \theta_0^C = 1/3$	2.079	1.303	2.483	1.166
$\sigma_i = 1.0; \theta_0^i = 3/5; \theta_0^C = 0.4$	2.047	1.287	2.287	1.177
$\sigma_i = 1.0; \theta_0^i = 3/5; \theta_0^C = 0.5$	1.997	1.263	2.088	1.182
$\sigma_i = 1.0; \theta_0^i = 3/5; \theta_0^C = 0.6$	1.951	1.244	1.951	1.244

Notes: Technology gap G_{12t} denotes China's hypothetical output/worker with India's technology divided by its estimated output/worker with its own technology. G_{21t} denotes India's estimated output/worker with its own technology divided by its hypothetical output/worker with China's technology. θ_0^C and θ_0^i denote China and India's capital share, respectively.
Source: Authors' calculations.

3/5. For comparative purposes, we set the same interval for the capital share for India as well.

Results of sensitivity analysis on the parameters γ_i^* and λ_i to changes of the elasticity of substitution σ_i and capital share θ_0 (or α_i) are shown in Table 3. Results in Table 3 show that, for China and India, the efficiency parameters γ_i^* decrease, but the growth rates of technological change λ_i increase with the elasticity of substitution σ_i from 0.3 to 1.2. For the US, the contrary is true. Further experiments show that the reason the US has a different relationship between γ_i^* and λ_i is because it is set as a reference country. The capital share θ_0 (or α_i) presents quite different effects to the parameters γ_i^* and λ_i. We can see from Table 3 that independent of whether $\sigma_i = 0.8$ or $\sigma_i = 1$, both for China and India, γ_i^* increases and λ_i decreases when θ_0 (or α_i) increases from 1/3 to 3/5. Considering differences in the initial gaps and the growth rates of technological change as shown in Table 3, our previous inference on changes in the technology gaps of China and India both with the US and with each other seems robust.

Results of the technology gaps G_{12_t} and G_{21_t} for China relative to India using different key parameters are shown in Table 4. Note that if the two economies have different capital share θ_0, then the technology gaps G_{12_t} and G_{21_t} may differ, and can no longer be simplified to A_{2_t}/A_{1_t}. We can see from Table 4 that, with any non-extreme values of key parameters elasticity of substitution σ_i and capital share θ_0 (or α_i), at least before the year 2008, the technology gap of China relative to India still remains in India's favour.

7 Conclusion

Our chapter reports calculations of the technology gaps for China and India compared both to the US and to each other between 1979 and 2008 using a CES framework. These gaps reflect differences between actual output per worker and hypothetical output using other countries' technology with domestic inputs. By comparing with the US, we investigate changes in the technology gaps between China and India through time, and also make comparisons of the efficiency or technology level of the two countries.

We find that the pairwise gaps between China and the US, and India and the US remain large while narrowing at a slower rate than GDP per worker. The technology gap between China and the US is significantly larger than that between India and the US for the period before 2008. Notably, the variations of China and India's technology gaps relative to the US present different behaviour. The technology gap for China relative to the US is narrowing much more rapidly than India. The calculations we report here also suggest that although China has a much higher growth rate of total factor productivity than India over the period, the bilateral technology gap between China and India is still in India's favour. India had higher initial income per worker than China in the 1970's, and China's much more rapid physical and human capital accumulation has allowed China to move ahead, but a bilateral technology gap remains.

These findings are noteworthy, since it seems that in the existing literature little attention is paid to the technology gap between China and India. Recent literature seems more inclined to emphasise the much higher growth rate of total factor productivity (or technological change) in China than that in India, and thus misses China's comparatively lower aggregate efficiency or technology level compared to India.

References

Barro, R. and J. Lee (2011), A New Data Set of Educational Attainment in the World, 1950–2010, NBER Working Paper No. 15902: http://www.nber.org/papers/w15902 (Updated Nov./2011), data available online at http:/www.barrolee.com/.

Bjurek, H. (1996), The Malmquist Total Factor Productivity Index, *The Scandinavian Journal of Economics*, 98(2), 303–313.

Bosworth, B. and S.M. Collins (2008), Accounting for Growth: Comparing China and India, *Journal of Economic Perspectives*, 22(1), 45–66.

Caselli, F. (2005), *Accounting for Income Differences Across Countries*, chapter 9 in the Handbook of Economic Growth 1A, P. Aghion and S. Durlauf (Eds.), North Holland.

Caves, D.W., L.R. Christensen and W.E. Diewert (1982a), The Economic Theory of Index Numbers and the Measurement of Input, Output and Productivity, *Econometrica*, 50(6), 1393–1414.

Caves, D.W., L.R. Christensen and W.E. Diewert (1982b), Multilateral Comparisons of Output, Input and Productivity Using Superlative Index Numbers, *The Economic Journal*, 92(365), 73–86.

Chirinko, R.S., S.M. Fazzari and A.P. Meyer (1999), How Responsive is Business Capital Formation to its User Cost? *Journal of Public Economics*, 74(1), 53–80.

Chirinko, R.S. (2008), σ: The Long and Short of It, *Journal of Macroeconomics*, 30(2), 671–686.

Duffy, J. and C. Papageorgiou (2000), A Cross-Country Empirical Investigation of the Aggregate Production Function Specification, *Journal of Economic Growth*, 5(1), 86–120.

Hall, R.E. and C.I. Jones (1999), Why do Some Countries Produce so Much more Output Per Worker than Others?, *The Quarterly Journal of Economics*, 114(1), 83–116.

Henningsen, A. and Henningsen, G. (2011). Econometric Estimation of the "Constant Elasticity of Substitution" Function in R: Package micEconCES. Frederiksberg: Institute of Food and Resource Economics, University of Copenhagen. (FOI Working Paper 2011 / 9). http://orbit.dtu.dk/files/6238545/Econometric%20estimation.pdf

Herd R. and S. Dougherty, (2007), Growth Prospects in China and India Compared, *The European Journal of Comparative Economics*, 4(1), 65–89.

Howitt, P. (2000), Endogenous Growth and Cross-Country Income Differences, *American Economic Review*, 90, 829–846.

Hsieh, C. and P.J. Klenow (2009), Misallocation and Manufacturing TFP in China and India, *The Quarterly Journal of Economics*, 124(4), 1403–1448.

Klenow, P.J. and A. Rodríguez-Clare (2005), *Externalities and Economic Growth*, chapter 11 in the Handbook of Economic Growth. 1A, P. Aghion and S. Durlauf (Eds.), North Holland.

Kmenta, J. (1967), On Estimation of the CES Production Function, *International Economic Review*, 8, 180–189.

Klump, R. and O. De La Grandville (2000), Economic Growth and the Elasticity of Substitution: Two Theorems and Some Suggestions, *American Economic Review*, 90(1), 282–291.

Klump, R., P. McAdam and A. Willman (2007), Factor Substitution and Factor Augmenting Technical Progress in the US, *Review of Economics and Statistics*, 89(1), 183–92.

Klump, R., P. McAdam and A. Willman (2011), The Normalized CES Production Function, Theory and Empirics, European Central Bank Working Paper Series No. 1294: https://www.ecb.europa.eu/pub/pdf/scpwps/ecbwp1294.pdf?9fcd5fddf87498417164716f2bbee9fd.

Klump, R. and H. Preissler (2000), CES Production Functions and Economic Growth, *Scandinavian Journal of Economics*, 102(1), 41–56.

Klump, R. and M. Saam (2008), Calibration of Normalized CES Production Functions in Dynamic Models, *Economics Letters*, 99(2), 256–259.

La Grandville, O. De (1989), In Quest of the Slutzky Diamond, *American Economic Review*, 79, 468–481.

Luoma A. and J. Luoto (2010), The Aggregate Production Function of the Finnish Economy in the Twentieth Century, *Southern Economic Journal*, 76(3), 723–737.

Marquetti A. and D. Foley (2011), Extended Penn World Tables Version 4.0, last updated in Aug./2011.

Thursby, J.G. and C.A.K. Lovell (1978), An Investigation of the Kmenta Approximation to the CES Function, *International Economic Review*, 19, 363–377.

Wang, J., D. Medianu and J. Whalley (2011), The Contribution of China, India and Brazil to Narrowing North-South Differences in GDP/capita, World Trade Shares, and Market Capitalization, NBER Working Paper No. 17681: http://www.nber.org/papers/w17681.

Wilson, D. and R. Purushothaman (2003), Dreaming with BRICs: The Path to 2050, *Goldman Sachs Global Economics Paper* 99.

Zhang, J. and S. Zhang (2010), Changes in Primary Income Distribution and Resulting Problems: A View of Labor Share in GDP, *Chinese Journal of Population Science*, 5, 24–35 (in Chinese; 张车伟、张士斌，中国初次收入分配格局的变动与问题——以劳动报酬占GDP份额为视角，中国人口科学，2010 年第 5 期，第 24–35 页).

Chapter 15

Heterogeneous Firms in a Product Fragmentation World[1]

Yue Gao
Shandong University of Technology, China
gaoyue01@163.com

John Whalley
Western University, Canada
Center for International Governance Innovation (CIGI) and NBER
jwhalley@uwo.ca

Abstract: This chapter analyses the ways in which product fragmentation (producing part of a product in onc country, and a part elsewhere) can be used by multinational firms which have different productivity to serve the market abroad when product chains can be internationally and arbitrarily fragmented. Product fragmentation is thus an additional option to serving markets abroad by either horizontal or vertical Foreign Direct Investment (FDI). Upon opening a market to trade, firms with the lowest productivity will exit, those with intermediate productivity will export, and those with higher productivity will choose fragmentation. Among the latter, the more productive a firm is, the more product chains are allocated abroad. Firms with the highest productivity will choose horizontal FDI. At a sector level, the more prone to fragmentation a sector is, the lower will be the ratio of exports to FDI sales.

[1] We are grateful for the financial support from the Ontario Research Fund (ORF) and the National Social Science Foundation of China (Project No. 15BJY064).

1 Introduction

During the past two decades, international fragmentation of production across locations by multinationals has become even more prevalent. Multinationals place different production phases of a product in different countries or regions, and set up a worldwide fragmentation network.

Fragmentation is not accounted for in the new trade theory based on Dixit–Stiglitz preferences where all firms export because of consumers' love of variety and the assumption is that there is no fixed cost for exporting. Available evidence indicates, that even within a sector, some firms export while many others do not (e.g., Head and Ries, 2003; Eaton *et al.*, 2004); a phenomenon not well explained by theory using an assumption of representative firms within industries.

Heterogeneous firms models present explanations for this phenomenon. The Melitz (2003) dynamic industry model with heterogeneous firms and fixed costs of exporting shows that exposure to trade induces only the more productive firms to enter export markets and simultaneously forces the least productive to exit. And among exporters, Melitz's model suggests that firms with higher productivity have greater sales. As a generalisation on Melitz, Helpman *et al.* (2004) (hereinafter referred to as HMY) introduce horizontal FDI into Melitz's model, and focus on a firms' choice between exports and horizontal FDI. They concluded that the least productive firms serve only the domestic market, that relatively more productive firms export, and that the most productive firms engage in FDI. In HMY, at a sector level, the more within-industry dispersion of firm productivity, the lower the ratio of exports to FDI sales. There is, however still no fragmentation in this structure.

This chapter extends the HMY model, and analyses the different ways multinational firms which have different productivity can serve the market abroad when product chains can also be internationally and arbitrarily fragmented. Besides exporting and horizontal FDI, firms face another choice which is to supply abroad through international fragmentation. In HMY, international fragmentation is absent, so firms only choose between exports and horizontal FDI to serve markets abroad. We first consider firms' choice when international fragmentation is possible but has a sole fixed cutoff point. We then analyse firms' choice when international fragmentation is possible, but there are two possible fixed cutoff points; and lastly the situation when product chains can be arbitrarily fragmented.

The main conclusions are the following: On exposure to trade, firms with the lowest productivity will exit, those with intermediate productivity will export, and those with higher productivity will choose fragmentation. Among these, the more productive a firm is the more of the production chains is allocated abroad. Firms with the highest productivity will choose horizontal FDI. At a sector level, the more prone a sector is to be fragmented, the lower the ratio of exports to FDI sales.

One of the most significant findings is that the ability of a country to fragment production internationally is a source of comparative advantage.

The remainder of the chapter is composed of four sections. The second is a literature review. In the third, we set up a model in which product chains can be arbitrarily fragmented and study the different choices of heterogeneous firms in supplying abroad. The last part is the conclusion.

2 Related Literature

This chapter is related to two strands of literature, one on heterogeneous firms (Melitz, 2003; Helpman *et al.*, 2004).[2] The other is fragmentation (Feenstra and Hanson, 1996, 1999; Deardorff, 2001; Yamashita, 2010). The former is about the different choices of the firms with different productivity, and the latter focuses on the effect of fragmentation on factors' prices, employment and welfare. This chapter is based on the HMY model, and the HMY model is based upon Brainard (1993) and Melitz (2003). Here we briefly review these chapters.

Brainard (1993) develops a "proximity-concentration" model to analyse the mode used by representative firms to supply abroad. In her study, there are two countries and two commodities. One is a homogenous product, and the other a differentiated product. The differentiated product sector is characterised by increasing returns at firm level since some inputs that have the characteristic of public goods, and scale economies at plant level so that concentrating production lowers unit costs. There is also a variable transport cost that rises with distance so that investment abroad can save transport costs. The decision to supply abroad via export or horizontal FDI depends on the trade-off between proximity advantage and concentration advantage. When proximity advantage has predominance over concentration advantage, a two-way investment equilibrium will arise. In contrast, when concentration advantage has predominance over proximity advantage, there will be a two-way trade equilibrium.

A two-way investment equilibrium is more likely to occur the higher are returns to scale at corporate level relative to plant level; the higher are transport costs across market, the greater is expenditure on differentiated products in the foreign market; and the higher is the elasticity of substitution between varieties in preferences. Under some circumstances, that is, for intermediate ranges of transport costs relative to plant level scale economies and of returns at the corporate level relative to the plant level, there exists a mixed equilibrium in which multinationals and international trade co-exists.

When a mixed equilibrium occurs, in Brainard's model, crowding out effects restrict the number of the firms that can supply abroad via horizontal FDI, so,

[2] Redding, (2010) provides a recent review of this literature.

firms that choose exports and horizontal FDI co-exist (Head and Ries, 2004). In Brainard, firms are homogenous. They choose to export or use FDI to supply markets abroad, but we do not know which firms choose to export, and which firms choose FDI.

Melitz (2003) later built a dynamic industry model with heterogeneous firms to analyse the intra-industry effects of international trade. Using heterogeneous firms with different firms have different productivity allows them to choose whether they supply abroad, and, we can distinguish between which firms supply abroad *via* export or FDI. His model suggests that exposure to trade induces only the most productive firms to enter the export market, the second most productive firms to serve only domestic market, and forces the least productive firms to exit.

To enter the market, firms must make an initial investment, and then draw their productivity from a common distribution. After firms know their productivity, they choose one of the following three choices: to exit, to supply the domestic market, or supply the domestic market and at the same time export. Firm needs to meet certain productivity requirements to make the two latter choices.

Melitz's model generates the following outcomes: Firms with high enough productivity can supply abroad via export because only these firms can afford the fixed export cost; exposure to trade forces the least productive firms to exit; market shares are reallocated toward more productive firms and contribute to an aggregate productivity increase.

Based on Melitz and following Brainard, Helpman *et al.* (2004) introduce an additional choice for firms into Melitz's model, namely horizontal FDI. They then focus on firm choices between exports and horizontal FDI in supplying abroad. In their structure, each firm decides whether to serve a foreign market, and whether to do so through export or local subsidiary sales. In their model, firms face a proximity-concentration trade-off as in Brainard. The two modes of market access have different relative costs: exporting involves lower fixed costs while FDI involves lower variable costs. They conclude that firms' choices are determined by their productivity, and that the least productive firms serve only the domestic market, that relatively more productive firms export, and that the most productive firms engage in FDI.

Helpman *et al.* (2004) thus highlight the role of within-sector firm productivity differences in explaining the structure of both international trade and foreign investment. In the HMY model, at a sector level, the more within-industry dispersion of firm productivity there is, the lower the ratio of exports to FDI sales. Helpman, Melitz and Yeaple thus then extend the proximity-concentration model of Brainard by introducing heterogeneous firms, and also extend heterogeneity model of Melitz by introducing horizontal FDI. This chapter goes further by extending the HMY model by introducing fragmentation into it.

Many papers have studied the phenomenon of fragmentation which means that various phases of a production process are physically separable and can be allocated in different places or nations. Jones and Kierzkowski (1990) believe that a production process is consisted of a series of production blocks which are connected and coordinated by service links, and that declining of service cost can stimulate the development of fragmentation at a great amount. When fragmentation takes place among different nations, trade in parts and components will happen. So, most of the papers use the imports of intermediate commodities to measure fragmentation. The existed papers in this field mainly concern the effect of fragmentation on factors' prices, employment and welfare. In a series of studies, Feenstra and Hanson develop a model that has the implication of an increase in outsourcing would lead to an increase in the relative wage of skilled labour in both the developed and the developing countries. In this chapter, we do not concern with the effect of fragmentation, but the firms' mode to serve the market abroad.

3 Theoretical Model

3.1 Demand

We assume the world consists of N countries, each producing goods in $H + 1$ sectors. H sectors produce differentiated products, and one sector produces a homogenous product which is the numeraire good. Labour is the sole factor of production, with country i endowed with L^i units of labour.

A fraction of β_h income is spent on differentiated products of sector h, the remaining fraction $1-\sum_h \beta_h$ is spent on the homogenous product. For a differentiated sector h, consumers have constant elasticity of substitution preferences. Demand for the differentiated sector h is $\left[\int_{v \in n_h} x_h(v)^{\rho_h} dv\right]^{1/\rho_h}$, $0<\rho_h<1$, where $x_h(\nu)$ is the demand for variety v in sector h, n_h is the available number of varieties in sector h, ρ_h measures the extent of consumers' love of variety, a smaller ρ_h indicates a stronger love of variety, and the elasticity of substitution between varieties is, σ_h, $\sigma_h = 1/(1 - \rho_h) > 1$.

3.2 Supply

We assume that the sector that produces the homogenous product is competitive. For simplicity, we assume every country has the same productivity in producing the homogenous product. There are no trade costs for the homogenous product in trade between countries. We assume $\sum_h \beta_h$ is small enough that every country produces the homogenous product and given competitive assumption and no trade costs the price is equal in every country. The price of the homogenous product is standardised so that the wage in every country is 1, and the total income of country i is L^i.

We next consider differentiated products. For a sector h that produces a variety h, we assume there are an infinite number of possible production chains which are evenly distributed over [0, 1]. These are arranged in descending order of fixed costs of setting up a plant. A firm can thus choose a cutoff point s in [0, 1]. Production chains over [0, s] are allocated to the home country i and intermediate products are made at home. Those over [s, 1] are allocated abroad, for example in country j,[3] and are made in country j. Firms export the intermediates produced at home, and production abroad uses these intermediates.[4] Though intermediates are introduced into the production and the whole of the production process is done in two nations, we assume this splitting does not affect a firm's production technology. This treatment appears in Table 2 and is further discussed later.

Table 1 reports the four categories of firms that this treatment implies. Firms in Category 1 only sell commodities at home, and neither export nor invest abroad. Firms in Category 2 supply abroad by exporting the final commodity, but do not invest abroad. Firms in Category 3 supply abroad using fragmentation. This means that production chains over [0, s] are used at home and those over [s, 1] are used abroad. Firms in Category 3 only export intermediates not the finally produced product. We label this fragmentation FDI, because there are fixed costs in setting up production chains in the foreign country. For firms in Category 4, they supply

Table 1. Categories of firms.

Category	s	How the commodity is supplied abroad	Export of home production	Category of FDI
1	—	not supply abroad	no export	no FDI
2	$s = 1$	commodity produced absolutely at home	the final commodity	no FDI
3	$s \in (0, 1)$	production chains over [0, s] produced at home; those over [s, 1] produced abroad	intermediates	FDI for fragmentation
4	$s = 0$	commodity produced absolutely abroad	no export	horizontal FDI

[3] This assumption will be clarified in the following analysis.

[4] When $s = 0$, all production chains are allocated abroad, and no intermediate is exported. When $s = 1$, all production chains are allocated at home, and the final commodity is exported.

Table 2. Fixed and marginal costs of different categories of firms.

Category	Fixed cost	Marginal cost of the commodity supplied to home	Marginal cost of the commodity supplied abroad
1	F_D	a	not supplied abroad
2	$F_D + F_1$	a	$a\tau$
3	$F_D + F_1 + f(s)F_D$	a	$\tau sa + (1 - s)a$
4	$2F_D + F_1$	a	a

the foreign country with the commodity produced fully abroad. There are no exports, but there is horizontal FDI. Categories 2 and 4 are two special cases of Category 3, with the cutoff points are respectively 1 and 0 in these two cases. Here we focus on the Category 3 in most cases.

To enter a sector h, potential entrants should pay a sunk entry cost of F_E units of labour. Once the sunk entry cost is paid, a firm draws its labour-per-unit-output coefficient a from a distribution $G(a)$. Once a firm has observed its productivity, it will choose between exiting and producing. A firm remaining in the industry will always serve its domestic market through domestic production, but it may also serve the foreign market. If so, it can choose to access the foreign market *via* export, fragmentation or horizontal FDI. This choice is driven by a proximity-concentration trade-off as in earlier literature: the more production chains are allocated abroad, the more transport costs can be saved, but it induces higher fixed costs. After entry, producers engage in monopolistic competition. In equilibrium, one firm chooses only one way to serve the foreign market.

Firms remaining in the industry should choose one of the four categories listed in Table 1. The fixed cost and the marginal cost of each category are indicated in Table 2. For all these four categories, we assume that there exists a fixed cost of F_D units of labour which is the cost of setting up a factory. For firms in Category 2–4 supplying abroad, we assume there exists an additional fixed cost F_I which is needed to selling products abroad. For example, firms may conduct market research in order to supply abroad. Since, firms in Category 4 supply abroad with the commodity produced fully abroad, we assume there is an additional fixed cost F_D for the foreign market which is the cost of setting up a factory abroad. Because we assume that production chains are uniformly distributed over [0, 1] in descending order of fixed cost of setting up a plant, we also assume that for firms in Category 3 there exists an additional fixed cost $f(s)F_D$ of setting up abroad, where $0 < f(s) < 1, f'(s) \leq 0$, when $s \to 0, f(s) \to 1$, and when $s \to 1, f(s) \to 0$.

The marginal cost of the commodity supplied to home for all four categories is a, since these firms always supply the home market *via* the domestically produced commodity. We next assume that there exist iceberg transportation costs for both the final commodity and the intermediates, which means τ units need to be exported for 1 unit to arrive.[5] The marginal cost of the commodity supplied abroad by firms in Category 2 is thus τa. For firms in Category 3, the marginal cost of the commodity supplied abroad consists of three parts, the first is sa that is incurred at home, the second is $(1 - s)a$ that is incurred abroad, and the third is transportation costs. The sum of the first two parts is a, since we assume a total of a labour input is needed to produce one unit of a commodity even if there is fragmentation. The sum of the three is $\tau sa + (1 - s)a$. For firms in Category 4, the marginal cost of the commodity supplied abroad is a.

Under an assumption of CES preferences, firms will maximise their profits by setting the price as a markup over marginal cost. Here, the markup factor is $\sigma/(\sigma - 1) = 1/\rho$. For firms in Category 3, the firm with labour-per-unit-output coefficient a will sell the commodity at home at the price of $p_D(a) = a/\rho$, and set the price at $p_1(a) = [\tau sa + (1-s)a]/\rho$ abroad. Firms in the other three categories also set the price at $p_D(a) = a/\rho$ for the commodity sold at home. Firms in Categories 2 and 4 set the price respectively at $a\tau\rho$ and a/ρ for the commodity sold abroad.

3.3 Choiced mode to serve the abroad market

We consider a firm with the labour-per-unit-output a in sector h in country i. After it observes its labour-per-unit-output as a, if it chooses to produce commodity, it will obtain profit π_D^i from home production.

$$\pi_D^i = (a)^{1-\sigma} B^i - F_D, \tag{1}$$

where $B^i = (1-\rho)A^i / \rho^{1-\sigma}$, $A^i = \left[\beta L^i / \int_0^{n^i} p^i(v)^{1-\sigma} dv\right]$ and A^i is the domestic demand faced by firm i.[6] If the firm is supplying country j, a firm in Category 3 will receive an additional profit:

$$\pi_I^{ij} = \left[\tau^{ij} sa + (1-s)a\right]^{1-\sigma} B^j - F_I - f(s)F_D. \tag{2}$$

[5] Here we assume a uniform iceberg transportation cost τ for all the intermediates. Therefore, production chains over [0, s] are allocated to the home country and those over [s, 1] are allocated abroad, because production chains over [0, 1] are arranged in descending order of fixed costs for setting up a plant.

[6] Helpman *et al.* (2004) use the expression of A^i, where L^i is the income of country i, n^i is the number of varieties of sector h available in country i, $p^i(v)$ is the price of variety v, $\int_0^{n^i} p^i(v)^{1-\sigma} dv$ is the price of composite goods $\left[\int_0^{n^i} x_h(v)^{\rho_h} dv\right]^{1/\rho_h}$.

Because categories 2 and 4 are two special cases of category 3, Equation (2) only reports the profits of firms in category 3.

We firstly consider a firms' choice when international fragmentation is prohibited, which means firms can only choose the categories 1–3. This is similar to Helpman *et al.* (2004). We next analyse a firm's choice when international fragmentation is possible, but there is only one fixed cutoff point. We then analyse a firms' choice when international fragmentation is possible but there are two fixed cutoff points. Lastly, we consider cases when product chains can be arbitrarily fragmented.

(1) When international fragmentation is prohibited.
As in HMY, when there is no international fragmentation, firms only choose among the categories 1, 2 and 4. For a firm in Category 2, the profit from sale to country j is

$$\pi_I^{ij}\big|_{s=1} = (\tau^{ij} a)^{1-\sigma} B^j - F_I. \tag{3}$$

For Category 4, the profit from sales in country j is

$$\pi_I^{ij}\big|_{s=0} = (a)^{1-\sigma} B^j - F_I - F_D. \tag{4}$$

Figure 1 represents firms' profits from the home market and abroad. In this figure, $(a)^{1-\sigma}$ is represented on the horizontal axis. The variable $(a)^{1-\sigma}$ increases monotonically with labour productivity and can be used as a productivity index. On the vertical axis is profit. π_D^i is the profit from the home market i, and $\pi_I^{ij}|_{s=1}$, $\pi_I^{ij}|_{s=0}$ are the respectively profits from country j when the firm choose export or horizontal FDI to supply j. All of π_D^i, $\pi_I^{ij}|_{s=1}$ and $\pi_I^{ij}|_{s=0}$ increase monotonically with $(a)^{1-\sigma}$. Under the assumption of equal demands between country i and country j, from (1), (3) and (4), we can see that $\pi_I^{ij}|_{s=0}$ and π_D^i are parallel, and that the slope of $\pi_I^{ij}|_{s=1}$ is less than $\pi_I^{ij}|_{s=0}$ and π_D^i. The profit lines π_D^i and $\pi_I^{ij}|_{s=1}$ cross the horizontal axis respectively at the point $(a_D^i)^{1-\sigma}$ and $(a_X^i)^{1-\sigma}$. The cross point of profit lines $\pi_I^{ij}|_{s=0}$ and $\pi_I^{ij}|_{s=1}$ have the abscissa of $(a_I^i)^{1-\sigma}$.

Helpman *et al.* (2004) use an assumption about fixed costs in order to make the firms' choice tractable, and here we make a similar assumption:

$$F_I(\tau^{\sigma-1} - 1) < F_D < F_I \tau^{\sigma-1}. \tag{5}$$

In Figure 1, $F_I > F_D$. We also can assume $F_I < F_D$, but if so, Equation (5) should hold.

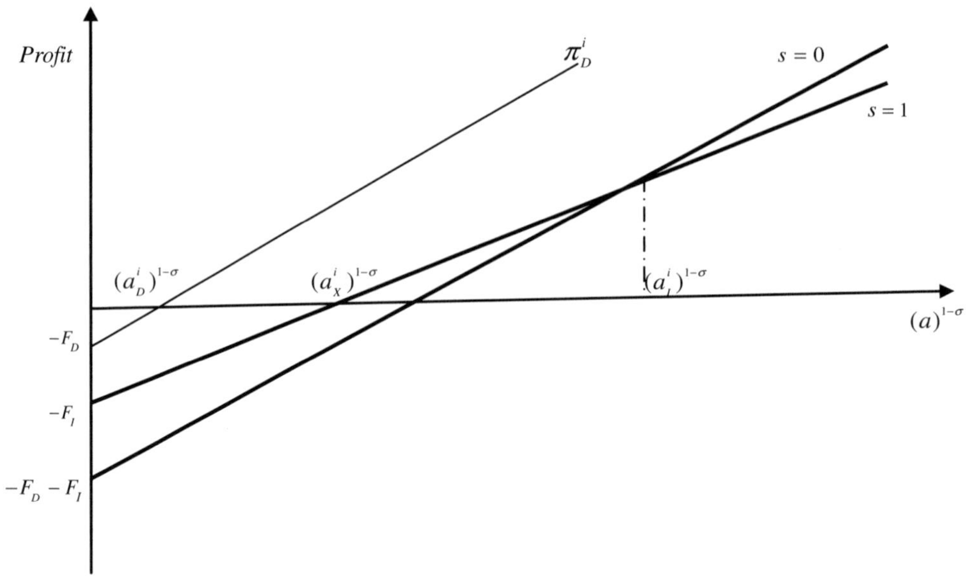

Figure 1. Profits of firms when international fragmentation is prohibited.

Notes: Profit lines $s = 0$, $s = 1$ denote respectively profit functions $\pi_I^{ij}|_{s=0}$ and $\pi_I^{ij}|_{s=1}$. This figure is similar to Figure 1 in Helpman *et al.* (2004) with a difference in the treatment of fixed cost and marginal costs relative to HMY.

Under these assumptions, from Figure 1, we can see

$$(a_D^i)^{1-\sigma} < (a_X^i)^{1-\sigma} < (a_I^i)^{1-\sigma}, \tag{6}$$

and firms with productivity index below $(a_D^i)^{1-\sigma}$ will exit because of negative net profits. Firms with productivity index between $(a_D^i)^{1-\sigma}$ and $(a_X^i)^{1-\sigma}$ will only supply the domestic market because export and horizontal FDI incur negative net profits. Firms with productivity index between $(a_X^i)^{1-\sigma}$ and $(a_I^i)^{1-\sigma}$ will not only supply domestic markets but also export to supply abroad. They will not adopt horizontal FDI, because exporting brings more profit than horizontal FDI. Firms with productivity index above $(a_I^i)^{1-\sigma}$ will not only supply the domestic market, but also supply abroad via horizontal FDI, because horizontal FDI brings more profit than exporting. These conclusions are as in Helpman *et al.* (2004).

(2) When international fragmentation is possible, but has only one fixed cutoff point.

Next, we consider cases where international fragmentation is possible but there is only one fixed cutoff point. We assume that a firm can only choose $s = s_1$ as a cutoff point if it chooses international fragmentation, as shown in Figure 2.

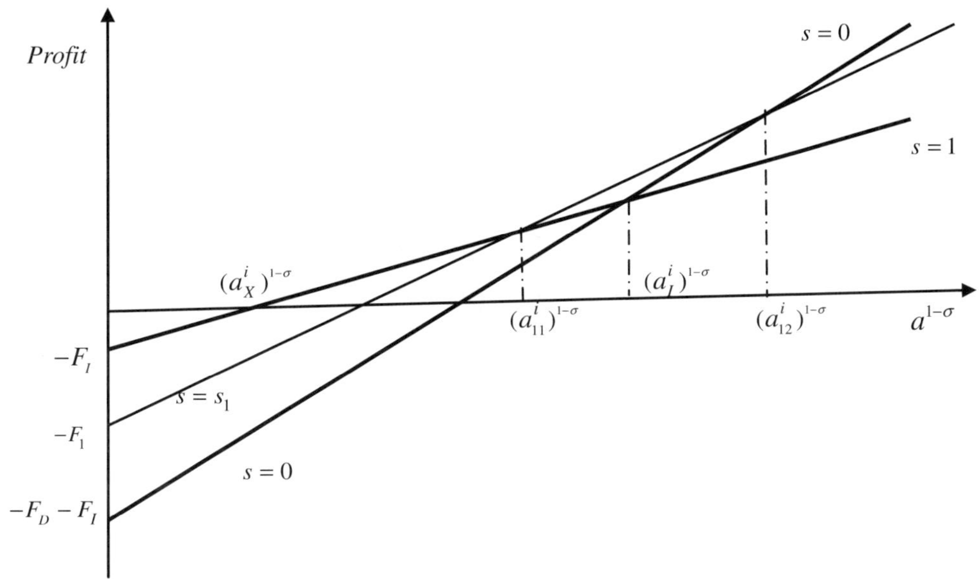

Figure 2. Profits of firms when international fragmentation is possible but only has one cutoff point.

To make the figure easier to follow, Figure 2 leaves out the line for π_D^i that is included in Figure 1.

From (2)–(4), we can see that the intercept $-F_1$ of the profit line $s = s_1$ is between $-F_I$ and $-F_D - F_I$ which are respectively the intercepts of the profit line $s = 1$ and $s = 0$. Also, the slope of the profit line $s = s_1$ is between the profit line $s = 1$ and profit line $s = 0$. In Figure 2, we can see the inequality $(a_X^i)^{1-\sigma} < (a_{11}^i)^{1-\sigma} < (a_I^i)^{1-\sigma} < (a_{12}^i)^{1-\sigma}$ is satisfied.[7] When we consider $s = s_1$ as a possible cutoff point, firms with their productivity between $(a_X^i)^{1-\sigma}$ and $(a_{11}^i)^{1-\sigma}$ still supply abroad via export. Firms with their productivity between $(a_{11}^i)^{1-\sigma}$ and $(a_{12}^i)^{1-\sigma}$ change to supply abroad via fragmentation. Firms with their productivity above $(a_{12}^i)^{1-\sigma}$ still supply abroad via horizontal FDI. So, when international fragmentation is possible, some firms that formerly chose export or horizontal FDI will now choose international fragmentation to supply abroad.[8]

---

[7]There is a possibility that this inequality does not hold. For example, when the cross point of profit line $s = s_1$ and horizontal axis is at the left of $(a_X^i)^{1-\sigma}$, but this does not affect the final conclusion. This paper considers the cases that Figure 2 describes.

[8]When $(a_{11}^i)^{1-\sigma} < (a_X^i)^{1-\sigma}$, part or all of the firms that previously only sold a commodity at home change to supply abroad *via* fragmentation; all of the firms that formally exported and part of the firms that formerly chose horizontal FDI change to supply abroad via international fragmentation. When $(a_{11}^i)^{1-\sigma} > (a_I^i)^{1-\sigma}$, the introduction of international fragmentation cannot change the choices of firms.

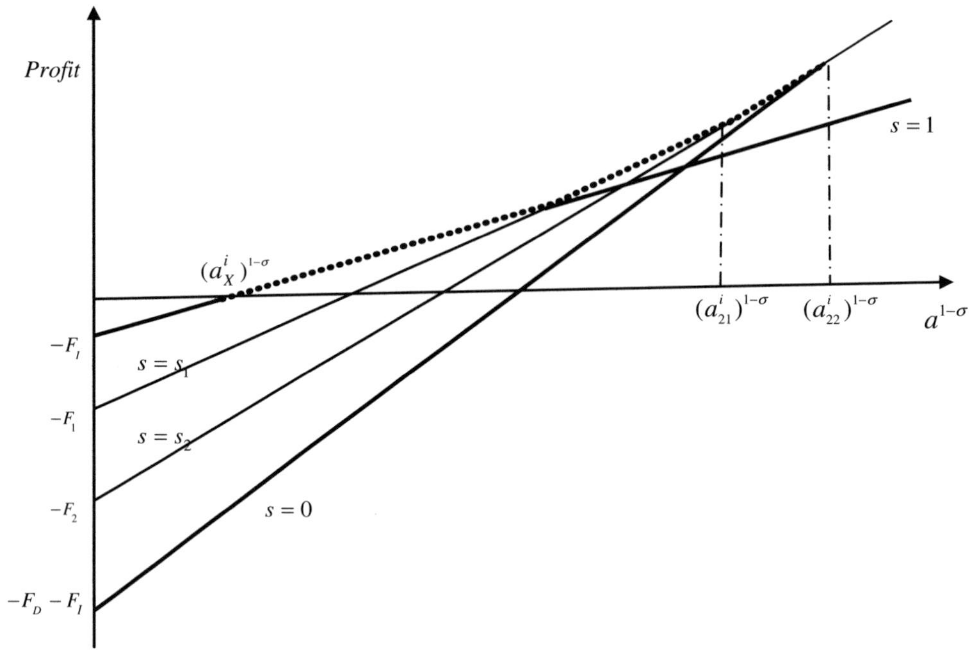

Figure 3. Profits of firms when international fragmentation is possible and has two possible cutoff points.

(3) When international fragmentation is possible but has two fixed cutoff points. Figure 3 depicts firm choices when there are two possible fixed cutoff points. Firms can choose the cutoff point $s = s_1$ or $s = s_2$ $(s_2 < s_1)$. From (2)–(4), we can see that the intercept $-F_2$ of profit line $s = s_2$ is between the intercepts of profit line $s = s_1$ and $s = 0$. Furthermore, the slope of the profit line $s = s_2$ is between the slopes of profit line $s = s_1$ and $s = 0$. In Figure 3, the following inequality holds[9]:

$$(a_{11}^i)^{1-\sigma} < (a_{21}^i)^{1-\sigma} < (a_{12}^i)^{1-\sigma} < (a_{22}^i)^{1-\sigma}.$$

When another cutoff point $s = s_2$ is added, firms with their productivity index between $(a_{11}^i)^{1-\sigma}$ and $(a_{21}^i)^{1-\sigma}$ will still supply abroad *via* international fragmentation and the cutoff point is still s_1. But firms with their productivity index between $(a_{21}^i)^{1-\sigma}$ and $(a_{22}^i)^{1-\sigma}$ that formerly choose the cutoff point s_1 now change to the

[9] In order to make Figure 3 concise, $(a_{11}^i)^{1-\sigma}$ and $(a_{12}^i)^{1-\sigma}$ that exist in Figure 2 do not appear in Figure 3.

cutoff point S_2. Firms with productivity index above $(a_{22}^i)^{1-\sigma}$ will still supply abroad via horizontal FDI. Thus, an additional cutoff point increases the proportion of the firms that perform fragmentation FDI.[10]

(4) When product chains can be arbitrarily fragmented.
Under the circumstances of international fragmentation, the more productive a firm is, the more product chains will be allocated abroad. This conclusion follows from: if the cutoff point could be an arbitrary number over (0, 1), in this ideal circumstance, the dashed line in Figure 3 would become a smooth curve that is convex to the origin. The more productive a firm is, the more profit it will obtain. Firms with the lowest productivity will exit, and those with lower productivity will choose export. Firms with higher productivity will choose fragmentation, among which, the more productive a firm is, the more product chains are allocated at abroad. Firms with the highest productivity will choose the horizontal FDI. With an increase in the numbers of possible cutoff points, the proportion of firms that choose fragmentation will increase, and the proportion of firms that choose exporting and horizontal FDI will decrease.

3.4 Equilibrium

In equilibrium, for country *i*,

$$(a_D^i)^{1-\sigma} B^i - F_D = 0, \tag{7}$$

where a_D^i is the dividing point of labour-per-unit-output for a firm to survive in the market. A firm with the labour-per-unit-output bigger than a_D^i will exit from the market and firms with labour-per-unit-output a_D^i will earn profits.

For all the $j \neq i$,

$$(\tau^{ij})^{1-\sigma} (a_X^{ij})^{1-\sigma} B^j - F_I = 0, \tag{8}$$

where a_X^{ij} is the dividing point of labour-per-unit-output for a firm in country *i* to supply country *j*. Firms with labour-per-unit-output smaller than a_X^{ij} will choose to supply abroad and firms with labour-per-unit-output a_X^{ij} earn zero profits by supplying country *j*.

---

[10] When $(a_{21}^i)^{1-\sigma} < (a_{11}^i)^{1-\sigma}$, part or all of the firms that formally exported change to supply abroad *via* fragmentation and choose the cutoff point s_2. All of the firms that formally choose the cutoff point s_1 and part of the firms that choose horizontal FDI will change to choose the cutoff point s_2. When $(a_{21}^i)^{1-\sigma} > (a_{12}^i)^{1-\sigma}$, the introduction of another cutoff point does not change the firms' choice.

The free entry condition is

$$\int_0^{a_D^i} (a^{1-\sigma}B^i - F_D)dG(a) + \sum_{j\neq i}\int_0^{a_X^{ij}} \left\{\left[\tau^{ij}sa + (1-s)a\right]^{1-\sigma} B^j - F_I - f(s)F_D\right\}dG(a) = F_E. \quad (9)$$

The first item on the left side of (9) is the expected profit gained from the domestic market i when a potential entrant's labour-per-unit-output is less than a_D^i . The second item on the left side of (9) is the expected profit gained from country j when a potential entrant's labour-per-unit-output is less than a_X^{ij}. (9) means that the expected profit is equal to the sunk entry cost F_E, which implies a zero expected profit for a potential entrant.

Firms that supply abroad via fragmentation FDI will choose such an s that they can make the highest profit. So, from, (2), we can get

$$\partial\pi_I^{ij} / \partial s = a^{1-\sigma} B^j(1-\sigma)(\tau^{ij}-1)\left[1-s+\tau^{ij}s\right]^{-\sigma} - f'(s)F_D = 0. \quad (10)$$

(7)–(10) implicitly implies the dividing point of a_D^i, a_X^{ij}, and the demand levels B^i, B^j.

3.5 The ratio of exports to FDI at the sector level

Next, let us look at the ratio of export to FDI for country i supplying country j at a sector level. Here FDI include horizontal FDI and fragmentation FDI. When product chains can be arbitrarily fragmented, from Figure 3 nearly all the firms supply abroad via fragmentation FDI and few firms choose export and horizontal FDI. In reality, product chains of a commodity may not be arbitrarily fragmented, which will mean that cutoff points firms can choose are limited.

From Figure 3, it follows that at the sector level, the more prone to be fragmented a sector is, the lower the ratio of exports to FDI sales is. The significance of this is that it suggests that the ability of a country to fragment product internationally is one of the origins of comparative advantage. A country that has a lower ability in fragmenting product internationally will have comparative advantage in this sector.

At a sector level, the ratio of export to FDI for country i to supply country j is determined by many factors. Among these are two that play an important role. One is the cross point with the minimum abscissa among all the cross points of all possible profit lines and profit line $s = 1$. The other is $(a_X^{ij})^{1-\sigma}$ which is the dividing point for firms to supply abroad. The distance along the horizontal axis

between these two points determines the ratio of exports to FDI. The larger the distance is, the bigger the ratio of export to FDI.[11]
From (2) and (3), we get

$$(\tau^{ij}a_{s1}^{ij})^{1-\sigma}B^{j}-F_{I}=\left[\tau^{ij}sa_{s1}^{ij}+(1-s)a_{s1}^{ij}\right]^{1-\sigma}B^{j}-F_{I}-f(s)F_{D},$$

which can be rearranged as

$$(a_{s1}^{ij})^{1-\sigma}=\frac{f(s)F_{D}}{\left[(1-s+\tau^{ij}s)^{1-\sigma}-(\tau^{ij})^{1-\sigma}\right]B^{j}}. \tag{11}$$

From (11), we see that the bigger τ^{ij} is or the smaller F_D is, the smaller $(a_{s1}^{ij})^{1-\sigma}$ will be.

From (8), we get

$$(a_{X}^{ij})^{1-\sigma}=\frac{F_{I}}{(\tau^{ij})^{1-\sigma}B^{j}}, \tag{12}$$

and the bigger τ^{ij} or F_I is, the bigger $(a_X^{ij})^{1-\sigma}$ will be.

The larger τ^{ij} is, the smaller the distance between $(a_{s1}^{ij})^{1-\sigma}$ and $(a_X^{ij})^{1-\sigma}$, and the larger τ^{ij} is, the smaller the ratio of export to FDI.

In (11), the smaller F_D is, the smaller $(a_{s1}^{ij})^{1-\sigma}$ is. When $(a_X^{ij})^{1-\sigma}$ is fixed, the smaller $(a_{s1}^{ij})^{1-\sigma}$ is, the smaller the distance between $(a_{s1}^{ij})^{1-\sigma}$ and $(a_X^{ij})^{1-\sigma}$ is, and hence the smaller is the ratio of export to FDI. In (12), the larger F_I is, the larger $(a_X^{ij})^{1-\sigma}$ is. When $(a_{s1}^{ij})^{1-\sigma}$ is fixed, the larger $(a_X^{ij})^{1-\sigma}$ is, the smaller the distance between $(a_{s1}^{ij})^{1-\sigma}$ and $(a_X^{ij})^{1-\sigma}$ is, and hence the smaller is the ratio of export to FDI.

Also at a sector level, the higher the transportation costs are, or the smaller the fixed cost for setting up a plant is, or the smaller the fixed cost for selling products abroad is, the lower the ratio of exports to FDI sales is. This extends the Proximity-Concentration model of Brainard (1993) in two ways. One is from the firm level to a sector level. The other is that the definition of FDI is extended to include horizontal FDI and fragmentation FDI.

[11] If $(a_{s1}^{ij})^{1-\sigma}<(a_X^{i})^{1-\sigma}$, all firms will choose FDI to supply abroad, no firm choose export. To make it general, in this essay, we assume $(a_{s1}^{ij})^{1-\sigma}>(a_X^{i})^{1-\sigma}$, so only part of firms choose FDI to supply abroad.

4 Concluding Remarks

This chapter builds on the HMY model to analyse different ways for multinational firms which have different productivity to serve the market abroad when product chains can be arbitrarily fragmented. Fragmentation is captured through the splitting of production chains across countries to yield a proximity advantage as in Brainard (1993), but with a fixed cost of fragmentation production in foreign countries.

The analysis generalises HMY by suggesting that while firms with the lowest productivity will exit, and those with lower productivity will choose to export, and those with higher productivity will choose fragmentation, among which, the more productive a firm is, the more product chains are allocated at abroad. Firms with the highest productivity will then choose horizontal FDI as in HMY. At a sector level, the more prone to be fragmented is an industry, the lower the ratio of exports to FDI sales is. Also at a sector level, the higher are transportation costs, or the smaller the fixed cost for setting up a plant, or the smaller the fixed cost for selling products abroad, the lower the ratio of exports to FDI sales.

By introducing fragmentation into the HMY model, this chapter looks at the choices of heterogeneous firms in supplying the market abroad in a product fragmentation world. When product chains can be arbitrarily fragmented, for the firms who choose fragmentation, the more productive a firm is, the more product chains are allocated at abroad. This suggests that the "proximity-concentration" hypothesis developed by Brainard (1993) can be applied even when product fragmentation occurs. For firms who choose fragmentation FDI, because more product chains allocated abroad incur more fixed costs, only more productive firms can allocate more product chains abroad.

One important implication of this chapter is that the ability of a country to fragment product internationally is a source of comparative advantage. At a sector level, the more prone for an industry to be fragmented, the lower the ratio of exports to FDI sales. For any sector, the country that has the most ability relative to others to fragment production internationally is more likely to supply markets abroad *via* fragmentation. Equally, this country will export fewer commodities for this sector; and the country that has less ability to fragment a product internationally is more likely to export.

References

Brainard S.L. (1993), A Simple Theory of Multinational Corporations and Trade with a Trade-off Between Proximity and Concentration, *NBER Working Paper No. 4269*.

Deardorff, A.V. (2001), Fragmentation in Simple Trade Models, *North American Journal of Economics and Finance*, 12, 121–137.

Eaton, J., S. Kortum and F. Kramarz (2004), Dissecting Trade: Firms, Industries, and Export Destinations, *American Economic Review*, 94(2), 150–154.

Feenstra, R.C. and G.H. Hanson (1996), Foreign Investment, Outsourcing and Relative Wages, in R.C. Feenstra, G.M. Grossman and D.A. Irwin (Eds.), *The Political Economy of Trade Policy: Papers in Honor of Jagdish Bhagwati*, MIT Press, 89–127.

Feenstra, R.C. and G.H. Hanson (1999), Productivity Measurement and the Impact of Trade and Technology on Wages: Estimates for the U.S., 1972–1990, *Quarterly Journal of Economics*, 114(3), 371–393.

Head, K. and J. Ries (2003), Heterogeneity and the FDI versus Export Decision of Japanese Manufactures, *Journal of the Japanese and International Economies*, 17(4), 448–467.

Head, K. and J. Ries (2004), Exporting and FDI as Alternative Strategies, *Oxford Review of Economic Policy*, 20(3), 409–423.

Helpman, E., M. Melitz and S. Yeaple (2004), Export versus FDI with Heterogeneous Firms, *American Economic Review*, 94(1), 300–316.

Krugman, P. (1980), Scale Economies, Product Differentiation, and the Pattern of Trade, *The American Economic Review*, 70(5), 950–959.

Melitz, M. (2003), The Impact of Trade on Intra-industry Reallocations and Aggregate Industry Productivity, *Econometrica*, 71(6), 1695–1725.

Redding, S.J. (2010), Theories of Heterogeneous Firms and Trade, NBER Working Paper No. 16562, http://www.nber.org/papers/w16562.

Yamashita, N. (2010), The Impact of Foreign Outsourcing on Wage Inequality in US Manufacturing: New Evidence, *Economics Letters*, 107(1), 46–48.

Index